PLATO'S *EUTHYPHRO*, *APOLOGY*, AND *CRITO*

Critical Essays on the Classics
Series Editor: Steven M. Cahn

The volumes in this series offer insightful and accessible essays that shed light on the classics of philosophy. Each of the distinguished editors has selected outstanding work in recent scholarship to provide today's readers with a deepened understanding of the most timely issues raised in these important texts.

Kant's *Critique of the Power of Judgment*
  edited by Paul Guyer
Descartes's *Meditations*: Critical Essays
  edited by Vere Chappell
Kant's *Groundwork on the Metaphysics of Morals*: Critical Essays
  edited by Paul Guyer
Mill's *On Liberty*: Critical Essays
  edited by Gerald Dworkin
Mill's *Utilitarianism*: Critical Essays
  edited by David Lyons
Plato's *Republic*: Critical Essays
  edited by Richard Kraut
Kant's *Critique of Pure Reason:* Critical Essays
  edited by Patricia Kitcher
The Empiricists: Critical Essays on Locke, Berkeley, and Hume
  edited by Margaret Atherton
Aristotle's *Ethics:* Critical Essays
  edited by Nancy Sherman
The Social Contract Theorists: Critical Essays on Hobbes, Locke, and Rousseau
  edited by Christopher Morris
The Rationalists: Critical Essays on Descartes, Spinoza, and Leibniz
  edited by Derk Pereboom
Kant's *Critique of the Power of Judgment*
  edited by Paul Guyer
The Existentialists: Critical Essays on Kierkegaard, Nietzsche, Heidegger, and Sartre
  edited by Charles Guignon
John Stuart Mill's *The Subjection of Women*
  edited by Maria H. Morales
Plato's *Euthyphro, Apology*, and *Crito*
  edited by Rachana Kamtekar

PLATO'S *EUTHYPHRO,* *APOLOGY,* AND *CRITO*

Critical Essays

Edited by
Rachana Kamtekar

ROWMAN & LITTLEFIELD PUBLISHERS, INC.
Lanham • Boulder • New York • Toronto • Oxford

ROWMAN & LITTLEFIELD PUBLISHERS, INC.

Published in the United States of America
by Rowman & Littlefield Publishers, Inc.
A wholly owned subsidary of The Rowman & Littlefield Publishing Group, Inc.
4501 Forbes Boulevard, Suite 200, Lanham, Maryland 20706
www.rowmanlittlefield.com

PO Box 317
Oxford
OX2 9RU, UK

British Library Cataloging in Publication Information Available

Library of Congress Cataloging-in-Publication Data

Plato's Euthyphro, Apology, and Crito / [edited by] Rachana Kamtekar.
    p. cm.—(Critical essays on the classics)
  Includes bibliographical references and index.
  ISBN 0-7425-3324-7 (cloth : alk. paper)—ISBN 0-7425-3325-5 (pbk. : alk. paper)
  1. Plato. Euthyphro. 2. Plato. Apology. 3. Plato. Crito 4. Socrates. I.
Kamtekar, Rachana, 1965– II. Series
  B370.P53 2005
  183'.2—dc22

                                                            2004014138

♾™ The paper used in this publication meets the minimum requirements of American
National Standard for Information Sciences—Permanence of Paper for Printed Library
Materials, ANSI/NISO Z39.48-1992.

Contents

Acknowledgments

Bostock, David. 'The Interpretation of Plato's *Crito*,' is reprinted from *Phronesis* vol. XXXV no. 1 (1990), pp. 1–20, with kind permission of Koninklijke Brill NV, Leider, The Netherlands, Phronesic, 1990.

Burnyeat, Myles. 'The Impiety of Socrates' is reprinted from *Ancient Philosophy* vol. 17 no. 1 (1997), pp. 1–12, by permission of the journal and the author.

Cohen, S. Marc. 'Socrates on the Definition of Piety: *Euthyphro* 10A–11B' is reprinted from *Journal of the History of Philosophy* 9 (1971), 1–13, by permission of the Johns Hopkins University Press and the author.

de Strycker, E. and S. R. Slings. '*Plato's Apology of Socrates*' is reprinted from *Plato's Apology of Socrates* (Leiden: Brill, 1994), pp. 1–25. Copyright 1994 by Brill Academic Publishers. Reprinted by permission of Brill Academic Publishers via the Copyright Clearance Center.

Geach, P. T. 'Plato's *Euthyphro*: An Analysis and Commentary,' is reprinted from *The Monist*, vol. 50 no. 3 (July 1966), pp. 369–82. Copyright c. 1966 The Monist: An International Quarterly Journal of General Philosophical Inquiry, Peru, Illinois, U.S.A. 61354. Reprinted by permission.

Harte, Verity. 'Conflicting Values in Plato's *Crito*' is reprinted from *Archiv für Geschichte der Philosophie* vol. 81 no. 2, pp. 117–47, by permission of the journal and the author.

Irwin, T. H. 'Was Socrates against Democracy?' is based on the article 'Socrates and Athenian Democracy', published in *Philosophy and Public Affairs*, vol. 32 i.1 (1989).

Kraut, Richard. '*Dokimasia*, Satisfaction, and Agreement,' is reprinted from Richard Kraut, *Socrates and the State* (pp. 149–93) c. 1984 Princeton University Press by permission of Princeton University Press and the author.

McPherran, Mark L. 'Justice and Pollution in the Euthyphro is reprinted from *Apeiron: A Journal for Ancient Philosophy and Science*, vol. 35 (2002), pp. 105–27, by permission of Academic Printing and Publishing and the author.

Morrison, Donald. 'On the Alleged Historical Reliability of Plato's *Apology*' is reprinted from *Archiv für Geschichte der Philosophie* vol. 82 no. 3, pp. 235–65, by permission of the journal and the author.

Smith, N. and T. Brickhouse. 'Socrates and Obedience to the Law' is reprinted from *Apeiron: A Journal for Ancient Philosophy and Science*, vol. 18 (1984), pp. 10–18, by permission of Academic Printing and Publishing and the authors.

Vlastos, Gregory. 'Socratic Piety' is reprinted from *Socrates, Ironist and Moral Philosopher*, pp. 157–178, edited by Gregory Vlastos. Copyright c. 1991 Cambridge University Press. Used by permission of the publisher, Cornell University Press.

Introduction

IN 399 B.C.E., SOCRATES WAS TRIED and sentenced to death on charges which, according to the report in Diogenes Laertius' *Lives*, ran: 'Socrates does wrong by not recognizing the gods the city recognizes and by introducing into it new gods; and he also corrupts the young' (II.40). Plato's *Euthyphro, Apology*, and *Crito*, the three works that are the subject of this volume, portray Socrates' words and deeds during these events. (How far Plato's portrayal departs from the historical Socrates' actual words and deeds is explored in several of the essays below.) Because Plato presents his readers with Socrates the individual, encountering particular individuals and particular situations, readers must work out for themselves what general principles to take away from the representation of Socrates' words and deeds: does Socrates hold that definitional knowledge is required for true judgments, or does he merely show his interlocutor's judgments not to be based on knowledge? Does Socrates believe that no citizen may disobey a law he cannot persuade his city is unjust, or is this exacting standard a personal one? Answering such questions requires attention to both the literary and the philosophical in Plato's writing and engages the reader's powers of imagination as well as analysis.

Plato's *Euthyphro* begins with Socrates approaching the office of the King Archon, the magistrate who will examine the charges against Socrates, just as he examines all cases involving violations of religious law to ascertain that the charges are valid and that the case can go to trial. Outside the office, Socrates encounters Euthyphro, who, unlike Socrates, has come to court on his own initiative. Euthyphro is there to prosecute his father for the murder of a servant. Socrates quizzes Euthyphro about the nature of piety—on the grounds that Euthyphro could only have the confidence to pursue such an unconventional suit (Euthyphro is prosecuting his own father and the servant is no relation of Euthyphro's) if he knows what piety is—and faults each of Euthyphro's attempts to say what piety is. As Mark McPherran shows in his 'Justice and Pollution in the *Euthyphro*', Euthyphro combines religious traditionalism with a progressive, even Socratic, attitude to piety: he is prosecuting his father because he believes, on the one hand, that a murderer pollutes those who associate with him unless he is brought to justice (4c), and on the other hand, that one should prosecute the wrongdoer whether he is a relative or not, that is, impartially (4b, 5d). Like Socrates, Euthyphro holds that there is one standard of virtue for gods and human beings and that only unjust killing could bring on pollution. Plato brings out these parallels between Socrates and Euthyphro to highlight their specific differences: although Socrates is the one on trial for corruption, it is Euthyphro who is a potential source of corruption and harm, presumably because he, and Socrates' prosecutor Meletus, are 'reckless extremists with a telling lack of belief-consistency, . . . guilty of allowing theological propositions [viz. about what piety is or demands] that they are demonstrated to be incapable of defending . . . to govern their treatment of others. . .' (p. 11).

Socrates' cross-examination of Euthyphro on the nature of piety (*hosiotês*, the abstract noun) or 'the pious' (*to hosion*, the neuter adjective used as a substantive), exemplifies his singular mode of ethical inquiry: he selects as an interlocutor someone whose professions or actions imply some special knowledge of virtue or excellence, extracts from this interlocutor some account of a virtue, and then proceeds to show that this account conflicts with the interlocutor's other commitments. Socrates says he does this so that he can learn what virtue is; in practice, he shows that others do not know what it is.

Euthyphro attempts several accounts of piety. (1) By his own example, and Zeus' and Kronos', it is prosecuting the unjust (5d). (2) It is that which is dear to [all] the gods (7a, 9d). (3) It is the part of justice having to do with care for or service of the gods (12e, 13d). (4) It is the knowledge of how to sacrifice and pray (14c). Each time, Socrates finds reason to reject his answer: against (1), that he is seeking not examples but 'that form itself which makes all pious actions pious' (6de); against (2) that the gods, as Euthyphro conceives of them, love opposite things, so Euthyphro's account would make the same thing pious and not-pious (7b-9c),[1] and that in any case, the pious cannot be the same as the god-loved since the cause of something's being god-loved is that the gods love it, so that the cause of the gods' loving it must lie in something other than the fact that they love it, such as the nature of the thing they love (10a-11b). Socrates' question, 'what is piety/the pious?' is not to be answered by giving the extension of 'pious' nor by stating the necessary and sufficient conditions for the application of that term. Socrates wants to be told what the nature of the pious is such as to make the gods love it. In response to (3) and (4), Socrates wonders how we can care for the gods since we can't benefit them (13c), or, if we care for them by serving them, what fine or good thing we assist them in making (13e), or what of value we can give to them in sacrifice (14e); when Euthyphro replies that we give them what is pleasing to them, Socrates accuses him of returning to (2) the account of the pious as the god-loved (15b).

Anglo-American philosophers in the 20th century have concerned themselves particularly with analyzing and evaluating Socrates' arguments against his interlocutors. Peter Geach argues, in 'Plato's *Euthyphro*: An Analysis and Commentary', that Socrates rejects Euthyphro's definition by example (1) because he assumes 'that if you know you are correctly predicating a given term "T" you must "know what it is to be T," in the sense of being able to give a general criterion for a thing's being T' and so 'it is no use to try and arrive at the meaning of "T" by giving examples of things that are T.' But, Geach objects, 'we know heaps of things without being able to define the terms in which we express our knowledge' (p. 25). Geach is also critical of Socrates' argument against Euthyphro's definition (2) that the pious is the god-loved. Socrates argues that the pious is not the same as the god-loved on the grounds that something's being god-loved cannot be the cause of, but must be caused by, the gods' loving it, and that the gods' loving it cannot be the cause of, but must be caused by, its nature (viz. the pious). Geach argues that the pious is not the cause of the gods' loving a thing, but rather, the characteristic in virtue of which they love it; the cause of the gods' loving a thing is their knowing (or believing) it to be pious. Further, Geach says, 'because' introduces a non-extensional context, into which co-referring expressions may not be substituted for one another without a change in truth-value. Still, Geach agrees with Socrates' conclusion: 'pious' and 'god-loved' can't mean the same thing; a thing must be loved by the gods in virtue of something other than its being god-loved. But, Geach asks, why couldn't the gods love a thing, as Euthyphro suggests in (4), because the thing is intended to please them?

Geach's criticism of Socrates' rejection of Euthyphro's definition (1) has prompted an extensive literature. There are several excellent discussions responding to Geach's criticism, which, for example, argue that Socrates is only making the methodological point that an example is not a definition; or distinguish between knowledge, for which knowledge of what it is to be T is necessary, from true opinion, for which it is not; or question the textual basis for attributing such a view to Socrates; or uphold such a view on philosophical grounds. These discussions range over other works in addition to the *Euthyphro, Apology*, and *Crito*.[2]

S. Marc Cohen's 'Socrates on the Definition of Piety: *Euthyphro* 10A-11B', focusses on Socrates' reply to Euthyphro's definition (2), that the pious is the god-loved; along the way Cohen answers Geach's criticism. According to Cohen, Socrates expects, not that co-referential expressions are intersubstitutable in non-extensional contexts without any change in truth value, but rather (and correctly) that a term and its definition be intersubstitutable in non-extensional contexts like 'because' without any change in truth value. However, Cohen points out that Socrates uses 'because' in two non-equivalent senses in contrasting statements of the following type:

(1) Something is a φ-d thing because it is φ-d by someone/because someone φ-s it,

and

(2) Someone φ-s something because it is a φ-d thing.

In statements of type (1), what follows the 'because' is a logically sufficient condition for applying the participial term 'φ-d thing', whereas in statements of type (2) what follows the 'because' is a reason for some action or attitude of φ-ing. Fortunately, despite his use of 'because' in these two senses, Socrates' argument doesn't depend on any equivocation between the two. For he argues that if 'god-loved' and 'pious' were the same, then one could infer from

P is loved by the gods because (reason) it is pious

to

(4) P is loved (by the gods) because (reason) it is god-loved

and from

(5) P is god-loved because (logical condition) it is loved by the gods

to

(6) P is pious because (logical condition) the gods love it.

The falsity of (4) is sufficient for Socrates to reject Euthyphro's definition of the pious as the god-loved; Socrates does not make anything of the apparently unproblematic claim (6). Socrates' argument proves that 'pious' cannot be defined as 'god-loved' if the gods' reason for loving what is pious is that it is pious (although it could be if they have some other reason for loving what is pious). For the major lesson of the *Euthyphro* is that 'If a moral concept M is such that there is an authority whose judgment whether or not something falls under M is decisive and is rationally grounded, then "M" cannot be defined in terms of that authority's judgment' (p. 45).

Gregory Vlastos's 'Socratic Piety' vivifies the revolutionary force of this theoretical lesson for Socrates' conception of piety. According to Vlastos, in presenting the gods as governed by objective norms—of goodness, of what to consider pious—Socrates is doing no less than rejecting the traditional Greek conception of the gods as powerful but ethically cavalier beings, and, along with this, the traditional conception of piety—the proper relationship between gods and human beings—as one in which human beings sacrifice to power- and honour-hungry gods in order to induce them to effect our wishes in the world; Vlastos dubs this rejected conception of piety 'magical'. Instead, Vlastos argues, Socrates in the *Euthyphro* suggests that the proper relationship of human beings to gods is as their assistants in benefiting human beings by perfecting their souls. As the *Euthyphro* and also the *Apology* show, Socrates embodies this ideal in his life of philosophizing: Socratic piety involves a commitment to rational inquiry. Vlastos explains this (to us) curious coupling of reason and religion by saying that although Socrates fully accepts the gods' authority, he also holds that critical reason is required to interpret messages sent from the gods; therefore, for Socrates, there cannot be any conflict between the gods' commands and reason's dictates, or any question of the gods' commands overriding reason's.

Let us turn to the *Apology*, where Socrates is in the courtroom before the assembled jury, defending himself not only against the official charges raised by the prosecution at his trial, that he wrongs the city by corrupting its youth, disbelieving in its gods and introducing new gods (24b), but also against the more longstanding and damaging rumours that he studies things in the sky and below the earth (like the physicists) and makes the worse argument the stronger (like the sophists) (18b).

Because Socrates' trial is an independently attested event (unlike his conversation with Euthyphro, for example), and because the trial was public, with at least 500 jurors present, scholars have wondered whether it gives us the actual words of the historical Socrates (rather than the Platonic voice-over that we may have in other dialogues). In the introduction to their magisterial *Plato's Apology of Socrates*, E. de Strycker and S. R. Slings explain why we should be skeptical about this possibility. They reconstruct the likely expectations of the readers of Plato's *Apology* by considering other ancient representations of actual speeches (write-ups of forensic oratory, of the speeches of great statesmen in the assembly, and so on); these texts suggest that Plato's audience would have expected not a verbatim record of what was said in the courtroom but rather, a spirited defence of Socrates (against his actual prosecutors as well as against those who criticized him after his death) that would be true to his image. De Strycker and Slings also argue that Plato intends the *Apology* to be not only a defence and portrait of Socrates, but also an exhortation to philosophy. The *Apology* is a very complex literary document, written and polished, they suggest, over a long time or at any rate completed only after 392 B.C.E. The analysis of the dialogue provided at the end of their piece helps us begin to engage with this complexity.

In 'On the Alleged Historical Reputability of Plato's *Apology*,' Donald Morrison argues that if the *Apology* does not contain Socrates' actual words, then we cannot even reconstruct Socrates' philosophy—'the general propositions he believed in and the intellectual methods he employed' (p. 106)—from the *Apology*. For example, it cannot (by itself or in combination with other Socratics' reports) tell us about Socrates' profession that he does not think that he knows anything fine and good (21d), what is the fine and good that he does not know, what are the standards for knowledge by which he judges that he does not know, whether such knowledge is in principle possible. Socrates may have been unclear or undecided about these matters, or his views about them may have changed over time.

Even if we cannot retrieve the original of Socrates from Plato's voice-over, the *Apology* raises historical questions. One such question is whether behind the official charges against Socrates there might not have been political motivations; perhaps Socrates' accusers thought that Socrates had provided ideological support for the violent oligarchic coup of 404 B.C.E. but could not prosecute him for this because of an amnesty declared by the restored democracy. This scenario may seem plausible because it is difficult to appreciate the seriousness of the official charges against Socrates in a secular society which guarantees freedom of conscience. Terence Irwin's 'Was Socrates against Democracy?' explains how the perception that Socrates was impious and a corrupter of the youth would have given the Athenians sufficiently serious reasons to want to prosecute him and Socrates' followers to want to exonerate him from the charges: Socrates' disbelief in the gods of Athens might cause the gods to look unfavourably upon an Athens suffering through the Peloponnesian War and the Plague; atheism can undermine people's commitment to justice; finally, as Plato himself suggests in the *Republic*, the kind of argumentation Socrates practiced can lead to a loss of faith in moral norms and practices. In addition to this discussion about what might have motivated the prosecution of Socrates, Irwin argues that Plato's Socrates does not provide ideological support for oligarchy, for Socrates' criticisms of democracy are largely theoretical and underdetermine what course of action an Athenian in his time ought to adopt (Socrates' chief criticism, that the people do not know their own interests and so are not qualified to rule, obviously applies to oligarchy as well).

Myles Burnyeat's 'The Impiety of Socrates' (which, despite its title, is in broad agreement with Vlastos's 'Socratic Piety') helps us to understand the official charges and Socrates' conviction from the perspective of a reasonable Athenian. The question before the jury is whether Socrates is guilty as charged, of doing wrong to the city by corrupting the youth, disbelieving in the city's gods, and introducing new gods (24b); Socrates himself asks the jury to consider nothing other than the justice of the case (17c). Burnyeat presents a strong case that Socrates is guilty of impiety: while Socrates may show that

Meletus' charge, that he introduces new gods, entails that he believes in gods, this does not show that he believes in the gods the city believes in; while Socrates may say that the God (*ho theos*) has ordered him to philosophize and is responsible for the voice that keeps Socrates from wrongdoing, he does not name any gods apart from two incidental references to Hera and Thetis. Finally, Socrates' announcement that the virtuous man cannot be harmed by the city, not even if they kill him (30bc), sounds like the claim that one can prosper solely as a result of one's own moral efforts—rather than, as traditional Greek religion would have it, if the gods please. Plato's own verdict, that if so good a man as Socrates was guilty of impiety under Athenian law, then Athenian religion was guilty of impiety, is a verdict about Athenian religion, but the question to Socrates' jury is whether Socrates was guilty under the law. And while a liberal might conclude from the case of Socrates that perhaps impiety ought not to be punishable as it was in Socrates' Athens, Burnyeat points out that Plato did not draw this conclusion, for the ideal city he describes in his *Laws* also imposes the death penalty for impiety on the terms of *its* religion.

That Plato in the *Laws* does not stand up for freedom of conscience and thought may not surprise the reader, but it is worth remarking that even in the *Apology*, Socrates does not defend the physicists for asking important questions or following reason wherever it leads, but instead distances his own activity from theirs. And if this isn't disappointing enough, the *Crito* seems to argue that unless a citizen can persuade the city that its law is unjust, he must obey it. (Of course, in context, Plato's point about Socrates might be that unlike the oligarchs of Athens' recent revolution, he is committed to obeying the law.) In the *Crito*, Socrates, awaiting his execution, explains to his friend Crito why he should not escape prison: he has a commitment to do no injustice, not even in return for an injustice (49bd), and he believes that it is unjust to break a just agreement (49e). In the voice of the Laws of Athens, Socrates says that it would be unjust for him to try to escape prison now because he would be trying to destroy the Laws and the city as far as he is concerned (50ab); he has agreed with the city to respect its judgments (50c); he may try to persuade the city to change its judgment, but if he fails he must obey it (51b); he is indebted to the city for his birth, nurture, and education, and may not retaliate against the city's punishments, just as a child may not against his parents' (50d).

Apart from its authoritarianism (to which we will return), this position seems to conflict with Socrates' attitude to obedience in the *Apology*: there, Socrates imagines the jury acquitting him on the condition that he cease practicing philosophy—and tells them what his reply would be: 'I will obey the God rather than you' (29ce). (Socrates also reports defying the order of the Thirty to participate in the arrest and execution of Leon of Salamis [32ce], but he may have thought that complying with this order would be unjust or even illegal.)

In 'Socrates and Obedience to the Law', Thomas Brickhouse and Nicholas Smith provide an elegant reconciliation of the conflict by appeal to Athenian law: the jury could not legally acquit Socrates but then impose a penalty (refraining from practicing philosophy) on him; in the case of a conviction, either the penalty was set by the law, or in cases like Socrates', where it was not, the prosecution proposed one penalty at the indictment, to which the defense could propose a counter-penalty after the conviction, but in no case could the jury propose its own penalty. So Socrates' imagined scenario is not one in which he will disobey the law; it is, instead, one in which he demonstrates his unconditional commitment to piety. Now one might think that a commitment to piety and a commitment to obey the law could easily come into conflict, so that Brickhouse and Smith have just been lucky to find a law that reconciles the conflict between them in this case. However, Brickhouse and Smith argue that the law itself commands piety, so that a case of such conflict would be a case of conflict internal to the law—and a legal system cannot expect anyone to obey two conflicting laws.[3] (One might then expect the law to claim that its interpretation of piety is authoritative—to deal, for example, with someone who says he is only obeying the law on piety in doing as his *daimonion* bids him.)

'*Dokimasia*, Satisfaction, and Agreement' is a chapter of Richard Kraut's essential book on the *Crito*, *Socrates and the State*. The book offers an unauthoritarian reading of the dialogue as a whole. One of its most influential arguments is the argument that by 'persuade or obey' the Laws mean that a citizen must obey a law unless he tries to persuade the city of the injustice of that law, in which case he may disobey it and suffer the consequences;[4] this gives Socrates a sort of theory of civil disobedience. However, '*Dokimasia* . . .' engages with a more fundamental topic in political philosophy, that of political obligation incurred by agreement. At the same time, it retains the dialogue's focus on what Socrates (rather than every citizen) is obligated to do. Kraut uses Socrates' principles (do no injustice, keep just agreements) to constrain any agreement Socrates can have made with the Laws, so that the Laws can only obligate him to keep an agreement that does not require him to commit injustice, if, in addition, the agreement is fairly made. The Laws' speech, then, demonstrates that the agreement (which may require Socrates to suffer injustice) is fairly made. To be fairly made, the agreement requires the parties to have full information and plenty of time. Kraut points out that Athenian citizenship was not automatic but involved an initiation called the *dokimasia* during which a young adult would be examined for his fitness to be a citizen; following this, the citizen would gradually become more and more aware of the city's laws; finally, a citizen would be taken to have agreed to obey the city's laws upon expressing satisfaction with them—which he need not do in so

many words, but, for example, by deciding to reside in the city over other reasonable alternatives, or by raising children there. This view of what constitutes
agreement has much to recommend it, both interpretively (it is consistent
with 'persuade and obey' and shows the relevance of the Laws' many appeals
to Socrates' satisfaction with Athens) and philosophically (agreement is not
implied by residence alone, nor does it depend on inner satisfaction). However, Kraut faults the Laws for equating satisfaction with the city and satisfaction with its laws, and for treating citizenship as a privilege—like membership
in a club—rather than a right.

By contrast with Kraut, in 'The Interpretation of Plato's *Crito*,' David Bostock treats the speech of the Laws as self-contained (rather than as committed to Socrates' initial principles at 49be) and argues that the *Crito* is so authoritarian in outlook as to demand obedience to the law even when it
commands the commission of injustice. If the Laws are arguing that it is unjust for Socrates to flee because to do so is to disobey the law that verdicts be
carried out, and to disobey this law is (for one's part) to destroy the whole system of laws, and *that* is unjust, then Socrates must obey the law to carry out
verdicts even if that requires him to commit an injustice. If the Laws are also
arguing that Socrates has made an agreement to abide by the Laws, then they
are emphasizing that he must do as they command because his agreement to
obey them was made under fair conditions—they make no exception for cases
in which he judges that what they command requires him to commit an injustice. Further, the agreement seems to be constituted by Socrates' residence
in Athens. If the Laws add to these arguments a third, that Socrates had the
opportunity to persuade them, then they must be claiming that if he tried but
failed to persuade them (as he did in the *Apology*), he must obey them—as a
slave who fails to persuade his master, or a child who fails to persuade his parent, must obey him. Bostock concludes with two further pieces of evidence for
authoritarianism in the *Crito*: that Socrates accords the same praise to the
customs and laws that he does to virtue and justice (53c), that the Laws distinguish themselves from the men who apply them and claim that Socrates'
escape would be directed at them, who did him no wrong (54b), which is a
basis for claiming that they can do no wrong. Finally, Socrates claims that in
order to decide the present case—whether it would be just for him to flee jail
and his execution—they should consult the moral expert; that expert must be
the Laws.

In 'Conflicting Values in Plato's *Crito*,' Verity Harte argues that the Laws'
speech conflicts with Socrates' principles[5]: whereas (Harte says) Socrates takes
all retaliation to be wrongful, the Laws claim only that retaliation is wrongful
in certain relationships—like that between parent and child and master and
slave—suggesting that in relationships of equality, retaliation would be just or

at least not unjust (50e-51a). Further, while Socrates holds agreements are binding only when what they require one to do is just, the Laws emphasize that Socrates has agreed to do whatever they command (51e)—and they could easily command some act of injustice. As for the Laws' appeal to Socrates' opportunity to 'persuade or obey', here the goal of persuasion is to get the laws to change (failing which he must obey), Harte says, not to legitimate acts of disobedience. What is the point of this conflict? Harte proposes that Crito, Socrates, and the Laws argue about the justice of Socrates' escape from three different perspectives. Still, the disagreement between Crito and the Laws can be bridged: Crito thinks of justice as a matter of doing one's duty within certain special relationships, especially with respect to one's family and friends; the Laws draw on an analogy between the household and the city to argue that the most important of these special relationships is with the city. By contrast, although Crito and Socrates agree on general principles of justice (one should never do wrong, not even in response to a wrong), their conceptions of what counts as harm, and thus as wrong, and thus as justice and injustice, and thus as the domain of justice are so different that there can be no 'common deliberation' (49d) between them. In representing these conflicting values, the *Crito* augurs Plato's own attempts to integrate individual and civic justice in later dialogues.

Plato's *Euthyphro, Apology,* and *Crito,* along with these varied articles about them, challenge readers to raise questions: what should we take away from these works—do they give us principles for inquiry and for the conduct of state and citizens, or do they simply testify to the way in which an extraordinary individual lived his life? Socrates describes his life of inquiry as prompted by a unique happening, the oracle's pronouncement of him as the wisest man alive (*Apology* 20e-23b). If Socrates philosophizes in order to follow the god's command, what are the implications for those who are not spoken to directly by the god? Does the importance of caring for our souls give the rest of us sufficient reason to philosophize? Under what conditions are we able to philosophize—do we need a Socrates to question us, or is his example sufficient, or do we need more than a Socrates? While we are seeking knowledge, what should our attitude be toward established authority? And does Plato's Socrates answer such questions?

Notes

1. Rather than treat this contradiction as an embarrassment for Euthyphro to rescue himself from, however, Socrates helps: he says, 'I did not ask you what same thing is both pious and impious' (8a). Saying of the same thing that it is both pious and impious is not simply affirming a contradiction; it is only failing to define the pious or the impious.

2. As a result, none of them have been included in this collection. Examples include: Benson, H. 'The Priority of Definition and the Socratic Elenchus.' *Oxford Studies in Ancient Philosophy* 8 (1990), pp. 19–65, reprinted in T. Irwin (ed.) *Classical Philosophy: Collected Papers* vol. 2, *Socrates and His Contemporaries* (New York: Garland, 1995), and 'Misunderstanding the "What-is-F-ness?" Question', *Archiv fur Geschichte der Philosophie* 72 (1990) pp. 125–42, reprinted in H. Benson (ed.) *Essays on the Philosophy of Socrates* (Oxford: Oxford University Press, 1992); Beverslius, J. 'Does Socrates Commit the Socratic Fallacy?' *American Philosophical Quarterly* 24 (1987), pp. 211–23; reprinted in Benson (ed.) *Essays on the Philosophy of Socrates*; Burnyeat, M. 'Examples in Epistemology: Socrates, Theaetetus and G.E. Moore,' *Philosophy* 52 (1977): pp. 381–98; Irwin, T. *Plato's Ethics* (Oxford: Oxford University Press, 1995), chapter 2; Nehamas, A. 'Confusing Universals and Particulars in Plato's Early Dialogues', *Review of Metaphysics* 29 (1975), pp. 287–306, and 'Socratic Intellectualism' *Proceedings of the Boston Area Colloquium in Ancient Philosophy* 2, ed. John J. Cleary (Lanham, Md.: University Press of America, 1987), pp. 275–316. Both reprinted in Nehamas, A. *The Virtues of Authenticity*; Santas, G. 'The Socratic Fallacy,' *Journal of the History of Philosophy* 10 (1972), pp. 127–41.

3. This discussion has been integrated into an excellent book-length study of the *Apology* by Brickhouse and Smith, *Socrates on Trial* (Princeton 1989). Another noteworthy book-length study of the *Apology* is C. D. C. Reeve's *Socrates in the Apology* (Indianapolis: Hackett, 1989).

4. *Socrates and the State*, (Princeton, 1984) ch. 3.

5. For an important book-length work distinguishing the voice of Socrates from the voice of the Laws, see Roslyn Weiss, *Socrates Dissatisfied: An Analysis of Plato's* Crito (Oxford, 1998).

1

Justice and Pollution in the *Euthyphro*

Mark L. McPherran

R EADERS OF PLATO'S *EUTHYPHRO* TYPICALLY FOCUS their attention on Socrates' elenctic examination of Euthyphro's five attempted definitions of piety (εὐσέβεια) (1) piety is proceeding against whomever does injustice (5d-6e), (2) piety is what is loved by the gods (6e-9d), (3) piety is what is loved by *all* the gods (9e-11b), (4) piety is that part of justice which assists the gods to produce their most beautiful product (11e-14b), and (5) piety is an art of prayer and sacrifice (14b-15c). But although these argumentative episodes do very much form the explicit philosophical substance of the dialogue, the complex motivations which drive its participants also deserve careful scrutiny if we are to fully understand both them and the overall import of the dialogue. It seems clear that Plato himself wishes to provoke this sort of examination, since he provides an unusually complex and long dramatic prologue, amounting to roughly one-third of the dialogue's length (one whose themes continuously inform the subsequent inquiry into piety). We would do well, then, to investigate one of the prologue's most puzzling and yet least-discussed elements; namely, Euthyphro's assertion that he is justified in prosecuting his father out of a concern for the μίασμα—the pollution—that attends homicides of the sort he imagines his father to have committed, and because impartial justice demands it (4b7-c3). In this paper I shall argue for a novel account of this appeal, one which shows Euthyphro to be more morally and theologically progressive than he has been thought but which also freshly illuminates the way in which the *Euthyphro* serves as an indirect, nonforensic defense of Socrates.[1]

The *Euthyphro*'s introduction consists of two parts, the first introducing the topic of Socrates' upcoming trial and the second detailing Euthyphro's own court case. For my purposes here I shall take the risk of assuming that in this first section and in what follows Plato portrays Socrates' motives for engaging with Euthyphro as relatively transparent, fully virtuous, and identical with those professed by the Socrates of the *Apology* (e.g., *Ap.* 22e-23b, 29c-31c): as this Socrates has it, the quest for knowledge of 'what the pious is' (15c-16a) ought never to be abandoned, since not only is this enterprise pleasurable (arguably an 'inconceivable happiness'; *Ap.* 41c3-4) and pious in itself, but coming to understand piety would allow one to 'live better the rest of one's life' (15e7-16a4), especially should its continuation be threatened by a charge of *im*piety (3b-d, 5a-c, 12e, 15e-16a).[2]

Naturally, some commentators have found such representations to be laced with brazen insincerity. According to John Beversluis, for example, the typical characterization of Euthyphro as a pretentious, dense, father-bashing, religious zealot who 'would have done well in the Nazi Youth Movement,' has drawn attention away from our noticing how abusive and ineffectual Socrates' examination of him actually is.[3] Socrates, we are told, first overwhelms Euthyphro with his idiosyncratic principles of proper definition (5c-d, 6d-e) and then elenctically drubs him on the basis of uncomprehending, merely verbal agreement. But however plausible this critique may be, it does not follow that Socrates is therefore guilty of impiously, unjustly, and hypocritically neglecting Euthyphro's soul (Beversluis, 184). Rather, *pace* Beversluis (176, 184), it seems most dramatically effective on Plato's part to have us think that Euthyphro's sudden departure at the end of the dialogue occurs *before* the court convenes, so that he thereby forfeits his ill-conceived suit (as later tradition had it; D.L. 2.29). Socrates' tactics thus benefit Euthyphro, his father, and his relatives by dissuading Euthyphro from pursuing a potentially damaging course of action. Be all this as it may, however, it is Euthyphro on whom I now wish to focus.

According to Plato's story, five years prior to Socrates' encounter with Euthyphro one of Euthyphro's hired farm hands (a πελάτης) had killed one of the family's household slaves (an οἰκέτης) during a drunken rage. Euthyphro's father had the killer bound and thrown in a ditch, and then—since the laborer was a murderer—neglected him while awaiting word from one of the Athenian religious advisors (ἐξηγηταί) on how to proceed. As a result, the laborer perished from hunger and exposure. In response, Euthyphro now brings before the Archôn Basileus a suit for homicide—a (δίκη φόνου)—against his father, in order to cleanse both his father and himself (and presumably his relatives) of the μίασμα that he sees attending this sort of unjust killing (4b-e).[4] Socrates is understandably astonished by this story. By suing his own father,

Euthyphro appears to be crazy (μαίνεσθαι, 4a1), since it would be most un-usual (if not actually impossible; see below) to prosecute a relative on behalf of an outsider. Moreover, doing so violates the norms of filial piety (4d-e, 9a-b, 15d).[5] Hence, Socrates insinuates, it could only be through the possession of a conception of piety superior to that of received tradition that Euthyphro could be so confident as to pursue such an unconventional and—one would think—potentially damaging course of action (4e; cf. 4a-b; 15d-e; damaging to Euthyphro, his father, and family in a variety of aspects [e.g., socially, psy-chologically, morally, and economically] if his father were to be convicted and sentenced to exile). Without the least hesitation, Euthyphro swallows the bait by agreeing with Socrates' suggestion, grandly laying claim to a 'precise' (ἀκριβῶς) knowledge of all such divine things. The characteristic setup of a Socratic interlocutor has thus been successfully stage-managed: if Euthyphro has such an exact understanding of divine matters, then surely he can spell out for Socrates just what piety is.[6]

Euthyphro's unusual suit has generated a great deal of scholarly debate, much of it focused on the issue of whether fifth-century Athenian homicide law was restrictive; that is, whether initiating a suit for homicide was restricted to those family members (or a slave his master or a woman her *kyrios*) speci-fied in Draco's law, or whether exceptions might be allowed (A. Tulin provides a good survey; see M. Gagarin 1997a for a review of Tulin). I shall bypass this issue here, and simply assume that Euthyphro's specific suit is legally permis-sible. For if it were not, we would expect that Plato would then have had his Socrates at least make note of Euthyphro's ignorance of the law for the sake of verisimilitude and dramatic plausibility. Likewise, Plato would not have por-trayed Euthyphro's relatives as being as troubled as they are (4a, 4d-e, 6a) were his suit in fact legally impossible.[7] Finally, the central discussion of whether Euthyphro's proposed prosecution is pious or not would be decidedly under-motivated if that prosecution posed no genuine threat to Euthyphro's father (*pace* J. Burnet, 104). In any case, the emphasis in the dialogue is placed not on the fact that Euthyphro is prosecuting on behalf of a non-relative, but that it is *his father* he is prosecuting on behalf of a non-relative (see 4b4-6).

Let us recall, then, how Euthyphro attempts to ground his unusual behavior:

It is laughable, Socrates, that you suppose that it makes any difference whether the dead man is an outsider [ἀλλότριος] or of the family [οἰκεῖος]rather than that one should be on guard only for whether the killer killed with justice or not; and if it was with justice, to let it go, but if not, to proceed against him—espe-cially if the killer shares your hearth and table. For the pollution is equal if you knowingly associate with such a man and do not purify yourself, as well as him, by proceeding against him in a lawsuit (4b7-c3; trans. after West and West).

Shortly thereafter, Euthyphro justifies and increases the scope of this principle of impartial justice:

> Piety is doing as I am doing; that is to say, prosecuting anyone who is guilty of murder, temple thefts, or of any similar crime—whether he be your father or mother, or whoever he may be—that makes no difference; and not to prosecute them is impiety. And observe, Socrates, what powerful evidence I can cite that this is the law . . . that one is not to give way to the impious one, whoever he happens to be. For do not men acknowledge Zeus as the best and most righteous of the gods?—and yet they admit that he imprisoned his father [Kronos] because he wickedly devoured his sons, and that he too castrated his own father [Ouranos] for the same sort of reason. Yet they are angry at me because I am proceeding against my father when he has done injustice, and so they contradict themselves both concerning the gods and concerning me (5d8-6a6; cf. 8b, 9a-b).[8]

Euthyphro is less than clear in communicating the principle of conduct he has in mind here and above, but he appears to hold that (P): [Pa] one who closely associates with an unjust killer becomes vulnerable to the pollution that attends such murderers;[9] hence, [Pb] in order to avoid becoming polluted oneself (or to purify oneself if already polluted), and to purify the murderer of his or her own pollution, one ought to prosecute, and thereby punish (typically: banish), that murderer irrespective of one's familial relationship to the killer.[10]

In view of Euthyphro's status as a μάντις (3b9-c3, 3e2-4), his initial concern with pollution, and his subsequent appeal to the behavior of Zeus and Kronos in justification of his suit (5d-6a), scholars have often been led to view him as simply Plato's mouthpiece for popular Athenian religion.[11] This interpretation, however, is only half right.[12] As I have argued elsewhere, Euthyphro's literary function is complex and two-fold: (A) Plato intends first that he should serve as a hubristic patient for the *elenchos* who, by prosecuting an older man on the grounds of piety and the justice of Homeric/ Hesiodic Zeus, can thereby serve as a paradigm of retrograde traditionalism and, thus, as a surrogate for Socrates' prosecutor Meletus as well; and (B) by suggesting various affinities between Socrates and Euthyphro—in particular, by casting Euthyphro as a *non*-traditionalist, religious innovator, and freelancing prophet (δεισιδαίμων)—Plato presents him as a dark Doppelgänger of Socrates, a lesson in what Socrates *is* and *is not*.[13] This interpretive outlook would thus suggest that Euthyphro's appeal to μίασμα in [Pa] is a manifestation of Plato's intention (A) to contrast Euthyphro's superstitious extremism with Socrates' own philosophically sound religious outlook. Oddly, though, it is this seemingly conventional notion of μίασμα that Euthyphro uses to explicate what appears to be a quite forward-looking, cosmopolitan principle of impartial justice (Pb) (Tulin, 81). Indeed—and although Euthyphro is portrayed as mildly chastising Socrates for possibly believing otherwise (4b7-c1)—the idea that one ought to proceed against those who do injustice, even if they are relatives, is a *Socratic* principle grounded in our texts (*Eu.* 8d-e; *Cr.* 49b, *Ap.* 28b; *G.* 480a-d). What appears to differentiate Euthyphro from Socrates here, then, is the incentive driving the principle of impartial justice constituted by Euthyphro's appeal to μίασμα; for surely *Socrates*, one might naturally suppose, would never endorse such a superstitious concern. Thus, we are to understand Euthyphro to be facing a moral and legal dilemma between the ancient demands of filial piety that would prohibit his prosecution of a relative (suggested at 4e, 9a-b, 15d), and the filial imperative 'that he free both himself and his father from the dangerous taint of pollution,' (Tulin, 84). As a typical instance of 'the superstitious man' (δεισιδαίμων) he thus chooses the latter course, but then paradoxically proceeds to represent it as grounding an enlightened principle of justice that anyone ought to heed.[14] To make sense of and resolve this puzzling, seemingly concocted conjunction, we must investigate Euthyphro's conception of pollution in light of the popular conception.

Constructing a brief, consistent, and accurate account of the fifth-century Greek understanding of pollution is, of course, highly problematic. However, it is fair to say that most Athenians would have understood μίασμα to have the following characteristics: it is a contagious defilement one may wittingly or unwittingly (as in the cases of Heracles and Oedipus) incur through unjust and impious conduct; it makes those affected ritually impure (thus unfit to enter a temple), it is dangerous since disasters attend upon it, and it can settle and spread like a disease to the innocent as well as the guilty (indeed, 'μίασμα' in its widest sense included disease).[15] Unlike curses, however, the gods are only indirectly involved in the suffering of those parties affected by the spread of μίασμα; for μίασμα is an impersonal, invisible material taint that polluted individuals transmit to others, although its origin can be divine animosity (R. Parker, 8-10; cf. *Il.* 1.1-102; Soph. *Ant.* 999-1047). The pollution that attends the killing of a human being—whether intended or not, just or unjust—is especially virulent: it takes the form of the victim's blood which in some sense clings to the hands of the murderer and spreads out from them to encompass the entire city (see, e.g., Soph. *Oedipus the King* [*OT*] 1-150; Antiphon, *Tetr.* 1.1.3, 2.1.2, 3.1.5). This blood carries the anger of the victim and/or attending avenging spirits and the victim's desire for revenge. Hence, there is legislation that proscribes associating with murderers so as to prevent the spread of their μίασμα (Demosthenes 20-21, 158). Sophocles' Oedipus is the most famous vector for this kind of μίασμα in Greek drama: as the unwitting, unpunished killer of his own father (King Laius), Oedipus bears a

μίασμα that has rendered his entire city infertile. But thanks to the information provided by Apollo, he is able to set out to banish (or kill) the unidenti-
fied polluter (*OT* 1-150,).[16] The remedy for μίασμα great or small is purification (καθαρμός) which can range from everyday ritual washing with
lustral water to the civic purification achieved through the expulsion of scape-
goats (see Parker, 23-31, and chs. 4 and 9).

In light of this and our knowledge of Athenian law, Euthyphro's suit and his
appeal to pollution and impartial justice emerge as non-traditional in several
respects:

1. Euthyphro appears to think that it should make no moral or civic difference whether a slain person is οἰκεῖος or ἀλλότριος as one determines how to proceed in a case of killing (M.J. Edwards, 216-17). Again,
by prosecuting his own father Euthyphro contravenes conventional
morality and risks doing something impious to his father and relatives
(namely, subjecting his father to the punishment of exile) (4e, 5b, 15d).
2. Euthyphro assumes that his father's neglect of the thrall amounted to
murder (φόνου; 4a10), even though many excused the father of deliberate homicide because of the individual's apparent guilt, because it was
inaction and not violence that killed the thrall,[17] and because that neglect was due in part to the father's attempt to consult with one of the
ἐξηγηταί.[18]
3. Euthyphro's view that only the justice of his father's deed is relevant rests
on the claim that it is *because* of the attendant pollution that one should
proceed against those unjust individuals who 'share one's hearth and
table.' But an allegation of pollution by itself carried virtually no legal
weight in Athens (Parker, 116; M. Gagarin and D.M. MacDowell, 18).
4. Euthyphro holds that if a killer kills justly then no pollution is incurred
(4b-c). Moreover, he appears to ground this novel idea on the equally
novel tenet that he and his action are pious because he acts in imitation
of gods (Zeus and Kronos). Euthyphro's appeal to the gods' behavior in
justification of his own is, of course, *extra leges*.
5. Euthyphro apparently holds that it is only through close association with
an *unjust* killer that one incurs pollution (4b7-c3).

In attempting to account for why Plato ascribes these particular innovations
to Euthyphro, the first obstacle to remove is the idea that Plato employs them
in order to cast Euthyphro as an unusually superstitious or archaic thinker (P.T.
Geach, 370) or an especially 'rigid adherent to traditional mores' (W.D. Furley,
206). For, as a few scholars have noted, Euthyphro anticipates in several respects the progressive view of pollution and civic justice represented in the

Laws by the Athenian Stranger (Edwards; cf. L. Versényi 1982, 36-7; see also *R.* 469e-470a). There we find it held that (a) non-relatives may prosecute on behalf of a stranger (866b, 871b) and that a kinsman who fails to prosecute on behalf of another is subject to pollution (871a-b) (*per* 1); (b) if a deed is just there is no wrongdoing and thus no religious sanction, and since the Stranger 'also holds that the civic laws should be underwritten by the gods (855b-c), he cannot fail to agree with Euthyphro that the only actions capable of polluting us are the ones that they [the gods] condemn,' (Edwards, 222) (*per* 3 and 4); and (c) pollution has very much to do with the state of one's soul, such that the morally corrupt person is impure of soul, and is in this way polluted (716d-717a) (*per* 4 and 5).[19] How, then, are we to square what now seems to be an attempt to cast Euthyphro as a forward-looking thinker on the topic of pollution, giving that notion a non-physicalist moral sense, with Plato's equally clear desire to make Euthyphro out to be philosophically deficient?

One answer holds that it is *Socrates*, not Euthyphro, who is initially made to pose 'as the mouthpiece of traditional partialities,' so that Euthyphro can then be seen as correct and cosmopolitan on the topic of civic justice (Edwards, 223). Euthyphro's failure to defend a coherent account of piety and its relation to justice in the face of Socrates' relentless elenctic examination is thus meant to signal that, unlike Socrates, he lacks the philosophical ability and self-knowledge required to defend his views. His purported mantic abilities may have given him a few true insights, then, but they manifestly fail to give him the ability to rationally defend them.

Although this interpretation is correct insofar as it takes Euthyphro to be both forward-thinking and (nonetheless) intellectually deficient when it comes to rational self-examination, it ought not to satisfy us entirely because of its failure to account for several of Euthyphro's other eccentricities (see n 13) and Socrates' own resistance to the theology that undergirds them. Moreover, it appears to be at odds with what I take to be the *sine qua non* of any adequate interpretation; namely, the dialogue's obvious pairing *per* dramatic intention (A) of Meletus—a seeming advocate of 'traditional partialities'—with Euthyphro. Socrates, then, should be compared to Euthyphro's father; for like Euthyphro's father, Socrates is elderly (*Eu.* 3a), 'goes to each Athenian like a *father*, persuading each to care for virtue' (*Ap.* 31b; my emphasis), and yet now finds himself rashly indicted by a younger man on the grounds of piety (5a-b) (McPherran 1996, 32-3, 181).[20] This analogical connection argues in turn that we are to pair Meletus' formal charge of corruption with Euthyphro's informal charge of pollution.[21] The text of the *Apology* also supports this pairing, for at 23d1-2 Socrates represents the informal allegation against him (that led Meletus to lodge the formal charge of corruption) as stating that 'Socrates is a most polluted fellow [μιαρώτατος] and corrupts the youth,' (with, presumably, a causal connection implied).

The key to making sense of this last pairing is to first note Socrates' surprising silence—tantamount to silent acceptance in view of our observations concerning the *Laws*—of Euthyphro's reliance on a non-traditionalist, moral conception of pollution. This acceptance stands, moreover, in sharp relief to Socrates' subsequent resistance to Euthyphro's appeal to the behavior of Zeus and Kronos and any other such stories of divine disagreement and conflict he might produce to justify his prosecution.[22] The uncommon hubris of this appeal[23] and, in particular, Euthyphro's agreement that there is but one sort of piety, however, does indicate that Euthyphro is no hide-bound traditionalist. Only someone with a relatively unorthodox intellectualist theology would simply presuppose that there is but one canon of virtue *for both gods and human beings*, as Euthyphro does with his 'powerful evidence' of Zeus' and Kronos' just, yet father-bashing, behavior (then confirmed by his acceptance of the idea of *generic* justice at 11e-12e). For the common view had generally held the gods not to be bound by human standards of conduct.[24] Together with his introduction of the notion that there is but *one* overarching property of piety, Socrates' pass over this unusual presupposition in utter silence indicates that he too thinks of piety—and so the other virtues—as universal, univocal concepts/ properties (such that both just gods and just humans are, for example, just in the same sense). He apparently also has no problem with the implicit, revolutionary, and (of course) very Platonic idea that one should attempt to model and justify one's own behavior in relation to that of a god (were one to have good evidence of what that behavior consisted in; *Eu.* 9a-c).[25]

Socrates' response to Euthyphro's 'proof' of the piety of his prosecution is, instead, entirely prompted by Euthyphro's conventionalist assertion that among the gods there exist many disagreements and battles similar to that experienced by Kronos and Zeus (6b; 6c); and to *this*, Socrates' reaction is swift incredulity (6a-c).[26] Indeed, he indicates that whenever anyone has said such things about the gods he has responded with a disbelief so unmistakable that he speculates that public awareness of this disbelief may be what has prompted his indictment on charges of impiety (6a-c). Thus, Socrates proceeds to show how Euthyphro's defenses of such later claims as 'piety is what gods love' (6e11-7a1) are inconsistent with his desire to retain both this popular conception of the gods as capricious, disagreeing rulers and the belief that the gods might also behave in a uniform and standard-setting fashion (e.g., that Zeus displays a standard of justice we should adopt and imitate [*Eu.* 5e-6a] and that the gods might all of them have a love for the same thing; 9e1-3).

I want to argue, then, that Socrates' silent acceptance of Euthyphro's use of a non-standard account of pollution in view of Plato's second dramatic intention (B) of drawing parallels between Socrates and Euthyphro strongly suggests that we are to understand Euthyphro's 'pollution' as conceptually equivalent to 'corruption' in the Socratic, moral sense; that is, a pollution of the soul we can label 'pollution$_m$'. This is the psychic pollution of inconsistent and false belief Socrates has in mind when he praises what philosophical activity and just punishment are able to eliminate from our souls (as forms of purification; *Ap.* 20d-23d, 29e-30b; *G.* 457c-458b, 476a-481b; *Phd.* 65e-69d, 80d-83d; cf. *R.* 611c-612a; *Crat.* 403d-404a; *Symp.* 211e-212a). Besides making dramatic sense, both terms—'pollution' (μίασμα)and 'corruption' (διαφθορά)—are first of all bound by linguistic and conceptual ties; both, for example, are to be understood as designating states of defilement and ruination (cf. Eur. *Bacchae* 1384; s.v. L&S) that can be remedied only through purification (cf. Soph. *OT* 1-150; Eur. *Hipp.* 601-606, 653-4, 946; *R.* 399e, 567c). Secondly, we have seen evidence that Euthyphro had come under new intellectualist influence, and such influence would have included the view exemplified in Antiphon's *Tetralogies* where 'pollution appears [in contrast to the traditional conception] as a stern and discriminating upholder of the moral order,' (Parker, 110; my bracketed phrase).[27] Finally, notice that rather than denigrating Meletus' charge of corruption, Socrates characterizes it as 'not ignoble or paltry, but weighty' (2c2-4; cf. 5b). Moreover, he then asserts that Meletus alone, of all the politicians, is proceeding correctly by paying attention to the moral development of Athens's youth and by proposing to 'weed out'—that is, expel from the city—those who corrupt them (2c-3a) (just as one does with those who carry μίασμα; cf. Parker, 264). Meletus rightly sees how Socrates could be a threat, since it is by teaching the young corrupting beliefs that they are corrupted (2c-3a, 3c-d). In the *Apology* as well, Socrates never complains that charges of corruption are illegitimate and (again) represents the informal allegation that led to the formal charge of corruption as stating that 'Socrates is a most polluted fellow [μιαρώτατος] and corrupts the youth,' (*Ap.* 23d1-2). Moreover, in the course of defending himself against the charge, Socrates reveals his own understanding of what corruption is, how it is spread, and how best to eradicate it.

Recall that according to the report of Diogenes Laertius (D.L. 2.40) and Xenophon (*Mem.* 1.1.1), and as Socrates himself recounts at *Apology* 24b8-c1 (cf. *Eu.* 3b-d), Meletus' writ of impiety (γραφὴ ἀσεβείας) consisted of three distinct charges:

(I). Socrates does not recognize (νομίζειν) the gods recognized by the state.

(II). Socrates introduces new divinities (καινὰ δαιμόνια).

(III). Socrates corrupts (διαφθείρων) the youth.

Socrates takes up the three formal charges in reverse order, considering the corruption charge first: (III) '[Socrates] also wrongs the youth by corrupting

them (ἀδικεῖ δὲ καὶ τοὺς νέους διαφθείρων)'. This allegation depends upon
the other two: it is *teaching* the doctrines specified by the other two charges
that constitutes the charge of corruption (see T.C. Brickhouse and N.D. Smith
1989, ch. 3). Socrates' initial response to it is to interrogate Meletus along two
lines of argument meant to establish the implausibility of the charge in its
own right, irrespective of what he is alleged to teach. The first tries to show
this by eliciting from Meletus the extremely unlikely claim that all the Athenians improve the youth while Socrates alone corrupts them (25a9-10; 24c-25c).
The second aims to defeat the corruption charge by arguing that since no one
wishes to be harmed (25d1-2), attempting to corrupt—that is, to harm
morally—those young people *with whom he associates* is something that
Socrates would never willingly do (25c-26a; cf. 37a; see, e.g., Brickhouse and
Smith 1989, 117-19, for discussion).

This second argument provides further reason for assimilating Euthyphro's
notion of μίασμα as pollution$_m$ to Socrates' sense of corruption; for here it
is argued that just as with pollution$_m$ (cf. [5] above), a person may expect to
be harmed by closely associating with those who are corrupt, and where for
Socrates this must refer to moral harm, moral corruption. On Socrates' account, while involuntary corrupters ought to be educated and not prosecuted
in order to change their behavior, those who intentionally corrupt ought to be
reformed through prosecution and punishment (cf. *Cr.* 51b; *G.* 480b-e; *Phd.*
113d).[28] Likewise, Euthyphro's seemingly retrograde idea that the pollution
posed by his father is 'caught' through *close* association with him ('sharing
hearth and table'), and can only be remedied through prosecution and punishment (non-traditional aspects 3, 4, 5), is thus arguably none other than
Socrates' own.[29] Since, then, as Euthyphro understands it, his father intentionally allowed his (Euthyphro's) laborer to perish from hunger and cold
without any dispensation from the religious advisors (ἐξηγηταί), prosecution followed by punishment—not instruction—is what is called for. Moreover, from his perspective, those who are aware of the questionable nature of
his father's behavior (viz., his relatives [4d-e]) and yet *continue to associate
with him* must themselves be morally blind and impaired, and thus, are very
much threatened with further damage to themselves. They are not, however,
endangered by the archaic, hobgoblin invisible physical taint of μίασμα, but
rather, by his father's evident influence and example: his teaching, so to speak
(so no wonder Euthyphro thinks that his relatives have no understanding of
true piety). Presumably these corrupting lessons would consist of whatever
justifications for his negligence his father might profess—citing his own fear
of the μίασμα carried by the thrall, for example (a wonderfully ironic twist,
if true)—something we may presume Socrates would himself find morally
objectionable, and so, teachings that are themselves instances of pollution$_m$.

Here, yet again, Plato invites us to see Euthyphro and Socrates as kindred spirits in the fight against the morality of the many.[30]

By drawing Socrates and Euthyphro close to each other in the above fashion, Plato forces his readers to identify the crucial differences between the two. One difference would seem to be that while Socrates is innocent of the charge of corruption, Euthyphro is not. Just as Socrates humorously hints at 5a-b, if he, Socrates, *were* to become Euthyphro's student in religion, he *would* be corrupted if he were to imbibe the tenets of conventionalist theology and other such inconsistency-producing beliefs at Euthyphro's feet; in which case Euthyphro's crime (corruption of the old) and consequent pollution$_m$ might well be appropriately dealt with by Meletus prosecuting and punishing Euthyphro. Euthyphro puts himself in danger of harming, not improving, his father and everyone who associates with him (including himself) by labeling his own father as a source of corruption on the basis of an inconsistent mix of cosmopolitan morality with errant, if popular, theology—one that he is clearly shown to be willing to teach to others, even Socrates and the members of the Assembly (3b-c). Because of his confused mix of advanced with traditionalist doctrines, Euthyphro is revealed to be a source of pollution$_m$ and a potential corrupter of both young and old (including his own father; cf. *Crito* 53c1). His examination by Socrates, moreover, ought to be seen as an example of how individuals ought to be purified and so healed of the pollution of hubris and contradictory belief by being 'put on trial' in the sort of private elenctic suit Socrates favors.[31] The *Euthyphro* thus also presages the *Sophist*'s discussion (226b-231b, 231e) of the sort of moral healing and purification (καθαρμός) the Socratic *elenchos* is able to provide.[32]

The outset of our dialogue can now be seen as implicitly declaring that, just as Euthyphro proposes to protect himself and others from the threat of moral pollution by suing and punishing his father, so likewise Meletus should be seen as proposing to purify and protect Athens by prosecuting and punishing Socrates. Both Euthyphro and Meletus initially appear to be young firebrands pushing an agenda of conservative social reform, but both are revealed to be reckless extremists with a telling lack of belief-consistency (cf. *Ap.* 26b-28a); they display a confusion emblematic of the tension between past and future that marked the last years of the Athenian fifth century. Specifically, both are guilty of allowing theological propositions that they are demonstrated to be incapable of defending (since they are inconsistent with their other beliefs) to govern their treatment of others: it is they who have 'made new gods' (*Eu.* 3b), not Socrates. Rather, on such theological details as the exact career of each god or goddess Socrates professes ignorance (while yet affirming basic truths, such as the wisdom, goodness, and non-quarreling nature of divinity) (6b, 14e-15a; cf., e.g., *Ap.* 21b-d; McPherran 1996, chs. 3.4, 5.2).[33]

Nevertheless, although Euthyphro may be an inept epistemologist, he is less a crackpot theologian and moralist than he has been thought; for he is also portrayed as forward-thinking through his principles of pollution$_m$ and impartial justice (P). Here we see, just as Socrates later notes at 14b8-c6, that it is possible for Euthyphro to almost 'get it right'. But with his subsequent unjustified and unjustifiable appeal to Zeus's treatment of his father he turns aside at the very moment when he might have at least plausibly defended the piety—or at least the justice[34]—of his own suit. Instead, he is shown to have his feet in two camps, the first morally progressive, but the second religiously antiquated, a position which rules out his ever producing a consistent defense of his behavior, let alone a Socratically-adequate definition of piety. Neither Euthyphro nor Meletus is the serious revitalizer of the past he takes himself to be; rather, that role is reserved for Socrates. It is Socrates—indicted for his philosophical service to Apollo (*Ap.* 20e-23c)—who is that god's own appointed guardian and interpreter of Athenian core values. It is he who is truly pious and pollution-free, and it is he who possesses the best measure of wisdom in respect of divine matters currently to be had in Athens. Or so, I submit, we are to think.[35]

Notes

1. It is not possible to address here the issue of whether we might legitimately use the testimony of Aristotle in conjunction with that of Plato and Xenophon to triangulate to the views of the historical Socrates in the manner of Gregory Vlastos (but see, e.g., Vlastos, chs. 2 and 3; and McPherran 1996, ch. 1.2). Rather, I will simply make the plausible and interpretatively useful assumption that the *Euthyphro* and the *Apology* (among other dialogues such as the *Crito*; those commonly labeled 'early', 'elenctic', 'aporetic', 'Socratic', and/or '*ad hominem*') constitute a mosaic of the characteristics, methods, views, and activities of a cross-dialogue, literary figure named 'Socrates' who manifests distinctly different philosophical attitudes from those expressed by the Socrates of the *Republic* and other such 'constructive' Platonic dialogues (cf., e.g., I. Kidd, 214). Such an approach avoids the issue of how we might accurately refer to the individual teacher of Plato, yet still allows us to confront most of the interesting questions Plato's works provoke (on the reasonable assumption, in this case, that the *Euthyphro* and *Apology* were meant to be read in concert with one another). Euthyphro does, however, strikes me as too multifaceted a character to have actually existed (on this, see below): he is probably more Platonic construction than historic interlocutor. There is also no evidence to support the idea that the Euthyphro of our dialogue is based on any particular historical individual, although most scholars agree that the character is the one mentioned in the *Cratylus*; see, e.g., W.K.C. Guthrie, 102 and n 2. As for the historicity of the conversation itself, Plato's calculated artistry and the bizarre nature of Euthyphro's legal case should give us pause. Ultimately, however,

there is no reliable way to decide if the conversation is historical, fictionalized, or simply fabricated; see the thorough discussion in A. Tulin, 65–71. Nevertheless, I take it to be part of Plato's maieutic, protreptic intention in writing dialogues to provoke his readers to raise and inquire into questions of the sort that the record of an actual conversation would raise (even, e.g., the question 'Where does Euthyphro go after his abrupt farewell?' [15e3-16a4]).

2. Moreover, Socrates' conversational activity is benevolent, something he would pay others to listen to (*Eu.* 3d). See M. McPherran 1996, chs. 2.2, 4.2, for a defense of the claim that for Socrates philosophical activity is pious. Note too that this Socrates also seems to hold the view that coming to a general conceptual understanding of piety is advisable, since without grasping and being able to use as a moral yardstick the definition of the one *eidos*/*idea* by which all pious things are pious (6d9-e7) one ought not to attempt actions whose performance poses a significant danger of impiety (and so injustice and harm) unless one has secure, countervailing reasons (4e4-8; 15d4-16a4); McPherran 1996, ch. 4.1, esp. 175–85.

3. R.F. Holland, quoted in J. Beversluis, 163; For Beversluis' view of Socrates' treatment of Euthyphro in general, see his ch. 8; for further discussion of Beversluis, see C. Gill and McPherran 200. For the argument that Socrates/Plato is even foisting the Theory of Forms onto Euthyphro at this point, see R.E. Allen, ch. 3.

4. On the precise legal, historical, and religious issues raised by this story, see J. Burnet, 82–107; R.G. Hoerber; D.M. MacDowell, 109–32, 192–94; W.D. Furley, 201–8; and I.G. Kidd. On μίασμα—a pollution, a defilement, that can settle and spread like a disease and upon which disasters attend—see R. Parker and below.

5. On which see, e.g., M.W. Blundell, 41. *Cr.* 50e-51a provides additional evidence that Socrates endorsed the traditional authority of fathers and the virtue of filial piety; see too *R.* 574a-c; *Mem.* 2.2.13; *Laws* 717b-718a, 869a-b, 931a; Aristophanes *Clouds* 1303–1453; and Ar. *EN* 1163b18 ff. According to the 'priests of old' endorsed by Plato's *Laws* (872c-873a), the 'karmic' relationship between children and parents is such that a child who commits the ultimate crime of murdering a parent will himself or herself be killed by one of his or her own children (in this incarnation or the next).

6. It is a common theme of the Socratic dialogues that the possession of knowledge of some concept confers the ability to give a Socratic definition of it; see, e.g., *Laches* 190c ff.

7. See I. Kidd, 215–16. He also notes, 219–21, that the man killed by Euthyphro was a πελάτης and hence, may well have possessed a legal status akin to that of a slave (thereby making Euthyphro's suit quite legally permissible).

8. Euthyphro's traditionalist focus here on the injustice of those who commit impious acts (viz., temple theft and *similar* crimes) and the piety and justice of proceeding against such malefactors is brought into question at 11e-14a (for here piety's relation to 'secular' person-to-person justice is raised as an issue; see McPherran 2000, 300–22).

9. Euthyphro also holds that the pollution posed by an unjust killer is the same for non-relatives as well as relatives so long as one's association with the killer is a knowing (συνειδώς; 4c2) one. Presumably the level of awareness this designates is not tantamount to a full knowledge of the killer's injustice (since, on Socrates' account at least, one would never knowingly associate with what one knows is sure to harm one;

see below). It seems a safe assumption that Euthyphro also believes that the potential for harm is even greater for those individuals who *unwittingly* have a close association with an unjust killer (on this, see below).

10. This seems the best account of Euthyphro's principle of conduct when considered in light of the only two reasonable alternatives: (i) all unjust killers (including one's relatives) ought to be prosecuted *by someone or other* and pay the penalty for their crime; and (ii) one ought to prosecute any unjust killer to whom one is related. (i) would hardly represent an innovation on Euthyphro's part; indeed, it is taken to be a trivial truth at 8e-9a. (ii) fails to recognize that for Euthyphro it is one's conscious and close association with a murderer, rather than one's biological relationship to him/her, that renders one susceptible to the pollution for which prosecution is the sole remedy. Of course, my rejection of (ii) in favor of P raises the question of why Euthyphro takes it upon *himself* to prosecute his father rather than simply *avoiding* his father, leaving it for another (esp. a relative) to prosecute, since he does not appear to think of himself as *already* polluted. I think the answer is that Euthyphro sees there to be a familial requirement on the part of some relative or other to attempt to 'decontaminate' the family by prosecuting, convicting, and exiling his father (over and above one's prudential reasons for decontaminating polluted individuals with whom one has direct or indirect contact, whether related to them or not). Since, however, he is the only member of the family who judges his father to be a source of pollution (4a, 4d), that task can currently only be assumed by him (because of what he takes to be the requirements of filial piety and justice, presumably, Euthyphro believes he will suffer pollution by failing to prosecute; this appears to be a requirement of justice for him because of his claim that he acts in imitation of the justice of Zeus when Zeus punished his father Kronos for Kronos' injustice [5e-6a]). [Pb], then, should be understood to contain an implicit qualification: one ought to prosecute a murderer irrespective of one's relationship to the killer only if one is already polluted by contact with the killer, or because failing to purify the killer through prosecution will create the same or greater amount of pollution for oneself through the neglect of a virtue (e.g., filial piety, justice).

Although Euthyphro leaves it unclear whether his proposed prosecution is sufficient to remove the pollution or whether actual conviction and punishment are required, the latter is implied when Euthyphro allows that no doer of injustice ought to go unpunished (8d-e).

11. See, e.g., Allen, 9; F.M. Cornford, 311; M. Croiset, 179; Furley; P.T. Geach, 370; G. Grote, 322; R. Guardini, 9, 26; and W.A. Heidell, 165.

12. Those who agree that Euthyphro has a non-traditionalist aspect include Burnet, 85–88; Hoerber, 95–98; J. Hoopes, 1–6; R. Klonoski, 123–39; F. Rosen, 105–9; and A.E. Taylor, 147.

13. For a defense and explication of this view of Euthyphro, see McPherran 1996, chs. 2.1.1, and 4.1.1. In brief, (A) Euthyphro's traditionalism is suggested by his endorsement of Homeric/Hesiodic conventions (e.g., the relationship between Zeus and Kronos, the existence of quarreling and epistemically deficient deities, and the correctness of *do ut des* prayer and sacrifice [14b; cf. *Il.* 9.497-501]); whereas his claims to precise knowledge of the 'divine things' (4e-5a), his appeal to Zeus' and Kronos' con-

duct in justification of his own (see below), and his proposed prosecution serve as evidence of his hubris. As for (B), Plato points to a number of similarities between Socrates and Euthyphro; e.g., he has Euthyphro take Socrates' side against the Athenians, has him accept—as a fellow μάντις (3b-c)—that the *daimonion* is harmless, grants Socrates' imputation of wisdom to himself (4b), and implicitly appeals at 5e-6a to the Socratic-Sophistic principle that the standard of morality for the gods is the same as for humans (against the tradition of a divine double standard; cf. *R.* 378b; see below). Plato also invites us to make the parallel when he has Socrates suggest that Euthyphro might take *his own place* in court (5a-c), and then when he has Euthyphro claim that his imagined court discussion would 'turn out to be much more about him [Meletus] than about me,' (5c2-3) a typically Socratic claim. And just as Euthyphro claims to know with precision an uncommon amount about divine things, so Socrates likewise regards such knowledge as an important matter (5a) to which he also makes a similar claim (though modest in extent; cf. 6b). Socrates, after all, seems to know with precision that he has been commanded by the gods to do philosophy (e.g., *Ap.* 33c), and both Euthyphro and Socrates regard the divine as a source of conviction on matters of virtuous conduct—one proceeding to prosecute his father on ostensibly religious grounds, the other proceeding to his trial and death for the sake of what he takes to be his pious obligation. Moreover, both believe that one should proceed against those who do injustice, even if they should be close relatives (4b-c, 5d-e, 8d-e; *Cr.* 49b8, *Ap.* 28b; *G.* 480a-d); see, e.g., Allen, 23; Burnet, 3, 23, 113; Furley, 202–4; Hoerber, 95–107; and Taylor, 16, 149 n 1.

14. Commenting on this grounding, R. Weiss, 265, claims that it reveals Euthyphro's leading motive to be not selfless devotion to impartial justice, but self-regarding fear of the kind of μίασμα that only a member of the household or a relative can inspire (irrespective of whether the slain person is οἰκεῖος or ἀλλότριος. I want to contend in response that not even Socrates would recommend *selfless* devotion to justice, since for him self-interest and justice perfectly coincide such that all our just actions derive from self-interested motives (cf. Brickhouse and Smith 1994, ch. 3.4). In any case, Weiss's claim appears to underrate 5d-6a, which—without making any mention of pollution—emphasizes the idea that any wrongdoer, relative or not, ought to be proceeded against (see also 8b-e, where the same point appears to be made, again, with no mention of pollution). There is also no reason not to suppose that Euthyphro acts out of a concern for his relatives as well as himself, and some reason to suppose he does (viz., his claim that pious actions preserve families; 14a-b). Hence, *pace* Weiss, Euthyphro arguably does advocate prosecuting 'just any unjust killer,' (265) but apparently places the responsibility for doing so on those for whom it is a (self-interested) requirement of piety and justice (neglect of which would pollute one; usually, of course, these will be the killer's relatives) (see n 10 above). On this count, at least, Euthyphro is a radical reformer of Athenian morality and law, which placed the burden of prosecution on the *victim's* family, not the killer's family. *Pace* Weiss (265 n 9), then, we should see Euthyphro as appealing to Zeus' impartial justice as evidence of his own impartial justice at 5e-6a. Finally, in my argument below, I shall contend that while it might be a self-regarding fear of pollution that drives Euthyphro primarily, since his conception of pollution is coextensive with Socrates' own revisionary conception of pollution as moral

corruption, that motive is one Socrates himself endorses. For, as Socrates sees it, moral pollution is something we should all fear and be motivated to eradicate (in oneself and others; *Ap.* 29b; *Cr.* 47c-d).

15. Parker, esp. chs. 7, 8, 9; E.R. Dodds, 35–37, 55 n. 43–44; W. Burkert, 147; Soph. *OC* 1482 ff., *Ant.* 773–76; Eur. *IT* 1218; cf. *Laws* 871b-e. See also R.J. Hankinson on the concept of pollution (37–40) and its relation to disease (27–37). As Dodds (36) famously put it, μίασμα operates 'with same ruthless indifference to motive as a typhoid germ.'

16. Hankinson, 39–40, notes that Sophocles' *Oedipus at Colonus* [*OC*] (226–36, 254–57, 1132–36) provides evidence that μίασμα can persist "even after punishment has been meted out" (39).

17. My interpretation of what is meant by Euthyphro's family's contention that the father did not kill (ὄυτε ἀποκτείναντι; 4d7) the thrall.

18. Neither Euthyphro nor Socrates make any mention of the possibility that Euthyphro's father may himself have been trying to avoid polluting contact with the thrall. This, in fact, seems likely to be the case, in view of the father's concern to be religiously correct as attested by his attempt to consult with the Athenian religious advisors (an especially scrupulous act, if he had caught the thrall in the act, since that gave him the right to execute the thrall on the spot; Allen, 21). There is reason, then, to see a 'like-father-like-son' story line at work here.

19. Edwards, 221–22. It should be noted, though, that the *Laws*'s notion of pollution is occasionally quite traditionalist: see, e.g., 759a-c, 865a-865c, 871b, 881b-882a, 946e-948b; cf. Parker, 113.

20. Mitchell Miller has pointed out to me that Plato's pairing of Socrates with Euthyphro's religiously scrupulous father may contribute to the *Euthyphro*'s apologetic agenda by leading us to view Socrates as not a Sophistic denier of religion but as a thinker who aims to renew its progressive character (this would be especially true if Euthyphro owes his progressive view of pollution to the teaching of his father). So the moral here would seem to be that Meletus and the citizens of Athens, having had their ignorance of virtues such as piety repeatedly brought home to them by Socrates, ought to retract their writ of impiety against him, just as Euthyphro ought to abandon his suit (despite his countervailing reasons; e.g., the importance of pursuing murderers impartially and of removing the pollution they engender). For in neither instance do the prosecutors understand what piety is, and since moral harm is incurred through unjust action (*Cr.* 47a-49e), the moral risk posed by a mistaken conviction means that neither set of prosecutors ought to employ the concept of piety as the basis of their respective lawsuits (see *Ap.* 30d-e).

21. Nicholas Smith has objected in correspondence to this pairing on the grounds that, unlike Euthyphro and his father, Meletus is not worried that Socrates' corruption of the youth will 'stain' him (Meletus) *personally*, whereas that seems to be an important element of why Euthyphro thinks he must prosecute his father. While I acknowledge this difference, it is not a telling one for my thesis; rather, it is explained by the fact that (i) Meletus is not related to Socrates and (ii) did not *closely associate* with him (see *Eu.* 2b; *Ap.* 26a) (as Euthyphro may have already done with his father, subsequent to the laborer's death). The parallel is in any case supported by the evidence that both men are prosecuting out of an alleged concern for others.

22. Socrates, Plato seems to be telling us, is especially unjustly charged with impiety if the basis of those charges lies in Socrates' doubts (6a-d) concerning the sorts of disagreeing gods Euthyphro appeals to in justification of his legal case. The stories of the gods' quarrels would have been received with skepticism by a number of Athenians, and if so, that is one reason for thinking that the charges against Socrates are unfairly brought (McPherran 1996, ch. 3.3–4).

23. In his *Trojans* (948), Euripides points out that the gods might be (wrongly) invoked to excuse or sanction human immorality in the way Euthyphro does by having Phaedra's nurse excuse her illicit passion with a reference to the example of Zeus and Eos, conquered by the power of Aphrodite; cf. Aeschylus *Eum.* 640. Plato makes the same point, in a clear reference to the *Euthyphro*, at *R.* 377e-378e (esp. 378b); cf. *Laws* 886c-d. Note too that even a critic of the new intellectualism like Aristophanes sees this same problem, but foists it onto the intellectuals, not the traditionalists (correctly so, since it is these individuals who are responsible for advocating a unitary conception of justice); e.g., in the *Clouds* he has Wrong Argument advocate using the example of Zeus to excuse one's own adulteries (1079–1084; cf. 904).

24. See, e.g., Guthrie 1950, 120–24; H. Lloyd-Jones, 176–79. This is true despite the fact that Zeus was generally understood to underwrite a code of just conduct for humans (see, e.g., Thuc. 5.104–5, and McPherran 1996, ch. 3.2), and that hence, what we term 'traditional Greek religion' carried within itself the seeds of its own reformation. In Hesiod, for example, we can find evidence that justice is already in the process of being raised to a universal. Nevertheless, Hesiod is himself a reformer who intends to 'elevate' Zeus, and so cannot be taken as emblematic of the entire body of ancient religious practice and belief that Gilbert Murray once labeled 'The Inherited Conglomerate' (Murray, 66 ff.). At any rate, if we do consider the whole of this Conglomerate what we find is that *Dikê* 'consisted first of all in doing what custom alone had established as being suitable for a particular station in life' (Guthrie 1950, 122), and on this view there is indeed a divine double standard of morality. On my picture, then, Euthyphro is very much a conflicted exemplar of a conflicted era: he is on the one hand drawn toward the developing-yet-still-new-fangled picture of a non-capricious deity inhabiting a *cosmos* unified by one over-arching principle of justice (against which even Zeus is to be measured)— a picture whose outlines begin to be drawn by Hesiod (and Homer, in one unique passage [*Il.* 16.384 ff.]). But his equally-intense attraction to the ideas that piety is established by divine *fiat* and that the gods quarrel also mark him out as what I would call a traditionalist.

25. This may explain why Aristophanes of Byzantium in the late second century B.C.E. produced an edition of Plato's dialogues that grouped the *Theaetetus* together with the *Euthyphro* and *Apology* (D.L. 3.61-62); although dramatic chronological considerations alone would justify this trilogy, it may be that Aristophanes saw a thematic connection between the *Euthyphro* and *Theaetetus* because of the latter's advocacy of 'becoming as like god as possible' through 'becoming just and pious, with wisdom' (176a-c); Allen, 7–8 (*pace* his claim that '. . . no reader, however ingenious, could draw such conclusions as these from the *Euthyphro* itself,' 8; cf. Hoerber, 107, who sees just such a connection).

26. Of course, rather than play the dogmatic, Socrates makes his typical confession (at 6b2-3) that his lack of knowledge on such subjects prevents him from affirming the truth of such stories; cf. *Phdr.* 229c-230a.

27. It is interesting to note on this score that, like Euthyphro, and despite his status as a Sophist, Antiphon seems to have been an 'ultraconservative . . . [and] enthusiastic supporter of the traditional religion' (Guthrie 1971, 294; cf. Gagarin 1997b, 9).

Hankinson, 40–46, notes that in the fifth-century text *On Breaths* (6, 3–22) the 'notion of *miasma* has . . . been taken over by rationalist medicine and thoroughly demythologized' (45) and that in Thucydides (2.47-58, 3.87) we find an implicit refusal to explain the Athenian plague (mainly 430–426 B.C.E.) in terms of *miasma* (whereas popular explanation would cite *miasma* and target Apollo, god of healing and illness, as its initial source; cf. *Il.* 1.1-102; Thuc. 3.104). Parker, 310, also claims that one can find in Euripides something of a contrast between his enlightened view in which 'pollution has lost its sting,' and the 'conventional piety of Sophocles.'

28. Brickhouse and Smith (unpublished) point out that the distinction Socrates makes at *Apology* 25e6-26a8 between those cases in which instruction but not punishment is appropriate and those other cases where a court trial and punishment are appropriate would make no sense if Socrates did not believe—despite his view that no one does wrong knowingly—that there are some individuals who do wrong with a culpable degree of awareness; see Brickhouse and Smith 2000, ch. 6.5, which argues for an interpretation of Socratic intellectualist moral psychology that is compatible with Socrates' apparent acceptance of corporal punishment.

As noted above (n. 11), Euthyphro holds that the pollution posed by an unjust killer is the same for non-relatives as well as relatives provided that one's association with the killer is a knowing (συνειδώς; 4c2) one. Presumably the level of awareness this designates is of the above Socratic kind; that is, not tantamount to full knowledge (which on Socrates' account is impossible, since no one would knowingly associate with what one knows is sure to harm one). Again, it seems safe to assume that Euthyphro thinks that the potential for harm is even greater for those individuals who *unwittingly* have a close association with an unjust killer, since that ignorance would only make it easier for the killer to infect—to teach them, that is—his or her injustice to them.

29. Although Socrates begins his *elenchos* of Meletus at *Apology* 25c-26a by addressing the charge that he corrupts *all* of Athens's youth (viz., 'those he dwells among'), his attention shifts immediately and solely to 'those who are closest to him and with whom he associates (συνόντων; as opposed to Meletus, who has avoided associating with Socrates),' a match for the close association Euthyphro adumbrates at *Eu.* 4b7-c3. In both cases, most clearly in the case of Socrates, the sort of potentially corrupting association that is envisaged is one that involves regular close contact of the sort that can transmit values by means of conversation and 'role-modeling' behavior.

30. Socrates' and Plato's appropriation and rational recasting of the notion of μίασμα as moral—that is, psychic—pollution is arguably part of their overall agenda of revisioning religious and medical conceptions in the service of philosophy. In the case of μίασμα, their move from a material to a moral contagion view of μίασμα is

natural since μίασμα (in the traditional sense) and guilt were closely associated ('. . . the imagery of pollution may be used to express moral revulsion'; Parker, 312; 312–17; cf. Aesch. *Supp.* 366, 375, 385 ff.). The move from moral to mental contagion is also natural, given the popular explanation of mental illness in terms of pollution (Parker, 128–29, 243–48, 318). Note too, e.g., how in the *Charmides* Socrates endorses the view of certain successful Greek physicians (probably the Hippocratics) who do not attempt to cure eyes by themselves, but only by means of treating the entire person (156b-c; similarly, the *Crito, Republic*, and *Timaeus* all treat body and soul 'as not merely parallel . . . but interdependent' [R.F. Stalley, 358]). As a result, the headache cure Socrates claims to possess—a medicinal leaf (*pharmakon*)—is only effective if accompanied by the singing of a charm, an *epôdê* (Greek medicine of the time commonly assumed that the application of drugs would precede or be joined with that of such chants [L. Entralgo, 1–107; J. Scarborough, 141–43; cf. *Tht.* 149c-d, 157c). According to certain Thracian physicians whom Socrates endorses, both leaf and charm are needed to effect a cure of both body and mind, but

> if the head and body are to be well, you must begin by curing the soul. . . . And the cure of the soul . . . has to be effected by the use of certain charms, and these charms are beautiful words, and by them temperance is implanted in the soul, and where temperance comes and stays, there health is speedily imparted, not only to the head, but to the whole body (*Charm.* 157a1-b1).

On this basis, some commentators have thought that more than any other of his dialogues, the *Charmides* shows Socrates/Plato to be the inventor of 'scientific verbal psychotherapy,' beside whom 'Gorgias and Antiphon are mere prehistory' (Entralgo, 137; cf. 126). See McPherran unpublished for an account of Socrates' diagnostic use of the *elenchos* and his rationalistic revisioning of charms as poetic *muthoi* that can moderate or still our childish fears (e.g., the concluding myth of *Phaedo* 107c-115a; cf. *Apology* 40c-41d and *Gorgias* 522c-527e). See McPherran 2003 for discussion of Socrates' relation to the healing god Asclepius.

31. Note how 2a-b makes the point that Socrates—in silent contrast to Euthyphro and Meletus—is not the sort of man to bring legal indictments against others. Rather, as we know from Plato's other works, he pursues private suits *via* the real politics of the one-on-one elenctic encounter (see, e.g., *Ap.* 22e-23c; *G.* 473e-474b); see H. Ausland on this. In view of the parallel Plato has invited readers to make between Socrates and Euthyphro's father, Socrates' 'trial' of Euthyphro can be understood to exemplify the law of just payback Plato sees as governing the relations between relatives (e.g., *Laws* 872c-873a): Euthyphro's attempt to prosecute his own father has resulted in Euthyphro himself being put 'on trial'.

32. Socrates also plays the role of elenctic physician in the *Charmides*; see above, n. 30, and McPherran unpublished. 'Purification' (καθαρμός) is the topic of Plato's sixth definition of the *Sophist* (226b-231b, 231e). There we are introduced to the art of Separation and the part of it concerned with the separation of better from worse, namely, 'purification'. This can be of body or soul, and for the two kinds of evil in the soul there are two kinds of purification: punishment for vice and instruction or education for ignorance. The worst and most pervasive ignorance is believing that one

knows what one does not, and here the best educational remedy is not rough reproof or gentle admonition (since ignorance is involuntary) but the *elenchos* as practiced by Socrates. No one can be said to be truly happy without having been cleansed by this greatest sort of sophistical purgation (cf. *G.* 470e): a sophistry that if it must be called such is still 'the Sophistry of noble lineage'. In view of Socrates' own intellectualist moral psychology, there is for him no difference between this intellectualist sense of purification and the moral sense of purification I have alluded to.

33. Socrates' suggestion that Meletus might put Euthyphro on trial in his (Socrates') place (5a-b), Euthyphro's retort to that idea (5b-c), and Socrates' parting words at 15e-16a indicate that, as they both see it, Euthyphro and Meletus share a similar traditionalist theology of imperfect, quarreling gods; Furley, 204, 207–8.

34. By having acknowledged that piety is but a part of justice concerned with our relation to the *gods* at 12a-13e (with 'secular', person-to-person justice as the remainder), Euthyphro can no longer straightforwardly claim that the prosecution of his father for an act concerning another *person* is just by reason of its piety. Rather, the case now appears to be a matter whose merits are primarily to be determined on the grounds of *secular* justice (although it remains possible on this view for an action to be not only secularly just but pious as well; see McPherran 2000). By presenting both Euthyphro and Socrates as involved in court cases whose crucial concern is pious action—yet where the search for a complete Socratic definition of piety fails—Plato may be attempting to tell us that since we as mere humans do not and perhaps cannot have complete knowledge of what acts serve the gods (nor a precise assessment of the intentions of any person), we should be extremely hesitant in judging someone's acts to be pious or impious. Hence, just as Euthyphro ought not to prosecute his father for a crime against another man on the unwarranted assumption (as revealed by Socrates' examination of him) that his prosecution is pious, neither should Socrates be charged with impiety. Such a charge is unwarranted, given our very fallible and incomplete understanding of the gods, and especially in view of Socrates' claims elsewhere that rather than acting impiously he is in fact operating under a divine mandate (see McPherran 1996, ch. 4.1).

35. My thanks to Mitchell Miller for his perceptive and useful commentary on a previous version of this paper, delivered at the Seventh Annual Arizona Colloquium in Ancient Philosophy on Plato, Myth, and Religion, held at the University of Arizona, February 15–17, 2002. I also owe a debt of gratitude to the editor of this journal (Jim Hankinson), Mary Margaret McCabe, Jennifer Reid, Nicholas Smith, Roslyn Weiss, and Paul Woodruff for their helpful comments on later versions. Finally, I am indebted to the National Endowment for the Humanities for the Fellowship (2001–2002) that afforded me the time to work on this and related projects.

Bibliography

Allen, R. E. 1970. *Plato's 'Euthyphro' and the Earlier Theory of Forms.* London.

Ausland, H. 2002. 'Forensic Characteristics of Socratic Argumentation', ch. 2 in G. Scott, ed., *Does Socrates Have a Method? Rethinking the Elenchus in Plato's Dialogues and Beyond.* University Park, PA.

Beversluis, J. 2000. *Cross-Examining Socrates: A Defense of the Interlocutors in Plato's Early Dialogues.* Cambridge.

Brickhouse, T.C., and Smith, N.D. 1989. *Socrates on Trial.* Oxford and Princeton.

———. 2000. *The Philosophy of Socrates.* Boulder.

———. Unpublished. 'The Myth of the Afterlife in Plato's *Gorgias*'.

Blundell, M.W. 1989. *Helping Friends and Harming Enemies.* Cambridge.

Burkert, W. 1985. *Greek Religion.* Cambridge, MA.

Burnet J. 1924. *Plato's Euthyphro, Apology of Socrates and Crito.* Oxford.

Cornford, F. M. 1952. (rpt. 1965) W.K.C. Guthrie, ed. *Principium Sapientiae.* New York.

Croiset, M. 1920. *Platon, Oeuvres Completes.* Tome 1, Paris.

Dodds, E. R. 1951. *The Greeks and the Irrational.* Berkeley.

Edwards, M. J. 2000. 'In Defense of Euthyphro'. *American Journal of Philology* 121:213–24.

Entralgo, P. L. 1970. *The Therapy of the Word in Classical Antiquity.* L.J. Rather and J.M. Sharp, trans. and ed., New Haven.

Furley, W. D. 1985. 'The Figure of Euthyphro in Plato's Dialogue'. *Phronesis* 30.2:201–8.

Gagarin, M. 1997a. 'Review of Alexander Tulin, *Dike Phonou: The Right of Prosecution and Attic Homicide Procedure*'. *Bryn Mawr Classical Review* 97.4.17.

———. 1997b. *Antiphon: The Speeches.* Cambridge.

Gagarin, M. and MacDowell, D.M. 1998. *Antiphon and Andocides.* Austin.

Geach, P. T. 1966. 'Plato's *Euthyphro*: An Analysis and Commentary'. *Monist* 50.3: 369–82.

Gill, C. 2001. 'Speaking Up For Plato's Interlocutors: A Discussion of J. Beversluis', *Cross-Examining Socrates*'. *Oxford Studies in Ancient Philosophy* 20:297–321.

Gomez-Lobo, A. 1994. *The Foundations of Socratic Ethics.* Indianapolis.

Grote, G. 1865. *Plato and the Other Companions of Sokrates.* v. 1, London.

Guardini, R. (B. Wrighton [trans.]) 1948. *The Death of Socrates.* New York.

Guthrie, W. K. C. 1950. *The Greeks and Their Gods.* Boston.

———. 1971. *The Sophists.* Cambridge.

———. 1975. *A History of Greek Philosophy.* v. 4, Cambridge.

Hankinson, R. J. 1995. 'Pollution and Infection: An Hypothesis Stillborn'. *Apeiron* 28.1:25–66.

Heidel, W. A. 1900. 'On Plato's *Euthyphro*': *Transactions of the American Philological Society* 31:164–81.

Hoerber, R. G. 1958. 'Plato's *Euthyphro*'. *Phronesis* 3:95–107.

Holland, R. F. 1981–82. 'Euthyphro'. *Aristotelian Society Proceedings* 82:1–15.

Hoopes, J. 1970. 'Euthyphro's Case'. *The Classical Bulletin* 47.1:1–6.

Kidd, I. G. 1990. 'The Case of Homicide in Plato's *Euthyphro*', 213–21 in E.M. Clark ed. *'Owls to Athens'; Essays on Classical Subjects Presented to Sir Kenneth Dover.* Oxford.

Klonoski, R. 1984. 'Setting and Characterization in Plato's *Euthyphro*'. *Diálogos* 44: 123–39.

Lloyd-Jones, H. 1971. *The Justice of Zeus.* Berkeley.

MacDowell, D. M. 1978. *The Law in Classical Athens.* Ithaca.

McPherran M. 1996. (pbk. rpt. 1999) *The Religion of Socrates.* University Park, PA.

———. 2000. 'Piety, Justice, and the Unity of Virtue'. *Journal of the History of Philosophy* 38.3:299–328.

————. 2001. 'Review of J. Beversluis' *Cross-Examining Socrates: A Defense of the Inter-locutors in Plato's Early Dialogues* (Cambridge, 2000)'. *Journal of the History of Philosophy* 38.4:583–84.

————. 2003. 'Socrates, Crito, and Their Debt to Asclepius'. *Ancient Philosophy*.

————. Unpublished. 'Socrates and Zalmoxis on Drugs, Charms, and Purification'.

Murray, G. 1946. *Greek Studies*. Oxford.

Parker, R. 1983. *Miasma: Pollution and Purification in Early Greek Religion*. Oxford.

Rosen, F. 1968. 'Piety and Justice: Plato's *Euthyphro*'. *Philosophy* 43:105–16.

Scarborough, J. 1991. 'The Pharmacology of Sacred Plants, Herbs, and Roots', 138–174 in C. Faraone and D. Obbink ed. *Magica Hiera: Ancient Greek Magic and Religion*. New York.

Stalley, R. F. 1996. 'Punishment and the Physiology of the *Timaeus*'. *The Classical Quarterly* 46.2:357–70.

Taylor, A. E. 1926 (rpt. 1960). *Plato: The Man and His Work*. London.

Tulin, A. 1996. *Dike Phonou: The Right of Prosecution and Attic Homicide Procedure*. Stuttgart and Leipzig.

Versenyi, L. 1982. *Holiness and Justice: An Interpretation of Plato's Euthyphro*. Washington, D.C.

Vlastos, G. 1991. *Socrates: Ironist and Moral Philosopher*. Ithaca.

Weiss, R. 1994. 'Virtue Without Knowledge: Socratic Piety in Plato's *Euthyphro*'. *Ancient Philosophy* 14:263–82.

2

Plato's *Euthyphro*:
An Analysis and Commentary

P. T. Geach

THE *EUTHYPHRO* MIGHT WELL BE GIVEN TO UNDERGRADUATES to read early in their philosophical training. The arguments are apparently simple, but some of them, as I shall show, lead naturally on to thorny problems of modern philosophy. Another benefit that could be gained from reading the *Euthyphro* is that the reader may learn to be forewarned against some common fallacies and debating tricks in moral disputes.

We may pass rapidly over the pages in which the stage is set for the discussion (2a-3e). Socrates and Euthyphro meet outside the office of the King Archon, where each has to "put in an appearance" respecting a legal action. Socrates tells Euthyphro how he is being prosecuted for impiety. Euthyphro is pained but not surprised; his own speeches in the Ecclesia are ridiculed when he speaks of things divine; no doubt Socrates' well-known divine sign has roused popular prejudice.

With some reluctance, if we may judge by the form of his answers ("I'm prosecuting. People will think me crazy. It's an old man; he won't fly away. It's my own father. For murder"), Euthyphro tells Socrates what his own cause is. Socrates is naturally astounded: surely then the victim must be some other member of the family, or Euthyphro would never have started the prosecution (3e-4b).

Euthyphro replies that whether the victim belongs to your own family or not does not really matter; what matters is whether the man was wrongfully killed. Then he tells the story. The man who died was a dependent of Euthyphro, a farm labourer on the family estate in Naxos. In a drunken brawl he quarreled with and killed one of the household slaves. Euthyphro's father, after having the killer tied up and thrown in a ditch, sent off to ask the authorities in Athens what was to be done—and then put the matter out of his mind. It was no concern of his if the fellow died. Before an answer came back from the mainland, the prisoner had in fact died from hunger, cold, and his bonds. Euthyphro felt he could not sit at his father's fireside and table as if nothing had happened; to the indignation of all his family, he thought himself obliged to prosecute his father; only so could he or his father be made clean of blood-guiltiness. The family protested that in fact the father had not murdered any-body; even if he had, the man was himself a killer and not worth considering; anyhow, it is impious for a son to prosecute his own father. This only shows, says Euthyphro, how little his relatives understood piety and impiety (4b-e).

Since the attitude of Euthyphro's relatives in the matter was likely to be shared by others and since Euthyphro knew that his own religious attitude at-tracted derision rather than respect, we may suppose Euthyphro to be well aware that his father would not in fact be in any serious legal danger; the pros-ecution is just a gesture. What sort of gesture? Some commentators call it superstition: even an accidental death—and this is practically the case in hand!—would bring on the man who caused it a contagious defilement, and Euthyphro is going through the proper motions to cleanse this away from the house. Others, just like Euthyphro's relatives, morally condemn him for mak-ing such a fuss, especially with his own father involved.

An unprejudiced reading shows that Euthyphro is not represented as merely superstitious about a ritual contamination; what upset Euthyphro was the way his father "was heedless and made little of the man, even if he should die." How far Euthyphro was from making a fuss about nothing comes out in the fact that in quite a number of civilized jurisdictions a man who acted like Euthyphro's father would be held guilty of a serious crime.

Euthyphro is represented as an earnest and simple believer in the old tradi-tional religion of the Hellenes. To him, therefore, the defence of a poor man's case may well have seemed a religious duty: Zeus of the Suppliant was there to hear the cry of the poor man with none to help him, and to punish those who walked in blind pride. Moreover, Euthyphro says, had not Zeus himself pun-ished his own father's wicked deeds?

Euthyphro's genuine belief in the old legend is something Socrates finds it hard to stomach (5e-6c), but he does not try to shake it. Instead, he adopts a line of argument that we find paralleled in many dialogues. If Euthyphro re-ally knows that his own action is pious, then he must be able to say what is pious; he must not just give examples of pious actions, like his own action or again the punishment of sacrilegious robbery, but say "what kind of thing it is that makes *whatever* is pious to be pious" (5d and 6d).

We need not here enter upon the vexed questions whether language like the piece I have just translated (6d 10-11) is meant to imply a full-blown theory of Forms, and whether we are to ascribe such a theory to the historical Socrates. Let us rather concentrate on two assumptions Socrates makes: (A) that if you know you are correctly predicating a given term 'T' you must "know what it is to be T," in the sense of being able to give a general criterion for a thing's being T; (B) that it is no use to try and arrive at the meaning of 'T' by giving examples of things that are T. (B) in fact follows from (A). If you can already give a general account of what 'T' means, then you need no examples to arrive at the meaning of 'T'; if on the other hand you lack such a general account, then, by assumption (A), you cannot know that any examples of things that are T are genuine ones, for you do not know when you are predicating 'T' correctly.

The style of mistaken thinking—as I take it to be—that comes from accepting these two assumptions may well be called the *Socratic fallacy,* for its *locus classicus* is the Socratic dialogues. Its influence has, I think, been greater even than that of the theory of Forms; certainly people can fall into it independently of any theory of Forms. I have myself heard a philosopher refuse to allow that a proper name is a word in a sentence unless a "rigorous definition" of "word" could be produced; again, if someone remarks that machines are certainly not even alive, still less able to think and reason, he may be challenged to define 'alive'. Both these controversial moves are clear examples of the Socratic fallacy; and neither originates from any belief in Forms.

Let us be clear that this is a fallacy, and nothing better. It has stimulated philosophical enquiry, but still it is a fallacy. We know heaps of things without being able to define the terms in which we express our knowledge: Formal definitions are only one way of elucidating terms; a set of examples may in a given case be more useful than a formal definition.

We can indeed see in advance why a Socratic dialogue so often ends in complete failure to elucidate the meaning of a term 'T'. If the parties to a discussion are agreed, broadly speaking, about the application of a term, then they can set out to find a criterion for applying it that shall yield the agreed application. On the other hand, if they are agreed on the criterion for applying the term, then they can see whether this criterion justifies predicating 'T' of a given example. But if there is no initial agreement either on examples of things that certainly are 'T' or on criteria for predicating 'T', then the discussion is bound to be abortive; the parties to it cannot know what they are about—they do not even know whether each of them means the same by saying 'T'. Any profit they gain from the discussion will be *per accidens; per se* the discussion is futile.

How harmful the rejection of examples may be we see from the *Theaetetus.* Theaetetus, asked what knowledge is, gives some instances of knowledge—geometry and shoemaking and the various crafts. Socrates objects that these are only examples, and he wants to know just what knowledge is. To give examples, each of which is the knowledge of so-and-so, is to miss the point—as though, asked what clay was, one mentioned potter's clay, brickmaker's clay, and so on (146d-147a). But of course any knowledge is knowledge of so-and-so; and a correct definition would have to run "Knowledge of so-and-so is . . . ," with the "so-and-so" occurring over again in the *definiens*. Moreover, the definition "Knowledge is sense-perception" could have been dismissed at once by looking to Theaetetus' examples of knowledge.

I am sure that imbuing a mind with the Socratic fallacy is quite likely to be morally harmful. Socrates, let us suppose, starts chatting with an ingenuous youth and says he has been puzzled about what injustice is. The youth says— "Well, that's easy; swindling is unjust." Socrates asks him what swindling is; no, examples will not do—a formal definition is required. Failing that, we don't know, do we?, what swindling is, or that it is unjust. The dialogue, we may suppose, ends in the usual *aporia*. The ingenuous youth decides that perhaps swindling is not unjust; he turns to ways of villainy, and ends as one of the Thirty Tyrants. After all, a number of Socrates' young men did end that way.

Pressed for a formal definition, then, Euthyphro comes out with this one: "The pious is what is liked by the Gods, the impious what is not liked" (6d 10). As in English, so in Greek, we must not take the negative word in the second clause for a bare negation: 'not liked', here, = 'disliked'.

The next argument Socrates uses has force only *ad hominem;* it explicitly depends on Euthyphro's traditionalist belief that stories about the quarrels of the Gods are literally true. What then, Socrates asks, do *men* quarrel about? For questions of fact—accountancy, measurement, weighing—there are agreed decision procedures. It is precisely questions of fair or unfair, right or wrong, that are undecidable and lead to quarrels. If, then, the Gods do quarrel, presumably they too quarrel about such questions; actions that one God thinks just another thinks unjust, and so they quarrel. Thus one and the same action may be both God-loved, and thus pious, and God-hated, and thus impious. Moreover, if we assume the truth of the traditional stories, different Gods may be expected to view with very different eyes acts like Euthyphro's: the chastisement of parents. Euthyphro's appeal to the example of Zeus is thus neatly turned against him (7b-8b).

This passage is of some historical interest; it may well be the first appearance in Western philosophy of the distinction between factual questions, for which there is a definite and accepted decision procedure, and moral questions, for which there is no such procedure. To my mind, this distinction is none the better for being an old one.

It very often happens that people who have no relevant disagreement about what ought to be done in given circumstances nevertheless quarrel bitterly, even go to law, because they disagree about the facts of the case. And of course they need not be irrationally ignoring some well known decision procedure; there may be no such procedure. The only eye-witnesses of an incident may grievously differ as to what happened, because men's observation and memory are both fallible; there is then no agreed decision procedure to settle the matter once and for all. It is mere thoughtlessness when a modern writer tells us that any purely factual premise of moral reasoning must admit of "definite tests (not themselves involving evaluation) for determining its truth or falsity."

So much for the decidability of factual questions; what about the undecidability of moral questions? Socrates just asserts this—or at least wins Euthyphro's assent to it by leading questions. There are many arguments now used to defend the position by prominent moral philosophers, which I have not space to discuss. We ought in any case to notice that the extent of moral disagreement both within and between civilized societies is often grossly exaggerated. As we may learn from Hobbes, no commonwealth will hold together without a great deal of moral consensus; if everyone made up his own morality by "free decision" and, as in the Book of Judges, every man did that which was right in his own eyes, then society would disintegrate. Between societies, too, there is a great deal of moral consensus, covered by the phrase 'the comity of nations'. Moral disagreements often do lead to enmity and conflict; but people who conclude from this that they could not be rationally resolved "argue as ill, as if the savage people of America should deny there were any principle of reason so to build a house as to last as long as the materials, because they never saw any so well built" *(Leviathan, c. 30).*

There is a reason why moral arguments often are inconclusive and lead only to quarrels: namely, people may start a moral disputation when, as regards one of the key terms, they are not initially in agreement *either* on a class of instances to which it applies or on criteria for applying it. I remarked just now that in that case disputants are pretty well bound to get at cross purposes. But of course such frustration of the purpose of discussion may come about for any sort of term, not just for an ethical term. In general, people cannot even use a term to express disagreement unless they are agreed on a lot of the judgments they would express with that term; for example, people cannot even disagree about an historical character, because they will not manage to refer to one identifiable person, unless they would agree on a good deal of what to say about him. There is no reason to think things are otherwise for a term 'T' whose meaning is "evaluative"; unless people have a great deal of moral consensus about judging actions to be T, they cannot sensibly use 'T' to express moral disagreement. Recent moral philosophers have devoted far too much attention to moral disagreements and perplexing situations and the alleged freedom to make up a morality for yourself; if instead they had concentrated on moral consensus, we might by now understand the rationale of that a lot better.

We ought not, then, to be impressed by the argument Socrates presents; it limps on both legs. Factual questions are not necessarily decidable; moral questions have not been shown to be essentially undecidable.

All the same, weak as his position is on this abstract issue, Socrates has a strong case *ad hominem* against Euthyphro; if Greek stories were literally true, as Euthyphro believes, then it would be all too likely that the Gods would take opposite sides about Euthyphro's action. Euthyphro does not attempt to defend himself on this, his really weak point; and Socrates does not press the attack further home.

Euthyphro protests, however, that all the Gods will agree that wrongful homicide must be punished. Socrates makes short work of this: everybody, God or man, will agree that homicide is to be punished if it is wrongful; but when is it wrongful? That is just where disagreements arise (7b-e).

This short passage of the dialogue illustrates a trap into which an unwary man of decent principles may fall when arguing with an adversary who knows his business. Euthyphro says that *wrongful* killing is odious to God—and man; and Socrates gets him in one move by saying: What killing is wrongful? In our time, we should more likely have A saying that the act he protests against is wrong because it is murder; his adversary B will then extract from him an admission that murder—unless the word is a legal term of art—is just wrongful killing; so that A has said no more than that the act is wrong because it is wrong. This move by Socrates, or by a contemporary B, is merely eristic; worthwhile discussion can only start if that feature of the act which Euthyphro, or A, really is objecting to is brought out into the open and carefully considered.

Socrates has no intention of doing any such thing. Instead (9a-b) he appeals to popular prejudices. Has a man been wrongfully killed when he is a *serf,* who killed somebody's slave, was tied up by the slave's master, and "happened to die first" before the master could ask the authorities what to do with him? Ought a son to prosecute his own father over such a man? Will all the Gods agree that the killing is wrongful and the prosecution righteous?

Euthyphro says he could make it plain that his cause is just, if only the judge would hear his reasons; "I suppose you find me slower of understanding," says Socrates—and does not ask what Euthyphro's reasons may be. Instead, he says in effect: "I *give* you that *all* the Gods hate what your father did; I waive the point about one God's hating what another God loves; if you like, say that the pious is what *all* the Gods love and the impious is what *all* the Gods hate, so as to be sure that the same act is not both pious and impious. Even so, will your account of piety and impiety stand?" (9c-e).

The next stage of the dialogue (10a-11b) purports to refute the thesis that *pious* is the same as *loved by the Gods,* regardless of whether "the Gods" means 'all the Gods' or 'some Gods'. The general scheme of the argument is plain. Euthyphro is got to agree that the following pair of propositions is true:

(1) What is pious is loved by the Gods because it is pious
(2) What is God-loved is God-loved because it is loved by the Gods

and the following pair false:

(3) What is God-loved is loved by the Gods because it is God-loved
(4) What is pious is pious because it is loved by the Gods.

Now we get (3) from (1) by putting 'God-loved' instead of 'pious', and (4) from (2) by the reverse substitution; so (3) and (4) ought both to be true if *God-loved* and pious were the same; "but in fact it is quite the opposite," so *God-loved* and pious cannot be the same.

The principle underlying the argument appears to be the Leibnizian principle that two expressions for the same thing must be mutually replaceable *salva veritate*—so that a change from truth to falsehood upon such replacement must mean that we have not two expressions for the same thing. Of course it would be anachronistic to see here a formulation of the Leibnizian principle; but it is not anachronistic to discern a *use* of the principle any more than it is anachronistic to call an argument a syllogism in *Barbara,* when it antedates even Aristotle, let alone Peter of Spain. Though some forms of argument have been invented by logicians, many existed before there was any science of logic; and this is no bar to logical classification of them *ex post facto.*

The validity of arguments using Leibniz's principle is one of the most thorny points in recent philosophical discussion. It is well known both that such arguments are liable to break down in contexts that are not securely extensional, and that propositions formed with 'because' give us non-extensional contexts. Indeed, the following pair of expressions, as used by a man X on a given occasion, need not be propositions agreeing in truth-value:

(5) I hit him because he was the man who had just hit me
(6) I hit him because he was my father

even if the term 'father of X' were coextensive with the term 'man who had just hit X (on the occasion in question)'. So the truth of (1) and (2) and the falsehood of (3) and (4) would perhaps not allow of our concluding that pious actions and men are not the same classes as God-loved actions and men; as the

truth of (5) and falsehood of (6) do not warrant us in concluding that the
man who had just hit the speaker was other than his father.

A reader may be inclined at this point to make Mill's distinction: what the
argument does validly derive from its premises is that 'God-loved' and 'pious'
have a different *connotation,* even if they *denote* the same men and actions.
But have we the right to ascribe any such distinction to Plato? I doubt if any
such distinction is anywhere even clearly exemplified, let along formally expounded.

Using more Platonic language, the reader might suggest that *God-loved* and
pious are supposed to be different Forms. But surely, for Plato, there could not
be a Form *God-loved*. Rather, the view we are meant to adopt is that 'loved by
all the Gods', unlike 'pious', answers to no Form whatsoever. Being God-loved
is something that the pious "has done to it"; there is no reason to suppose that
'God-loved' expresses what something is, in that sense of 'what so-and-so is,'
which would mean, for Plato, that we are laying hold of a Form.

It is possible that the present argument is *supposed* to prove that the two
terms 'God-loved' and 'pious' differ in *application;* for at the end of the dialogue
Euthyphro is supposed to have contradicted his own previous admission by
saying that pious acts are dear to the Gods, loved by the Gods (15a-c). If what
the present argument is meant to prove were what some would express nowadays by saying that two terms differ in *connotation,* this criticism of Euthyphro
by Socrates would be an unfair debating trick. But we need not impute deliberate unfairness; we need only suppose that at this stage in philosophical
thought the different kinds of difference in meaning were not well sorted out.
We could scarcely be confident that they are really well sorted out even today.

Let us now look at the way the premises of the argument are reached. It is accepted by Euthyphro without demur that (1) is true and (4) false. The truth of
(2) and the falsehood of (3) are deduced by a tricky argument, relating to passive verbs in general. Plato of course could not use a grammarian's terms of art;
they hardly existed when he wrote, and it would have spoiled the dialogue to introduce them if they had existed. So he has to make Socrates convey the general
principle to Euthyphro by a series of examples; from these, Euthyphro is meant
to get the application of the principle to the verb 'to love' in particular.

Here we come up against a linguistic obstacle. Taking 'φ pass' as representing the ordinary inflected third-person singular passive of a verb, and 'φed' as
representing the passive particle of the same verb, we may say that what Plato
gives us are a series of examples in which these two propositions are contrasted:

(7) A thing φ pass. because it is φed

(8) A thing is φed because it φ pass.

The successive interpretations of 'φ' are 'to carry', 'to drive', 'to see', and finally 'to love'. But as regards the first two, it is extraordinarily hard to make out what the point is. In Greek, the expressions I have schematically represented as 'φ pass.' and 'is φed' are of course different; but in English both are naturally rendered by the ordinary present-tense passive form. One might try using the plain passive for the 'φ pass.' form and a periphrastic expression for the 'is φed' form; for example, one would get some such pair as this:

(9) A thing is carried because *carried* is what it is.
(10) Because a thing is carried, *carried* is what it is.

But this is just whistling in the dark; we just do not know how Plato conceived the difference between the forms I provisionally translate 'so-and-so is carried' and '*carried* is what so-and-so is', nor why it is supposed to be obvious that (10) is true and (9) is false.

Fortunately there is no need for us to try and solve this problem; for the supposed parity of reasoning between 'carried' and 'loved' just does not exist. Socrates is made to treat both as examples of "what things have done to them." We get the same assimilation in the *Sophist* (248d-e), where the Eleatic Stranger argues that being known is something the Forms "have done to them" (the same Greek verb is used as in the *Euthyphro*) and they therefore are not wholly changeless. But this assimilation is certainly wrong; among grammatically transitive verbs, verbs like 'know', 'love', and 'see' are logically quite different from verbs expressing that something is shifted or altered.

We need not try to delineate this difference, which has been the theme of much recent philosophical writing. It will be enough to concentrate on the peculiar use of 'because' in one of the premises of the main argument:

(11a) What is pious is loved by the Gods because it is pious. The conjunction 'because', and the corresponding word in Greek, occur in a lot of logically different sorts of propositions. To avoid confusion, I shall slightly rephrase (11a):
(11b) What is pious is loved by the Gods in respect of being pious.

This way of speaking—that something is the object of an attitude *in respect of* this or that characteristic—is one that I owe to McTaggart *(The Nature of Existence,* vol. ii, Section 465). Following close in his footsteps, I shall try to show the difference between propositions like (11b) and ordinary causal propositions.

The most obvious difference is that a person can have an attitude towards something in respect of its being X when the thing is not X but is mistakenly regarded by him as being X; I may e.g. admire a man in respect of his courage when he was in fact a great coward—and then his courage cannot be a cause or part-cause of my admiration. What is a cause or part-cause of my admiration is his *being believed by me* to be courageous; which is quite different from his being courageous, even if he is. And I certainly do not admire people in respect of *this* characteristic—being believed by myself, rightly or wrongly, to be courageous; that is not a characteristic I find admirable. No doubt the Gods would never falsely believe a man to be pious who was in fact impious; but we could still draw the distinction—the Gods would love him in respect of his piety, not in respect of his being *known to the Gods* as a pious man; that would only be the cause of the Gods' loving him, not the characteristic in respect of which they loved him.

Let us now rephrase (3) in the same style:

(12) What is God-loved is loved by the Gods in respect of being God-loved.

If (11b) is true, as Euthyphro surely wishes to say, and (12) is false, then 'pious' and 'God-loved' must somehow differ in meaning—in fact, there must be a big difference. And surely (12) is false; nobody, God or man, can love a thing simply *for*, in respect of, being loved by himself. Similarly, nobody can fear a thing simply *for* its being fearful to him; if the Church approves the Bible *for* being inspired, then 'being inspired' cannot simply mean 'approved by the Church'; and so in general. The principle illustrated by the falsehood of (12) does seem to be both sound and sufficient to serve as a premise in the way Plato intended. Failing a rigorous account of verbs of attitude (intentional verbs, as they are now sometimes called), we cannot quite clearly see the rationale of this principle; all the same, it surely is a sound principle.

The remainder of the dialogue is of less interest. Socrates gets over to Euthyphro, with some difficulty, the idea that though anything pious is just, it does not follow that everything just is pious; he does this by the "You might as well say" technique familiar to readers of *Alice*—you might as well say that if all shame is fear, all fear is shame, or that if everything odd is a number, every number is odd (12a-d). We thus get the question: What sort of just acts are pious? Euthyphro replies: Those which concern the service of the Gods rather than men (12e).

Socrates professes himself unable to understand this answer. Huntsmen serve, or look after, hounds; drovers look after cattle, and so on; presumably this consists in helpful actions, actions that are for the betterment of that which is served. Then is piety aimed at the betterment of the Gods? Euthyphro of course protests that this is not at all the kind of service he meant; rather, we serve the Gods as slaves their masters (13a-d).

Socrates does not reject this answer, but raises further questions about it. The work of a subordinate is ordered to the particular end of his master; for a doctor the servant's work will be directed towards health, for a shipwright towards voyaging, for an architect towards building, and so on. What then is the magnificent work of the Gods in which we play a subordinate role as their servants? Or at least, what is the chief end of this work, as victory is the general's chief end and winning food from the soil is the farmer's? (13e-14a).

Euthyphro cannot answer this question; and we should notice that he is not logically committed to doing so. If men are the slaves of the Gods, then by obeying them men will fulfil the Gods' ends, whatever these may be; but men can know that without knowing in what particular the Gods' ends are. "The servant knoweth not what his lord doth"; and Euthyphro would account himself only a servant, not a friend, of the Gods.

Instead of answering the question, then, Euthyphro states which actions specially constitute giving the Gods their due: prayers and sacrifices and the like. The answer is seriously meant, and deserves to be taken seriously if any theological discourse does. We may notice that for Aquinas the virtue of "religion" is the part of justice that gives to God what is specially due to him, and that he conceives the characteristic acts of "religion" as Euthyphro does. There are, of course, serious objections that can be raised about the rationale of acts like prayer and sacrifice. Socrates raises none of these; his retort is, as commentators say, "playful." At that rate, piety would be a skill of bargaining with the Gods ("If you choose to call it that," Euthyphro interjects), and the bargain is a bad one for the Gods, since only we and not they are benefited (14b-15a).

Euthyphro says, as he has said before, that of course our pious acts cannot benefit the Gods; they are acts of honor and courtesy (*charis*) that *please* the Gods. At this point Socrates charges him with going back to the old rejected explanation of pious acts as acts that the Gods love. The charge, as I said, need not be deliberately sophistical, but at least is far from having been logically made to stick. We may see this quite simply if we use the Mactaggartian apparatus of 'in respect' of that I introduced just now. Though the Gods cannot be pleased by an act in respect of its being pleasing to the Gods, they logically could be pleased by an act in respect of its *being intended* to be pleasing to them, as human parents are by the acts of their children. And Euthyphro's act in prosecuting his father could be pleasing to the Gods both as an act of human justice and as an act of piety; both in respect of its avenging a poor man's wrong, and in respect of its being intended to please the Gods.

Socrates presses Euthyphro to try again to define piety; surely he would not have ventured, without knowing what piety is, to . . . Here Euthyphro has to listen again to Socrates' appeals to conventional prejudices—including the class prejudice against a "serf fellow." But he has heard enough, and says he is too busy for further talk. The commentators seem to agree that the dialogue ends with a moral victory for Socrates. I should prefer to think that, to use Bunyan's language, Mr. Right-Mind was not to be led a-wandering from the straight path.

3

Socrates on the Definition of Piety:
Euthyphro 10A-11B

S. Marc Cohen

Pₗₐₜₒ'ₛ *Eᴜᴛʜʏᴘʜʀᴏ* ɪs ᴀ ᴄʟᴇᴀʀ ᴇxᴀᴍᴘʟᴇ of a Socratic definitional dialogue. The concept to be defined is that of holiness or piety (τὸ ὅσιον); the need for a definition is presented in a manner characteristic of the early dialogues. Euthyphro is about to prosecute his father on a charge of murder, Socrates expresses surprise at Euthyphro's action, and Euthyphro defends himself by saying that to prosecute his father is pious, whereas not to prosecute him would be impious. Socrates then wonders whether Euthyphro's knowledge of piety and impiety is sufficient to guarantee that he is not acting impiously in prosecuting his father. The trap has been set; Euthyphro's vanity is stung, and the search for a definition begins. The outcome of the search is also familiar; all of Euthyphro's efforts miscarry. The dialogue ends with no satisfactory definition of piety either produced or in the offing.

The central argument in the dialogue is the one Socrates advances (10a-11b) against Euthyphro's definition of piety as "what all the gods love." The argument is interesting on several counts. First, the argument is sufficiently unclear as to warrant discussion of what its structure is. Second, it is at least open to question whether there is any interpretation or reconstruction of the argument according to which it is valid and non-fallacious. Third, there are a number of points of contemporary philosophical interest that inevitably arise in any adequate discussion of the argument. Fourth, the argument has been traditionally thought to have an important moral for contemporary ethical theory, and not just for ancient theology. Before beginning a detailed examination of the argument itself, I will comment briefly on the moral the argument has been traditionally thought to have.[1]

For Euthyphro, the question whether or not he ought to prosecute his father is to be settled by determining whether or not it would be pious for him to do so. Whether or not his doing so would be pious is determined by finding out whether all the gods love it, or, as we might now say, approve of it. For Euthyphro, then, moral questions (such as "Ought I prosecute my father?") are settled by appeal to moral authorities—the gods. Euthyphro is offering an authoritarian normative ethical theory. But he apparently wishes to offer an authoritarian meta-ethical theory as well, since 'pious' is for him *defined* in terms of the approval of an authority. Moreover, Euthyphro's authorities must have been thought of by him to be pre-eminently wise and rational; after all, they are the gods. Their wisdom and rationality is part of what makes them moral authorities. It is their wisdom and rationality that enables them to perceive, where mere mortals may fail to perceive, whether a given act is pious. Socrates' argument may then be thought of as having the following force. If 'pious' is to be defined in terms of the gods' approval, then the piety of a given act cannot be that upon which the gods base their approval of it. If the gods' approval of a pious act has any rational basis, then, it must lie in their perception of some *other* features of the act. And then it is *these* features in terms of which 'pious' should be defined. In general, if one's normative ethics are authoritarian, and one's authorities are rational and use their rationality in forming moral judgments, then one's meta-ethics cannot also be authoritarian.

I want to argue in support of this somewhat traditional interpretation of the *Euthyphro*. I shall try to show that Socrates' arguments should be taken as supporting this conclusion (indeed, that they cannot be taken to support anything else).

I

Socrates begins his argument against Euthyphro's proposed definition by asking him this question: "Is the pious loved by the gods because it is pious, or is it pious because it is loved?"[2] Socrates hopes to get Euthyphro to affirm the first and deny the second of these two alternatives, but Euthyphro fails to understand the question. Socrates agrees to "speak more plainly" (σαφέστερον φράσαι) and then produces the most baffling part of the argument. Before examining the explanation that Socrates offers, we might note that it seems somewhat surprising that Euthyphro does not realize that he cannot, consistent with his own definition, deny the second of these alternatives. For if 'pious' is to be defined as 'loved by all the gods', then surely, in some sense of 'because', it will be because it is loved that the pious is pious. But I think it is easy to see why Euthyphro cannot be expected to have realized this. First of all, it has not been explicitly stated that Euthyphro was to be offering a *definition*. When the question was first raised, Socrates simply asked Euthyphro to "say what the pious is" (τί φῂς εἶναι τὸ ὅσιον: 5d7); later, Socrates asks for "the characteristic in virtue of which everything pious is pious" (τὸ εἶδος ᾧ πάντα τὰ ὅσια ὅσια ἐστιν: 6d10-11). And it is not hard to imagine that Euthyphro, not appreciating the force of the phrase τὸ εἶδος ᾧ, would find it sufficient to produce a formula which he feels will serve to pick out all and only pious things. After all, the philosophical topic of definition was just being invented, and Euthyphro could hardly have been at home in it. And part of Plato's point will surely be that the definition of a term 'F' cannot be *just* a formula which applies to all and only F things. If this is a mistake that Plato wants to show up, then Euthyphro must surely be given the opportunity to make it. At this point in the dialogue Euthyphro is content to say that pious things are the ones the gods love; and if this is what he wishes to say, then he need not be expected to answer Socrates' question "Is the pious pious because it is loved?" in the affirmative, even if he understood the question. But he has not even claimed to understand it.

II

The next part of Socrates' argument, in which he tries to explain to Euthyphro what his question meant, has produced more confusion on the part of commentators and translators than has anything else in the dialogue. Everything starts out well enough: Socrates notes that we speak of a thing being carried and a thing carrying, a thing being led and a thing leading, etc., and that the first member of each pair is different from the second.[3] The first member of each pair is a passive participle *(pheromenon, agomenon, horômenon)* and the second an active participle *(pheron, agon, horôn)*.[4] The distinction is surely intended to be a grammatical one; as has been frequently noted, the grammatical terminology in which the distinction between active and passive voices would be expressed had not been invented at the time Plato was writing. The distinction is then applied to the verb relevant to Euthyphro's definition; being loved *(philoumenon)* is distinguished from loving *(philoun)*. So far, so good. The distinction Socrates wishes to draw is clear, even if what he is up to is not.

But having distinguished between active and passive participles, Socrates immediately drops the active member from the discussion and contrasts, instead, the passive participle with the inflected third-person singular passive. The distinction Socrates is after has to do with how these forms fit into sentences of the form 'p because q'. He wants to say that substituting the participle for 'p' and the inflected passive for 'q' will yield a truth, whereas substituting the inflected passive for 'p' and the participle for 'q' will yield a falsehood. Thus a thing carried *(pheromenon)* is (1) *pheromenon* because *pheretai*, but not (2) *pheretai* because it is a *pheromenon*. The trouble is that whereas Socrates' first distinction was between active and passive voices, this second distinction is between two different passive forms. Thus, it is hard to see how the first distinction is meant to bear on the second. An even greater difficulty is that when we try to translate Socrates' words when he draws this distinction, we are faced with the fact that *both* of these forms are normally translated the same way into English—'is carried', 'is led', etc. If we try to translate what Socrates says, then, we get: "a thing carried is (1) carried because it is carried, but not (2) carried because it is carried." But this makes Socrates' point nonsense.

This difficulty has reduced translators to babble and driven commentators to despair. Let me give one example of each. In one translation of the *Euthyphro* we read: "a thing is not carried because it is in a state of being carried: it is in a state of being carried because it is carried."[5] But even if one can find this intelligible, it is still hard to see why it is supposed to be true. Geach[6] tries translating what Socrates wishes to deny as "a thing is carried because *carried* is what it is" and what he wishes to affirm as "Because a thing is carried, *carried* is what it is" and then gives up, saying that

> this is just whistling in the dark; we just do not know how Plato conceived the difference between the forms I provisionally translate 'so-and-so is carried' and *'carried* is what so-and-so is', nor why it is supposed to be obvious that [the second] is true and [the first] is false.

I think that we can do better by way of both translation and interpretation. Indeed, unless we can understand what Plato is up to here we will be in no position to assess his argument.[7]

Two important points need to be noted if we are to grasp Plato's point. The first is that the passive participle can function as part of a noun phrase or, by itself, nominally. *Pheromenon ti* means "something carried"; a *pheromenon* is something which is carried. The second point is that the inflected passive entered the discussion in place of the active participle. *Pheretai*—"it is carried"—can, in general, have the sense of "one carries it" or "something carries it"; and it clearly must have that sense in Socrates' argument.[8] It now becomes tempting to try to put Socrates' point this way: the passive participle of a verb introduces the notion of an alteration in something—a thing's being in an altered state or condition. The inflected passive of the verb introduces the notion of a process which results in that alteration—a thing's having been acted on in such a way that it is altered as a result. Then Socrates would be saying that a thing's having been acted on in a certain way explains why it is in an altered condition, whereas a thing's being in an altered condition does not explain why it underwent the process which results in that alteration. Socrates would be seen as putting forward a rudimentary causal doctrine having to do with the relative explanatory powers of causes and effects.[9]

But to try to interpret Socrates' point in this way invites the obvious objection that, owing to a clear disanalogy between the verb 'love' and the others that Socrates first considers, the point Socrates wishes to make using those other verbs cannot be applied to the verb 'love'. For whereas a thing that is carried or led is altered by being carried or led, a thing that is loved need not be altered by being loved.[10]

Let me try to present what I take to be Socrates' point in a way that will leave it immune to such an objection. Let us represent the passive participle of a verb 'φ' as 'φ -ed thing' or 'is a φ -ed thing', and the inflected passive of the verb either as 'is φ -ed by x' where the subject, x, is specified or as 'is φ -ed (by something)' where no subject is specified.[11] Then Socrates' point is that, where 'φ' is a verb, a φ -ed thing is

(α) a φ -ed thing because it is φ -ed (by something)

not:

(β) φ -ed (by something) because it is a φ -ed thing.

Our job now is to try to see whether this claim can be understood in a fairly natural way such as to make (α) true and (β) false. Clearly, this will depend upon the force we assign to the crucial word 'because'.

It is not hard to see that, on a natural reading of (α) and (β), 'because' must be understood to have different senses in the two sentence-forms.[12] Let us begin with (β). We may be at a loss in trying to understand (β), I think, unless we remember that the inflected passive, 'is φ -ed (by something)', entered the argument in place of an active form.[13] If we are to understand the earlier distinction between active and passive participles to have any bearing on the later distinction between two passive forms, we must, I think, give the inflected passive in (β) an active sense. Transforming (β) in this way we get:

(β*) Someone or something φ -s a φ -ed thing because it is a φ -ed thing.

If we understand the context governing the first occurrence of 'φ -ed thing' in (β*) to be transparent, we can read (β*) as:

(β* 1) Someone or something φ -s a thing (which is, in fact, a φ -ed thing) because it is a φ -ed thing.

Leaving out the parenthetical clause we get:

(β*2) Someone or something φ -s a thing because it is a φ -ed thing.

Concentrating on just the first part of (β*2), "Someone or something φ -s a thing because. . . ," it is easy to see that the 'because' should be thought of as introducing a reason for some action or attitude. What sort of reason is being introduced will, of course, depend on the verb that replaces 'φ'. Where the verb is one which will properly take 'someone', but not 'something', as the subject (such as the key verb in the argument 'love'), the reason introduced will have to be a person's reason for having a certain attitude or performing a certain action.[14] The first part of (β*2) can therefore be understood as introducing a reason which would serve to answer a question of the form "Why does someone φ . . . ?" The form of answer, "Someone's reason for φ -ing is that . . . ," is clearly what is intended by the first part of (β*2), in which 'because', rather than 'reason for', occurs. (β), then, can be understood as the claim that someone's reason for φ -ing x is that x is a φ -ed thing. I think that this is a natural reading for (β); that (β), so read, is an unacceptable principle I hope to show later.

   The 'because' in (α), on the other hand, cannot be thought of as introducing a person's reason for some attitude or action. The first part of (α), "A φ -ed thing is a φ -ed thing because . . . ," does not suggest that what is needed to fill the blank is the specification of a person's reason. Rather, it suggests that what is needed is, at least, a logically sufficient condition for applying the participial term 'φ -ed thing' to something. Perhaps even more is needed. For we ought to understand (α) to be an answer to the question "Why is a φ -ed thing a φ -ed thing?" And this question seems to require an informative answer which provides logically necessary and sufficient conditions for applying the term 'φ -ed thing' to something. Transforming (α) by replacing the inflected passive with the corresponding inflected active, as we did with (β), will not alter this reading of (α). Transforming (α) in this way we get:

(α*) A φ -ed thing is a φ -ed thing because someone or something φ -s it.

Once again understanding the context governing the first occurrence of 'φ -ed thing' to be transparent, we can read (α *) as:

(α *1) Something (which is, in fact, a φ -ed thing) is a φ -ed thing because someone or something φ -s it.

Again leaving out the parenthetical clause we get:

(α*2) Something is a φ -ed thing because someone or something φ -s it.

(α*2), like (α), must be thought of as purporting to provide an informative answer to the question "Why is something a φ -ed thing?", an answer which provides logically sufficient (and perhaps also necessary[15]) conditions for applying the term 'φ -ed thing' to something. In what I take to be the natural readings of (α) and (β), then, 'because' is used equivocally. We must now determine whether, on these readings, (α) is an acceptable principle and (β) unacceptable.

We can see why (α) should be affirmed and (β) denied by examining some of Socrates' examples. "A carried thing is a carried thing because it is carried (by something)" has this force: the fact that something or someone carries x is an informative, logically sufficient condition for calling x a carried thing. This seems unobjectionable. The condition is logically sufficient because it follows from the fact that x carries y that y is a carried thing. It is informative because it might instruct someone in the use of the expression 'carried thing'. 'Carried thing' is to be applied to something, y, when there is something, x, which carries y. By contrast, "A carried thing is carried (by something) because it is a carried thing" has this force: a reason why x is carried by someone or something (i.e., a reason why someone or something carries x) is that x is a carried thing. But this is clearly objectionable; that x is a carried thing cannot be anyone's reason for carrying x. The same point seems to carry over to the verb Socrates is interested in. The fact that someone loves x is an informative, logically sufficient condition for x's being called a loved thing; but the fact that x is a loved thing does not explain why someone loves x. It cannot be anyone's reason for loving x that x is a loved thing.[16] Thus, for Socrates' claim to be made intelligible and acceptable, the *hoti* ('because') in *philoumenon hoti phileitai* and *phileitai hoti philoumenon* must be understood to be used equivocally. But whether this equivocation proves fatal to Socrates' argument remains to be seen.

III

At this point (10d1) Socrates once again poses his original question, and this time Euthyphro is willing to answer. What he says is that the pious is

(a) loved by the gods because it is pious

not:

(b) pious because it is loved (by the gods[17]).

('Loved' translates the inflected passive *phileitai*; the participle *philoumenon* does not appear here.) Now a new term is introduced: *theophiles,* or 'god-loved'.

From the manner of its introduction it is clearly serving as a specific filler for *philoumenon.* To be *theophiles,* I take it, is to be a *philoumenon* which *phileitai hupo theôn.* Next a pair of *hoti* statements, like (a) and (b) above, is put forward (by Socrates, with Euthyphro's assent) about *theophiles.*[18] The god-loved is

(a') god-loved because it is loved by the gods

not:

(b') loved (by the gods[19]) because it is god-loved.

Euthyphro has now agreed that (a) and (a') are true while (b) and (b') are false. Socrates claims that this shows the pious and the god-loved to be "different from one another" (ἕτερον τοῦτο τούτου), for "if they were the same" (εἴ γε ταὐτὸν ἦν), (b') would follow from (a) and (b) would follow from (a'). The warrant for this inference, not stated by Socrates, can only be that the substitution of 'god-loved' for 'pious' in (a) yields (b') and the substitution of 'pious' for 'god-loved' in (a') yields (b). At this point it will be wise to stop and assess the argument.

First of all, what does Socrates mean when he says that the pious and the god-loved are different from one another? Does he think he has shown that the class of pious things and the class of god-loved things are not co-extensive? If he does think this, he is clearly mistaken. His argument depends on substituting the terms 'pious' and 'god-loved' for one another in sentences agreed to be true, where the substitutions produce sentences which are agreed to be false. But this result will not show that the terms 'pious' and 'god-loved' apply to different instances unless the sentences in which the substitutions are made are clearly extensional. And sentences of the form 'p because q' are not extensional, whether 'because q' is thought of as introducing a person's reason for acting or a logically sufficient condition for the application of a term to something.

But there is no reason to think that Socrates took himself to be showing that these two classes are not coextensive. He has already told Euthyphro that he is not interested in an enumeration of things that are pious, but rather wants to know the characteristic in virtue of which (τὸ εἶδος ᾧ) each pious thing is pious (6d9-11). Clearly, the point must be that 'god-loved' does not introduce τὸ εἶδος ᾧ a thing is pious. And this point is quite consistent with 'god-loved' applying to the same things to which 'pious' applies. Also, Socrates gives some indication, at the end of his argument, that he realizes he can grant Euthyphro that 'pious' and 'god-loved' apply to the same things without putting his main point in jeopardy.[20]

So Socrates is trying to show that 'god-loved' does not introduce τὸ εἶδος ᾧ a thing is pious. And I think it is safe to say that the phrase which *does* introduce τὸ εἶδος ᾧ a thing is pious would be the definition of 'pious'. So the principle which Socrates' argument depends on is not, as Geach thinks, "the Leibnizian principle that two expressions for the same thing must be mutually replaceable *salva veritate*,"[21] but rather a principle which might be formulated roughly as follows: two expressions, one of which is a definition of the other, must be mutually replaceable *salva veritate*. We might call this the principle of substitutivity of definitional equivalents, understanding definitional equivalents to be a pair of expressions one of which is a definition of the other. And while perhaps both principles can be shown to break down in some intensional contexts, the principle of substitutivity of definitional equivalents does not seem to be one which will break down in the intensional contexts in question, even if the Leibnizian principle will. So if there is a flaw in Socrates' argument, it does not lie in the intensionality of 'because'. But it may lie in an equivocation on 'because'.

We saw earlier that in order to render Socrates' claims about the use of participles and inflected passives in 'because' contexts intelligible, we had to interpret *hoti* equivocally. It is clear that we will have to do the same here if we are to see why (a) and (a') are to be accepted as true, and (b) and (b') rejected as false. Let us then disambiguate the troublesome word *hoti* in the following way: *phileisthai hoti* (clearly equivalent in the context to *phileitai hupo theôn hoti*) will be rendered as 'the reason the gods love it is that . . . ;' *hosion hoti* and *theophiles hoti* as 'a logically sufficient condition for applying the term 'pious' to it is that . . .' and 'a logically sufficient condition for applying the term 'god-loved' to it is that . . ,' respectively. The referent of 'it' will be supplied by the subject of each sentence in which these phrases occur. The four sentences can now be reformulated as:

(Ra) The reason the gods love what is pious is that it is pious.
(Rb) A logically sufficient condition for applying the term 'pious' to what is pious is that the gods love it.
(Ra') A logically sufficient condition for applying the term 'god-loved' to what is god-loved is that the gods love it.
(Rb') The reason the gods love what is god-loved is that it is god-loved.

We may now turn to the question whether (Ra) and (Ra') should be accepted by Euthyphro as true, but (Rb) and (Rb') rejected by him as false.

Since (Ra) is what is going to get Euthyphro into trouble, by turning out to be inconsistent with his definition, one might feel that he should not accept it. But Euthyphro's acceptance of it must be taken to indicate that he thinks the gods do have a reason for loving pious things, that they do not love pious things irrationally, and that *their being pious things* is precisely this reason. (Ra') seems clearly acceptable; that the term 'god-loved' correctly applies to something ought to follow from the fact that the gods love it. (Rb), however, should not have been rejected by Euthyphro; for his rejection of it is clearly inconsistent with his definition and it is not apparent that he must reject it in order to maintain that the gods have a reason for loving the pious. But as we will see, Socrates' conclusion does not depend upon Euthyphro's rejection of (Rb); whether Socrates saw that a rejection of (Rb) was superfluous, however, is another matter. But (Rb) must certainly be rejected. For although a person's reason for loving something, x, may be that x has a property P, it is absurd to suppose that this could hold when P is the property of being loved by him. For x's having this property amounts to nothing more nor less than the fact that he loves x. And one's *reason* for loving something cannot be that he loves it. Imagine the following dialogue:

A: "She mistreats you terribly. Why do you love her?"
B: "Just because I do."

B's answer, which amounts to saying "I just love her," is clearly a rejection of A's question. B is saying, in effect, that he has no reason for loving her; he just does. Thus, since being god-loved amounts to nothing more nor less than being loved by the gods (a point Euthyphro can be assumed to have at least a dim awareness of, in view of his acceptance of (a'), (Rb') is certainly false. The gods' *reason* for loving something cannot be that they love it.

Socrates, we have seen, equivocates on *hoti* in the course of his argument. But this is not to say he commits the fallacy of equivocation in the argument. Let us call the *hoti* which serves to introduce a person's reason a "reason-*hoti*," and the one which serves to introduce logically sufficient conditions for the application of a term a "logical-*hoti*." Then for Socrates to be committing the fallacy of equivocation would be for him to infer, by substitution, from a sentence which must be understood to contain a reason-*hoti*, one which must be understood to contain a logical-*hoti*, or *vice versa*. But Socrates does not do this. Although he equivocates on *hoti* in the argument, the word is used univocally within each of the *inferences* that Socrates draws. Socrates' argument, as we have interpreted it, was that if 'pious' and 'god-loved' are definitionally equivalent, then (a) entails (b') and (a') entails (b). But the *hoti* in both (a') and (b) is the logical-*hoti*; the one in both (a) and (b') is the reason-*hoti*. Socrates' argument, then, does not commit the fallacy of equivocation.[22]

Nor does the argument depend upon Euthyphro's dubious rejection of (b). For the conclusion, that 'pious' and 'god-loved' are not definitionally equivalent, follows from the acceptance of (a) and rejection of (b') alone.[23] If 'pious' meant 'god-loved', then something's being pious could not be a reason for the gods to love it, since something's being god-loved cannot be a reason for the gods to love it. The *hoti* that is crucial for Socrates' argument is the reason-*hoti*. But the logical-*hoti* still plays an important, if subsidiary, role in the argument. For the acceptance of (a'), in which the logical-*hoti* occurs, paves the way for the rejection of the absurd (b').

IV

What, then, does Socrates' argument prove? It does not prove that 'pious' cannot be defined as 'god-loved'. It only proves that 'pious' cannot be defined as 'god-loved' if the gods' reason for loving what is pious is that it is pious. Does this amount to proving that 'pious' cannot be defined as 'god-loved' if the gods have a reason for loving what is pious? No; the gods might have other reasons for loving what is pious. But this implication is clear at any rate: if the gods do have reasons for loving what is pious, it is to these reasons that we should look in trying to define 'pious'. If the gods have a reason for loving pious acts, it will be that these acts have, or are thought by the gods to have, certain features. It is these features, then, that should serve to define piety. The fact that the gods have a rational love for what is pious may be relevant to the problem of defining piety. But then it would be in the rationality, and not in the love, that the answer to this problem lies.

The more general point I take to be this: If a moral concept M is such that there is an authority whose judgment whether or not something falls under M is decisive and is rationally grounded, then 'M' cannot be defined in terms of that authority's judgment. This may be taken to be a generalization of the conclusion of the central argument in Plato's *Euthyphro*.[24]

Notes

1. Cf. A.E. Taylor, *Plato the Man and his Work* (London: Methuen, 1949), p. 151, and Robert G. Hoerber, "Plato's *Euthyphro*," *Phronesis*, III (1958), 95–107, esp. n. 1, p. 102, and p. 104.

2. ἆρα τὸ ὅσιον ὅτι ὅσιόν ἐστιν φιλεῖται ὑπὸ τῶν θεῶν, ἢ ὅτι φιλεῖται ὅσιόν ἐστιν (10a2-3). Translations, unless otherwise noted, are my own.

3. Λέγομέν τι φερόμενον καὶ φέρον καὶ ἀγόμενον καὶ ἄγον καὶ ὁρώμενον καὶ ὁρῶν καὶ πάντα τὰ τοιαῦτα μανθάνεις ὅτι ἕτερα ἀλλήλων ἐστὶ καὶ ᾗ ἕτερα (10a5-8).

4. In what follows I shall transliterate the Greek terms a Greekless reader will find it useful to identify in following the argument.

5. F. J. Church, revised by Robert D. Cumming (New York: Liberal Arts Press, 1956), p. 12.

6. P.T. Geach, "Plato's *Euthyphro:* An Analysis and Commentary," *The Monist,* July 1966, p. 378.

7. This opinion is not shared by Geach. Cf. *ibid.,* bottom.

8. This has been noted by some translators of the *Euthyphro. Pheretai* is translated by Fowler (Loeb Classical Library) as "one carries it" and by Cooper (*The Collected Dialogues of Plato,* Hamilton and Cairns, ed.) as "something carries it."

9. Indeed, Socrates' generalization of his examples has often been interpreted as giving voice to just such a doctrine. Socrates' generalization is this: εἴ τι γίγνεται ἤ τι πάσχει, οὐχ ὅτι γιγνόμενον ἐστι γίγνεται, ἀλλ' ὅτι γίγνεται γιγνόμενόν ἐστιν (10c1-3). Cooper translates these lines as follows: "Whenever an effect occurs, or something is effected, it is not the thing effected that gives rise to the effect; no, there is a cause, and then comes this effect." This mistranslation gives rise to an erroneous interpretation of Socrates' point. It seems to me that Socrates is trying, without an adequate logical vocabulary, to generalize on his earlier examples; lacking the notion of a variable, Socrates uses the all-purpose verb γίγνεσθαι, in effect as a verb-variable. The result of reading Socrates' sentence in this way—with 'φ' as a verb-variable in place of γίγνεσθαι—is my pair of principles (a) and (b) below.

10. Cf. Geach, *loc. cit.,* pp. 378–379. A further reason for not taking Socrates' point in this way is that the verb 'see', which occurs in the *epagoge,* is, like the verb 'love', disanalogous to the others in this respect.

11. Bearing in mind that 'is φ -ed by x' is taken to be equivalent to 'x φ -s it' and 'is φ -ed (by something)' to 'something φ -s it'.

12. J. L. Ackrill is reported (in a footnote in John H. Brown, "The Logic of the *Euthyphro* 10A-11B," *Philosophical Quarterly,* Jan. 1964, p. 13) to have suggested an interpretation much like the one I develop at length below. The interpretation I offer, however, was arrived at independently of Ackrill's.

John C. Hall ("Plato: *Euthyphro* 10a1-11a10," *Philosophical Quarterly* [Jan. 1968], pp. 1-11) also considers the possibility of understanding the argument to employ 'because' equivocally, and even tries out the "person's reason" sense of 'because', in much the way that I do below. But he winds up rejecting such an interpretation, on what seem to me to be mistaken grounds. Cf. n. 22 below and Brown, *loc. cit.*

13. Cf. above, p. 4.

14. Where the verb can take 'something' as well as, or rather than, 'someone' as a subject, the 'because' might introduce all or part of a purely causal explanation, and not a person's reason. I shall ignore this complication in what follows, as it is not relevant to the point at issue.

15. That Plato thought of (α) as providing a necessary condition as well seems likely. At 10b1-2 Socrates asks Euthyphro whether a *pheromenon* is a *pheromenon* because it *pheretai* "or because of something else" (ἤ δι'ἄλλο τι). Euthyphro's answer, οὔκ ἀλλὰ διὰ τοῦτο, must be understood to mean that *pheretai* and only *pheretai* specifies an informative sufficient condition for being a *pheromenon,* thus making it necessary as well as sufficient.

16. One might offer the following objection to this claim. My reason for loving x cannot be that *I* love it, but it can be that *others* love it. And if a loved thing is one that people generally love, then perhaps I *can* give as my reason for loving x that it is a loved thing, i.e., that it is generally loved. Socrates' argument, as we shall see, neatly avoids this difficulty by replacing *philoumenon* ('a loved thing') with *theophiles* ('god-1oved') before the discussion of why the *gods* love what they do begins.

17. Plato does not actually say *hupo theôn*—'by the gods'—here, but that qualification is clearly intended.

18. Whether the ὅτι statements about τὸ θεοφιλές enter the argument at 10d9-10 or only later at 10e5-7 is open to question. I have followed Bast and Schanz in amending 10d10 by adding the words τὸ θεοφιλές as the subject of the sentence, which then amounts to an assertion of (a'). If the manuscript tradition is accepted, the subject of the sentence is an implicit τὸ ὅσιον, which would carry over from 10d1. Socrates' point would then be that *what is pious* is god-loved because it is loved by the gods. The reason for preferring the emendation is not that this last point would be unacceptable to Socrates (it would not), but that without the emendation the speech at 10d9-10 would have no place in the argument. The construction at 10e2-7 (ὁμολογοῦμεν τὸ μὲν ὅσιον . . . τὸ δέ γε θεοφιλές . . .), where (a') and the negation of (b') are explicitly asserted, indicates that at least one if not both of (a') and (b') have been explicitly formulated already. Burnet, for some reason, feels that the emendation "spoils the argument by making τὸ θεοφιλές the subject instead of 'τὸ ὅσιον" (John Burnet, *Plato's Euthyphro* [Oxford: Oxford University Press, 1924], p. 49). How this would spoil the argument is unclear to me. But even without the emendation the argument is not spoiled; we need only take the agreement at 10e5 to refer back to 10c9-11, where φιλούμενον ὅτι φιλεῖται is affirmed and φιλεῖται ὅτι φιλούμενον is denied. But this would make the place of 10d9-10 in the argument somewhat mysterious.

19. Cf. n. 17.

20. 11b2-4. Socrates says that the question of what piety is (τί ποτε ὄν τὸ ὅσιον) arises even if the pious is loved by the gods (εἴτε φιλεῖται ὑπὸ θεῶν); and he adds that he and Euthyphro will not disagree about this last point (οὐ γὰρ περὶ τούτου διοισόμεθα) i.e., will agree that what is pious is loved by the gods.

21. Geach, *loc. cit.,* p. 376.

22. Brown, *loc. cit.,* claims that Socrates' argument is equivocally fallacious because, he feels, the negation of (b) is *inferred* by Socrates from (a); he similarly feels that Socrates infers the falsity of *pheretai hoti pheromenon* from the truth of *pheromenon hoti pheretai,* etc. As I have presented the argument, the denials of (b) and (b') are put forward independently of the assertions of (a) and (a'), not inferred from them. If this is right, there is no reason to suspect that some inference in the argument is equivocally fallacious.

There is, however, some reason for thinking that the negations of (b) and (b') are inferred from (a) and (a'), respectively. For although no inferential particles precede the introduction of the negations of (b) and (b') into the argument, the situation seems to be different in the *epagoge.* There an instance of (α) is put forward, after which the negation of the corresponding instance of (β) is introduced preceded by the (weak) inferential particle ἄρα (10b4-8). And since the truth of both (a) and (a') and the falsity of both (b) and (b') seem to be inferred from the *epagoge*, the inferential connection between (α) and not-(β) might be thought to carry over to the later pairs.

Since the inferential particle is the weak ἄρα, rather than the strong οὖν, one might argue that Socrates is speaking somewhat carelessly and is not supposing that there is a logical connection between (α) and not-(β). But the success of my interpretation does not depend on such an argument, for I think it can be shown that even if not-(β) is being inferred from (α), the inference is not fallacious *despite* the equivocation on *hoti*.

The sense of (α), as I have interpreted it, might be put in this way:

Being a φ -ed thing is not a property that a thing can have (or be thought to have) independently of being (or being thought to be) φ -ed by someone or something.

The sense of (β) would be:

Someone's reason for φ -ing something is (or can be) that that thing has the property of being a φ -ed thing.

But despite the obvious equivocation on 'because' in (α) and (β), it still seems quite correct to *infer* not-(β) from (α). For if *both* (α) and (β) were true, then it would be possible for someone, x, to f something, y, and have as a reason for φ -ing y that y has a property which, it turns out, y cannot even be *thought* to have independently of x's φ -ing it. The absurdity of this seems to be that it conflicts with the following, which I take to be a conceptual truth. If x's reason for φ -ing y is that y has property P, then it must be possible for y to have property P independently of being φ -ed by x. Otherwise, x's "reason" turns out to be no reason at all. Cf. above, p. 11.

23. Cf. Lynn E. Rose, "A Note on the *Euthyphro, 10–11,*" *Phronesis,* X (1965), 149–150, for a brief discussion of the multiplicity of inconsistencies into which Euthyphro falls.

24. I have benefited from discussions of earlier versions of this paper with members of the philosophy departments of the University of California, Irvine and Dartmouth College. I owe a special debt of gratitude to Gareth B. Matthews for his help in bringing the paper to its present form.

4

Socratic Piety[1]

Gregory Vlastos

SOCRATES' COMMITMENT TO REASONED ARGUMENT as the final arbiter of claims to truth in the moral domain is evident throughout Plato's Socratic dialogues. He refers to it in the deliberation by which he justifies to Crito the decision to remain in prison and await execution:

> T1 *Cr.* 45B: "Not now for the first time, but always, I am the sort of man who is persuaded by nothing in me except the proposition which appears to me to be the best *when I reason* (λογίζομένῳ) about it."

And yet he is also committed to obeying commands reaching him through supernatural channels. When explaining at his trial why the state's power of life and death over him could not scare him into abandoning the public practice of his philosophy, he declares

> T2 *Ap.* 33C: "To do this[2] has been commanded me, as I maintain, by the god through divinations and through dreams and every other means through which divine apportionment has ever commanded anyone to do anything."

Between these two commitments—on one hand, to follow argument wherever it may lead; on the other, to obey divine commands conveyed to him through supernatural channels—he sees no conflict. He assumes they are in perfect harmony.[3] Can sense be made of this? I want to argue that it can. This will be my first task in this chapter. But what concerns me even more is a larger objective: to understand Socrates' conception of religion. So before closing I shall be returning to the point in the *Euthyphro* at which the search

for the definition of piety is sidetracked in that dialogue.[4] I shall push that
search a step further in the direction indicated there.

   Let us begin by facing a fact about Socrates which has been so embarrass-
ing to modern readers that a long line of Platonic scholarship has sought—in
the most recent book-length study of the *Euthyphro*[5] is still seeking—to explain it away: Socrates' acceptance of the supernatural. I shall waste no time
arguing against these scholars. The fact they are denying is so firmly attested
in our principal sources—Plato's and Xenophon's Socratic writings—that to
cut it out of them would be surgery which kills the patient. If we are to use
Plato's and Xenophon's testimony about Socrates at all we must take it as a
brute fact—as a premise fixed for us in history—that, far ahead of his time as
Socrates is in so many ways, in this part of his thought he is a man of his time.
He subscribes unquestioningly[6] to the age-old view that side by side with the
physical world accessible to our senses, there exists another, populated by
mysterious beings, personal like ourselves, but, unlike ourselves, having the
power to invade at will the causal order to which our own actions are confined, effecting in it changes of incalculable extent[7] to cause us great benefit,
or, were they to choose otherwise, total devastation and ruin. How they act
upon us we cannot hope to understand. But the fact is that they do and their
communications to us through dreams and oracles is one of the inscrutable
ways in which they display their power over us. Born into this system of religious belief, Socrates, a deeply religious man, could not have shrugged it off.[8]
And he could not have reasonably denied it without good reason: when a belief pervades the public consensus the burden of justifying dissent from it falls
upon the dissident. And here his problem would be aggravated by the fact that
the religious consensus has legal sanction. To flout it publicly is an offense
against the state punishable by death.

   A succession of brilliant thinkers, from Anaximander to Democritus, had
solved this problem with the utmost discretion. From their new picture of the
world they had expunged the supernatural quietly, without ever naming it in a
critique: the Greek ancestor of our word for it was not in their vocabulary[9] and
they did not need to invent it in order to obliterate its referent. They did the job
in attending to their own business of *physiologia*, "science of nature," by so ex-
panding the concept of nature as to make nature encompass all there is,[10]
thereby creating a new conception of the universe as a cosmos, a realm of all-
encompassing, "necessary"[11] order whose regularities cannot be breached by
interventionist entities outside it because outside it there is nothing.[12] What
room is there for god or gods in this new map of what there is? For supernatural gods there is none. For natural ones there is ample room—for gods existing not beyond nature, but in it. Not all of the *physiologoi* preserve deity
under this name, for their world-picture is crafted to meet primarily scientific,

not religious, needs; in principle they could complete it without any reference to god or gods. But they are not antireligious. Their temper is not that of the village atheist. When they postulate a cosmic intelligence to account for the intelligible order of their cosmos, most of them call it "god." So did Xenophanes, Heraclitus, and Diogenes of Apollonia, though not Anaxagoras:[13] in none of his fragments is the ordering mind which creates the world termed "god."

Thus in Ionian *physiologia* the existence of a being bearing that name becomes optional. What is mandatory is only that to have a place in the real world deity must be naturalized and thereby rationalized, associated with the orderliness of nature, not with breaches of its order, as it continued to be for the vast majority of Greeks. Even someone as enlightened as Herodotus was content to minimize supernatural intervention in history without excluding it in principle. When he tells the story of the prodigiously high tide that overwhelmed the Persian army at Potidaea he endorses the local belief that it was caused by Poseidon punishing the invaders for desecrating his shrine.[14] Should we ever forget how tiny is the band of intellectuals who accept *in toto* the point of view of the *physiologoi*, we should recall what happened on the plain of Syracuse on August 27, 413 B.C. When immediate evacuation of the Athenian forces had become imperative, and the departure had been decided by Nicias, their commanding general, the full moon was eclipsed, whereupon, writes Thucydides,

> T3 Thuc. 7.50.4. The mass of the Athenians was greatly moved and called upon the generals to remain. . . . And Nicias, who was rather too given to divination and the like, refused to even discuss the question of the departure until 27 days had passed, as the diviners prescribed.

Remain they did, with the result that Nicias' army was wiped out.

From Plato's *Laches* we learn that Nicias knew Socrates well[15] and had been influenced by his moral teaching: in that dialogue Nicias is made the champion of the Socratic definition of courage. Nicias could not have acted as he did at Syracuse if his teacher had been Anaxagoras instead. That influence would have swept the supernaturalist view of eclipses clean out of his mind.[16] His association with Socrates had left it in place.[17] And we can see why. The way the new "science of nature" had opened up out of that whole morass of superstition Socrates could not have taught to his companions because he had not found it himself.[18] From the investigations of the *physiologoi* he had stood aloof.[19] Putting all his energies into ethical inquiry,[20] he took no more interest in natural philosophy than in metaphysics, epistemology, ontology, or any other branch of investigation that falls outside the domain of moral philosophy.

To be sure, it was bruited about that he pursued *physiologia* in private[21] and Aristophanes made immortal comedy of the canard. But our most reliable sources leave no doubt that the talk is groundless. Aristotle is so sure of this that he disposes of the matter in a parenthetic clause:

T4[22] Aristotle, *Metaph.* 987b1-2: But Socrates, occupying himself with ethical questions, *and not at all with nature as a whole* (τῆς ὅλης φύσεως) . . .

In Plato's *Apology* Socrates repudiates as slander the Aristophanic caricature of the man in a basket up in the air scanning the skies.

T5 Plato, *Ap.* 19c: "Of such things I know nothing, great or small. Not that I would speak disparagingly of such science, if anyone really has it. . . . But the fact is, O Athenians, that I have no share in it."

Xenophon, with his proneness to apologetic overkill[23] pulls out all the stops to clear Socrates of the suspicion of having been a crypto-*physiologos*, representing him as scornfully hostile towards natural inquiry:

T6 *Mem.* 1.1.11: Nor did he discourse, like most others, about the nature of the universe, investigating what the experts call "cosmos" and through what necessary causes each of the celestial occurrences are generated. *Those who did so he showed up as idiots.*[24]

Thus from Xenophon, no less than Plato and Aristotle, we get good reason for withholding credence from the representation of Socrates in the *Memorabilia*[25] as a dabbler in teleological cosmology in the style of Diogenes of Apollonia, producing a physico-theological argument for divine providence predicated on the man-serving order of a variety of natural phenomena, from the structure of the human organism to the solstitial motions of the sun.[26] Cosmological argument for the existence of god is the cosmologist's business. Why should Socrates produce such argument when cosmology is none of his?

To be sure, Socrates could hardly insulate his religious faith from the formidable energies of his critical intellect. But to find scope for these in his conception of the gods he would not need to desert moral inquiry for physics and metaphysics. He could require his gods to meet not metaphysical but ethical standards. The Ionians had rationalized deity by making it natural. From within the supernaturalist framework which they reject, Socrates makes a parallel move: he rationalizes the gods by making them moral. *His gods can be both supernatural and rational so long as they are rationally moral.* This, I submit, is his program. Given his obsessive concentration on ethics, a *natural theology* he could not have produced. But he could, and did, produce a *moral theology,* investigating the concept of god no further than is needed to bring it into line with his ethical views, deriving from his new vision of human goodness norms binding on the gods themselves.

Here is the first of the "outlines of theology," τύποι θεολογίας as Plato calls them, in book II of the *Republic:*

> T7 R. II, 379B: "Is not god truly good, and must he not be so described? . . .
>   "And surely nothing good can be harmful? . . . And what is not harmful does not harm? . . . And what does not harm does no evil? . . . And what does no evil could not be the cause of any evil? . . . And is not the good beneficent? . . . Hence the cause of well-being? . . .
>   "*So god cannot be the cause* of *all things, but only of good things; of evil things he is not the cause?*" . . .[27]

I have italicized the final step in this sequence of inferences, the crucial one:[28] god cannot be the cause of everything in the life of men, but only of the good things in it. God's causation of those good things Socrates makes no effort to explain. Only the boldest of metaphysicians could have tried to excogitate how a supernatural being may produce any changes, good or bad, in the natural order. Socrates, no metaphysician, sticking to his own last, the moralist's, taking the fact of such causation for granted, is content to do no more than clamp on it moral constraints, reasoning that since god is good, he can only cause good, never evil.[29]

But why should god be credited with such unexceptionable beneficence? Is it because of the superlative wisdom which Socrates,[30] in common with traditional Greek sentiment,[31] ascribes to the gods? No, not just because of that. To allow one's gods infinitely potent intellect is not of itself to allow them flawlessly moral will. It may only lead one to conclude, with Heraclitus, that god transcends the difference between good and evil[32] and, with Aristotle, that to ascribe moral attributes to god is to demean him.[33] Why should Socrates reach the opposite conclusion? Because, I suggest, for him the highest form of wisdom is not theoretical, but practical.[34] And it is of the essence of his rationalist program in theology to assume that the entailment of virtue by wisdom binds gods no less than men.[35] He could not have tolerated a double-standard morality,[36] one for men, another for the gods: this would have perpetuated the old irrationalism. If Socrates is to rationalize the moral universe as relentlessly as the Ionian *physiologoi* had rationalized the physical universe when they made a cosmos out of it, he would have to match in the moral domain their unstated axiom that the regularities discernible in terrestrial events hold for all events everywhere: if fire radiates heat and light in our fireplace, it must do the same in the remotest star, and the bigger the fire, the greater the heat and the brighter the light that it would have to generate.

To be sure, Socrates never states the moral analogue of this axiom. Do we know that he would stand by it? Would he want to say that principles discoverable by elenctic argument on the streets of Athens will be universally valid,

holding for all moral agents, even if they are gods? There is evidence in the
Euthyphro that he would. He asks there:

> T8 *Eu.* 10A: "Is piety loved by the gods because it is piety? Or is it piety because
> the gods love it?"

He is pressing Euthyphro to agree that the essence of piety—its rationally discoverable nature—has no dependence on the fact that the gods happen to love
it.[37] So he is assuming that what piety is depends no more on what they, or
anyone else, feel about it, than does the nature of fire depend on what anyone,
god or man, happens to think that fire is. Piety, and by the same token, every
other virtue, has an essence of its own which is as normative for the gods as it
is for us: it determines what virtue is in their case as strictly as it does in ours.
Thus Socrates would reason that if knowledge of good and evil entails moral
goodness in a man it would entail the same in a god. And since the god's wisdom surpasses greatly that of the wisest man, god's goodness must surpass no
less greatly that of the most virtuous man. And since he holds that goodness
in a man can never cause evil to anyone[38] he is bound to hold that *a fortiori*
neither can goodness in a god: since god can only be good, never evil, god can
only cause good, can never be the cause of evil to anyone, man or god.

   To heirs of the Hebraic and Christian traditions this will hardly seem a bold
conclusion. For those bred on Greek beliefs about the gods it would be shat-
tering. It would obliterate that whole range of divine activity which torments
and destroys the innocent no less than the guilty, as careless of the moral
havoc it creates, as is, for instance, Hera in Greek traditional belief, who per-
secutes Heracles relentlessly throughout his life beginning with infancy, when
she sends snakes to finish his life almost before it has started, and so on repeatedly thereafter until the day of his death, when she dispatches Lyssa, the
divinity of madness, to unhinge his mind so that he murders his own wife and
children in a fit of insanity—all this simply because Heracles had been the offspring of one of her consort's numerous infidelities: the calamities she con-
trives for Zeus's bastard is one of the ways in which she makes the son pay for
his father's offenses to her.[39] It would be hard to find a human female acting
more viciously than this goddess does in the myths.[40] What would be left of
her and of the other Olympians if they were required to observe the stringent
norms of Socratic virtue which require every moral agent, human or divine,
to act only to cause good to others, never evil, regardless of provocation? Required to meet these austere standards, the city's gods would have become un-
recognizable. Their ethical transformation would be tantamount to the destruction of the old gods, the creation of new ones—which is precisely what
Socrates takes to be the sum and substance of the accusation at his trial:

T9 *Eu.* 2B "They say I am a god-maker. For disbelieving in the old gods[41] and producing new ones Meletus has brought this indictment against me."[42]

Fully supernatural though they are, Socrates' gods could still strike his pious contemporaries as rationalist fabrications, ersatz-gods, as different from the ancient divinities of the cult as are the nature-gods worshiped in the godless Thinkery of the Aristophanic caricature.

Socrates could hardly have moved so far from the ancestral faith unless he had adhered uncompromisingly to the authority of reason, brooking no rival source of knowledge on any matter whatsoever, about the gods no less than about anything else. How could he have done so while believing, as we saw in T2 above, that communications from gods come regularly through extra-rational channels—reaching him, in particular, through dreams and through his personal "divine sign"?[43] Should this incline us to believe that Socrates is counting on two disparate avenues of knowledge about the gods, rational and extra-rational respectively, yielding two distinct systems of justified belief, one of them reached by elenctic argument, the other by divine revelation through oracles, prophetic dreams, and the like?[44] If we did, then, since, as I remarked a moment ago, he shares the common Greek view that god's wisdom is vastly superior to man's,[45] we would have to conclude that he would look to the intimations of his *daimonion* as a source of moral knowledge apart from reason and superior to it, yielding the certainty which is conspicuously lacking in the findings of his elenctic searches.[46] I want to argue that, however plausible it may seem on first encounter, such a view is unsupportable by textual evidence and is in fact inconsistent with that evidence.

First let us look at the way Socrates views those dreams of his which he construes as divine monitions. Consider the one in the *Phaedo* (60E-61B):[47] He says that he had "often" had a dream "urging" and "commanding" him to "make music"[48] and that formerly he had *assumed* (ὑπέλαβον) that this meant he should be doing philosophy "since philosophy is the highest music" (61A), but that now in prison it has occurred to him that what the dream has been enjoining on him is "to make music in the popular sense of the word" (61A), i.e. to versify. So it has now "*seemed*" (ἔδοξε) to him that "it would be safer not to depart [from life] before fulfilling a sacred duty (πρὶν ἀφοσιώσασθαι) by composing verses in obedience to the dream." The words he uses—"I assumed" in the first case, "it has seemed to me" in the second—are not those he would have chosen for knowledge-claims.[49] From what he relates and from the language he uses in relating it we can infer that he thinks of the dream as conveying to him a sign from the god susceptible of alternative interpretations, the choice between them left entirely to his own good sense.[50]

That he thinks of oracles too in the same way we can tell from his conception of divination. Though he never expounds this directly, we can reconstruct it from the theory of poetic inspiration which he develops with great gusto in the *Ion*,[51] alluding to it also in the *Apology*.[52] In the epic the poet had claimed confidently that he puts into his verse knowledge imparted to him— "breathed into him"[53]—by his divine mentor.[54] To this claim Socrates responds with a characteristic ploy. His reply is, in effect: "Yes, what the inspired poet puts into his poem is a wonderful, god-given thing; but *it isn't knowledge*—it can't be knowledge for it is mindless." The poet's claim to be the direct beneficiary of divine prompting, Socrates accepts; he allows it at its strongest, conceding that at the moment of inspiration the poet is ἔνθεος, "has god in him":[55] he is "god-possessed" (κατεχόμενος).[56] But the very form in which Socrates allows inspired poetry, a superhuman source, debunks its claim to constitute knowledge:[57]

> T10 *Ap.* 22B-C: "I soon perceived that *it is not through knowledge* that poets produce their poems but through a sort of inborn gift[58] and in a state of inspiration,[59] like the diviners and soothsayers, who also speak many admirable things but *know nothing of the things about which they speak.*"[60]

In Socrates' view the effect of the god's entry into the poet is to drive out the poet's mind: when the god is in him the poet is "out of his mind," ἔκφρων,[61] or "intelligence is no longer present in him";[62] so he may find himself saying many things which are admirable (πολλὰ καὶ καλά)[63] and true[64] without knowing what he is saying. Thus to think of the poet as a recipient of divine *revelation*, i.e. as the beneficiary of "disclosure of *knowledge*"[65] to him by the god, would be to contradict Socrates' description of him as "speaking while *knowing nothing* of what he speaks": one who "has no knowledge of what one speaks" cannot have been given knowledge.[66]

That this mediumistic theory of inspired poetry Socrates would apply also to divination follows directly from the fact that he regards divination as the theory's primary field of application: it is because he is *like* the diviner[67] that the inspired poet is "out of his mind" and "knows nothing of the things of which he speaks." So neither could Socrates think of the diviner as receiving knowledge in his mantic states: how could a mental state in which there is no νοῦς, no understanding, in which a person "knows nothing of what he speaks," constitute *knowledge*? For Socrates diviners, seers, oraclegivers, poets are all in the same boat. All of them in his view are know-nothings, or rather, worse: unaware of their sorry epistemic state, they set themselves up as repositories of wisdom emanating from a divine, all-wise source. What they say may be true; but even when it is true, they are in no position to discern what there is in it that is true. If their hearer were in a position to discern this, then *he* would have the knowledge denied to them; the knowledge would come from the application of *his reason* to what these people say without reason.

Though Socrates does not apply this theory explicitly to prophetic dreams or to his own "divine sign" the connection with the latter is unavoidable, since he refers to the functioning of his *daimonion* as his "customary divination" and to himself as a "seer,"[68] without ever denying, directly or by implication, that what is true of divination generally would also apply to that homespun variety of it with which "divine dispensation" has favored him. So all he could claim to be getting from the *daimonion* at any given time is precisely what he calls the *daimonion* itself—a "divine sign,"[69] which allows, indeed requires, *unlimited scope for the deployment of his critical reason* to extract whatever truth it can from those monitions.[70] Thus without any recourse to Ionian *physiologia*,[71] Socrates has disarmed the irrationalist potential of the belief in supernatural gods communicating with human beings by supernatural signs. His theory both preserves the venerable view that mantic experience is divinely caused *and* nullifies that view's threat to the exclusive authority of reason to determine questions of truth or falsehood.[72]

Thus the paradox I confronted at the start of this paper dissolves: there can be no conflict between Socrates' unconditional readiness to follow critical reason wherever it may lead and his equally unconditional commitment to obey commands issued to him by his supernatural god through supernatural signs. *These two commitments cannot conflict because only by the use of his own critical reason can Socrates determine the true meaning of any of these signs.* Let me apply this result to the signs from the god on which Socrates predicates his philosophic mission in the *Apology*.[73]

Some scholars have expressed bafflement, or worse, incredulity, that from the Pythia's "No" to the question "Is there anyone wiser than Socrates?" he should have derived the command to philosophize on the streets of Athens.[74] Wouldn't that be pulling a rabbit out of a hat? Quite so. And is there any difficulty about that, if you are licensed to put the rabbit into the hat yourself in the first place? Socrates makes no secret of how subjective had been the process by which the god's command[75] had reached him:

T11 *Ap.* 28E: "The god commanded me, as *I supposed and assumed,* to live philosophizing, examining myself and others."

Here again the same language as in recounting the dream in the *Phaedo* where he had "assumed" *(Phd.* 60E) that "make music" meant "do philosophy." So even if that oracle from Delphi had been the only sign Socrates had received from the god, he could still have pried out of the Pythia's "No," the command to engage all and sundry in philosophic discourse: he could do so by "supposing and assuming" that this had been the hidden meaning in the riddling declaration[76] that no one alive was wiser than himself, though he was painfully "aware of being wise in nothing, great or small" (21B). But in point of fact that oracle was by no means the only sign Socrates had received. It was only the first of many. Let me cite T2 once again:

> T2 "To do this has been commanded me . . . *through divinations and through dreams and every other means through which divine apportionment has ever commanded anyone to do anything.*"

So there had been more divinations (some of them no doubt from his own *daimonion)* and more than one prophetic dream. Suppose that one of these had spelled out fully what the god wanted him to do, ordering him to do it in the very words in which he describes his own activity:

> T12 *Ap.* 30A-B: "I do nothing but go about persuading you, young and old, to have your first and greatest concern not for your body or for your money but for your soul, that it should be as excellent as possible."

Suppose the dream had ordered him to do just that. Would this have given him the certainty that the command comes from god? How would he know that this is not one of those lying dreams which the gods have been traditionally thought to send to men when they want to deceive them?[77] And how could he tell that it does not come from his own fancy instead? There is only one way he could have proceeded to still that doubt. He would have had to ask himself: Do I have *reason* to believe that this is work the god wants done by me? Is he that sort of god? What is his character?

Fully explicit in the text is one item in the character Socrates imputes to the god upon first hearing the report Chaerephon brought back from Delphi:

> T13 *Ap.* 21B: "Surely he is not lying. That would not be right (θέμις) for him."

Why so? The gods in whom the city believes have no such scruples. They have been lying since Homer.[78] Why should Socrates think his god would be so different? Because, as we saw earlier, unlike their gods, Socrates' god is invariantly good, incapable of causing any evil to anyone in any way at any time. Since to deceive a man is to do evil to him, Socrates' god cannot be lying. And since his goodness is entailed by his own wisdom,[79] which is boundless, his goodness must be boundless too. And since his good will is directed to Socrates' fellow-townsmen in Athens, no less than to Socrates himself,[80] he must wish that, they should put the perfection of their soul above all of their other concerns.

How could the god implement this wish for them? How could he bring everyone in Athens to see that "they should have their first and greatest concern for their soul that it should be as excellent as possible?" He could send them signs to that effect, dreams and oracles galore. But *unless they brought the right beliefs to the interpretation of those signs, they would not be able to read them correctly.* And they could not have come by those right beliefs unless they had already engaged in the quest for moral truth.[81] So the god is stuck. . . . Vastly powerful in innumerable ways though he is, in this matter he is powerless to give effect to his will by his own unaided means.[82] He must, therefore, depend on someone who does have the right beliefs and can read signs correctly to assist the god by doing on his behalf for the people of Athens what the god in his boundless good will for them would be doing himself in person, if he only could. This being the case, is it not understandable that Socrates should have seen his street-philosophizing as work done on the god's behalf and should, therefore, have a rational ground for "believing and supposing" that this is what the god is commanding him to do, declaring that no man is wiser than Socrates, not to give Socrates cause to preen himself on that account,[83] but to make it possible for him to guess that a unique responsibility was laid on him to use in the god's service what little[84] wisdom he has?

We can now move to that point in the *Euthyphro* to which I said at the start of this chapter I would return near its close. In the search for the answer to "What is piety?" Euthyphro had got as far as saying that piety is "service" to the gods.[85] But when pressed to say what sort of service this would be, he could only regurgitate the traditional answer:

T14 *Eu.* 14B: "Speaking and doing what is pleasing to the gods by praying and sacrificing—this is piety."[86]

Sniffing out here the age-old *do ut des* conception of worship—swapping gifts of sacrifice for prayed-for benefits—Socrates rebuffs it brutally. He says that, if so, piety would be "an art of commercial exchanges between gods and men" (ἐμπορικὴ τις τέχνη, 14E6), exchanges which would make no sense since they would be so one-sided: the gods stand in no need of gifts from us, while we are totally dependent on their gifts to us—"there is no good in our life which does not come from them" (15A)—so we would be the exclusively advantaged party; if piety is holy barter it is a bargain for us, a swindle for the gods. So the definition in T14 is decidedly on the wrong tack. To forestall that wrongheaded, diversionary move Socrates had asked:

T15 *Eu.* 13E10-11: "In the performance of what work (ἔργον) does our service to the gods assist them? . . . In Zeus's name, tell me, what is that glorious[87] work the gods perform by using us as their servants?"

That is the critical point in the search. Socrates remarks a moment later that if that question had been answered correctly, the goal of the search would have been reached: Socrates would have learned what piety is.[88] That is a very broad hint. But how could Euthyphro have taken advantage of it? The clue he is offered is lost to him because the notion that the gods have work to do,[89] work in which human beings could assist them, is foreign to Greek religion.[90]

But just suppose that Euthyphro had been allowed a preview of the speech Socrates was to give at his trial—that part of it which recounts the oracle story and Socrates' response to it. Would it be too much to hope that even Euthyphro's sluggish mind would have picked up the needed clue? For then he would have realized that Socrates saw his own work in summoning all and sundry to perfect their soul as work he did at the god's command, as his own service (λατρεία, ὑπηρεσία) to the god.[91] And that Socrates did consider this a "glorious work" could hardly have escaped Euthyphro if he had heard Socrates assuring the judges

> T16 *Ap.* 30A: "I believe that no greater good has ever come to you in the city than this service of mine to the god."

With these pieces of the puzzle before him Euthyphro should have been able to see what piety means in Socrates' own life: doing on the god's behalf, in assistance to him, work the god wants done and would be doing himself if he only could.[92] To derive from this a definition of piety Euthyphro would then have had to generalize, contriving a formula that would apply not only in Socrates' case but in every possible case of pious conduct. This is a tall order and it is by no means clear that Socrates himself would have been able to fill it. But this technical failure would not shake—would scarcely touch—the central insight into the nature of piety with which, I submit, we can credit Socrates on the strength of what Plato puts into his mouth in the *Apology* and the *Euthyphro*. *Piety is doing god's work to benefit human beings*—work such as Socrates' kind of god would wish done on his behalf, in service to him. Whether or not a formula could be devised to encapsulate this insight in an elenctically foolproof definition, this much should be already clear: Socrates has hit on a new conception of piety, as revolutionary in the religious domain as is his nonretaliatory conception of justice in the moral one.

How radical, how subversive of traditional Greek belief and practice this conception of piety would be we can see if we reflect that what had passed for religion to date had been thick with magic. By "magic," I understand[93] the belief, and all of the practices predicated on it, that *by means of ritualistic acts man can induce supernatural powers to give effect to his own wishes.* In black magic one exorcises supernaturals to do evil to one's enemy. In white magic one seeks to prevail on them through prayer and sacrifice to do good to one-self and to those for whom one cares—one's family, friends, nation, and the like: good which, but for those ritualistic performances, the gods would have withheld. As practiced all around Socrates, religion was saturated with just that sort of magic.[94] From religion as Socrates understands it magic is purged—all of it, both white and black. In the practice of Socratic piety man would not pray to god, "My will be done by thee," but "Thy will be done by me." In this new form of piety man is not a self-seeking beggar beseeching self-centered, honor-hungry gods, cajoling them by gifts of sacrifice to do good which without that gift their own will for good would not have prompted them to do. Man addresses gods who are of their very nature re-lentlessly beneficent: they want for men nothing but what men would want for themselves if their will were undividedly will for good.

If some such thing as this is what Socrates' conception of piety would do for Greek religion, we may still ask what it would do for Socrates himself. What is it that doing god's work on god's behalf to benefit his fellow-towns-men brings to Socrates' own life and character that would not otherwise be assured for it? Here is my answer in nutshell form: it brings a release from that form of egocentricity which is endemic in Socratic eudaemonism, as in all eudaemonism. In that theory the good for each of us is unambiguously our own personal good: the happiness which is the final reason for each of our intentional actions is our own personal happiness.[95] To what extent we should care for the good of others will then depend on those contingencies of blood or fortune which so bind their good to ours that we can perceive their good as our good, their happiness as a component of ours. In Socratic piety that link between our good and that of others is made non-contingent through devotion to a disinterestedly benevolent god who, being already per-fect, does not require from us any contribution to his own well-being but only asks each of us to do for other persons what he would be doing for them himself if he were to change places with us. To the spiritual toxins in eudae-monist motivation high religion here provides an antidote. Were it not for that divine command that first reached Socrates through the report Chaerephon brought back from Delphi there is no reason to believe that he would have ever become a street-philosopher. If what Socrates wants is part-ners in elenctic argument, why should he not keep to those in whose com-pany he had sought and found his eudaemonist theory—congenial and ac-complished fellow-seekers after moral truth? Why should he take to the streets, forcing himself on people who have neither taste nor talent for phi-losophy, trying to talk them into submitting to a therapy they do not think they need? The physician who seeks out people who fancy themselves in the best of health, taking it on himself to persuade them that they are mortally sick is undertaking a thankless task. Would Socrates have given his life to this task if his piety had not driven him to it?

In closing let me offer a passage which is a far cry from Socrates' own world and shows what his piety would be like if transposed into the language of an altogether different religious creed and practice:

T17 *The Book of the Perfect Life:*[96] When men are enlightened by the true light they renounce all desire and choice and commit and commend themselves to the Eternal Goodness, so that every enlightened man would say: "I fain would be to the Eternal Goodness what his own hand is to a man."

The language is that of mystical religion, and Socrates is no mystic. And "renunciation of all desire and choice" would be decidedly out of the question for him as a declared eudaemonist. But this much he would have in common with that medieval mystic. He too would fain be to an infinitely wise and benevolent being what his own hand is to a man or, better still, what a man's argumentative voice is to a man.[97]

Notes

1. This is a corrected and expanded version of a paper read to the B Club of the Classics Faculty in Cambridge in May 1988, published in the *Proceedings of the Boston Area Colloquium* (vol. v, 1989). Parts of it had been included in a Gifford lecture on "Socratic Piety" at St. Andrews (1981) and a Townsend Lecture at Cornell (1986).

2. I.e. to "live philosophizing; examining himself and others" (*Ap.* 28E, cited as T5 in chapter 4, and as T2 in chapter 5 above; cf. the comment on this text in those chapters).

3. As they must, since what is "commanded" him by the god in T2 is to engage in the activity which pursues the commitment to reason affirmed in T1.

4. At 14B-C Euthyphro is told that if he had answered the question he had been asked at 14A9-10, Socrates would have "learned piety [i.e. learned what piety is]": "you came right up to the point and turned aside." Cf. T. C. Brickhouse & N. D. Smith, "*The Origin of Socrates' Mission,*" *Journal of the History of Ideas* 4, 1983: 657–66, at 660.

5. By the late Laszlo Versenyi, *Holiness and Justice: An Interpretation of Plato's* Euthyphro, New York (1982). For effective critique see Mark L. McPherran, "Socratic Piety in the E*uthyphro,*" *Journal of the History of Philosophy* 23, 1985: 292–7.

6. In Plato's Socratic dialogue the gods' existence and power are never called in question—not even as an abstract possibility. In the *Memorabilia* the farthest anyone ever goes in that direction is to disbelieve in the power of the gods and their care for men (Aristodemus at 1.4, Euthydemus at 4.3), For Xenophon's and Plato's Socrates, as for the vast majority of Greeks, the gods' existence is almost as much of a "given" as is that of the physical world.

7. But by no means infinite extent. In striking contrast to the Hebraic and Christian deity of traditional theology, Greek gods are not omnipotent.

8. As did Thucydides, whose thoroughly secularized outlook makes it possible for him to ignore it, except as such beliefs afflict the subjects of his narrative.

9. ὑπερφυσικός is a late, Neoplatonic, concoction. As I have pointed out elsewhere (1975: 20) "the demolition of the supernatural is accomplished [in Ionian *physiologia*] without a single word about the victim."

10. This assumption is built into the very phrase by which they commonly designate their subject-matter: "the all" or "all things." Cf. the Word-Index in Diels-Kranz, *Die Fragmente der Vorsocratiker*, 6th ed., 3 vols., Berlin, 1952 (hereafter "DK"), *s.v.*τὸ πᾶν, τὰ πάντα, expanded into "the nature of all things" (ἡ τῶν πάντων φύσις), in Xenophon, *Mem* 1.1.11 (quoted in part in T6 below) and 1.1.14.

11. Cf. the Word-Index in DK, *s.v.* ἀνάγκη: and cf., "necessary [causes]" in Xenophon's description of "what the experts call 'cosmos'" at T6 below.

12. For parallel accounts of the destructive impact of natural philosophy on the traditional religious world-view see "Die Wirkung der Naturphilosophie" in Olof Gigon, *Grundprobleme der antiken Philosophie*, Berne, 1959: 51–9; and "The Displacements of Mythology" in Lloyd, 1987b: 1–49.

13. Nor yet Anaximander, the true founder of Ionian *physiologia*, though this is controversial: cf. Vlastos, 1952: 97ff., at 113; *contra* Jaeger, 1947: 29ff. and 203ff.

14. 8.129.3: "in my opinion at any rate, they [*sc.* the Potidaeans] speak well in saying that this was the cause." For other examples see Lloyd, 1979: 30, nn. 102–3.

15. Note especially *La.* 187D-188C: he had evidently known at close quarters the power of Socrates' elenchus to "examine" the life, no less than the beliefs, of his interlocutors: cf. Vlastos, 1983a: 37. Cf. also *La.* 200C-D (cited as T11 in additional note 1.1). *The reference is to G. Vlastos, *Socrates: Ironist and Moral Philosopher*, Cornell, 1991.

16. As it did for Pericles: through his association with Anaxagoras, says Plutarch *(Life of Pericles* 6), he "was made superior to the fearful amazement which superstition produces on those who are ignorant of the causes of events in the upper regions."

17. Not that Socrates would have approved Nicias' decision to follow the advice of the diviners in defiance of military prudence. In the *Laches* (198E-199A) Socrates reminds his interlocutors that the law requires the diviner to obey the general, not the general the diviner. Thucydides (7.48.4: cf. W. R. Connor, *Thucydides*, Princeton, 1984: 237) enables us to recognize the moral weakness which left Nicias vulnerable to the promptings of superstition at the fatal moment.

18. It is, therefore, a gross error to think of Socrates as a "typical representative of the Greek Enlightenment" (Karl Joël, *Gesichte der antiken Philosophie*, vol. I, Tübingen, 1921: 759). As we know from the case of Pericles and Euripides, it is to natural philosophers, like Anaxagoras, that the partisans of the Enlightenment would look for leadership. Nor is it right to think of Socrates as "the intellectual leader of Athenian intellectuals" (Heinrich Maier, *Sokrates*, Tübingen, 1913: 463). Certainly Plato does not so picture him: in his *Protagoras* the great sophist compliments Socrates on his future promise, not on his present achievement: "I would not be surprised if you were to become highly distinguished for wisdom" (361E).

19. Which is not to say that he was scornful of it, as Xenophon would have us believe (T6 below). In Plato's *Apology* Socrates expressly repudiates that sentiment (T5 below). This is one of several cases (cf. de Strycker, 1950: 199ff. *passim)* in which, faced

with a conflict between Xenophon's and Plato's testimony, we have good reason to prefer Plato's: he is less prone than Xenophon to tailor his representation of Socrates to
apologetic ends (cf. n. 23 below).

20. Cf. Thesis 1A in chapter 2.

21. In Aristophanes' comedy he teaches behind well-guarded gates. At his trial (*Ap.*
19B-D) Socrates appeals to members of the jury (which was bound to contain many
men of his own age or even older) to speak up if any of them has ever heard him discuss such things, confident that no one has. John Burnet (*Greek Philosophy: Thales to
Plato*, London, 1914, in his note to 19D4) cites parallels from Andocides and Demosthenes which show that such an appeal would not be out of line with Athenian judicial procedure.

22. T9 in chapter 3.

23. For the strongly apologetic animus of the *Memorabilia*, which determines even
the form of its construction, see Hartmut Erbse, "*Die Architektonik im Aufbau von
Xenophon*," *Memorabilien Hermes* 89, 1961: 17ff.

24. *Mem.* 1.1.1. In his account of Socrates' attitude to astronomy *(Mem. 4.7.4-7)*
Xenophon makes Socrates side with the obscurantists, warning his associates that "he
who ponders such things risks going mad like Anaxagoras."

25. 1.4.1ff. (dialogue with Aristodemus); 4.3.3ff. (dialogue with Euthydemus).

26. As W. Jaeger (*The Theology of the Early Greek Philosophers*, Oxford, 1947: 167
and notes) has pointed out, the arguments for the natural theology which Xenophon
here attributes to Socrates "are undoubtedly not Xenophon's own." Following Theiler
(1925: 18ff.), Jaeger suggests that the source is Diogenes of Apollonia. In accepting the
suggestion (*pace* Vlastos, "Theology and Philosophy in Early Greek Thought," *Phile-
sophical Quarterly* 2, 1952: n. 84) we should heed Theiler's caveat (1925: 168) against
reading into that source Xenophon's own naively anthropocentric theodicy: there is no
indication in Diogenes (DK B3) that the imposition of "treasures" on celestial motions
was made for man's benefit. Xenophon, producing his natural theodicy *ad hoc* in the
interests of piety, is all too likely to have used borrowings from Diogenes for edifying
purposes of his own. The axiomatic faith of the cosmologists in the unexceptionable-
ness of the order of nature is alien to Xenophon's thought. He is as likely to see evi-
dences of the gods' care for men in providential breaches of the natural order as in its
maintenance for man's benefit: he believes (*Mem.* 1.4.15) that the gods send "portents"
(τέρατα) to enable men to foretell future events through the practice of divination.

27. This comes from a passage in book II of the *Republic* where Plato lays down the
first of the articles of theology to which all references to the gods by the poets should
conform. What is presented here in a dialogue of Plato's middle period is pure Socratic
heritage *employing no premises foreign to the thought of the earlier dialogues.* Only after
this first τύπος θεολογίας has been staked out does Plato make Socrates go beyond
it (380Dff.), introducing the new, distinctively Platonic, metaphysical premise that
gods cannot change, because this would involve "departure from their own form"
(380D; cf. *Ti.* 50B; *Cra.* 439E), deriving from this the conclusion that gods cannot lie,
since this would involve them in change.

28. Reiterated for emphasis at 379C2-7: "thus, since god is good, he is not the cause
of all things that happen to human beings, *as the many say,* but of few of these: of
many of them he is not the cause." I italicize the phrase in which Plato highlights the

great novelty in Socratic theology by setting it off in defiant contrast to what is commonly believed, just as he highlights the great novelty in Socratic morality, the rejection of the *lex talionis*, by representing it as held in lonely opposition to the common view: it is not just to do evil to those who have done evil to us, *"as the many believe"* (*Cri.* 49D).

29. Of this cardinal feature of Socratic theology, which would obliterate the whole of the apotropaic aspect of Greek religion, there is not a word in Xenophon, understandably so, for there is no place for it in the conception of piety he ascribes to Socrates, which departs no further from vulgar notions than to teach that "modest sacrifices from persons of modest means are no less acceptable to the gods than frequent and lavish ones from those who have great possessions" and "the greater the piety of the giver the greater is god's pleasure in the gift" (*Mem.* 1.3.3), but still adheres to the *do ut des* rationale of sacrificing (cf. *Mem.* 4-3.17, quoted in additional note 6.3 below), as also to the conventional belief that the gods "have power to do *both good and evil*" (*Mem.* 1.4.16).

30. *Ap.* 23A-B. When Socrates discovers the true meaning of the oracle Chaerephon had received at Delphi he sees that compared with the divine wisdom man's "is worth little or nothing." In the *Hippias Major* (289B) Socrates endorses the saying of Heraclitus that "the wisest man is to god as an ape is to a man"; cf. Charles Kahn's gloss (*The Art and Thought of Heroditus*, Cambridge, 1979: 183–5) on this fragment (no. 68 in his book).

31. Even subordinate divinities, like the Muses, are credited with cognitive powers vastly superior to the human (*Iliad* 2.485–6: "You are goddesses, you are present, you know everything," whereas what men know is only κλέος ('hearsay'); divine beings are privileged with that perfectly "clear" insight (σαφήνεια) which is denied to man (Alcmaeon, DK 24B1).

32. DK 22 B102: "For god all things are beautiful and good and just, but men have thought some things unjust, others just." Of all the Presocratics it is Xenophanes who might be credited with "moralizing divinity" (cf. Vlastos, 1952: 97ff., at 116). Certainly none protested more strongly the *immorality* imputed to the gods in traditional belief (DK 21 B11 and B12). But this is dictated by his protest against anthropomorphism (DK B23 and its immediate sequels in Clement, DK B14 and B15), *not* by the ascription of a specifically moral will to god as in Socrates' premise at T7 (ἀγαθὸς ὅ γε θεὸς τῷ ὄντι τε καὶ λεκτέον οὕτω, 379B1). I must, therefore, demur at the suggestion (Flashar, 1958: 109, n. 2) that the τύποι θεολογίας expounded in Rep. 379A-383C "have been taken over from Xenophanes." This first τύπος certainly has not, and whether even the second has is doubtful: there is appreciable difference between the denial of motion to god in Xenophanes (B 26) and the denial of "departing from his own form" (τῆς ἑαυτοῦ ἰδέας ἐκβαίνειν) in Plato: Xenophanes builds on a cosmological premise, Plato on a metaphysical one.

33. *Nic. Eth.* 1178b8: holding that "perfect happiness" (τελεία εὐδαιμονία), could only consist of purely theoretical activity, he infers that we would make the gods "ridiculous" if we imputed to them actions to which moral predicates apply.

34. *Moral* wisdom is clearly what he has in view in the doctrine that all the virtues "are" wisdom (*Pr.* 361B; cf. Aristotle, *Nic. Eth.* 1145b23, *Eud. Eth.* 1215b1; *Magna Mor.* 1182b15). So if god's wisdom is perfect (n. 31 above) so must his virtue be.

35. This would follow from the unrestricted generality of the principle that "form is everywhere the same" (ταὐτὸ πανταχοῦ εἶδος, *Meno* 72D). And cf. the next note.

36. His search for definitions is predicated on the assumption that if any moral character *F* is correctly defined, the definitions will apply to *every* action characterizable as *F* (cf. *Eu.* 5D: "Is not piety the same as itself *in every action?*").

37. Cf. A. C. Crombie, *An Examination of Plato's Doctrines*, vol. 1, *Plato on Man and Society*, London, 1962: 209–10; A. E. Taylor, *Plato: The Man and His Work*, 3rd. ed., London, 1929: 151–2; S. Marc Cohen, "Socrates on the Definition of Piety" [this volume, chapter 3], 1971: 158–76.

38. *R.* 335d: "Is harming anyone, be he friend or not, the function (ἔργον) of the just man, or of his opposite, the unjust?" This is a crucial premise for his rejection of the *lex talionis* in the Crito: to return harm for harm is unjust, because "to harm a human being is no different from being unjust to him" (*Cr.* 49C).

39. I take the example from Mary Lefkowitz, "Impiety and Atheism," *Classical Quarterly* 39, 1989a. She argues forcefully that such conduct by divine beings is portrayed in Euripides' plays not because the poet is "trying to get his audiences to question the gods' traditional nature, but because increased fears and resentments expressed by the characters are an aspect of Euripides' celebrated realism."

40. Another example from Euripides: because Hippolytus had provoked Aphrodite's enmity she destroys not only him but two third parties as well, Phaedra and Theseus, who had done no wrong whatever and had caused her no offense. In comments on my paper Professor Lefkowitz observed that in so acting the goddess "is playing by well-established rules" because "when there are many gods all should be honoured." But *this* rule is far too general. To fit the case the rule would have to be that a god or goddess offended by a mortal may destroy, along with him, innocent persons who had no hand in the offending action. Could there be a rule more obnoxious to the Greek, no less than our own, sense of decency?

41. I.e. the gods of the public cult ("the gods of the state") in whose existence he disbelieves according to the formal indictment (*Ap.* 24B; Xenophon, *Mem.* 1.1.1). Not once in Plato's *Apology* does Socrates plead innocent to this charge: that he believes in gods he makes clear enough; that he believes in the gods of *the state* he never says, as he does in Xenophon to rebut the charge *(Mem.* 1.1.2; *Ap.* 11 and 24). Here, as elsewhere (cf. n. 19 above), when Xenophon's testimony conflicts with Plato's we would be wise to believe Plato rather than Xenophon, whose Socrates, a model of conventional piety ("most conspicuous of men" in cult-service to the gods of the state, *Mem.* 1.2.64), would never have been prosecuted for impiety in the first place and, if he had been, would have had no trouble reassuring the jury (which was bound to be as heavily weighted on the traditionalist side as the mass of the army at Syracuse was weighted on the traditionalist view of eclipses: Cf. T3 above) that in the abundance of his sacrifices the piety of his life compared favorably with theirs.

42. And cf. his subsequent remark (*Eu.* 6A), "Isn't this why I am being prosecuted—because when such things are said about the gods [tales of savage strife between them], I find them hard to stomach." Socrates would know that he was not alone in objecting to such tales (Euripides, for example, puts the objection in the mouth of Heracles, Hera's victim *(Her. Fur.* 1340–6). What would be held against him, Socrates thinks, is that by pressing such objections in his *teaching* he undermines traditionalist faith ("the

Athenians don't mind anyone they think clever, so long as he does not teach his wisdom; but if they think he makes others like himself, they get angry" *Eu.* 3C7-D1).

43. On Socrates' *daimonion* see additional note 6.1.

44. He does not specify the further means, to which he refers at T2 above by the phrase καὶ παντὶ τρόπῳ ᾧπέρ τις ποτε καὶ ἄλλη θεια μοῖρα ἀνθρώπῳκαὶ ὁτιοῦν προσέταξε πράττειν. But we should note that he never attaches such significance to any of the extraordinary *physical* events which the Greeks consider "portents" (τέρατα: cf. Xenophon, *Mem.* 1.4.15, cited in n. 26 above)—unusual occurrences of lightning, thunder, earthquakes, floods, plagues, famine, eclipses, and the like—which figure so prominently as "signs" from the gods in the traditional religious view of the world (for examples see Vlastos, *Plato's Universe*, Oxford, 1975: 11–13); as I remarked above, in Plato's earlier dialogues Socrates never alludes to anything of that sort as a divine "sign."

45. Cf. n. 30 above.

46. In chapter 4 (as also previously in 1985: 1ff., at 17–18 *et passim*) I stressed the shortfall in certainty in what Socrates expects to find through elenctic searching.

47. The passage is embedded in the piece of Socratic biography which introduces the philosophical argument of the dialogue: cf. ch. 1, n. 44.

48. The dream "urging" and "commanding" (61A2, τὸ ἐνύπνιον ἐπικεύειν, 61A7, προστάτοι τὸ ἐνύπνιον) are, of course, contractions: it is the god that does the "urging" and "commanding" through the dream (Cf. *Ap.* 33c5-6). Nonetheless it is significant that in Plato (less so in Xenophon) Socrates avoids as much as possible locutions which would suggest that god speaks to him, instead of merely giving him signs whose interpretation is left to him.

49. Socrates uses similar language in relating an occurrence of his "divine sign" in *Phdr.* 242B-C: "When I was about to cross the river . . . my customary divine sign came to me . . . and I *thought I heard* a voice (φωνὴν ἔδοξα ἀκοῦσαι), forbidding me to leave the spot until I had made atonement for some sin to god. Well, I am a seer (μάντις)—not a very good one but, like a poor reader, good enough for my own purposes."

50. The same is true in the case of the dream recounted more briefly in the *Crito:* it too, like the first dream in the *Phaedo,* employs allegory: in the verse of the *Iliad* (9.363) which foretells Achilles' death Socrates reads a prophecy of his own death; and here too he speaks only of "belief" or "seeming" (ἐδόκει, 44A10; ὥς γέ μοι δοκεῖ, 44B4).

51. See additional note 6.2 on the *Ion* below.

52. T10 below.

53. Hesiod, *Th.* 31ff.

54. For references see E. R. Dodds, *The Greeks and the Irrational*, Berkeley, 1951: 80–82 and notes.

55. The Greek word comes through the translations feebly as "inspired," losing its literal force (for which see e.g. Burkert, 1985: 109–11: he takes *entheos* to mean "within is a god"). Similarly weakened in translation is ἐνθουσιάζω, "to be inspired or possessed by a god, to be in ecstasy" (LSJ, *s. v.*); when ἐνθουσιασμός is anglicized as "enthusiasm" it becomes "ardent zeal" (*O.E.D.*); "frenzy" might come closer to its force.

56. The poets are described as "possessed by the god" (κατεχόμενοι: 533E7, 534A3-4 and E5); "possessed [by the god]" (κατεχόμενοι, 534A4 and 5); it is said that they βαγκεύουσι ("speak or act like one frenzy-stricken," LSJ, *s. v.* βαγκεύω).

57. And most particularly, the supposed knowledge which had made Homer "the educator of Hellas," widely thought to deserve "to be constantly studied as a guide by which to regulate our whole life" (R. 606E, Cornford's tr.; cf. W. J. Verdenius, "L'Ion de Platon," Mnemosyne 11, 1943: 233ff. at 248).

58. Φύσει τινι, "by a kind of native disposition" (Allen); "some inborn talent" (Grube). Cf. Burnet, Plato's "Euthyphro," "Apology of Socrates," and "Crito," Oxford, 1924: note on Ap. 22C1: "The word is used here in the sense in which it is opposed to habituation and instruction. It is the φυά which Pindar (Ol. 2.24) opposes to the ineffectual efforts of poets who have been taught, and is in fact 'genius' in the proper sense of the word."

59. ἐνθουσιάζοντες. Cf. additional note 6.1.

60. ἴσασιν δὲ οὐδὲν ὧν λέγουσι: "know nothing of the things they speak" (Allen); speak "without understanding of what they say" (Grube). The same phrase is applied to statesmen in the Meno (99c) when likened to the oracle-givers and seers who are bracketed with the poets in the Apology.

61. "Out of his mind, beside himself" (LSJ, s. v. ἔκφρων, principal use)—not ἄφρων, "silly," "stupid," as would have been the case if he had retained his own mind, albeit in an impaired condition.

62. Ὁ νοῦς μηκέτι ἐν αὐτῶ ἐνῆ. . . οἷς νοῦς μὴ πάρεστιν (Ion 534C-D).

63. T10 above. So too in the Ion: in the state of divine possession "admirable" (καλά: 533E7, 534E4) sentences are uttered by poets—which is scarcely surprising since it is "god himself who speaks to us through them" (Ὁ θεὸς αὐτοός ἐστιν Ὁ λέγων, διὰτούτων δὲ φθέγγεται πρὸς ἡμᾶς, 534D3-4). It is reassuring to learn that Socrates did not consider inane or foolish the great poetry he hears on the stage or reads in Homer, whose words he has at his finger-tips and quotes freely (see the numerous listings s.v. ὅμηρος and its inflections in L. Brandwood, Word Index to Plato, Leeds, 1976). His stubborn resistance to the popular Greek view that one may learn how to live by reading, hearing, and memorizing the poets (cf. n. 57 above), instead of searching critically for the truth, does not keep him from admitting that there is much wisdom in poets who speak "by divine grace" (θεία δυνάμει, 534C) and are used by god as his mouthpiece (534D3-4).

64. Ion 534B: καὶ ἀληθῆ λέγουσι.

65. O.E.D., s. v. "revelation." On this see further additional note 6.1 on the daimonion.

66. He might have true beliefs, yet lack that understanding which would enable him to see why they are true and draw the right inferences from them. The knowledge denied to the poets is reserved to the god who speaks through them or in them: Ion 534D: "it is not they [the inspired poets] who utter those priceless words while bereft of understanding (οἷς νοῦς μὴ ἐνῆ), but that the god himself is the speaker (Ὁ θεὸς αὐτός ἐστιν Ὁ λέγων)."

67. Ap. 22B-C: "they compose their verses not by skill but by a sort of natural endowment and divine inspiration, like the diviners and oracle-givers" (ὥσπερ οἱ θεομάντεις καὶ οἱ χρησμωδοί). In the Ion (534C) god uses poets and oracle-givers and "those of the diviners who are divine" as his servants by "taking away their understanding from them" (ἐξαιρούμενος τούτων τὸν νοῦν). We should note that both passages speak of "oracle-givers," not of the "oraclemongers" (χρησμολόγοι), who are treated with such scorn by Aristophanes and whom Socrates ignores as unworthy of any notice at all.

68. *Ap.* 40A; *Phdr.* 242C (cf. n. 49 above).

69. Cf. additional note 6.1.

70. It is in this direction that Plato develops his own theory of divination in *Ti.* 71E: a god-given sop to human weakness (ἀφροσύνῃ θεὸς ἀνθρωπίνῃ δέδωκεν), enabling us to enjoy divinatory powers in certain abnormal states (dreams, or illness, or enthusiasm) whose import we may try to understand when we revert to a normal condition: "it is for the rational nature (τῆς ἔμφρονος φύσεως) to comprehend (συννοῆσαι) the utterances, in dream or waking life, of divination and possession."

71. As does Democritus, producing a naturalistic theory of divination (DK 68A136-8), the complement of his naturalistic theory of poetic inspiration that fine poetry is produced by its creators "with enthusiasm and a holy spirit" (DK 63B18; cf. B21). The divine influx into the poet's mind is explained, like everything else in Democritus' natural philosophy, in corpuscularist terms (Plutarch, *Moralia* 734F-735C: cited as Democritus' fragment A77 in DK, with which A79 and B166 in DK should be compared). For a detailed exposition of the Democritean theory see Delatte (1934: 28ff.) who, however, assumes (56ff.) that the theory of inspiration in the *Ion* was derived from Democritus—a groundless guess, which would have had considerable plausibility if we knew that Socrates had been receptive to the speculations of the *physiologoi*, while, as we know, he insisted that he had no truck with them (*Ap.* 19C).

72. It is hard to find a clear recognition of this in any account of Socrates' view of divination in the scholarly literature: James Beckman's (*The Religious Dimension of Socrates' Thought*, Waterloo, Ontario, 1979: 84–5) comes closest to doing so, for he rightly credits Socrates with "a strict refusal to grant the status of knowledge to any such 'revelations.'" But he stops short of allowing Socrates a clean break with the traditional view, remarking that nonetheless Socrates retains "an orthodox view of divine inspiration" (*loc. cit.*). How so, when the assumption that divine inspiration yields *knowledge* was of the essence of the orthodox view?

73. I shall be following exclusively Plato's version of the oracle story. In Xenophon's *Memorbilia* there is no reference at all to the oracle Chaerephon brought back from Delphi (a curious discrepancy with the Xenophontic *Apology*, where the oracle story forms the centerpiece of Socrates' defense), and the whole motif of a command from God is suppressed—understandably so, given the apologetic animus of the former work: for that purpose the claim to have received a divine commission would be counter-productive—it would be seen as self-serving megalomania, which is indeed how Socrates fears it is being viewed by many of his judges in the Platonic *Apology*: "if I were to say that this [abandoning his mission to obtain acquittal] would be to disobey the god and this is the reason why I could not keep silent; you would not believe me, thinking that I was shamming" (37E). (Further comment on the difference between Plato's and Xenophon's versions of the oracle story in additional note 6.3.)

74. R. Hackforth (*The Composition of Plato's "Apology,"* Cambridge, 1933: 88ff.) is greatly exercised over this, as are the other commentators to whom he refers. He claims that to make sense of the narrative in Plato's text "we must deduct from that story the element of the imperative in the oracle" (93). The claim is refuted convincingly by Brickhouse & Smith, 1983: 657ff. (cf. n. 4 above).

75. The wording in T11 (τοῦ θεοῦ τάττοντος) and the analogy with the orders on which a soldier is assigned to his "post" (*loc. cit.*) as well as the reiteration of the idea

in T2 above (προστέκταται) leave no doubt on this point. I cannot understand why Brickhouse & Smith (*loc. cit.*) follow Guthrie in claiming that "Socrates sees the oracle as a 'message' and not as a 'command'" (1983: 663, n. 14).

76. Which he had found so baffling on first hearing (21B): "I kept thinking: What does the god mean? What is he hinting at? . . . For a long time I was baffled . . ." (Cf. Burnet's note on 21B3.)

77. As e.g. in *Iliad* 2.6ff.

78. See e.g. Karl Deichgräber, *Der listsinnende Trug des Gottes*, Göttingen, 1952. That the traditional gods think nothing of deceiving each other is one of the first criticisms the Ionian rationalists directed against the deities of popular belief (Xenophanes B11). Would such gods scruple to deceive men? "Athena has deceived me," Hector reflects (*Il.* 22.299) in that duel with Achilles which is to be his last.

79. Cf. p. 164 above.

80. Socrates assumes that he had been commissioned to be Athens' gadfly because of the god's care for the Athenians (30E–31A).

81. As Socrates already had, else *he* could not have read correctly the signs the god sent him. Scholars who think that Socrates' moral inquiries begin with his receipt of the Delphic oracle (W. D. Ross, "The Problem of Socrates," *Proceedings of the Classical Association* 30, 1933, in Andreas Patzer, *Der historiche Sokrates*, Darmstadt, 1987: 227; John Ferguson, "On the Date of Socrates' Conversion," *Eranos*, 1964: 70–3) seem unaware of this fundamental point.

82. A parallel (and entirely independent) use of this idea is made by C. C. W. Taylor, 1982: 109ff., at 113: "But there is one good product which [the gods] can't produce without human assistance; namely good human souls." That Socrates sees the pious man as a kind of craftsman" who aims at the production of an "all-glorious" *ergon* in service to the god is rightly stressed by Brickhouse & Smith (1983: 665; cf. n. 4 above).

83. As he does in the Xenophontic *Apology of Socrates* (15–17) where mention of the oracle (blown up to declare that "no one is more liberal, more just, or wiser" than Socrates), triggers a lengthy outburst of self-congratulation.

84. "Human wisdom," he calls it, admitting that this much he *can* claim (20D-E) in the very context in which he declares that he "is not aware of being wise in anything, great or small" (21B: cf. additional note 1.1).

85. 13D: ὑπηρετικὴ . . . τις θεοῖς (13D7).

86. This is virtually the same as the definition of "piety" Xenophon puts into Socrates' mouth in the *Memorabilia:* "The pious man is rightly defined as 'he who knows the νόμιμα concerning the gods'" (4.6.14); these νόμιμα are the lawfully prescribed sacrifices (1.3.1).

87. πάγκαλον, "all-beautiful," "marvellously fine."

88. Cf. n. 4 above.

89. The imputation of an *ergon* to the gods has been thought a conclusive objection to taking the question in T15 as a true lend to the discovery of what piety is: Burnet, Allen, Versenyi have claimed that Socrates could not have predicated his search on a notion which is so patently foreign to the common Greek conceptions of the gods: for refutation of this claim see Brickhouse & Smith, 1983: 660–2 (cf. n. 4 above) and McPherran, 1985: 292–4 (cf. n. 5 above).

90. The nearest thing to it in Greek mythology is the "labors" of Heracles. Socrates, clutching at a straw, alludes to them at one point in his defense: he speaks of the hardships of his mission (22A) "as if they were labors I had undertaken to perform" (ὥσπερ πόνους τινὰς πονοῦντος), choosing to ignore, the fact that Heracles' labours had been a torment inflicted on him by the ill-will of Hera, while Socrates' labors had been the source of the greatest possible happiness in his life (38A). (Professor Lefkowitz in her comment reminds us of Ion's "labor" (πόνον, Eur. *Ion* 128) for Apollo; but this case is not illuminating: Ion is a religious professional, a temple-servant.)

91. 23B-C (in T16) τὴν τοῦ θεοῦ λατερίαν, and 30A6-7: τὴν ἐμὴν τῷ θεῷ ὑπηρεσίαν. The former had especially strong religious evocations; cf. *Phdr.* 244E, "prayer and service to the gods" (θεῶν εὐχάς τε καὶ λατερίας) for "religious activity."

92. Cf n. 82 above.

93. The primary sense of "magic" according to the *O.E.D.* is "the pretended art of influencing course of events by occult control of nature or of spirits"; among the senses for "occult" that dictionary lists "mysterious, beyond the range of ordinary knowledge, involving the supernatural." Taking "occult" in this sense of the word, petitionary prayer whose efficacy is predicated on the incinerating of a sacrificial offering on an altar in accordance with the established ritual, could very well be reckoned magic (white if benign, advancing the welfare of the petitioner or his friends, black if malevolent, causing harm to his enemies).

94. Most petitionary prayer accompanying sacrifice, as conceived by the Greeks, would have to count as white magic: the sacrificial gift to the gods is designed to elicit a reciprocal favor to the worshiper. See additional note 6.4.

95. As I point out in chapter 8, n. 14, this assumption is so deeply embedded in Socratic eudaemonism that no need is felt to make it explicit, but its presence is easily detectable when the text is closely read. Thus in explaining the general principle that in all our actions we pursue the good, Socrates moves from "because we think it better" (*G.* 468B, οἰόμενοι βέλτιον εἶναι) to "because we think it better for us" (οἰόμενοι βέλτιον εἶναι ἡμῖν) without any apparent awareness that what is expressed in the second phrase is substantially different from what is expressed in the first.

96. By an unknown German mystic of the fourteenth century.

97. In revising this essay for publication I have benefited from Professor Lefkowitz's comments on it (1989b) and have made some revisions in my text in the light of remarks of hers which I consider just. But I am puzzled why she should think the gods she has in view here (and in her paper [1989a] to which I refer in n. 39 above) worthy of *reverence* (σέβας: piety *is* εὐσέβεια). Think of Hippolytus. Eccentric in his straitlaced abstention from "the works of the night" over which Aphrodite presides (fornication and adultery these would be in his case, since he is unwed), he commits no moral wrong: chastity is no crime, even when it is overdone. Can he *revere* the deity who destroys him—"powerful, proud, intolerant, and quite without scruple or pity" (Barrett, 1964: 155)? Fear of her power would have given him reason enough to refrain from provoking her fury. But could such concessions to power devoid of moral quality be reckoned εὐσέβεια, and the sentiment which animates it σέβας?

5

Plato's *Apology* of Socrates

E. de Strycker and S. R. Slings

The Historicity of the Platonic Apology

BURNET's 'INTRODUCTORY NOTE' TO HIS COMMENTARY of the *Apology* opens with this sentence: 'The first question we have to ask about the *Apology* is how far we may regard it as an historical document' (p. 63). Many scholars have indeed considered this the basic problem. From this standpoint, the interpretation of the *Apology* is ancillary to the reconstruction of the historical Socrates. It is not evident, however, why this question should be the first one to ask about the *Apology* and not about the *Phaedo* and the *Symposium* as well. There is no a priori reason why we should not examine every work of Plato's primarily as a work of Plato's, with Plato's literary and philosophical aims, and apply a method that, taking due account of the peculiarities of each work, is essentially the same everywhere, viz. to look for the signals that the author himself gave us in order to lead us to a correct understanding of what he wrote.

Now, Burnet thinks that, in the *Apology,* Plato's statement that he was present when Socrates delivered his defense in court (34a1, 38b6-9) is a significant indication of Plato's intention. For Plato's aim was 'to defend the memory of Socrates by setting forth his character and activity in their true light'[1]. And since many of the potential readers had attended the trial, Plato 'would have defeated his own end if he had given a fictitious account of the attitude of Socrates and of the main line of his defence' (63-64). This reasoning implies that a reader of the Platonic *Apology* would have expected to find there not simply such an account of Socrates' reaction to the indictment and of his attitude toward the possible outcome of the trial as would be consonant with his whole life and character, but an objective record of what he actually said in the courtroom, though not, of course, a verbatim report. Now, in order to determine whether the audience for which Plato intended his work entertained such expectations, we should consider the *Apology* in the context of the prose literature of the fifth and fourth centuries. Of course, there is no room here for more than a rapid survey, and much of what follows has been said many times already, but some elements of information need to be mentioned again in order to dispel unfounded presuppositions.

We shall start with the historians. With Herodotus, the critical method in history is still in its early stages; he tries to ascertain facts by testing the reliability of his sources, but in reporting speeches and conversations he still follows the model of poetry closely. Thucydides was the first to see a problem in this method: he points out that it is more difficult to remember speeches than events. His account of the former will therefore differ from his account of the latter. In his rendering of the speeches he will stick to the general trend (τῆς ξυμπάσης γνώμης) of what was actually said and develop it as he thinks the situation demanded from the orator (i 22,1). He does not aim at a reproduction of the speaker's own words, because this would not only be virtually impossible but would run counter to his basic manner of composition, which involves extreme compression. Thus, for example, he gives us three speeches of Pericles, one delivered before the outbreak of the war (i 140-144), another (ii 35-46) in which the Athenian leader explains what his fellow-citizens are fighting for and what spirit guides them in peace and in war, and a third (ii 60-64) about the tenacity and sang-froid they should display in difficult moments. There can be no doubt that Pericles repeatedly spoke before the Assembly on such matters; what is important is Pericles' main idea, not the question whether he actually addressed all the issues in each of the three speeches on their several occasions, nor whether, on these occasions, he spoke on some further points that Thucydides did not find worth mentioning. When even Thucydides takes these liberties, we would expect Xenophon to be even more careless about a close correspondence between the actual spoken words and the speeches in the *Hellenica* and the *Anabasis*, since he takes far less trouble to discover historical truth and indulges freely in rhetoric[2].

The problem is much more complicated in the case of oratory and I cannot here examine all the different circumstances in which a speech could be written, delivered or published as a pamphlet[3]. Especially interesting are occasions when a politician wrote a speech that he intended to deliver himself, either before the Assembly or in a courtroom, or that he intended to be used in a lawsuit by one of his political allies. Not infrequently, the author published his text afterwards in the hopes of further arousing public opinion against his adversaries or in favour of his own political line. If it suited him, he could adapt it to these new purposes. It was even possible, as is the case with Demosthenes' *In Meidiam* (xxi), that an orator wrote out a complete accusation, then accepted a settlement out of court, and none the less published his text some time later, after having larded it with new material[4]. The public asked no questions, as it was interested in the lively arguments, not in painstaking conformity with what had actually been said at the time by either party[5].

As for epideictic speeches, they were but loosely concerned with historical reality. Works like Gorgias' *Defence of Palamedes* were the result of pure imagination. In the *Olympicus*, Gorgias himself probably addressed the crowd gathered for the Panhellenic festival, but his *Funeral Oration* he cannot have delivered at the official Athenian celebration of the men killed in action, since he was a foreigner. The speeches which Isocrates did not write at the request of a litigant are all fictitious, since, as he himself admits (xii 10), he lacked both the strong voice and the daring that were necessary for an orator. This fact, however, did not prevent him from presenting some of his works as speeches before the Assembly (vii, viii, xiv) or a jury (xv). In the *Nicocles* (iii), the Cypriot king of that name advises his subjects about their duties: but nobody will have imagined that this text reflected the king's own ideas, and even less his tone and style, rather than those of Isocrates himself.

This brings us at once to the various *Defences of Socrates* that were published roughly between 395 and 375 B.C. In addition to those by Plato and Xenophon, we know that there was another one by Lysias[6] (another by Theodectes of Phaselis cannot be precisely dated, but it is not improbable that it is later than 375 B.C.[7]). Now these *Apologies* were certainly not the only ones that were written in those years, as appears from Xenophon *Apol.* 1 γεγράφασι μὲν οὖν περὶ τούτου (about Socrates' attitude towards his judges and towards death) καὶ ἄλλοι, καὶ πάντες ἔτυχον τῆς μεγαληγορίας αὐτοῦ. If Xenophon had had only Plato and Lysias in mind, he would not have spoken of πάντες. So we may be sure that in this period there were several *Apologies* in circulation, in each of which Socrates' tone was in some way haughty. On the other hand, they must have been different enough from one another to make it worthwhile for each author to publish a new work and for the public to read it. Manifestly, the members of the Socratic circle could not stomach Socrates' condemnation, and after a few years their protest took the form of literary polemics similar to the posthumous defences of politicians like Theramenes and Alcibiades[8].

Not only did Socrates' friends defend his person and his ideas; his adversaries attacked him in their turn. We learn from Isocrates (xi 4) that the sophist Polycrates published a Σωκράτους κατηγορία, about which we are relatively well informed[9]; it was written after, probably shortly after 394 B.C. Anytus is supposed to have been the speaker; he accused Socrates, amongst other things, of inciting the young to contempt for the Athenian laws and to violence in order to overthrow those laws, of having had among his pupils Critias and Alcibiades, who had committed the worst crimes against the Athenian civic community, of undermining young people's respect for their fathers and for the traditional values of their class. Now, Anytus, as a leader of the moderate Athenian democrats, cannot have reproached Socrates for his connections with men who were dead when the amnesty was voted. Polycrates' Κατηγορία is in fact a fictitious speech, in which mention is made of the rebuilding of the Athenian Long Walls, an undertaking that was started only in 394/3 B.C. It was probably published two or three years after that date, and shortly after or before Plato's *Gorgias*. It is within that same polemical framework that the several *Defences of Socrates* were published. Since each author wrote according to his own conception of what kind of man Socrates had been and of the beneficial or harmful effects of his ideas, they could scarcely aim at an exact reproduction of the speeches of either Anytus or Socrates. Nor would the public have expected any of these works to keep close to the actual words that were spoken in the courtroom in 399 B.C.

As regards the accuracy with which Socrates' arguments are reproduced by Plato, some scholars postulate a basic difference between the *Apology* and the dialogues. According to such an authoritative scholar as W.K.C. Guthrie *(Hist. Gr. Phil.* iv 73), 'the dialogues of Plato are avowedly fictitious, or at least imaginative' while 'the *Apology* is an entirely different category'. It is true that 'many of the dialogues are represented as taking place when Plato was unborn or a child'. This, of course, is not the case with the *Apology*. Two passages in the *Apology* tell us that Plato was present at the trial, but exactly what do they tell us? The first time (34al), Plato's name is mentioned in a list of seven fathers or elder brothers who, accompanied by their charges (Plato is one of the latter) appeared in the courtroom to support Socrates because they themselves had experienced his influence and believed that it was beneficial to the young. In the second passage (38b6-9), Plato is mentioned with three other men who were prepared to post bail for Socrates in the event that the jury sentenced him to a fine of 30 minas. In neither case is there any hint that Plato's presence would especially qualify him as a witness, capable of reporting the content of Socrates' defence with the utmost accuracy.

It is instructive to compare these casual references to Plato's attendance of the proceedings with the opening of the *Phaedo*. There, Echecrates asks the question: Αὐτός, ὦ Φαίδων, παρεγένου Σωκράτει ἐκείνῃ τῇ ἡμέρᾳ ἧ τὸ φάρμακον ἔπιεν ἐν τῷ δεσμωτηρίῳ ἢ ἄλλου του ἤκουσας; Phaedo answers: Αὐτός, ὦ Ἐχέκρατες (57al-4). After Phaedo enumerates which friends of Socrates were and were not present on that last day, Echecrates asks him to give as exact an account as possible of every particular: ἀλλὰ πειρῶ ὡς ἄν δύνῃ ἀκριβέστατα διεξελθεῖν πάντα (58d8-9). If we are prepared to admit that the *Phaedo* is 'avowedly fictitious, or at least imaginative', I do not see why we might not say the same about the *Apology*.

Words like 'fictitious' and 'imaginative' are, of course, ambiguous. I feel quite sure that Plato presents, both in the *Apology* and in the dialogues, an eminently truthful image of Socrates' character and activity, and especially that the biographical particulars contained in those works should be accepted as historical, unless there is (and this is hardly the case) indisputable proof to the contrary. But this introduction is not the place to reopen the 'Socratic question' as a whole, and elsewhere ('Les temoignages . . .')* I have given my opinion on that subject and the arguments on which it is founded. What I wish to say here is that no work of Plato's is intended to be a faithful report of the particular line of thought that Socrates followed in any individual conversation or speech. This statement will be clarified further in the next paragraphs and in § 2.

The most conclusive proof that Plato, when writing his *Apology,* did not feel bound to stick as closely as possible to the main lines of what Socrates had actually said in court is, in my eyes, its exceptional literary quality. Most scholars who think that Plato aimed at reproducing, with some exactitude, Socrates' own speech will readily agree that the style is Plato's own. The problem, however, should not be considered on the level of style in the narrow sense of the word. It principally concerns the composition, and by that I mean not only the general structure, but the way in which the structure is worked out in detail: each idea gets its proper place and emphasis, and the relations of the parts to one another give the whole its articulation on the one hand, and its unity on the other.

Detailed discussions of Plato's intentions and achievements in that respect will be given in the Analyses of the various sections of the *Apology.*† Here I shall restrict myself to a few illustrations. When Socrates describes his examination of the clever men of Athens, he distinguishes three classes in such a way that the account of his conversations with them will be divided into three stages. This three-stage development has an important theoretical and literary significance. Each of the three moments is treated in quite a different manner, in order to prevent monotony and to create the impression that we break new ground each time. Moreover, the distribution of the σόφοι over three groups makes it possible to suggest a chronological sequence, as is normally expected in the narration of a forensic speech, although there is no objective reason

---

* The reference is to E. de Stryker, S. J., "Les témoignages historiques sur Socrate," *Melanges Henri Grégoire* ii (Brussels 1950), *Annuaire de l'Institut de philologie* et *d'histoire orientales et slaves* 10 (1950), 199–230. [ed.].
† Here and below there are references to discussions in further chapters of E. de Strycker and S. R. Slings, *Plato's Apology of Socrates* (Leiden: E.J. Brill, 1994), from which this introductory chapter is excerpted, [ed.].

why Socrates should refrain from questioning some poets or craftsmen before he had examined all the politicians. When the conclusion about the meaning of the oracle has been drawn in 22e6-23c1, it might seem normal for the speaker to pass immediately to the Refutation of the New Accusers, but this would have led to a break in the psychological and literary continuity. At the end of the paragraph 22e6-23c1, the tone is most serious and one feels intensely the depth and sincerity of Socrates' religious sense. Before he can strike the playful note that characterises the 'interrogation' of Meletus, a transition is needed. Plato makes the transition with some reflections about the young friends of Socrates who imitate his testing of clever men and thus aggravate the resentment against him (see Chapter V 69-70). As a whole, the Refutation of the Old Accusers, and especially the Narration, gives a description of Socrates' activity, but in fact only its negative and elenctic side is illustrated. The positive and protreptic aspect is reserved for the Digression, which will emphasise how the two sides complement one another.

Meanwhile, the cross-examination brings a diversion, first through the dialectical method, secondly through the ludicrous effect of the accuser's imprudent answers. Its two parts seem to parallel each other, yet they differ greatly in content and method. The Digression is the core of the *Apology,* the part that uncovers the hidden source of Socrates' unconquerable courage, his care for his fellow-men and his devotion to God. At the same time, although it is not immediately apparent, the Digression contains the true refutation of the indictment, but with the two charges treated in reverse order to the charges in the Ἐρώτησις. The rich content of this part, and the care with which the ideas are marshalled and illustrated by a mythological example, by humorous comparisons borrowed from daily life, by the narration of dramatic events in the life of Socrates, is treated in the Analyses. Here I break off this all too long enumeration. Jejune as it is, it will justify my claim that none but the most skillful literary artist could construct a speech such as the Platonic *Apology,* and that such a refined piece of work can only be the fruit of long deliberation and patient polishing. It would be a grievous error to think that its apparent simplicity and straightforwardness lack the conscious artistry that is at work in every section and every sentence.

A last remark on the *Apology's* putative reliability as a historical document. Since the *Apology* is obviously not purely a product of Plato's imagination, as are e.g. Gorgias' *Defence of Palamedes* and Xenophon's *Hieron,* many attempts have been made to distinguish between parts that can be considered relatively faithful renderings of what Socrates said in his defence and others that are Plato's inventions[10]. What I have said above shows that, in my eyes, all such efforts are futile. I am confident that Socrates' proposal of a fine of 30 minas (38b6-9) was certainly made by Socrates in court, in whatever form he may have done this (see Chapter X 198-199); I am also confident that there cannot have been an opportunity for delivery before the court of the first half of the Third Speech (38c1-39d9; see Chapter XI § 1)[11]. For the rest, I would dare to assert that there is, on the one hand, no single sentence[12] in the Platonic *Apology* that Socrates could not have actually pronounced, and on the other, that the published work contains no passage so specifically un-Platonic that it cannot be Plato's work. Therefore, I shall, neither here nor elsewhere in this book, enter upon such discussions.

The Intention of the Platonic *Apology*

What Plato intended his readers to find in his *Apology* we cannot decide a priori. A careful examination of the text will show that it displays different but closely interwoven aspects. For the sake of clarity I will treat them successively; the order in which this will be done is not one of increasing or diminishing importance; it is chosen simply for the sake of convenience of exposition.

The *Apology* as a Defence

Socrates has been found guilty, condemned to death and executed. Plato sets himself the task of writing a speech that will have the outward appearance of a defence delivered in court to an Athenian jury. Actually, however, the audience he has in mind is the Athenian public at large, and even other Greeks, if they are interested. The plan of the speech conforms overall to that of contemporary forensic oratory. In many passages Socrates makes use of the commonplaces devised by the teachers of rhetoric; in others, he conspicuously, indeed explicitly, refuses to do so, or else he gives their practices a new turn, exactly opposite to their original and intended use[13]. He quotes the terms of the indictment and undertakes to refute, in the form of a cross-examination of Meletus, the two charges brought against him, viz. that of deviating from the official religion and that of corrupting the young. In the subsequent sections of the *Apology,* Socrates' general attitude remains the same: by describing what he actually does he tries to show that the suspicions entertained and the accusations lodged against him are unfounded. In other words, the *Defence* should make clear to the reader that the members of the jury were totally mistaken in their verdict and that Socrates was not at all guilty of the offences of which he was accused.

Plato, however, unambiguously shows in the *Apology* that he is not interested in the three official accusers and their indictment. What we know about them has to be collected from other sources. We can make reasonable guesses about what exactly their charges meant, and even about what motivated them to indict Socrates (see Chapter VI § 3 and 4), but our guesses can scarcely be based on Socrates' words[14]. Nor does he say anything significant about the content of his opponents' speeches[15].

The first idea expressed in the *Apology* is that the accusers told many lies and did not care for truth at all; they did not rely on serious argument but on the magic of rhetoric (17al-c5). This already implies that a thorough scrutiny of what they have said is not worthwhile. It is not surprising, then, that in the Proposition Socrates declares that the official indictment rests exclusively on the prejudices spread among the masses over many years by a continuous campaign of slander. The anonymous calumniators associated Socrates to the new-fangled intellectuals who were active in Athens in the second half of the fifth century B.C., natural philosophers and sophists. The ideas disseminated by these men were considered by the traditional Athenians to amount to atheism and to the subversion of common morality[16].

If Socrates, however, denies that the rumours about him have any foundation in fact (19d4-el), he should explain why they are so readily accepted and why he is an object of aversion to so many people. This is what he does in the Narration, the story of the oracle about him which was given to Chaerephon by the god of Delphi, and of the examination to which he decides to submit all clever people (20c4-24b2). This section is very important because it gives a detailed account of Socrates' everyday activity, although only, as I said above, 7, of its elenctic aspect. The complementary, protreptic aspect is described, with full particulars, in the Digression, especially in the first half (28b3-31c3). These two sections give us the gist of what Plato wishes to convey in his *Apology*; they are quite independent of the charges formulated by Meletus. The Refutation of the New Accusers (24b3-28a1) is sandwiched between them. As Burnet was the first to point out (100), 'this part of the speech does not contain the real defence of Socrates', precisely because Plato wishes us to realise that Meletus has not tried to ascertain what Socrates was aiming at with all his questioning and discussing and therefore Meletus' accusation and speech have no real significance and do not merit a serious refutation.

But if the common belief that Socrates is a natural philosopher and a sophist is rejected very summarily (19c2-d7. 20b9-c3), and the accusations of Meletus are treated playfully, are we still entitled to say that the *Apology* is intended as a defence? We are, for what Plato defends Socrates against is neither that popular misunderstanding nor the technical content of Meletus' indictment; it is what remained after the verdict in the mind of the man in the street: that Socrates had been condemned to death by a jury of five hundred of his fellow-citizens as irreligious and as a corruptor of the young. The average Athenian did not exactly know of what specific crimes Socrates had been found guilty, because Socrates was in every respect a very uncommon man

whose behaviour and opinions were often incomprehensible. But the jury did
not inflict the supreme penalty upon him only because he was an eccentric;
the trial must somehow have brought to light that under the cover of eccen-
tricity Socrates concealed a most dangerous wickedness. It was Plato's intention to show that Socrates was, on the contrary, the only truly religious man,
in comparison with whom all other people were but superficially pious, and
the only true educator, since he directed everybody, young and old, towards
authentic ἀρετή by means of a method quite different from that of the
sophists. This is the proper object of the central sections of the *Apology*, viz.
the Narration and the Digression, and in both parts of the latter Plato makes
it clear that Socrates' statements absolve him once and for all from the charges
on which he was condemned. By portraying Socrates' conduct as a whole,
rather than any particular action of his, Plato has achieved a most effective defence of his master.

The *Apology* as a Portrait

   The *Apology* as a whole is a portrait of Socrates. This is in a sense especially
true of the two sections just mentioned, the Narration and the Digression; but
every page of the work contributes to the same end. It does so in a way quite
different from that followed by a historian like Xenophon or a logographer
like Lysias[17]. In order to draw a picture of Cyrus the Younger, Xenophon (*An.*
i 9) starts with anecdotes about the childhood of his hero and then amasses
details that illustrate the qualities which enabled him, as an adult, to gain the
confidence of the Greek city-states of his satrapy, to restore order and safety
to the countryside, to encourage efficient men and to win trustworthy friends.
Lysias, in writing a speech (i) for a man who revenged himself by killing the
seducer of his wife, makes his client tell, in full detail, the story of his domes-
tic life since the time of his marriage; in all of these details both his naivete and
his astuteness manifest themselves. Both authors work primarily with external
actions which gradually reveal the personality that lies behind them.

   In the *Apology*, Socrates seldom speaks of what he has done, but regularly of
what he thinks about specific human situations and problems, and of what he
says about those matters to other people. Therefore, the portrait in the *Apology*
has nothing to do with a biography and does not at all strive for completeness.
Little attention is paid to the chronology of his life. As we will see below (Chapter V 74-75), we cannot determine the date of the oracle given to Chaerephon;
the three battles in which Socrates took part (28e2-3) are not listed in their
chronological order, and the text gives no clue as to how many years elapsed
between those military achievements and the manifestations of Socrates' civic
courage mentioned in another context (32a9-d8). Plato is so indifferent to

chronology because he records most of these events in order to acquaint us not with the person and character of Socrates, but with his ideas, and with their relation to his actual conduct.

Now, what is typical of Socrates' ideas is, first, that they do not bear on specialised and impersonal questions as those of the natural philosophers do, but on questions that arise from everyday life and on decisions we should take; second, more often than not they contradict flatly what most people would consider truisms. According to common opinion, a defendant will use any means to secure his acquittal and, more generally, an orator is a man who, by his inborn or acquired skill, will succeed in persuading an audience even when he tells lies or, as they say, in making them believe that the moon is made of green cheese. But for Socrates the orator *par excellence* and the litigant in particular is the man who speaks the truth and cares only for justice (18a3-6), regardless of the consequences. What is more, Socrates presents these paradoxes as self-evident, as if everybody would share his acceptance of them. When he comes up with them, the hearers scarcely believe their ears and they wonder whether Socrates is serious or wishes to make fools of them. Not only are they perplexed, but angry too. He always has a group of young men listening to him, but he contends that he is no teacher and cannot provide education (19d9-e1, 20c1-3, 33a5-b6). How are we to take such an assertion? How can Socrates, by asking his seemingly innocuous questions, checkmate every clever man and still pretend that he is wholly ignorant of the matter under discussion? (23a3-7). Not only will those whose incompetence he has exposed be indignant, but the bystanders as well (21e1-2, e3-4, 22c6-8, e6-23a5, c7-8, 24a7). Everybody feels that he has been fooled and that Socrates is not honest.

And still the reader can hardly help feeling that Socrates is deadly serious. In order to live up to his paradoxical principles, he has accepted a life of poverty and repeatedly sets his life at stake. In his defence he will say nothing that is not relevant to the case, and he will refrain from flattering and beseeching his judges. There is no inconsistency between the rules he adopts for himself and proclaims for others, and his actual conduct. We come under the spell of that unparalleled consistency, that strength of purpose, that indifference towards personal advantage and disadvantage. Socrates' whole attitude offers the prospect of a more noble, full, and genuine way of life. And what makes it all the more impressive is that Socrates does not consider himself important. He does no more than fulfill his duty and follow the call of God.

How will the public react to these seemingly contradictory aspects of Socrates' personality? Will they cling to the views that they have always held, that everybody should seek his own profit first, use every means to that end and take no unnecessary risks? Or will they accept Socrates' own scale of

values, radically different though it is from theirs and despite the sacrifices it
requires? Will it be possible for Socrates to bring them around to *his* view of
life and death, and in such a short time (cf. 37a6-b2, 19a1-2)? He doubts it,
and the outcome will prove that his misgivings were well-founded. But he is
not disillusioned (36a2-3) and does not regret having lived and spoken as he
has (38e2-5, 39b7-8, 41d46-7).

This ambiguity in the portrait of Socrates is essential to what Plato intended in the *Apology.* He had to explain how a majority of Athenian citizens,
people who had met Socrates every day, could sentence to death a man who,
to use Plato's own words, 'was of all people we are acquainted with the most
noble and simply the most sensible and the most just'[18]. They could only do
this if they totally misunderstood him, and if his conduct led them inevitably,
as it were, to such a misunderstanding. Socrates' uncompromising attitude
was, in reality, the result of his strong belief in the absolute character of moral
duty and in the urgency of what God asked of him. But the man in the street
could hardly see things in this way. When, in everything he said and did,
Socrates seemed to choose deliberately to depart from the common course,
what could that be but a sign of intolerable arrogance and haughtiness[19]? Jurors expected a defendant to behave with the utmost modesty. Even as proud
a man as Demosthenes would be at pains, when he described his policy of resistance to Philip as the only one worthy of Athens' glorious past, to emphasise that this policy was not *his* but the city's (xviii 206). There was nothing of
that kind in Socrates' attitude and the judges felt this as a provocation. This is
precisely what Plato's mastery consists in, that he not only makes us understand the reaction of the jury, but makes us feel that it was unavoidable.
Socrates was not found guilty because he was irreligious or a corruptor of the
young, but because the judges could not admit that his lofty religious and educational ideals were genuine and sincere.

The *Apology* as an Exhortation to Philosophy

In drawing a portrait of Socrates in the *Apology* Plato did not simply or
even principally intend to keep the memory of a great man alive. As we saw
above, it is not Socrates' deeds, nor his idiosyncratic individuality to which he
calls the reader's attention, but Socrates' ideas about the problems of human
conduct. Socrates is convinced that the answer to such questions can only be
discovered by consistent reasoning and open discussion; this discovery is the
object of his dialectical activity. He does not search for the truth with an eye
to himself alone. The god has entrusted him with the mission to test his
fellow-men and the reliability of their views on 'the most important matters'
(see note on 22d7). When it becomes apparent that their opinions cannot

stand close scrutiny, they will realise their own ignorance and he will urge them not to rest until they have found a satisfactory answer.

This is what Socrates lives for and, now that he is seventy years old, he does not feel that his task is accomplished. He is perfectly aware that his examinations arouse bitter resentment in many, but he does not think of giving up. Even when threatened with death, he declares emphatically: 'As long as I live, as long as I can, I will never cease to search for the truth and to address to you my reasonings and my admonitions' (29d4-6) and he concludes: 'And now, Athenians, you can listen to Anytus or not, you can let me free or not, but this you should know, that I am not prepared to change my conduct even if I should die many deaths' (30b7-c1). When, after having been found guilty, he again examines the possibility of staying in Athens but without continuing his discussions and research, he categorically rejects the very idea, although he knows that the members of the jury will not be convinced by his motives:

> If I say that this amounts to disobedience to the god, you will not believe me and think this to be just a pretence; if, on the other hand, I say that this is the highest felicity for a man, every day to devote his conversations to virtue and to the other subjects you always hear me talking about and examining myself and others, and that a life without examination is not bearable for a man, *that* you will still less accept from me. (37e5-38a6)

In these conversations, Socrates exhorts his partners always to put the higher goods above the lower and to take their decisions exclusively in accordance with an objective scale of values (29d7-e3. 30a7-b3. 36c5-d1). Persuading others to strive for the supreme good and to examine both their opinions and their behaviour is nothing else than winning them over to philosophy (28e5-6. 29d4-e3). This was Socrates' mission, but it does not follow that the protreptic activity to which he had devoted his life should come to and end with his death. He is so convinced of the need for its continuation that, in his very last words (41e2-7), he asks the judges to treat his sons, whom he will leave orphans, exactly as he treated them himself, exposing their ignorance if they prove to be conceited and reproaching them if they pursue money and other inferior goods more eagerly than what is truly worth-while. But he also thinks about the city as a whole; if the judges do away with him, there is still a possibility that the god, in his solicitude for the well-being of Athens, will send another man to take over the task which Socrates could not continue to perform (31a6-1). Further, there are Socrates' young friends, who may try to carry on his work, although they can by no means be compared with him (cf. 23c2-7. 39c-d3). Indeed, what does Plato do in his dialogues, and most conspicuously in the *Apology,* but to pass on the message of Socrates to those who did not hear the master himself?

A superficial reading of the *Apology* might leave us with the impression that it is just a portrait, a vivid representation of the unique personality of Socrates. This has led not a few scholars to the conclusion that it is not a philosophical work, at least not in the sense that it 'discuss(es) impersonal philosophical problems' (Hackforth *Composition* 46 n.1). But is any of Plato's works about such impersonal problems? All the dialogues are concerned with the attitude man should adopt towards his own states of mind, his sensations, his thoughts, his joys and griefs, hopes and fears, desires and aversions, the attitude he should adopt towards the influence that his friends and foes exercise upon him, towards the civic community and the cosmos to which he belongs. The questions treated in the dialogues are of a surprising variety, but they all have a bearing on the individual and his choices. To be sure, they are not all strictly ethical, but they all have an ethical dimension.

In the *Apology*, Plato deals with the basic problems of ethics, because the essential issues could be set forth with a minimum of technical language. A defence in court is not the proper setting for specialised debate; it gives no opportunity for a systematic application of the dialectical method[20]; it does not allow the leisurely kind of talk that is necessary to prevent misunderstandings or resolve them if they arise[21]. So we should not be disturbed by the differences in approach, content and literary technique between the *Apology* and the other works of Plato, nor should we conclude from these differences that only the latter are relevant to Plato's philosophy. Actually, as Aristotle emphasises in a celebrated argument at the beginning of his *Protrepticus*[22], anyone who asks the question whether one should search for insight (φιλοσοφεῖν) is already searching for insight. Therefore the *Apology*, which is an exhortation, a προτρεπτικός λόγος, to philosophy[23], is by that very fact a philosophical work. And as such it is the more interesting because Socrates so frankly expresses his own favourite ideas, whereas when we read the aporetic dialogues we often wonder whether what he says is an expression of his deep conviction or only a challenge to elicit a contradiction. In that respect, the *Apology* complements the early works that have so exercised the ingenuity of the interpreters[24].

Although the philosophical importance of the *Apology* lies primarily in its forceful and unambiguous formulation of the fundamental principles of ethics, it also touches on various specific tenets that are typical of Socratic philosophy. To close this section I give a list of these tenets; for their significance and impact I refer to the analyses of the sections and to the commentary.

1. An educator should possess knowledge: 20a6-c1. 25a12-c1.
2. Virtue has a civic as well as a personal aspect: 20b4-5. 30b4. 36c7-8.
3. There are three states of mind with regard to knowledge, (a) conceited ignorance (ἀμαθία), (b) consciousness of one's ignorance and striving

for insight (φιλοσοφία), (c) perfect knowledge (σοφία, φρόνησις): 20d6-23b4. 29d4-6. Only God possesses perfect knowledge: 23a5-7, cf. 20d7-9.

4. Talent and inspiration are not knowledge: 22b8-c6[25].
5. Skill, as competent within the limits of a determined field and concerned with means, is different from knowledge about τὰ μέγιστα, that is, about ultimate ends: 22c9-e1.
6. Nobody harms himself knowingly and willingly: 2543-26a1.
7. Examination of oneself is essential for virtue (insight) and for happiness: 28e5-6. 38a1-6.
8. Virtue or goodness, that is, insight[26], legitimises power: 29b6-7.
9. In virtue, the intellectual and the volitional aspect are inseparable: 29d5-6[27].
10. There is a threefold scale of values, viz. wealth, glory[28], knowledge. Virtue consists in acknowledging the superiority of the higher good to the lower one: 29d7-e3; cf. 30a8-b4. 36b6-dl. 41e4-5.
11. Inferior goods depend on superior goods: 30b1-4. 41d1-2.
12. Virtue cannot be automatically transferred from teacher to pupil and it is always the object of personal choice: 33a5-b6.

The *Apology* does not touch on the problem of the unity or multiplicity of virtues. In practical terms, ἀρετή is insight into the good, the acceptance of the right scale of values, and this is identical to σοφία or φρόνησις: compare 29e1 with e5, 30a8-b4, 31b5, 36c3-8 with 38a3-6.

It is remarkable that the terms εὐδαίμων and εὐδαιμονία are only found in contexts with little philosophical significance (36d9. 41c4 and 5). We do find, however, ὀρθῶς ζῆν (39d5), which is to be compared with the well-known εὖ ζῆν in *Crit.* 48b6.

The Date of the Platonic *Apology*

As is well known, analysis of style has shown that Plato's dialogues can be arranged in three chronological groups: early, mature and late. Many scholars might further divide the early dialogues into a 'Socratic' and a 'transitional' subgroup[29]. Admittedly, there is not much in the stylistic evidence to justify this division. Two fairly significant arguments, however, can be adduced. First, the 'transitional' dialogues seem to involve a more elaborate treatment of philosophical problems which have some significance in their own right and not only as a part of the comprehensive question about the 'good life'. Second, Socrates' role as a constructive thinker receives more emphasis in relation to his elenctic role. Since these two characteristics are even more conspicuous in the 'mature' works, these scholars consider the 'transitional' dialogues to be later than the 'Socratic' ones. But even if we accept this view, it cannot be decided whether the *Apology* belongs to the 'Socratic' or to the 'transitional' works. The fundamental difference in genre between a defence and a dialogue should prevent us from assessing the stylistic features of both by the same standards and, with regard to the content, the relationship of a defendant and his judges cannot be put on a par with that between participants in a dialogue.

Critics who believe that Plato's intention in the *Apology* was to give a faithful record of what Socrates had actually said in court are understandably inclined to assign it an early date, when the event was still fresh in the author's memory. Furthermore, the approach to philosophical issues in the *Apology* is more closely related to that of the early dialogues than to the later ones, so that it can be called 'the logical preface' to all the works of the early group.[30] On the basis of these two premises, it has been concluded that the *Apology* was probably Plato's 'first work, written not long after the event'[31]. If, however, as I have argued above, § 1, Plato did not aim, in the *Apology*, at anything like documentary authenticity, there is no special reason why we should consider the work to be particularly early. Any place within the early group, including the putative 'transitional' group, is acceptable.

In recent times, Erbse ('Entstehungszeit') has made the only attempt at dating the *Apology* more precisely. His argument is very complex and not very well organised, but its main thesis is that the attitude, the method and the assertions of Socrates as depicted in the *Apology* cannot be satisfactorily understood without a knowledge of all the early dialogues, including the *Gorgias* and the *Meno,* and that Plato intended this new work for an audience that was acquainted with his earlier writings. I do not think that Erbse has succeeded in establishing this point[32] and shall show with a few examples why I am not convinced.

The *Apology* tells us, Erbse says, that Socrates engages people in discussions, asking them questions and exhorting them to take care of their souls, but 'how this questioning functions logically, how it has an educational value for the mind and what its significance is for the discovery of moral and political truths remains obscure' (350, my translation). How the questioning functions is, however, evident in the story of Callias (20a4-c1) and in the first half of the discussion with Meletus (24c9-26a7). Erbse (350 n.20) objects to an appeal to the Ἐρώτησις because its function is only to expose Meletus' levity. That is indeed its overt intent, but nevertheless it illustrates the dialectical technique with its use of induction and of the *argumentum a minore ad maius,* and, although Meletus does not perceive the fact, it leads to the important educational and ethical conclusions mentioned above, 15, under numbers 1 and 6.

With regard to Socrates' protreptic activity, Erbse thinks (350) that the *Apology* does not specify what the 'care for the soul' exactly is. He argues that this becomes clear only when it has been established *(Prot.* 354e3-357e8) that wrong action proceeds from wrong thinking, because only then do people realise that our principal concern ought to be to acquire correct insight. That, however, is just what the *Apology* explicitly says: φρονήσεως δὲ καὶ ἀληθείας καὶ τῆς ψυχῆς ὅπως ὡς βελτίστη ἔσται οὐκ ἐπιμελῆ οὐδὲ φροντίζεις (29e1-3)[33] in a context in which Socrates characterises his activity as a 'searching for insight' (29d5 φιλοσοφῶν). Further, Erbse says (356) that the *Apology* only makes fun of Meletus and does not refute his charges. He seems not to have noticed that the Digression contains Socrates' real answer to the accusations. Finally, Socrates' refusal to beseech the judges may appear to the reader of the *Apology* to betray arrogance. From the early dialogues, however, he will have learned, according to Erbse (357), that Socrates' attitude is determined by an absolute desire for objectivity. But that is precisely what the *Apology* asserts (35b9-d5): moreover, it was certainly Plato's intention that there would be something defiant in the tone of Socrates' defence, as I said above, 12-13.

The reader probably expects me to give my own opinion now. I shall do so, although I know how risky the matter is. The first reflection I wish to submit is that, both in its content and in its structure, the Platonic *Apology* must be a work that matured over a long time. The figure of Socrates appears before our eyes with an exceptionally forceful though far from solemn compactness. There are no anecdotes, no descriptive details that are merely picturesque, amusing or moving, as those which we know from Alcibiades' speech in the *Symposium*, even though these were certainly dear to Socrates' devoted admirers. Every feature is subordinate to the character as a whole and the character itself embodies the fundamental ideas that, according to Plato, modelled the whole life and thought of Socrates. These ideas are few and receive full high-lighting, although Socrates, as the early dialogues show, was interested in a great variety of topics. Here, too, one finds a simplification which gives the intellectual figure of Socrates, as it is depicted in the *Apology,* a density that surpasses all his characterisations in Plato's other works.

It seems to me that, in order to isolate in his own mind the essential core of Socrates' personality and philosophy from its many fascinating manifestations, the author must have needed a long time, but probably still more to discover how he could present it in such a literary form that the readers would at every moment experience the flexibility of life and at the same time the weight and solidity of Socrates' moral and intellectual consistency. I think that to achieve this Plato needed more than solitary meditation: he needed to try out his intentions and first tentative efforts in discussions with others, enemies of Socrates as well as friends, and see how they reacted. In this way he could gradually discover which of the many aspects of Socrates' personality to include, and which to discard, as well as how to organise the *Apology* as a defence, a portrait and an exhortation to philosophy, so that these three elements would not be merely juxtaposed but integrated with one another. This would, in my opinion, require more than a couple of years; I should rather think five to ten and it could be still more, but for stylometric reasons one should refrain from crossing the boundary into the mature period. I am well aware that this estimate, even if it might be acceptable in the case of an average author, would not therefore apply to a genius like Plato.

Of more use than such guesses, whose value is difficult to assess, will perhaps be two details in the text that have so far gone unnoticed and could be of help in dating the *Apology*. The first is found in the Narration, where Socrates, after having examined the politicians and found that they did not possess knowledge, passes on to the poets and makes a similar discovery. There is, however, a difference: thanks to a natural gift or divine inspiration the poets really have the ability to cast a spell 'on their audience, whereas nothing has been said about an irrational capacity in the case of the politicians. The whole argument is strongly reminiscent of a similar argument near the end of the *Meno* (99b5-e2), although in that dialogue the two groups mentioned are the politicians and the *soothsayers*, not, as in the *Apology*, the politicians and the *poets*. Yet the similarity with the *Meno* remains because what is said of the poets in the *Apology* (22c1-3) is identical with what is said of the soothsayers in the *Meno*. The sentence in *Meno* 99c2-5 repeats practically verbatim *Apol.* 22c1-3: one must depend on the other. Now, a few lines earlier in the *Apology*, Socrates had declared that he has realised *again* and with regard to the poets *too* (b8-9 ἔγων οὖν αὖ καὶ περὶ τῶν ποιητῶν) how their ability is based upon an irrational force, not upon insight. Actually, however, Socrates had said nothing in the *Apology* about what politicians could achieve, whereas in the *Meno* their talents are fully acknowledged and characterised as irrational. In short, the passage in the *Apology* depends on that in the *Meno* and therefore the *Meno* must be earlier than the *Apology*.[34]

The second piece of evidence occurs in the most inspiring and important passage of the *Apology*. Answering an anonymous objector Socrates begins by illustrating, through the example of Achilles, a rule that is dear to him, viz. that a man of honour will never deviate from what he sees as his duty out of fear of death. Then, supposing that the judges might be prepared to spare him on the condition that he ceases his elenctic and protreptic activity, he gives a passionate reply, the longest sentence of the whole work (it runs to twenty lines). He starts with a conditional protasis, which he reiterates twice, making the hypothesis more specific each time, and ends with a solemn statement of his adamant resolution:

> Truly, men of Athens, I respect and love you, but I shall listen to God rather than to you and, as long as I live, as long as I can, I shall never give up searching for the truth and addressing to everyone of you whom I may meet my reasonings and my admonitions, saying as I am accustomed to do: "My excellent man, you, an Athenian, who belong to a city, the most important for her culture and her power, are you not ashamed to care for money, of which you try to get ever more, and for fame and marks of honour; but for insight, for truth, for your soul that it may become as virtuous as can be, do you not care for that nor give it a thought?" (29d2-e3)

Socrates appeals here to the pride of the Athenian citizens, the descendants of the heroes who fought at Marathon and Salamis, and the daring and enterprising men who, under the leadership of Pericles, made Athens the first city of Greece, and he asks whether it is not a disgrace if such men entertain petty views and purposes and do not strive for the highest ideals. It is essential for the dynamism of this sweeping sentence that the reader should apply to himself every word that Socrates speaks, without being distracted by any other consideration.

But can he? And can Plato himself have felt so? He cannot, in my opinion, if he wrote this passage at any time between 399 and 394, because the words πόλεως τῆς μεγίστης εἰς ... ἰσχύν would have sounded like a sneer at that time and the reader's attention would have been diverted from Socrates' intention, and, as a result, the whole effect of his passionate exhortation would have been lost. In 404, at the end of the Peloponnesian war, the defeated Athenians were forced to tear down the Long Walls and to hand over their fleet to the Spartans. It was the end of a period of more than sixty years during which they had dominated the seas. Now Athens was reduced to the status of a second- or third-class city, while Spartan harmosts controlled the islands and many strategic points. This humiliation was bitterly resented by the citizens, as appears from what Andocides says in a defence speech delivered in 399 B.C.: his personal foes find it absurd that he wishes to come back to Athens: 'Does he not see in what a situation our city finds itself?' (i 4).

The position of Athens scarcely improved till the summer of 394. But then there was an unexpected reversal: the Athenian admiral Conon, who had been given the command of the Persian navy, crushed the Spartan fleet off Cnidos. In the shortest possible time, the harmosts were expelled from the cities of Asia Minor and from the islands. In 393, under Conon's leadership, the Long Walls were rebuilt, a new fleet came into being and soon many cities and islands again sought an alliance with Athens. This revival lasted several years,[35] until it came to an abrupt end in 386 with the King's Peace, by which the King of Persia decreed that all Greek cities should be autonomous and were not allowed in the future to establish permanent leagues. Anyhow, from 392 or 391 until 386, Athens again felt herself as the first power of Greece and her citizens forgot the humiliating period 404-394 as if it were a dark episode, after which their city had recovered what rightfully belonged to it. I would suggest that it was during the years 392-387 that Plato wrote the long sentence which I have discussed, and the whole of the *Apology*[36].

I would, of course, be glad if I could establish the date of the *Apology* on a less narrow basis than these two details. Since, however, this is not the case, the argument above may make a significant contribution to the dating of the *Apology*.

The Plan of the Platonic *Apology*

It is Burnet's great merit to have seen that the first or main speech consists of five parts; he provides relatively short but important preliminary remarks for each of them. These parts are not specific to the Platonic *Apology*, but belong to the standard structure of Greek forensic oratory. So far, I fully agree with Burnet, but I think that parts III[37], IV and V should be further subdivided, not with the pedantic aim of presenting a complicated survey, but because each of the lesser sections has its proper and well-defined function and is carefully marked off from the preceding and the following ones by appropriate particles, summaries, changes of address, transitional formulas and other stylistic means. Each of these will be examined at its proper place in the analyses. Manifestly, Plato composed his *Apology* with deliberate artistry, and if one fails to notice his technique, one will not fully appreciate the coherence of the whole.

Surprisingly enough, scholars who wrote after Burnet's commentary was published paid little attention to his division of the First Speech[38]. What they say on this matter is generally speaking neither clear nor complete and it often conflicts with the explicit indications given by the text[39]. It can therefore not be used as a basis for the interpretation of the work.

First Speech
On the Question of Guilt

I. Exordium (προοίμιον)
Socrates contrasts the artful eloquence of his accusers, which is deceitful and aims only at persuasion, with his own artless and straightforward way of speaking, which simply tries to tell the truth (17a1-18a6).

II. Proposition (πρόθεσις)

Socrates makes a distinction between two groups of accusers; he will defend himself first against the older ones, and afterwards against the new (18a7-19a7).

III. Refutation (λύσις)

A. *Against the old accusers.*

   1. Negative part: what Socrates is not.

     a) He is not a natural philosopher (19a8-d7)

     b) He is not a sophist (19d8-20c3).

   2. Positive part: what Socrates really is, or the origin of the slander against him. NARRATION (διήγησις)

     a) The oracle (20c4-21a8)

     b) The investigations

       i. Introduction (21b1-9).

       ii. The politicians (21b9-e2).

       iii. The poets (21e3-22c8)

       iv. The craftsmen (22c9-e5)

     c) The results of the investigation:

       i. Origin of the slander-campaign (22e6-23a5)

       ii. Socrates understands that Apollo has entrusted him with a mission (23a5-c1)

       iii. Imitators of Socrates arise, and this increases the hatred of him (23c2-e3)

       iv. This leads to the indictment by Meletus (23e3-24b2)

B. *Against the new accusers.* 'INTERROGATION' (ἐρώτησις)[40].

   1. Introduction (24b3-c3).

   2. Meletus has never concerned himself with educational problems.

     a) First error, regarding the question who makes one better (24c4-25c4).

     b) Second error, regarding the question whether it is possible to corrupt willfully (25c5-26a7).

   3. Meletus contradicts himself in his indictment.

     a) Interpretation of the indictment: Socrates corrupts the young by teaching them atheism (26a8-e1).

     b) So understood, the indictment is a joke, for it contends that Socrates both does and does not believe in gods (26e7-27e3).

   4. Conclusion (27e3-28a1).

C. *General conclusion of the Refutation* (28a2-b2).

IV. DIGRESSION (παρέκβασις)

A. *First Objection:* The way of life Socrates has chosen is dangerous. The answer to this gives the proof of his piety.

    1. Considerations taken from 'the honourable' (τὸ καλόν).
      a) General principle: duty should be valued above life (28b3-d10).
      b) Application to Socrates: no peril of death will prevent him from fulfilling his mission (28d10-30c1).
    2. Considerations taken from the 'advantageous' (τὸ ὠφέλιμον).
      a) The accusers cannot do any harm to Socrates (30c2d5).
      b) Socrates' mission was entrusted to him for the advantage of Athens (30d5-31c3).
  B. *Second Objection:* Socrates should have taken part in political life. The answer proves his influence on the young to have been salutary.
    1. Socrates has been warned off by his 'divine sign' (31c4-d6).
    2. Honesty in politics is impossible in Athens (31d6-32e1).
    3. Therefore Socrates keeps within the bounds of individual conversation, from which he excludes nobody (32e2-33b8).
    4. His influence on the young has been salutary (33b9-34b5).
V. Peroration (ἐπίλογος)
Socrates will not address supplications to the jury.
    1. This would be honourable neither for himself nor for Athens (34b6-35b8).
    2. It would not be just (35b9-c7).
    3. It would not be consistent with piety (35c7-d8).

Second Speech
On the Question of Penalty

  A. *Introduction:* Socrates has been found guilty only by a narrow majority (35e1-36b2).
  B. *A proposal according to principle:* Socrates will make a proposal in accordance with what he deserves.
    1. He is a benefactor of the city, and a poor one (36b3-d4).
    2. Therefore he deserves to enjoy public maintenance (36d4-37a1).
  C. *A proposal according to the feasible:* what sentence is the jury prepared to pronounce on him?
    1. Socrates does not deserve punishment; banishment, in particular, will in his case be no solution (37a2-38b1).
    2. If the jury insists on a 'punishment', Socrates proposes a fine of one mna; the proposal is changed to one of thirty mnas (38b1-9).

Third Speech
Final Reflections

  A. *To the members of the jury who voted for a death sentence.*
    1. Introduction: their responsibility (38c1-d2).

2. Comparison between Socrates and his accusers (38d2-39b8).
3. The activity of Socrates will be continued by his followers (39c1-d9).
B. *To the members who voted for acquittal*: significance of death for Socrates.
1. The 'divine sign' has not warned him of any evil (39e140c3).
2. Two popular views of death (40c4-41c7).
3. Socrates trusts in Providence; he begs the jury to take care of his sons (41c8-42a5).

Notes

1. This could seem to be a truism, on which everybody would agree. But, as will appear from § 2 of this introduction, Plato's aim was not exclusively, and perhaps not even primarily, retrospective. He was not only concerned with the *memory* of Socrates, but also with the question whether Socrates' view of life and death was the right one, and was the one that everyone should adopt to attain τὸ εὖ ζῆν *(Crito* 48b6; cf. *Gorg.* 512d8-e5). Plato's intention was not properly historical, but protreptic. This does not imply, of course, that Plato took liberties regarding the facts of Socrates' life.

2. Cf E. Delebecque *Essai sur la vie de Xénophon* (Paris 1957) 56–57, 264–265, 271–272 (on the *Hellenica); * 96–98, 292 (on the *Anabasis).*

3. The various possibilities are discussed exhaustively and very thoroughly for the whole of Athenian forensic oratory in an excellent chapter ('Client and Consultant') in K. J. Dover *Lysias and the Corpus Lysiacum,* Berkeley–Los Angeles, 1968, 148–174.

4. This has been doubted, most recently by D.M. MacDowell *Demosthenes, Against Meidias* (Oxford 1990) 23–28. Cf. contra Dover *Lysias* 172–174.

5. It seems relevant here to quote a few sentences of Dover's *(Lysias* 170–172) which can be fruitfully compared with what John Burnet *(Plato's Euthyphro, Apology of Socrates, and Crito,* Oxford, 1924) says in his 'Introductory note' 63–64 (see above, 1–2): 'Scholars who seriously believe that the reputation of a Greek orator would be diminished by the detection of inaccuracies and distortions in his published speeches must be singularly blind to the workings of the world in which they themselves live, and in particular to the fact that in political life it is so much more important to score off an opponent than to assess his conduct judiciously . . . I therefore find it difficult to see that substantial alteration of a speech before it was put into circulation would seem to either the consultant or the litigant likely to diminish his political and artistic reputation in any significant respect.'

6. Cicero *(De Or.* i 54, 231) and Diogenes Laertius (ii 40) state that Lysias wrote this defence for Socrates to deliver in court, but that Socrates refused to make use of it because it was rhetorical rather than philosophical. This story, however, belongs to the kind of Hellenistic anecdotes in which literary data are converted into biographical facts. In the same way the ὑπόθεσις of Isocrates' Busiris (xi) anachronistically says that Polycrates furnished Anytus and Meletus with a speech against Socrates; cf. Diog.

Laert. iii 38. Lysias' *Apology*, too, was probably a piece of epideictic oratory. Cf. Dover *Lysias* 192–193.

7. Theodectes was a 'pupil' of Plato and Isocrates and took part in the rhetorical exercises that Aristotle led when still in the Academy. He seems to have been born about 405–400 B.C. According to F. Stoessl *Kleine Pauly s.v.* Theodectes, he died after 334; before 334 according to E. Diehl *RE s.v. Theodectes* 1, 1725–1726. Since Theodectes' rhetorical activity falls primarily in the early period of his life, it is not impossible that the 'Ἀπολογία was a work of his youth, but a late date is not to be excluded either. Cf. L. Radermacher 'Θεοδέκται' AAWW 76 (1939) 62–69. See also Chapter VII n.51; note on 27e5.

8. *P. Mich.* inv. 5982, cf. R. Merkelbach - H. Youtie, *ZPE 2* (1968) 161–169 has been interpreted as a pamphlet defending Theramenes by A. Andrewes, *ZPE 6* (1970) 35–38. The literary polemic about Alcibiades is attested for us by Isocrates' *De bigis*, by Orations xiv and xv of Lysias, by the *Against Alcibiades* of the Pseudo-Andocides and by an anonymous speech (or later declamation?) *P. Strassb.* inv. 2346, cf. N. Lewis *EPap* 3 (1936) 79–87; the *Symposium* of Plato and the *Alcibiades* of Aeschines of Sphettus are probably related to the same debate.

9. For a short and reliable account of the available data, see E. R. Dodds *Plato: Gorgias*, Oxford, 1959. 28–29; A. H. Chroust *Socrates: Man and Myth*, London, 1957, ch. iv has many more details, but is insufficiently critical.

10. As far as I know, the most systematic effort along that line is to be found in chapter V (80–134) of R. Hackforth *Composition of Plato's Apology*, Cambridge, 1933.

11. Of course, I do not wish to deny that some ideas developed in the Third Speech may have been touched upon by Socrates in another section of his defence. - See also below, n.35.

12. I say *sentence* because, as I have argued, whole paragraphs and sections are so artfully composed and stand in such complex relations to what precedes and follows them that they cannot be separated from the whole.

13. Cf. Chapter II 32–34; Chapter VI 103; note on 35c5-6.

14. What we read 23e3-24a1 is just playful.

15. In the *Exordium* (17a5-bl), he mentions that his adversaries had warned the members of the jury to be on their guard lest Socrates deceives them, since he is a clever speaker. In the Digression (29c1-5), he recalls an assertion of Anytus: now that legal proceedings have been started against Socrates, the judges have no choice but to condemn him to death, since otherwise all the young will be irretrievably corrupted. That is all, since the remark about the relation between the δαιμόνια καινά of which the indictment speaks and Socrates' δαιμόνιον σημεῖον (31d1-2) is based upon the text of the γραφή, not upon the speech of Meletus.

16. Hackforth *Composition* 81 says that 'there is . . . nowhere else in Plato's writings or elsewhere any suggestion that Socrates had long been the victim of popular misrepresentation'. He certainly was misrepresented in Aristophanes' *Clouds*. The view that Socrates was a natural philosopher and therefore despised the gods is combated in Xenophon's *Memorabilia i* 1, 11–14. About half a century after Socrates' death, it is said in the *Laws* that the man in the street (οἱ πολλοί) thought that the study of astronomy and related sciences led to atheism (xii 966d6-967a8, quoted in the note on

18c2; 967c5-d2). Anytus' violent outburst against the sophists (*Menu* 91b2-9242) aptly illustrates the bad reputation of this second group of intellectuals; in the later works of Plato (e.g. the *Sophist)* and in those of Aristotle the term σοφιστής has acquired a pejorative connotation. The orator Aeschines calls Socrates a sophist (i 173, quoted Chapter VI 94). It is no wonder that Socrates' partners in the dialogues do not identify him with the φυσιολόγοι or the sophists; they do not belong to οἱ πολλοί, but to the cultivated class, or even to the professional intellectuals.

17. On the relation between Plato's technique of portrayal and that of the other prose writers of his time see Chapter V § 4.

18. *Phaed.* 118a16-17; cf. *Epist.* vii 324e1-2.

19. Cf. *Apol.* 34d9-el οὐκ αὐθαδιζόμενος, ὦ ἄνδρες 'Αθηναῖοι, οὐδ'ὑμᾶς ἀτιμάζων; 37a3 ἀπαυθαδιζόμενος.

20. The cross-examination of Meletus (24c9-28a1) is not meant as a serious piece of dialectic.

21. On the importance of 'leisure' in the dialectical discussions in contra-distinction to forensic oratory, see *Theaet.* 172c3-173b3, and cf. J.L. Stocks 'Σχολή' *CQ* 30 (1936) 177–187, and Gaiser *Protreptik and Paränese* 208–209. Cf. Chapter II 35 and n.26; note on 37a6.

22. Fragment 2 (Walter, Ross), Testim. A 2–6 (Düring).

23. This is not to say that the *Apology* belongs to the literary genre of protreptic, its intention is, like many Platonic dialogues, to be implicitly protreptic. See Chapter XI 217.

24. On this see my essay 'The Unity . . .',

25. The terms ὀρθή and & ἀληθὴς δόξα do not occur in the *Apology.* Cf. Chapter V 66; Chapter XI 215–216; note on 22b8.

26. Ὁ Βελτίων (29b6) is equivalent to σοφώτερος, as appears from the whole context.

27. I may refer once more to 'The Unity. . .'.

28. In a variant, glory is replaced by the body (30a8). Cf. Chapter VII 137–138 and n.36.

29. The mature group consists of *Republic, Parmenides, Theaetetus, Phaedrus* (not necessarily in this order, although it is the most probable one), the late group of *Sophist, Politicus, Timaeus, Critias, Philebus, Laws* (it is disputed whether the pair *Soph. - Polit.* or the pair *Tim. - Critias* comes first in this group). Candidates for the 'transitional' subgroup include *Gorgias, Meno, Phaedo, Symposium, Cratylus.* It should be emphasised that there is no stylometric evidence whatsoever for the inclusion of any member of this transitional subgroup in a 'middle' group, despite repeated allegations to the contrary (e.g. W. K. C. Guthrie *A History of Greek Philosophy, Plato*, Cambridge, 1975, iv 50; Gregory Vlastos *Socrates: Ironist and Moral Philosopher*, Cornell University Press, 1991, 46–47). The most recent works on the subject are G.R. Ledger *Recounting Plato, A Computer Analysis of Plato's Style* (Oxford 1989) and L. Brandwood *The Chronology of Plato's Dialogues* (Cambridge 1990; revision of an unpublished dissertation, London 1958). Both authors maintain the tripartite division, and both betray uneasiness about the existence of a separate Socratic subgroup within the early group. From a philosophical point of view, C.H. Kahn's paper 'Did Plato write Socratic Dialogues?' *CQ* 31 (1981) 305–320, seems well on its way to be epoch-making. See the

doxography in H. Thesleff 'Platonic Chronology' *Phronesis* 34 (1989) 1–26, esp. 2–3 and notes.

30. A. Diès *Platon* (Paris 1930) 85–86; Diès refrains from speaking of a preface written *before* the early dialogues.

31. Guthrie *Hist. Gr. Phil.* iv 72. It should be emphasised that the author proposes this opinion with great caution and that he adds: 'but certainty is impossible'.

32. Although, of course, a knowledge of the early dialogues, and of later ones too, is of great help for a full understanding of many passages in the *Apology*, as the whole of the present book will show abundantly.

33. Cf. 36c5-7 μὴ πρότερον . . . τῶν ἑαυτοῦ μηδενὸς ἐπιμελεῖσθαι πρὶν ἑαυτοῦ ἐπιμεληθείη ὅπως ὡς βέλτιστος καὶ φρονιμώτατος ἔσοιτο.

34. The point is discussed fully in the extensive note on *Apol.* 22b8.

35. The momentum of the Athenian 'imperial' recovery in those years is well described by G. Glotz and R. Cohen *Histoire grecque* iii (Paris 1936) especially 87–88 and 94–95. Recent scholarship tends to stress Athens' economic problems in the years between Cnidos and the King's Peace, as shown by the obsession with poverty in Aristophanes' *Ecclesiazusae* and *Plutus,* and certainly the revival after Cnidos did not bring back the golden days of the fifth-century empire, but politically, Athens resumed a major role. See B.S. Strauss *Athens after the Peloponnesian War* (Ithaca 1987) 121–178, esp. 163–167.

36. For the same reason as I explained above, it would have been impossible for the historical Socrates to utter these words in his defence. And the readers of say 390 will not have remembered, when reading the *Apology,* that Socrates had spoken in a dark time.

37. In part III Burnet himself distinguishes three sections, the first of which corresponds to my III A, the second to my III B 1 and the third to my III B 2–4. Moreover, Burnet counts 28a2-b2 as belonging to part IV, whereas I think that these lines belong as C to part III.

38. Still more striking, perhaps, is the fact that in Hackforth's *Composition* nothing at all is said about the structure or plan of the work.

39. Thus e.g. the *Exordium* and the Proposition are put together by Friedlander *Platon* ii 146–147, who further adds to that part the sub-section III A 1; the same happens with the Proposition and the Refutation of the Old Accusers in Guthrie *Hist. Gr. Phil.* iv 80; with the Digression and the Peroration in P. Friedländer *Platon,* Berlin, 1957–1960, 154. While recognising the validity of Burnet's division, C. D. C. Reeve *Socrates in the Apology,* Indianapolis, 1989(3–4) perceives a tripartite structure in the *Apol.* as a whole, which is worth mentioning: (1) the false Socrates, negative (17a1-24b2); (2) the defense against Meletus, negative, but containing the positive component of ἔλεγχος (24b3-28a1); (3) the true Socrates, positive (28b3-42a5). Cf. Chanter VI & 9.

40. Since neither 'interrogation' nor 'cross-examination' is an adequate translation, I will use the Greek term throughout this book.

6

On the Alleged Historical
Reliability of Plato's *Apology*

Donald Morrison

SOCRATES IS THE PATRON SAINT OF PHILOSOPHY. He has functioned in our tradition as the paradigm philosopher, and his life has served as a model of a
philosophical life. In some sense or other, he was the first philosopher; and so
philosophy, whatever it is, is what Socrates did and what he started. Saints are
often martyrs. Socrates, the patron saint of philosophy, gave his life rather
than betray his calling.

Students of hagiography know that saints' lives tend to be legendary. So also
in the case of Socrates. The Σωκρατικοὶ λόγοι, the 'Socratic discourses' produced by Socrates' friends and followers, contained a great deal that was fictional. The surviving Socratic writings, both whole works and fragments, contain enough anachronisms and inconsistencies and other sorts of historical
implausibilities that we can be confident the constraints of this genre were
rather loose, and authors were entitled and expected to put a great deal into
the mouth of their character 'Socrates' which the historical Socrates never said
and never would have said.[1]

Sometimes our efforts to reconstruct the lives of saints are aided by the
writings of the saints themselves (though of course these must be handled
with care) and by contemporary documentary and other relatively neutral
sources. Our efforts to reconstruct the life of Socrates cannot be so lucky.
Socrates himself wrote nothing; and the contemporary or near-contempo-
rary sources about him are all either hostile or friendly. Practically the only
documentary evidence we have is the precise wording of the indictment
against Socrates, available to us in a second-hand report in Diogenes Laertius (2.40).

Thus the problem of the historical Socrates is like the problem of the historical Jesus: it is vitally important to our sense of ourselves, as well as to our sense of the civilization to which we belong, that we obtain a historically reliable picture of who this man was and what he was like. But this task is dismayingly difficult and perhaps impossible. 'The problem of the historical Socrates' has benefitted from the intelligence and labor of many fine scholars over more than two centuries. Perhaps unsurprisingly, they have arrived at depressingly diverse results.

But in recent decades a group of the most outstanding scholars of the subject, who disagree with each other about much else, have come to agree at least on this: that Plato's *Apology of Socrates* is a historically reliable source for the reconstruction of Socrates' character and opinions. The views of these scholars are subtle and nuanced, and they vary as to just how reliable the *Apology* is and in what aspects. These variations will concern us later. But the basic idea, that Plato's *Apology* is a reliable source for forming our picture of the historical Socrates, seems to have become the dominant view. It is what Aristotle might have called 'the most reputable opinion'.

The most recent defender of this view is Charles Kahn. In his magnificent new book *Plato and the Socratic Dialogue* Kahn is sceptical of the historical value of the Socratic dialogues, on the grounds that the conventions of that genre allow great freedom for invention. But Kahn argues that the *Apology* belongs to a different genre, being a defense speech rather than a dialogue. At one point he sums up: "It is likely, then, that in the *Apology* Plato has given us a true picture of the man as he saw him."[2] For his own reconstruction of the historical Socrates' philosophy, therefore, Kahn relies almost exclusively on Plato's *Apology*.

The foremost German scholar of Socrates is Klaus Döring, author of the monograph on Socrates and the Socratics in the New Ueberweg-Flashar history of philosophy.[3] Döring also bases his presentation of the historical Socrates "on the basis of the assumption, which I hold to be correct, that the picture of Socrates in the *Apology* is in its basic features authentic".[4] Like Kahn, though for partly different reasons, Döring holds that the other dialogues contain Platonic material and are therefore not as reliable as guides to the philosophy of the historical dialogues.

The most important and influential scholar of Socrates in the English-speaking world during the last several decades was Gregory Vlastos. He believed that all of the 'early' writings of Plato are, within certain limits, reliable evidence for the philosophy of the historical Socrates. This group includes the *Apology*. In his magisterial book on Socrates, Vlastos did not give special attention to the status of the *Apology*. But in an earlier, influential essay Vlastos gave a separate argument for "accepting the *Apology* as a reliable re-creation of the thought and character of the man Plato knew so well".[5]

Is Plato's *Apology* a reliable source for the philosophy of the historical Socrates? These three distinguished scholars, along with many others,[6] argue 'yes'. I shall argue 'no'.

But before proceeding to detailed arguments, a few distinctions are in order. The *Apology* can be used as evidence for (1) certain events in Socrates' life; (2) certain features of Socrates' character and his characteristic activities; (3) Socrates' 'philosophy' in the modern sense: his beliefs and intellectual methods. Examples of these categories include: (1) Chaerephon's question to the oracle at Delphi and its answer; (2) Socrates' disdain for money and honor; (3) Socrates' profession of ignorance, and his quest for definitions. Those who regard the *Apology* as a reliable source of evidence for the historical Socrates employ it, reasonably enough, as evidence for all three categories. But what they—and we—as historians of philosophy are chiefly interested in is the third category, Socrates' philosophy.

My own scepticism about Socrates is a moderate one.[7] I believe that we can have reasonable confidence about certain events in Socrates' life, and about certain general features of his character; and I believe that the *Apology* takes its place alongside other texts in providing evidence for these. But what I deny, and shall argue against here, is that Plato's *Apology* gives us grounds for confidence that we know anything very precise about what we most want to know, namely Socrates' philosophical views.

My discussion will be divided into two parts. The first part will consider arguments for the historicity of the *Apology* based on its special literary characteristics and circumstances. My primary focus in this part will be on Kahn's, and secondarily Vlastos's arguments. The second part will treat arguments based on a comparison between the *Apology* and other sources. Here I shall concentrate on Döring.

Arguments from Genre and the Special Circumstances of the *Apology*

I shall begin with Kahn's version of what has become a traditional argument:

> [W]e are struck by the fundamental contrast between the *Apology* and the rest of Plato's work. There is first of all a sharp difference of literary form. The *Apology* belongs to a traditional genre, the courtroom speech revised for publication; the dialogues all belong to the new genre of "Conversations with Socrates". But underlying this literary contrast is a more fundamental difference. The *Apology* reflects a public event, the trial of Socrates, which actually took place, and at which Plato and hundreds of other Athenians were present. The dialogues represent private conversations, nearly all of them fictitious . . .

The situation is quite different for the *Apology.* As the literary version of a public speech, composed not by the speaker but by a member of the audience, the *Apology* can properly be regarded as a quasi-historical document, like Thucydides' version of Pericles' Funeral Oration. We cannot be sure how much of the speech as we have it reflects what Socrates actually said, how much has been added or altered by Plato. But if, as we imagine, Plato composed the speech to defend Socrates' memory and to show to the world that he was unjustly condemned, it was essential to present a picture of Socrates in court that could be recognized as authentic.[8]

Kahn is a sophisticated intellectual historian. One reason why he disagrees with e.g. Vlastos on the historical reliability of the early Platonic dialogues is that the conventions of the genre 'the Socratic dialogue' permitted authors to put their own views into Socrates' mouth. Kahn argues that Plato made use of these liberties throughout his career, even in the earliest dialogues.

But the *Apology,* Kahn argues, belongs to a different genre. Does it? Let us leave aside the important question whether and to what extent the notion of 'genre' can validly be applied to the literary productions of classical Greece. Kahn's claim still faces the problem that we have no other surviving text which belongs to *precisely* the same type as Plato's *Apology.* We know that there was a 'genre' of defenses and accusations of Socrates in antiquity, and we have one other example, Xenophon's *Apology of Socrates.* But Plato's *Apology* does not have precisely the same literary form as Xenophon's, because Plato's *Apology* is in direct speech. It pretends to be the speech which Socrates himself gave. By contrast, Xenophon's *Apology* does not pretend to be Socrates' own words. Instead it presents Xenophon's defense of Socrates: Xenophon's account of why Socrates spoke as he did, and Xenophon's account of why Socrates was not guilty.

It is hard to know what exactly the conventions were which governed Plato's *Apology,* since we have no precisely comparable surviving text. We do not even know that there were any such conventions, since for all we know Plato's may have been the first defense of Socrates which took the literary form of a direct speech. Kahn claims that because the *Apology* is a speech and not a dialogue, it is not governed by the conventions of the genre, the Socratic dialogue.

But we do not know that the Σωκρατικοὶ λόγοι which are spoken of by Aristotle[9] were not understood to include the *Apologies* of Plato and Xenophon, as well as the various dialogues. Σωκρατικὸς λόγος just means 'Socratic discourse'; and this label applies to the apologies just as well as to the dialogues. So we do not have good grounds for thinking that fourth-century Athenian authors and readers would have regarded Socratic 'apologies' as belonging to a genre distinct from Socratic 'dialogues'.

The genre in which Kahn places Plato's *Apology* is anyway mistaken. He claims that the *Apology* belongs to the genre of courtroom speeches revised for publication. But this traditional genre is one in which the author writes a speech which he either delivers himself, or gives to another to deliver, before a court, and then revises later for publication. Unless one believes that Plato actually ghostwrote Socrates' speech for him—which so far as I am aware no scholar has claimed—then Plato's defense speech is of a different type. The gap between a speech that is actually delivered in a courtroom, and the revised version which a proud and creative author might eventually publish, can of course be great. The published version may contain arguments and appeals which the author did not include at the time, but later comes to think he should have. But there is a natural and organic relation between the original speech and the published version in such a case, which there is not between a literary version written by one person of a speech which was originally composed and delivered by someone else.

Thucydides' version of Pericles' funeral oration is an interesting parallel, because there is a narrow 'genre' into which both it and Plato's *Apology* might fit: "the literary version of a public speech, composed not by the speaker but by a member of the audience".[10] This genre is narrower than the category 'forensic speech, revised for publication', since it excludes both speeches written to be delivered at a particular occasion, and entirely fictive speeches, written for a nonexistent occasion. *If* we were in a position to be confident that literate Athenians of the classical period recognized this type of literary production as a genre to itself with conventions of its own; and *if* we were in a position to know what those conventions were, in particular what amount of historical license was expected or allowed; *then* the argument for the historicity of the *Apology* on the grounds of genre might be sustainable. But unfortunately, the evidence to support this argument is lacking. We know very little about the circumstances of composition of most surviving speeches from classical Greece, so as to know which of them belong to this narrow genre; and we have very little independent evidence with which to compare them.

Kahn seems confident that the funeral oration is a "quasi-historical document". Among scholars of Thucydides, this is controversial. And those who doubt, as I do, that we have good grounds for believing in the historicity of the funeral oration, will also doubt that the parallel between it and the *Apology* does anything to help establish the historicity of the latter.

Like other scholars before him, Kahn stresses the public and prominent character of the historical event, Socrates' trial, as a ground for believing that Plato's version of Socrates' speech is historically faithful. There are in fact several different reasons why the public character of the event might be thought to be relevant, which Kahn does not explicitly distinguish. The argument most clearly suggested by his remarks is that Plato observed a genre distinction between Socratic writings which depict well-known historical events, and those which do not. For fictitious events, one is free to invent fictitious views and arguments, but for historical events, one is tied to history. As Kahn recognizes, this principle falls foul of the *Phaedo,* which depicts the death of Socrates, yet contains what most scholars agree is mature Platonic philosophy. Kahn suggests that the *Phaedo* is exempt because Plato makes clear in the dialogue that he was not present.[11] But the resultant literary convention, "Feel free to put your own ideas into the main character's mouth, unless you are portraying a prominent historical event (unless you make clear that you weren't an eyewitness, in which case it doesn't matter)", is implausibly cumbersome.

Before looking at further reasons why the historical character of the trial might be relevant to the *Apology's* historicity, it is important to distinguish three basic views of the relation between Plato's *Apology* and Socrates' actual speech. (Each of these types could be further subdivided; and there are other possibilities. But this tripartite distinction will suffice for my purposes.) One view is that Plato's *Apology* is an attempt to reproduce faithfully the speech which Socrates gave. According to this view Plato intends his *Apology* to differ from the actual speech only insofar as he 'cleans up' Socrates' expression and exposition. According to a second view, Plato does not intend his *Apology* to be a faithful, albeit more polished, representation of the speech that Socrates gave. Rather, he intends it to present the substance of the defense which Socrates actually gave, though presented in language and organization different from Socrates' own. A third view is that Plato is not attempting to reproduce Socrates' actual speech at all. He is putting into Socrates' mouth the defense which he, Plato, thinks is best. On this view Plato's *Apology* aims to present, not Socrates' actual speech, but the speech which Socrates ought to have given. It aims to be faithful to the historical Socrates, but to Socrates the man, and not to his speech.

All three types of view have been defended.[12] Yet scholars are not always careful to distinguish sharply between them. It is important to keep them separate, because the further one moves from the first view, the less reliable the *Apology* becomes as evidence for the historical Socrates.

One argument contained in Kahn's remarks which might be thought to rely, in part, on the public nature of the trial, is this. Since Plato wrote the *Apology* to defend Socrates' memory and to show that he was unjustly condemned, it is essential that the picture of Socrates contained in the *Apology* be recognized as authentic. This argument depends, however, not on the fact that many people were present at the trial, but that many people who would be reading Plato's *Apology* knew Socrates personally, or were otherwise well-informed about his character and opinions. What this argument implies is not that the *Apology* must be faithful to Socrates' speech, but that it must to some degree be faithful to the character and attitudes of Socrates the man. This argument is therefore naturally suited to the third view. Even if Plato's purpose was to give the 'true' defense of Socrates, the defense which Socrates should have given of himself but did not, to be effective this defense must still have been recognizably a defense of the historical Socrates. It must have been faithful enough to the beliefs and character of the historical Socrates to have been convincing to a large number of readers who knew him well.

However, the accumulated experience of more than two thousand years of political propaganda and criminal defense practice shows that this argument is very weak. Dramatic misrepresentation of the facts and of one's client's character can be extremely helpful in public exoneration, even if one's client is a celebrity. Let us assume, plausibly, that prominent among Plato's aims in writing the *Apology* was to acquit Socrates in the court of public opinion. This aim, taken by itself, is compatible with very great historical misrepresentation.[13]

If one assumes, more strongly, that Plato's aim was a rhetorically effective public defense of Socrates' character and opinions *as he, Plato, remembered them*, then a much stronger conclusion of historical reliability is warranted. But Kahn and the other defenders of the historicity of the *Apology* are trying to argue to the conclusion that Plato was aiming at historical faithfulness in the *Apology*, and to base their argument on this stronger assumption would be question-begging.

Another reason why the public and prominent character of the trial might be thought to ground the historicity of the *Apology* is not explicit in Kahn's account, and I hesitate to attribute it to him. This justification is more clearly present in Gregory Vlastos' argument in his famous essay "The Paradox of Socrates":

> Plato's *Apology* has for its *mise en scène* an all-too-public occasion. The jury alone numbered 501 Athenians. And since the town was so gregarious and Socrates a notorious public character, there would have been many more in the audience. So when Plato was writing the *Apology*, he knew that hundreds of those who might read the speech he puts into the mouth of Socrates had heard the historic original. And since his purpose in writing it was to clear his master's name and indict his judges, it would have been most inept to make Socrates talk out of character.[14]

Vlastos stresses that the trial was a public event, which hundreds of Athenians attended. What would make this fact relevant is the thought that the *Apology* aimed, or would have been expected to aim, at reproducing the essence of the speech given at the trial, so that if Plato had deviated very far from this, his audience would have recognized the deviation, and the *Apology* would have been a failure. This is an argument *for* the second type of view that I have distinguished, and *against* the third type of view.[15] The availability of hundreds of witnesses to the trial is a constraint on the historicity of the *Apology* only if it was expected to reproduce at least the gist of what was actually said. If not, if the 'rules of the game' were that authors of Socratic apologies were entitled to present the defense speech which Socrates ought to have given but did not, then widely recognized divergences between the actual speech and Plato's *Apology* would be irrelevant.

Both Kahn and Vlastos are careful to dissociate themselves from the first view, that in writing the *Apology* Plato is functioning as a combination reporter and vigorous editor. Certainly this view is not popular nowadays: most people who defend the historical reliability of the *Apology* acknowledge that Plato is not reproducing Socrates' actual speech, but somehow re-creating it. But this is a dangerous admission, since the more creativity one attributes to Plato in writing the speech, the less valuable it is as historical evidence.

One widely recognized reason for admitting that Plato is not merely reporting Socrates' speech has, I believe, stronger implications than are usually noticed. Plato's *Apology* is a literary masterpiece. This literary excellence is often recognized to be the result of Plato's extraordinary talent, rather than Socrates'. But the point can be pressed further. As Reginald Allen has shown, the *Apology* is not merely a masterful piece of writing. It is a quietly ironical parody of the standard defense speech of its day. Socrates' speech contains an exordium, prosthesis, statement of the case, refutation, digression, and peroration, the same formal parts which a student of rhetoric would have been taught to produce.[16] This is a highly literary device. It fits Plato's massive literary talent and carefully developed skill at imitating many different styles. It does not very well fit Socrates the oral philosopher.

Of course we are not in a position to know that Socrates did not use such a complex literary form for his speech. The judgement that this is unlikely is based on commonsense psychological probabilities, nothing more. Still, if we accept that the structure and organization of Socrates' speech in the *Apology* is probably not true to the original, but is rather due to Plato, then we must accept that the *Apology* will immediately have struck a contemporary reader who had been present at the trial, or who knew Socrates well, as very different from the original speech. Just from its literary form, the *Apology* will have appeared as Plato's complex rhetorical project, and not as Socrates'. This runs counter to Vlastos's suggestion that Plato aimed to make Socrates talk in character. 'Talking in character' includes both style and content. If Plato's intention had been to present the gist (though not the exact language) of Socrates' speech, in such a way that readers who had been present at the trial would recognize the Socrates they heard in his words, then it would have been rhetorically counterproductive for him to have chosen a literary form and organization which was so obviously different from the one which Socrates actually used.[17]

The literary form of the *Apology* gives us reason, therefore, to reject not only the first of the there views which I have distinguished, but also the second. Plato seems—characteristically—to have been driving his own agenda when he wrote the *Apology*. He was aiming to defend his beloved friend and mentor Socrates, to be sure. But he chose literary means which made it clear to his contemporary audience, and also clear upon reflection to us, that he is defending Socrates in his own way.

Perhaps one reason why some scholars might think that it is not necessary to distinguish between arguments why Plato would have made the *Apology* faithful to Socrates' actual speech, and arguments why he would have been faithful to Socrates' character, is that this difference might seem to make no difference to the historicity issue. Since what we are interested in is Socrates' philosophy (and not the details of his speech), Plato's *Apology* will be good evidence either way.

But that is not right. One thing we can be sure of about Socrates is that he was a deep and mysterious and utterly extraordinary man. Socrates was a puzzle: Vlastos rightly put that fact at the center of *Socrates: Ironist and Moral Philosopher*. What follows from this is that, even if we could be sure that Plato in the *Apology* intended to give the best defense of Socrates as he saw him, and even if Plato is a strong and insightful judge of character, nonetheless Plato's Socrates may not be what a sober historian would judge to be a historically accurate version of Socrates. Plato's 'take' on Socrates will certainly be a profoundly interesting version of Socrates. But it may differ quite a bit from Antisthenes' view of what was essential to Socrates' character and philosophy, or Aeschines', or Xenophon's. And a careful historian of today who was able *(per impossibile)* to interview extensively everyone who knew Socrates well, would very likely come up with a version which differs significantly from each of theirs.

By contrast, if Plato's *Apology* were a sincere attempt to re-create the speech which Socrates actually gave, that would give us good evidence about Socrates' self-presentation at that crucial moment. And Socrates' self-presentation at his trial is excellent evidence concerning his character, for two reasons. First, it was likely to be sincere. (Socrates was not courting favor.) Second, while Socrates' self-presentation should not be accepted at face value as good evidence for what his character was actually like (no one knows himself that well); still, the fact that Socrates would present himself in this way is a very important and revealing fact about his character. Thus, whether Plato aims in the *Apology* to reproduce Socrates' self-presentation at the trial, or to give his own defense of Socrates against the charges, makes a large difference to its status as historical evidence for Socrates' character.

The gap is even greater when evaluating the *Apology*'s value as evidence for Socrates' philosophy. Socrates' 'philosophy' in the modern sense consists in the general propositions he believed in and in the intellectual methods he employed. ('Philosophy' in Socrates' and Plato's sense was a way of life. So much the better for them, and worse for us.) Now a person can easily be badly mistaken about his own character; but it is less easy to be mistaken about which philosophical propositions one holds true. If Socrates said in his speech, "Neither I, nor any other mortal I am acquainted with, knows anything important", that statement could be taken over pretty straightforwardly onto the list of Socrates' epistemological opinions. So, on the assumption that Socrates did make philosophical remarks at his trial, a reliable report of Socrates' defense speech would be even better evidence for Socrates' philosophy than for his character.

In philosophy, the precise wording matters enormously. It matters a great deal whether Socrates said, "I knew that I know nothing" (the legendary misconstrual of Plato's version) or "I do not think that I know anything fine and good" (Plato's version) or "I do not know anything divine" (Xenophon's version). In writing the *Apology,* the more Plato re-created Socrates' speech, as opposed to merely reporting it, the less valuable it is as evidence for Socrates' philosophy. Further, the more Plato gives his own defense of Socrates, instead of reproducing the essence of Socrates' own self-defense, the worse still. Plato was a great and perceptive and creative philosopher who had the ability to see potentialities in the views of his predecessors and contemporaries to which they themselves were blind. Plato's estimate of the essence of a person's outlook, whether that person be Parmenides or Hippias or Socrates, is certain to be very interesting philosophy. But there is no reason to think that it will be a historically reliable account of the views that the person actually held.

Once again, in philosophy the precise wording matters. And the deeper and more penetrating the diagnosis of someone's philosophical position, the less likely it is to be verbally faithful. The truth in the traditional objection against Plato as a source of evidence that "Plato is too creative a philosopher to be historically reliable" is not that Plato was so creative that he would have irresistibly put his own views into Socrates' mouth (though that may also be right); it is that Plato's sincere efforts to present the essence of Socrates' views are likely to be so philosophically penetrating as to be unreliable guides to the views which Socrates actually expressed and would assent to.

If we assume that Plato's goal was to give the best defense possible for the Socrates that he knew, then what he was trying to do was to defend the character and actitivities of the historical Socrates, and not to reproduce his philosophical views. This is important, because these two goals can easily conflict. Suppose that Socrates did think that he had a certain amount of important moral knowledge. But suppose further that Plato thought that Socrates was wrong about this, that (judged by proper standards, which may have been implicit in Socrates' activity but were not properly appreciated by him) what Socrates had was not knowledge after all. In that case, Plato may well have thought that the best defense of Socrates would involve having him point out that he knows nothing important. Plato could have thought this, even while being aware that Socrates himself thought that he did have some moral knowledge.

Arguments Based on a Comparison of the *Apology* with Other Sources

A very different type of argument has recently been used by Klaus Döring and others to demonstrate the special historical reliability of Plato's *Apology*. These scholars employ the resources of traditional 'source-criticism', comparing the reliability and doctrinal content of the various ancient sources concerning Socrates.[18] In this section I shall focus my attention on Döring's version of the argument, since it is the most fully developed and presented.

Before beginning, I must issue both an apology and a warning. Arguments based on a comparison of sources by their nature depend on the details. In order to refute Döring's case, I shall have to examine various parallels he puts forward, one by one. This will make the exposition more complicated than I would like, and I beg the reader's patience.

Next a warning: the failure of Döring's parallels to establish the historicity of the *Apology* does not by itself prove that no such parallels exist. Other scholars have put forward other examples, and no argument of principle can establish that no convincing set of parallels could be discovered. Since Döring is an outstanding scholar, and his effort to employ source-critical methods to establish the historicity of the *Apology* is the best one so far, the failure of his argument (if I do succeed in refuting it) is indicative. But it is not conclusive.

Methodological Preliminaries

Döring calls his version of the method (following H. Maier): "historical inference from effect to cause".[19] The idea is that Socrates is the prime intellectual influence on the Socratic movement. Socrates himself did not write anything. But his followers did. We possess numerous complete writings by two of his followers, Plato and Xenophon, along with some fragments and testimony of others. If a certain view is shown by a comparison of all of the surviving sources to be characteristically 'Socratic' in the sense of being characteristic of the Socratic circle, then we are entitled to attribute it to Socrates. Where the sources conflict with each other, perhaps further consideration will allow us to reject one as unreliable and accept the other as reflecting the historical Socrates. (Thus Vlastos argues against Xenophon in favor of early Plato in cases of conflict, and Kahn argues against the early Plato in favor of the *Apology*). Where such conflicts cannot be resolved, we must suspend judgement.

This method is both sound and appropriate. But as any scientist or engineer will testify, reasoning from effect to cause within a complex, uncontrolled system can be rather difficult. The case of Socrates and his followers is a case of intellectual influence, during a period of remarkable ferment and creativity. If all of the Socratics believe X or are preoccupied with X, does this show that Socrates himself believed X and was preoccupied with X, or only that Socrates had certain beliefs and preoccupations which, when reflected upon and further developed by his companions, led them to believe X and concern themselves with X? Which of these one thinks is most plausible will depend on the details of the example, but the latter cannot be ruled out *a priori*.

Recall the special difficulty of establishing through indirect means a person's philosophical views, given the importance of the precise verbal formulation in what constitutes those views. Socrates and his followers clearly were, and saw themselves as, a distinctive moral community, which dissented from the dominant surrounding culture in important values. Socrates and his followers thought that most people value money and fame much more highly than they should, and that they value virtue and good character much too little. Socrates and his followers believed that mere reliance on tradition for one's most important beliefs is wrong. Instead, one ought to subject one's own beliefs, and those which are prominent in one's culture, to searching examination. These characteristically Socratic values are important values, and the propositions which express them are philosophical propositions. But as philosophical theses go, they are vague.

Example: Attitude toward Physics

The case of Socrates's attitude toward natural philosophy is instructive. A great historian of Athenian democracy, M. Hansen, has recently argued that Socrates' denial that he takes any serious interest in natural philosophy must have been an ingredient in the historical trial.[20] Hansen bases his argument on similarities between Plato's and Xenophon's defenses of Socrates, which he believes were written independently.

Even if Hansen (following von Arnim 1923) is correct that Plato's and Xenophon's accounts of the trial are independent, any attempt to use that independence to establish Socrates' attitude toward natural philosophy at the time of his trial faces two (by now familiar) problems.

First, Plato's and Xenophon's testimonies count as independent witnesses to the actual trial only if their aims were to be faithful to the trial, or at least to present some of its essential features. If their goal was instead to present the best defense of Socrates they could (regardless of what defense Socrates actually presented), then the fact that they both make Socrates repudiate natural philosophy is evidence of what they both thought about the historical Socrates' philosophical activity and attitudes. It is not good evidence for what went on at the actual trial.

The second problem is that 'denies any serious interest in natural philosophy' is a phrase too vague to be useful in writing the history of philosophy.[21] Plato and Xenophon put very different content into their denials. Plato has Socrates say (in the *Phaedo*) that he used to study physics, but then gave it up completely. Xenophon has Socrates deny that an interest in physics for its own sake is sensible *(Mem.* 1.i.11-15). But Xenophon's Socrates takes cosmology seriously enough to deploy it for ethical purposes in an argument from design.

The commonality between Plato's and Xenophon's accounts is perhaps sufficient for us to say that some sort of disdain or contempt for physics, or for the physicists, was part of the image of the historical Socrates. But what precise philosophical views justified or generated that negative attitude, we cannot know.

Example: Choosing the Good

Consider a series of four propositions:

1. A person should not be frightened by death or loss of fortune, but should rather only be concerned with doing what is right.
2. In acting, a person should always choose the good, i. e. what is most in his or her own interest, properly understood.
3. In acting, a person should always choose the good, i. e. what is morally right.
4. In acting, a person should always choose the good, i. e. what will bring about the best consequences for everyone, all things considered.

Socrates was a person of great moral courage and astonishing self-control. But these are traits of character, and not philosophical opinions. Nonetheless, the method of reasoning from effect to cause, applied to the surviving texts, does suggest that Socrates probably did say things like, "One should always do what is right", and "One should always choose the good". The problem comes in deciding what, if anything, more philosophically precise the historical Socrates had in mind when he made such remarks. On the basis of Plato's texts, scholars have often attributed to the historical Socrates thesis (2), the attitude of ethical egoism. Also on the basis of Plato's texts, scholars have often attributed to the historical Socrates thesis (3), a kind of moral absolutism. Those who have been inclined to find both positions implied by the texts have struggled mightily to show how the two positions can be reconciled within a consistent view. Xenophon's portrait of Socrates suggests position (4), a kind of consequentialism or utilitarianism.

A suitably cautious application of the method of reasoning from effect to cause relieves one of the need to choose between these alternatives. For it is perfectly easy to imagine that Socrates was convinced, and often said, that it is always right to do right, and always good to choose the good, without himself ever having a clear idea about how these apparent truisms should be interpreted and applied. A variety of scenarios are plausible, and we have no grounds to choose between them. Socrates himself may have stuck to the truisms, and it was left to various of his followers to work out one or another version and run with it. Or Socrates may have settled on one version, leaving others for others to explore. Or Socrates may have subscribed to one version during one phase of his philosophical activity, and another version during another phase.

Why Believe in a Unitary Socratic Philosophy?

This last possibility has not been adequately attended to in the literature on the historical Socrates. There is a large body of scholarship on Plato's development, and a large body of scholarship asserting the lack thereof. But the literature on the historical Socrates typically assumes that there is a single, uniform philosophical personality there to be discovered. Yet there is no good reason to make that assumption.

The tradition of scholarship does make two main exceptions to this assumption, but these exceptions do not go far enough. There is first the notorious question whether Socrates experienced an intellectual revolution, abandoning the study of physics for an exclusive concern with values, and with what we would call moral philosophy. I have already expressed scepticism about this. But even if Socrates at some point turned from physics to moral philosophy, there is no reason to suppose that his views in moral philosophy became fully formed and as precise as they would ever be, within a few months of his conversion.

The other exception to the general tendency to ignore questions of Socrates' development belongs to an earlier stratum of scholarship on Socrates. Antisthenes was older than Plato, and attained philosophical prominence sooner. It used to be thought by some that Antisthenes was a better witness to the historical Socrates, in part because he knew Socrates and began his literary production earlier than Plato. (It was also thought that Xenophon was therefore a better witness than Plato, because of Xenophon's presumed borrowings from Antisthenes.)

If Socrates' philosophical views developed significantly, either through changing his mind, or by adding precision and elaboration to views which were already present *in nuce,* it is perfectly possible for different Socratics, even if they *were* all aiming at reliable portraits, to present different images of Socrates. Many of the alleged 'incompatibilities' between Plato's Socrates and Xenophon's of which Vlastos made so much[22] could be reconciled in this way. Any inconsistencies within Xenophon's portrait might also be reconciled on the assumption that Xenophon was drawing on his own memories and on reports of conversations with Socrates which occurred at various times and with varying interlocutors. (As all philosophers know from personal experience, conversations with different interlocutors tend to bring out different aspects of one's views. And there is no guarantee that these different aspects are mutually consistent!)

A cautious and sophisticated application of the method of inference from effect to cause to the case of Socrates must allow for the possibility that the cause in question—Socrates' philosophical personality—may have changed its character over time.

On the other hand, one might argue that this complication does not much affect the question of the reliability of Plato's *Apology.* First, the thought that Socrates' philosophical personality may have changed over time expands the range of possibly historical material in the writings of the Socratics, rather than reducing it. Where the *Apology* contradicts Xenophon or Aeschines or other Platonic writings, the explanation may be, not that the *Apology* is unhistorical or that both conflicting sources are, but rather that both portrayals reflect the historical Socrates, but in different moods or moments. Where the *Apology* agrees with all of our sources, then, we have more reason to suppose that it reflects a strong and enduring trait of the historical Socrates.

Second, if Plato intended his *Apology* to portray Socrates as he really was, Plato will have intended it to portray Socrates at one stage of his life and intellectual development, namely at or near the very end. The whole question of Socrates' philosophical development can be avoided if we take the question of the 'historical Socrates' to be a question about the fully mature Socrates, i. e. the Socrates who stood on trial for his life.

These two arguments have weight. However, the second argument is undermined if one supposes that Plato intended to present the defense speech that Socrates ought to have given rather than to represent the one which Socrates actually gave. Plato was a powerful intellectual personality, surely capable of independent judgment from an early age. What if in his view Socrates' recent changes of mind and revisions in the formulation of his beliefs were mistaken? What if Plato thought that the way Socrates put his moral principles five years before his death was best, though the way he formulated his sense of his own ignorance was better two years later, after his moral views had already changed? If Plato were aiming to present the best defense of Socrates he could, using only formulations which Socrates himself had actually uttered, nonetheless Plato may have given us a portrait which is not a reliable portrait of any one 'Socrates-stage', i. e. of Socrates at any one stage.

The reader may feel that the speculations in the last paragraph are too complicated and elaborate, and have gone too far afield, for us to have good reasons for giving them substantial weight. I agree; that is part of my point. The idea that Socrates changed his mind frequently concerning the precise formulation of his views, and that Plato picked and chose among them for his portrayal of Socrates, is speculative and we have no good grounds for assigning it a particular probability of being correct. But the reverse idea, that Socrates did not change his mind in philosophically crucial respects, is equally speculative and we have no good grounds for assigning it a particular probability either.

The Comparison of Sources on Care of the Soul

The more precisely a statement of Socratic philosophy is formulated, the more difficult it is to attribute it with confidence to the historical Socrates.

Consider this series of propositions:

1. Most people value money too much, and the state of their souls too little.
2. Money is intrinsically neither good nor bad for a person.
3. Only states of the soul are intrinsically either good or bad for a person.
4. The soul is a person's true self.
5. Moral perfection is the only important value.

Döring attributes (4) and (5) to the historical Socrates, on the strength of passages like 29d7-e3, 31b5, and 36c5-d1 in the *Apology,* together with similar expressions elsewhere in Plato and in the other Socratics.[23] These are rather strong and precise philosophical theses. (4) is also a metaphysical thesis, and not (or not merely) a moral one.

The method of reasoning from effect to cause entitles us to conclude that the historical Socrates held thesis (1). Part of what made the Socratic circle different from the rest of society was that they valued money much less and spiritual improvement much more than the dominant culture did.

The possibility of historical development undermines the argument that the historical Socrates held (4) and (5), or even (2) and (3). The process by which Plato and other Socratics came to hold (4) and (5) might have been that they took them over from Socrates. But it equally well might have been that Socrates himself believed something vaguer and weaker, and the stronger theses are a further development by his followers.

Consider an example. If only states of the soul are intrinsically good or bad for a person, and moral perfection is the only important value, then physical health is not an intrinsic or significant good for a human being. Plato and Aristippus and perhaps some other Socratics seem to have deprived physical health of the value given to it by common-sense.[24] In order to explain the origin of their views, do we need to assume that Socrates himself thought that physical health is of no significant value? No we do not. It is enough that Socrates insisted that the state of one's soul is much more important than most people consciously realize. If Socrates also thought, reasonably enough, that physical health is also a significant good, then what may have happened was that Plato and others thought that Socrates did not go far enough, and in depriving physical health of any significant value they further radicalized his thought.

That the historical Socrates attempted to convince the gifted young men whom he met that they were leading thoughtless lives, and that they ought to devote themselves to philosophy and the quest for virtue, is probable. This image of Socrates is conveyed by both Plato and Xenophon, as well as by fragments from the other Socratics, above all Aeschines.[25] But any effort to attribute philosophically precise theses to Socrates is frustrated by the scarcity of sources and the difficulty of inferring a certain precisely formulated doctrine from a biographical anecdote or differently worded expression.

Döring is well aware of these dangers. Yet the evidence he relies upon does not escape them. Döring cites the *Gorgias* (468a ff.) and the *Phaedo* (64a ff.) to supplement the *Apology*.[26] But these dialogues are usually thought to contain a great deal of Plato himself. The motto in the *Phaedo*, 'philosophy is practice for death', can perhaps be used, by reasoning from effect to cause, to confirm that Socrates was concerned with the health of the soul. But we have no particular reason to attribute this motto to the historical Socrates. And if we cannot attribute these words to Socrates, we cannot attribute the confidence in immortality and the exclusive emphasis on the soul which they imply to him either.

In Aeschines' *Alcibiades,* Socrates praises the virtue and foresight of the great leader Themistocles. He humbles Alcibiades, convincing him that he has a great deal to learn before he could hope to match the wisdom of someone like Themistocles.[27] Döring cites the dialogue—rightly—as evidence of Socrates' concern for 'care of the self'.[28] Ample evidence from many sources suggests that Socrates believed that many people think they know things that they do not know, and that realizing their ignorance is a first step toward learning what they need to learn.

But the *Alcibiades* does not support Döring's stronger claim that Socrates thought that moral perfection is the only important thing, and that a person's highest task is the improvement of his soul. To the contrary: as Döring recognizes[29], Themistocles' 'virtue' is conventional Greek virtue. What Socrates praises and Alcibiades envies is the cleverness and prudence which make one an effective leader and promotes worldly success. Perhaps Socrates does tacitly disagree with Themistocles' values, but there is no direct evidence of that in what survives of the text.

Alcibiades thinks that worldly success is the most important value, and Socrates convinces him that a devotion to education and self-improvement is a necessary means to that end. Recognition of one's own ignorance is a doubly instrumental value: it is necessary in order to acquire the devotion to self-improvement which is necessary for success. By helping Alcibiades to realize his own ignorance, Socrates makes him better. But this is because recognition of one's own ignorance is instrumentally valuable, not because it is 'the most important thing', or even just intrinsically good.

Döring cites a scene at the beginning of Phaedo's *Zopyrus* as evidence that care of the soul played a central role for Socrates.[30] This is a scene in which Socrates admits that he has a violently passionate nature, which he has overcome by insight and discipline. This passage confirms ample other evidence that Socrates was renowned for his self-control. But self-control is a feature of Socrates' character, not his doctrines. It is somehow psychologically probable that a person who had Socrates' level of self-control also thought that self-control is a valuable trait. But exactly what place Socrates thought self-control to have in the spectrum of human values is left open by this story in the *Zopyrus.*

According to Döring, Aristippus constitutes an exception among the Socratics.[31] What Aristippus believes is the most important goal in life is not virtue, but pleasure. Döring explains that Aristippus' difference from the others is due to his epistemological doctrine that all we can know are our private sensations.

If we state the characteristically Socratic attitude more vaguely and generally than Döring does, we can see that Aristippus is not an exception. If what

Socrates held and passed on to his companions is a conviction that care of the soul is much more important than most people think it is, and money and fame much less important, then Aristippus fits right in. Pleasure is after all a soul-state. Neither money nor the good opinion of others are intrinsically valuable, on Aristippus' view. Of course pleasure is a popular value; both ordinary people and tyrants were thought to seek pleasure. But Aristippus' view need not have been a popular, non-Socratic view. He may well have thought that a great deal of virtue, including self-control, were needed in order to maximize pleasure. The *Protagoras* and the *Philebus* suggest that Plato thought this.

Socrates held that virtue is more valuable and worthy of more attention than most people thought. Did he also hold that virtue is the most valuable good and the only thing good in itself, or did he hold that virtue is valuable instrumentally, e. g. for its help in maximizing pleasure? The mixed and fragmentary state of the evidence does not allow us to decide.

Finally, the case of Antisthenes. Döring cites the statement by Antisthenes in Xenophon's *Symposium:* "I believe that men have their wealth and poverty, not in their homes but in their souls" (IV, 34). There is the problem how much of this statement should be attributed to the historical Antisthenes, or rather to Xenophon. But for the method of working back from effect to cause, this is a subtlety we can hope to leave aside. What is important for us is whether the character Antisthenes implies here that virtue is the only or the most important good.

In the remainder of his speech Antisthenes defends his claim by pointing out that many people who have great quantities of material goods do not have enough to satisfy their desires, whereas he, who has little, has enough. Antisthenes does not explicitly define what he means by 'wealth' or what he understands to be 'good'. But what his remarks imply is an instrumental view of wealth, according to which wealth is what enables one to satisfy one's desires. Antisthenes' wealth is in his soul, because what enables him to satisfy his desires is the fact that his desires are few and rationally controllable. The view of the good which is suggested by his remarks is that the good, for human beings, is desire-satisfaction. Desire-satisfaction is the goal for which wealth, whether material or spiritual, is instrumental. Yet desire-satisfaction is not virtue; it is not even (usually) a state of the soul. Desire-satisfaction is a relational complex involving a state of the soul (the desire) and another state-of-affairs which satisfies it. Of course, what precise view (if any) Antisthenes had about the metaphysics of desire-satisfaction is hidden by the mists of time. But the view of virtue which is implied by this passage is that virtue is an instrumental good. The idea that virtue is the most important instrumental good was clearly circulating in the Socratic movement. Whether the historical Socrates

himself thought that virtue is the most important instrumental good, or
something weaker or stronger, is impossible to tell.

Socratic Ignorance

In the *Apology* Socrates denies that he has wisdom, and that he knows anything fine and good (21c-d). Most recent interpreters put Socratic ignorance
at the center of their portraits.[32] Döring lists Socratic ignorance as the second
of the "main ideas" which the *Apology* allows us to attribute to the historical
Socrates. According to Döring, Socrates is convinced that "since it is impossible for a human being to attain secure knowledge of what the good is, he must
continually strive afresh to clarify, insofar as he can, what the good is here and
now".[33]

The historical evidence concerning Socrates' ignorance is similar to the evidence for his emphasis on moral perfection. We have good reason to attribute certain characteristic activities and intellectual interests to the historical
Socrates, but no grounds for confidence in attributing to him anything like a
precise philosophical thesis.

Socrates' claims of ignorance in the *Apology* are notoriously unclear. What
he says is that, in contrast to a certain politician, he knows that he knows
nothing fine and good (21d). And unlike craftsmen, who know many fine
things, he knows almost nothing (22d-e). What kinds of knowledge count as
'fine and good'? What little bit of knowledge is left open by the phrase 'almost
nothing'? The answers to these questions are far from obvious.

Döring's version of Socratic ignorance is far more precise than the text of
the *Apology*. Socrates says nothing about 'knowledge of the good' (as opposed
to 'knowing good things'), and he says nothing about 'secure knowledge' (as
opposed to mere 'knowledge'). According to Socrates, neither he nor anyone
he has yet encountered know these 'fine and good things'. He does not say that
knowledge of them is impossible for human beings, as Döring's interpretation
requires.[34] Whether the Socratic search for wisdom was viewed by him (or
Plato) and in principle completable or not, is an enormous question which is
not settled by the text of the *Apology*.

Moreover, what can be clearly inferred from Socrates' claims does not
quite support Döring's account. The fine and good things of which Socrates
disclaims knowledge at 21d are things which some politician has claimed to
know. But politicians do not characteristically claim to know what 'the good'
is, in the sense of being able to answer the general Socratic question, 'What is
the good?'. They characteristically claim to know whether it is good to go to
war or make a treaty or impose a tax, or to prosecute and convict someone

for a crime. Some politicians may claim certainty for their opinions, but they need not.

There is a distinction between having great confidence in one's opinions, and claiming certainty (though many politicians will not be sophisticated enough to make that distinction). In at least some cases, Socrates has great confidence in his own evaluative views: e. g. that he, Socrates, deserves to be acquitted. Would Socrates claim to know this with certainty? The text does not yield an answer to this question.

The craftsmen know something 'fine'. Socrates does not say that they know something 'good', and perhaps this omission is significant. In any case, what craftsmen know is how to make certain things or produce certain results. Socrates claims to have little or no knowledge of that kind. But this sort of ignorance is very different from a lack of certain knowledge of what the good is.

Döring's interpretation of Socratic ignorance is, therefore, not supported by the text of the *Apology* taken by itself. But the question remains whether his interpretation, or some other reasonably precise interpretation, is supported by the *Apology* and the surviving evidence from the minor Socratics taken together.

Socrates went around questioning peoples' claims to knowledge, and showing those claims to be unfounded. This aspect of Socrates' activity stands out in our sources. From this it follows that Socrates probably thought that rhetors and rhapsodies and maybe even Homer did not know what they claimed to know. This is one important epistemological opinion which we can attribute to the historical Socrates.

If the rhetors and even the poets do not know what they claim to know, then knowledge and expertise must be harder to acquire than most Athenians recognize. One natural effect of Socrates' activity would be to raise the standards for knowledge, and also to raise, in a pressing way, the question what the proper standards are. Thus one effect of Socrates' philosophizing would naturally be that his followers were concerned with epistemological issues, including scepticism. But here as elsewhere the method of inferring from effect to cause yields imprecise results. Socrates cast the standards for knowledge that were dominant in his culture into question, in such a way that his followers were still discussing and disagreeing about these standards for decades after his death. But what Socrates himself actually thought the proper standards were; and whether or to what extent he thought he met them; or even whether Socrates had clear and consistent views on this question over time, the evidence of his followers does not permit us to decide.

Döring argues that the minor Socratics generally agreed with the Socrates of the *Apology* that knowledge about moral concepts is impossible. Furthermore, they went beyond him in advocating a global scepticism: we cannot

have certain knowledge about what anything is. This interpretation of the Socratics' attitude toward knowledge permits two slightly different arguments
for the historical faithfulness of the *Apology*. (1) Since scepticism about moral
concepts is common to all, this must be the historical core which we should
attribute to Socrates himself.[35] (2) Since the global scepticism of the Socratics
is a generalization of the moral scepticism of the *Apology,* the former is probably a historical development of the latter. This suggests that the moral scepticism portrayed in the *Apology* belonged to the historical Socrates.[36]

But the various negative attitudes towards knowledge on the part of the
minor Socratics are generally not good evidence that they denied anyone can
have 'wisdom concerning the greatest matters', as Socrates puts it in the *Apology.* The evidence Döring cites from the other Socratics as confirmation of Socratic ignorance is really just evidence of a pervasive concern among the Socratics with epistemological questions.

Antisthenes is said to have denied that we can have knowledge of essences
(frags. 50, 44A Caizzi). This is a denial that we can have knowledge of the sort
of thing which Plato thought we needed to know in order to have wisdom.
This is evidence—however, shaky, as later testimony about earlier philosophers always is—of a philosophical disagreement about knowledge between
Plato and Antisthenes.

But how and whether these fragments bear on Socratic moral ignorance is
not at all clear. These fragments do not mention moral concepts at all. They
do not say or imply that Antisthenes thought that knowledge of essences was
necessary for wisdom; or that Socrates thought so; or that either Antisthenes
or Socrates thought that they knew nothing fine.

Antisthenes is portrayed as a sceptic only about essences. He could recognize things when he saw them (fr. 44), and he could explain what things are
like, even if not what they *are.* There is no evidence, either here or in the ethical fragments, that Antisthenes saw himself as lacking in wisdom. (Recall that
the Socrates of Plato's *Republic* cannot say what the good is, but only what it
is like!)

When asked what one must do to become good, Antisthenes is said to have
replied, "Learn from those who know that your faults are to be avoided" (fr.
175). This advice implies that there are those who know, from whom one can
learn. This is not the advice of a moral sceptic.

Aristippus is said to have held that we can only know our private sensations.
If we can only know our private sensations, then there is a lot we cannot know.
Aristippus' view is scepticism of a kind. But Aristippus apparently thought
that his view does allow us to know what the good is, namely pleasure.[37]
Therefore Aristippus' scepticism seemed to him compatible with knowledge
of the good, and even wisdom.

If the Socratics, though disagreeing with each other about other matters, all agreed that no one knows anything fine and good, one might suppose that they got this latter view from Socrates. But despite certain elements of scepticism, neither Antisthenes or Aristippus—nor of course Plato—have inherited from Socrates the kind of scepticism which the Socratic ignorance of the *Apology* seems to represent.

Döring also cites the case of Euclides. Euclides is said to have attacked the method of reasoning by analogy. What this shows is that Euclides concerned himself with epistemology. If, as seems plausible, the historical Socrates characteristically reasoned by analogy, this may also show that Euclides had reason to think that Socrates was more poorly off, epistemologically, than Socrates himself realized. But it is no evidence at all that Socrates thought himself to be ignorant.

A fragment of Aeschines provides the strongest confirmation in the surviving Socratic literature of the *Apology's* Socratic ignorance:

> Through the love I felt for Alcibiades I experienced a kind of Bacchic inspiration. When the Bacchants are filled with the god's power they draw milk and honey from wells which do not even yield water to others. I have no learning to teach anyone and help him in that way, but I thought that through just being with him my love for him might make him better. (fr.11 Dittmar)

Döring rightly argues that Aeschines' Socrates is especially similar to the Socrates of the *Apology*.[38] Of course two out of seven are a weak consensus. A clear parallel between three or four sources would make a stronger case; and it would help if the remaining sources were silent on the issue rather than conflicting with the first group. Aeschines' Socrates says that he has nothing to teach. But Antisthenes and Aristippus and Xenophon's Socrates all *do* seem to think that they have something to teach.[39]

But the important difficulty is that, even if we assume that Aeschines and Plato meant their portraits to capture the truth about Socrates, we have no way to decide between two alternatives. Do Plato and Aeschines make Socrates declare his ignorance because the historical Socrates actually did declare his ignorance? Or do they make him declare his ignorance because they, i. e. Plato and Aeschines, think that he was ignorant (and maybe even that he was ignorant by his own standards, or by the standards implicit in his activity, even though he did not realize it)?

The evidence of Plato's dialogues suggests that Plato thought Socrates was quite ignorant. The historical Socrates was most unlikely to have met the standards for wisdom which Plato lays out in the *Republic*.[40] If Plato thought that Socrates knew nothing fine and good, and Plato was attempting in the *Apology* to give the best defense of Socrates that could plausibly be given, then

Plato had good reason to make Socrates in the *Apology* declare his ignorance. This is so, even if the historical Socrates thought that he knew some important moral truths, and aggressively said so to the jury at the trial.

Like Plato's *Apology,* the Aeschines fragment can easily be read as Aeschines' own diagnosis of Socrates' condition. Suppose Aeschines, like Plato, thought that Socrates was ignorant. Socrates' ignorance raises a problem for his defense to which Plato in his *Apology* does not adequately respond: if Socrates is so ignorant, how can his influence be beneficial? If Socrates does not know that the knows anything fine and good, is it not criminally negligent of him to seek out and influence impressionable young boys?

Plato's response in the *Apology* to these questions is that Socrates passes on his conviction of ignorance, and coming to realize that one does not know what one does not know is enormously beneficial. No sensible person will find this response very comforting. There is a great deal more to human thought and behavior than one's assessment of one's epistemological position. What the Athenian jurors wanted to know, and what any sensible person would want to know, is whether association with Socrates made his young companions more or less likely to strike their fathers and mutilate herms. What Socrates says in the *Apology* leaves this central concern unaddressed.

The fragment of Aeschines does address this concern. What Aeschines says is that although Socrates had nothing to teach, simply his presence and his love for his companions made them better, as if by a kind of inspiration. This response is not very philosophically satisfying. But unlike Plato's, Aeschines' response does address the issue, because 'made them better' here means 'morally better'. Moreover, Aeschines' appeal to inspiration will have been much more persuasive in his cultural context than in ours.

Aeschines is saying what Xenophon says in the *Memorabilia,* that while Alcibiades was with Socrates he was a better person than he would otherwise have been, and than he later became.[41] The Socrates of Aeschines' fragment 11 resembles the Socrates of Plato's *Apology,* but he also resembles the Socrates of Xenophon's *Memorabilia.* And Xenophon's Socrates is regarded by Döring and others as a dogmatic Socrates, incompatible with the portrayal in the *Apology.*

In Plato's *Apology* Socrates contrasts 'a sort of human wisdom', which he says he has, with 'more than human' or divine wisdom, which neither he nor anyone whom he has met possesses. A parallel contrast is attributed to Socrates in Xenophon's *Memorabilia,* between those matters which it is given to human beings to understand by their own efforts, such as carpentry and arithmetic, and those matters which are dark to human beings and known only to the gods, such as whether it is wise to join the army or to marry a certain person (I.1.6-9).

This parallel raises the question whether the two authors are presenting somewhat different interpretations of something the historical Socrates actually said. As I have said before, it is quite possible that they are, and also quite possible that they are not. A loose parallel between two authors is suggestive, without being enough to warrant confidence.[42] But let us suppose, for the sake of discussion, that the historical Socrates did habitually draw a contrast between human and divine wisdom, and maintained that neither he nor any other human being known to him has divine wisdom, which is the kind that really matters. Can we build on this supposition to infer anything very precise or interesting about Socrates' philosophical views?

Unfortunately, we cannot. As I discussed earlier, what Plato makes Socrates say in the *Apology* is remarkably under-specified. Socrates tells us virtually nothing about what kind of knowledge would count as 'fine and good'. He admits—but does not seem sure—that awareness of one's own ignorance is 'a kind of human wisdom'. He later says that craftsmen do know things, namely their crafts. Is knowledge of a particular craft a kind of human wisdom also? Socrates does not say, nor does he say anything which implies an answer.

Scholars have been naturally and appropriately ingenious in supplying detailed interpretations of what Socrates' contrast between divine and human wisdom amounts to. But given Plato's presumably intentional reticence on this topic in the text of the *Apology,* these interpretations are inherently speculative. People like Vlastos and Döring and others have given philosophically powerful and precise interpretations of what the contrast between divine and human wisdom involves. Most of these would have been interesting and worthy contrasts for the historical Socrates to have drawn—though of course they are mutually incompatible. But for any one scholar to believe that his philosophically powerful and precise interpretation is not only the correct specification of what Plato had in mind, but also reaches through the mediation of Plato's interpretation of Socrates to be the correct specification of what the historical Socrates had in mind, would be to have remarkable confidence in one's own powers of divination.

Perhaps it will be useful for me to close with a reminder, not directed at any one scholar's arguments in particular, but applicable to many different arguments in general, of just how slim and fragmentary our evidence for classical antiquity often is, and how dramatically this affects the degree of confidence we are entitled to have in our conclusions.

There is, after all, an all-too-human temptation in historical scholarship to underestimate what happens when probabilities multiply. Let us imagine an honest and self-critical scholar of Socrates who will admit that this interpretation of Socrates' ignorance in the *Apology* has a 40% chance of being right. The other, say, 19 interpretations which are not incompatible with the evidence each have significantly poorer probabilities, as judged by our imagined scholar. Since the nearest competitor to his interpretation has a probability of (let us say) only 20%, his interpretation is much the most likely of the group.

Suppose further that our scholar believes the odds that Plato was trying to give an accurate portrayal of Socrates' thought and character are 60%. And suppose he thinks the odds that Plato got it reasonably right are also 60%. These are generous odds. I myself would not give any detailed interpretation of Socrates' ignorance a 40% chance of being correct, and I do not believe that it is more likely than not that Plato's aim was an accurate portrayal of Socrates or that he got it right. But a more optimistic scholar than I am, a Vlastos or a Döring or a Kahn, might well assign these odds. Even so, on such an optimistic view, our imagined scholar must admit that the odds of his account of Socratic ignorance being true of the historical Socrates are merely 40% times 60% times 60%, or 14.4%.[43] Not a very inspiring number.[44]

Notes

1. The best survey of these issues is now Kahn 1996, ch.1.

2. Kahn 1996, 97. Whether 'a true picture of Socrates as Plato saw him' is a reliable guide to the historical Socrates himself is of course a further question. (On this see notes 1–12 below.) Concerning this question Kahn is cagey. He says that the *Apology* is "the most reliable guide of all our testimonies concerning Socrates" (79) and that "insofar, then, as we can know anything with reasonable probability concerning Socrates' own conception of philosophy, we must find this in the *Apology*" (79). These two statements are compatible with an admission that the *Apology* is not a reliable guide to the historical Socrates (the other testimonies are even worse), and that we cannot know anything at all with reasonable probability concerning Socrates' own conception of philosophy.

3. Döring 1998. This fine monograph reached me as I was making the last revisions to this paper, and so I have not been able to take full account of it here. Döring's basic position on the Socratic question remains unchanged from his earlier writings.

4. Döring 1992, 3; cf. Döring 1987.

5. Vlastos 1971, 4 = Vlastos 1995, 6. The core of this argument is endorsed in a footnote to the book: Vlastos 1991, n. 5. See also Vlastos 1989, 1393 = Vlastos 1995, 25.

6. For a list of scholars on each side of this question, see Brickhouse and Smith 1989 n. 9 and n. 19.

7. For example it is not as extreme as that of Gigon 1947.

8. Kahn 1996, 88–89.

9. *Poetics* 1447b11. One textual complication deserves mention. A report in Athenaeus regarding Aristotle's lost work *On the Poets* uses the phrase 'Socratic dialogues' (διάλογοι) rather than 'Socratic discourses' (λόγοι) *(De Poet.* Fr. 3 Ross = Rosel 72 = Ath. 505c). But the word διάλογος might easily have been introduced by Athenaeus or his source, so this parallel by itself is not good evidence that Aristotle recognized a genre which included Socratic dialogues but not Socratic speeches.

10. Kahn 1996, 88.

11. Kahn 1996, 88.

12. (1) This view is not popular; A. Patzer goes so far as to say that no one believes it nowadays (1984a, 442). But W. D. Ross seems to have endorsed it: he claims that it is improbable that Plato would have much altered the "main lines" of Socrates' actual speech (1933, 23 = Patzer 1984b, 238). (2) Vlastos 1971, 3. (3) A. Patzer 1984a, in Patzer 1984b.

13. An argument similar to Kahn's (though less cautiously expressed), which fails for this same reason, can be found in H. Patzer 1965, 26.

14. I quote the version reprinted in Vlastos 1971, 3. The original 1957–58 publication differs slightly: see the bracketed phrases in Vlastos 1995, 6.

15. As Ross realized (1933, 23 = Patzer 1984b, 238).

16. Allen 1980, 5–6. See also Lezl 1992, 82.

17. In the Introduction to his study and commentary to Plato's *Apology* (edited and completed by S. Slings), Father E. de Strycker, S. J. argues that Plato's aim cannot have been to reproduce Socrates' actual speech, since the elaborate literary character of the *Apology* can only be Platonic (1994, 6–7). Yet de Strycker concludes by expressing his faith in the Socratic content within the Platonic form: "For the rest, I would dare to assert that there is, on the one hand, no single sentence in the Platonic *Apology* that Socrates could not actually have pronounced, and on the other, that the published work contains no passage so specifically un-Platonic that it cannot be Plato's work" (1994, 8). It is a sign of de Strycker's meticulous scholarly honesty that he marks this assertion as 'daring'. (Wilamowitz expressed basically the same view [1919, II, 52–53] in vastly more confident tones.)

18. Kahn employs these methods to argue against the historical reliability of "early Plato" apart from the *Apology,* and thus uses them in an indirect way to argue for the historicity of the *Apology.*

19. Döring 1992, 2; Maier 1913, 153.

20. 1995, 6. Hansen traces ten items back to Socrates' trial, based on similarities between Plato's and Xenophon's accounts. Of these only one concerns Socrates' philosophy: his denial of any serious interest in natural philosophy (Hansen cites Pl. *Ap.* 26D and Xen. *Mem.* 1.1.11–15; *Ap.* 19C–D should be added).

21. Of course, writing the history of philosophy was not Hansen's aim; his prime interest is the history of Athenian democracy.

22. Vlastos 1971, 1–2; Vlastos 1991, 99–106, 288–300.

23. Döring 1987, 77, 84–87.

24. Xenophon presents an argument according to which nothing is good simpliciter, but only good *for something (Mem.* III.viii; cf. IV.ii.35–36). This passage in Xenophon is evidence that the Socratic circle was actively exploring the question of what is or is not intrinsically valuable. The method of reasoning from effect to cause can allow us to conclude that Socrates' philosophizing was of such a sort as to provoke this topic of investigation, but it cannot allow us to infer that he personally subscribed to one or another answer.

25. For Xenophon, see above all his conversations with Euthydemus in Book IV; for Aeschines, the *Alcibiades.* A fragment of Euclides (fr. 14D) cited by Döring (1987,

p. 86) implies that most men care too much about food and clothing, and too little about their attitudes. It does *not* imply that food and clothing are unimportant.

26. Döring 1987, 85.

27. Fr. 8 Dittmar; 50 Giannantoni.

28. Döring 1987, 85; see esp. fr. 8, 1. 52 Dittmar; 50, 1. 42 Giannantoni.

29. 1984, 20–21.

30. Döring 1987, 85. The evidence for the *Zopyrus* is presented and discussed in Rossetti 1980.

31. 1987, 86–87.

32. See e. g. Nehamas 1985 and 1986, reprinted in Nehamas 1999.

33. 1981, 84.

34. Döring cites 20c1-3, d6-e3, 23a5-6, and b3-4 as evidence. But in these texts Socrates says only that no one (or no one whom he has met) has this sort of wisdom, not that in principle no human being could ever have it. At 20d6-e3 he even holds out the possibility that some people might have it! (Of course, how ironically to take this statement is a delicate matter.)

35. This is the argument stressed in Döring 1987 (see esp. p. 90).

36. This argument is more explicitly present in Döring 1998 (156).

37. D. L. II, 87–88. Attributing this view to Aristippus himself requires that we accept, as Döring does, later reports concerning the Cyrenaics as evidence for the view of Aristippus. Thus Döring also thinks that Aristippus' scepticism was combined with the claim to have a criterion of truth (1987, 89).

38. 1987, 90. See also Döring 1984.

39. Concerning Xenophon's Socrates, see Morrison 1994.

40. Note that the character Socrates in the *Republic* probably also does not meet the standards for wisdom he sets out. Döring contrasts the Socrates of the *Apology* with the Socrates of the other Platonic dialogues, on the grounds that the latter does know what the former does not. But this is not clear. The Socrates of the *Republic* has a strong opinion concerning what justice is, but he cannot define the good. Judged by his own standards, does the Socrates of the *Republic* know anything noble? Is he wise?

41. *Mem.* I.ii.24. This and related texts are discussed in Morrison 1994.

42. Kahn would rule out any argument based on parallels between Xenophon and Plato on the grounds that Xenophon is dependent on Plato, so that he is not an independent witness. To this two brief responses: (1) Many of the examples of dependence which Kahn lists in his appendix (393–401) are not convincing. The strongest case for dependence is the one made by A. Patzer (1984a) for the dependence of certain features of Xenophon's account of dialectic on Plato. (2) But more importantly, even if Xenophon's account is dependent on Plato in some places, indeed in all of the places where Kahn finds dependence along with others, this does not mean that Xenophon's account of Socrates is of no independent value, as Kahn mistakenly argues. First, Xenophon may well have chosen to borrow certain material from Plato (or Antisthenes, or whomever), because what he finds in that author squares well with his own memories of Socrates and his general impression from years of conversations with other companions of Socrates about their beloved mentor. Second, from the fact that Xenophon's account derives from Plato's in some places and for some features, it does

not follow that Xenophon's account derives from Plato's in all places and in all features. And so long as the latter is false, Xenophon's account has independent value. Kahn's strongly dismissive conclusion overlooks principles familiar from textual criticism. An eclectic manuscript which derives largely from lost archetypes, but partially from one surviving archetype, has independent value in constituting a text.

43. This particular calculation assumes that the component probabilities are independent. But even if they are not, the basic trend remains.

44. Thanks are due to Helen Lang, Hilary Mackey, Ineke Sluiter, Harvey Yunis, and the readers for this journal, for helpful written comments which led to welcome improvements.

Bibliography

Allen, R. E. (1980): *Socrates and Legal Obligation*. Minneapolis.

von Arnim, H. (1923): *Xenophons Memorabilien und Apologie des Sokrates*. Copenhagen.

Brickhouse, T. and N. Smith (1989): *Socrates on Trial*. Princeton.

de Strycker, E. (1994): *Plato's Apology of Socrates: A literary and philosophical study with a running commentary*. Leiden.

Döring, K. (1984): "Der Sokrates des Aeschines von Sphettos and die Frage nach dem historischen Sokrates", *Hermes* 112, 16–30.

———. (1981): "Der Sokrates der Platonischen Apologie und die Frage nach dem historischen Sokrates", *Wfirzburger Jahrbiicher far die Altertumswissenschaft, Neue Folge*, 14, 75–94.

———. (1992): "Die Philosophie des Sokrates", *Gymnasium* 1992, 1–16.

———. (1998): "Sokrates, die Sokratiker und die von ihnen begründeten Traditionen", in H. Flashar, ed., *Grundriss der Geschichte der Philosophie: Die Philosophie der Antike*, Band 211, 141–364.

Gigon, O. (1947): *Sokrates*. Bern.

Hansen, M. (1995): *The Trial of Socrates—from the Athenian Point of View*. Royal Danish Academy of Sciences and Letters. Historisk-filosofiske Meddelelser 71. Copenhagen.

Kahn, C. (1996): *Plato and the Socratic Dialogue: The philosophical use of a literary form*. Cambridge.

Lezl, W. (1992): "Il processo a Socrate in due libri recenti", Universita di Firenze, *Annali del dipartimento di filosofia*, VIII, 1992, Florence.

Maier, H. (1913): *Sokrates. Sein Werk and seine geschichtliche Stellung*. Tubingen.

Morrison, D. (1994): "Xenophon's Socrates as Teacher", in P. Vander Waerdt, ed., *The Socratic Movement*, Ithaca, 181–208.

Nehamas, A. (1985): "Meno's Paradox and Socrates as a Teacher", *Oxford Studies in Ancient Philosophy 3*, 1–30.

———. (1986): "Socratic Intellectualism", *Proceedings of the Boston* Colloquium *in Ancient Philosophy 2*, 274–285.

———. (1999): *Virtues of Authenticity:* Essays *on Plato and Socrates*. Princeton.

Patzer, A. (1984a): "Sokrates als Philosoph", in Patzer 1984b, 434–452.

———, ed. (1984b): *Der historische Sokrates*. Darmstadt.

Patzer, H. (1965): "Die philosophische Bedeutung der Sokratesgestalt in den platonischen Dialogen", in K. Flasch, ed., *Parusia: Studien zur Philosophie Platons und zur Problemgeschichte des Platonismus,* Frankfurt, 21–43.

Ross, W. D. (1933): "The problem of Socrates", *Proceedings of the Classical Association,* 30, 7–24.

Rossetti , L. (1980): "Richerche sui `dialoghi socratici' di Fedone e di Euclide", *Hermes* 108, 183–200.

Vlastos, G. (1957–58): "The Paradox of Socrates", *Queen's Quarterly* 64, 296–516.

———. ed. (1971): *The Philosophy of Socrates.* Garden City, NY.

———. (1989): Review of Brickhouse and Smith, *Socrates on Trial, Times Literary Supplement,* No. 4, 524, Dec. 15, 1989, p. 1393.

———. (1991): *Socrates: Ironist and Moral Philosopher.* Ithaca.

———. (1995): *Studies in Greek Philosophy II.* Ed. D. Graham. Princeton.

Wilamowitz-Moellendorff, U. (1919): *Platon.* Berlin.

7

Was Socrates against Democracy?[1]

T. H. Irwin

The Significance of the Trial of Socrates

IT IS DIFFICULT TO RESIST THE TEMPTATION to introduce Socrates to students by discussing Plato's *Apology*. But however tempting this may be, it has the disadvantage of presenting us with some historical questions that are difficult to answer. Is the *Apology* historically accurate? Are any of our other sources on the trial of Socrates historically accurate? Was Socrates prosecuted for religious reasons, or for political reasons, or for both sorts of reasons? Did many Athenians believe that he was an opponent of democracy? Was he in fact an opponent of democracy?

These questions are difficult to answer because of the simple fact that we lack the evidence that would justify complete confidence in any answers to these questions. We have no contemporary accounts of the trial that would allow us to confirm or to correct the *Apology*. Some sources that seem to offer us plain statements of fact turn out on further examination to be less straightforward than they seem.

This situation is familiar to historians of ancient Greece, who are used to weighing probabilities on the basis of their assessment of the value of fragmentary and conflicting sources. The trial of Socrates, however, has produced an unusual degree of disagreement among modern critics about which evidence is reliable and which is open to suspicion. For any critic who treats a given source as a sound basis for historical reconstruction, we can find another critic who regards it as a fabrication.

A sceptical position on the historical facts might be right. Perhaps we simply know too little to decide whether the *Apology* or some other source should be trusted. If this is the right verdict on our evidence, we can at least free ourselves from some pseudo-history about Socrates. But if we can give reasonable, though disputable, answers to some of our questions, we might be better able to understand the impression that Socrates made on his contemporaries.[2] Though it would be a mistake to focus entirely on the trial and death of Socrates, as though nothing else about his life and philosophical activity could have mattered to the Athenians, it is not altogether surprising that some modern writers have treated this dramatic episode in Socrates' life as a means of understanding his significance.[3]

It is useful, in any case, to examine the available evidence on Socrates' trial so that we can avoid some rash inferences. Some have drawn sweeping conclusions about the stupidity of Athenians, the vices of Athenian democracy, or even the vices of democracy in general. In considering these partisan verdicts we need to remind ourselves that (if we believe the *Apology*) Socrates was convicted by a fairly narrow margin. Since it was quite a close case, it may not betray any deep and inevitable conflict between Socrates and Athens; and we know so little about the trial that it is peculiarly unwise to draw large conclusions from it.

According to one view, the trial is significant because it reveals Socrates' anti-democratic outlook, and the Athenians' reaction to it. This view may be expressed in three claims.[4]

1. Socrates was prosecuted, and the prosecution succeeded, mainly because many Athenians suspected him of having influenced leading members of the Thirty, the oligarchic regime that ruled Athens in 404-3.
2. The suspicions were correct. Critias and other leading oligarchs believed that Socrates advocated oligarchy, and their belief encouraged them in their anti-democratic activities.
3. The influence rested on a correct understanding of Socrates. For Socrates' political views, correctly understood, implied that an oligarchic regime such as the Thirty was better than the democracy that it replaced.

The first two claims require mostly historical argument. The third requires some philosophical argument, since it depends partly on interpretation of Plato's dialogues. All three claims are open to fatal objections. I will discuss all three claims, and in the course of this discussion will answer the initial questions about Socrates.

The Charges against Socrates

According to the Platonic Socrates, the prosecutors charged that he committed injustice by corrupting the young men and by not recognizing the gods whom the city recognized, but new and different divine beings (*Ap.* 24b8–c1). Though Socrates does not directly quote the indictment,[5] the source that purports to quote it directly gives us the same two counts in the reverse order.[6] Socrates answers the two formal charges, and he connects them with the informal charges of his 'older accusers' (18de), which contain similar allegations (19b). He does not, therefore, confine himself to the indictment, but goes back to the circumstances that led to it.

Socrates' description of these circumstances omits events that, in the view of some modern critics, aroused the hostility of many Athenians towards him. According to these critics, the formal charges do not state the main reason why Socrates was prosecuted, or the main reason why a majority of the jury voted to convict him. These critics believe that Socrates was prosecuted and convicted because of his association with some leading members of the regime of the Thirty.[7]

The evidence for the political dimension of the trial comes from outside the *Apology*.[8] Xenophon mentions an 'accuser' who alleged that Socrates caused his associates to despise the established laws, and recalled that he was a companion of Critias, one of the Thirty, and Alcibiades, the most dangerously uncontrollable citizen under the democracy (*Mem.* i 2.9–12). If 'the accuser' was one of the accusers at the trial, the trial had an explicit political dimension.

Other evidence for the political dimension appears in a speech by Aeschines, delivered in 345. Aeschines reminds the jury of an incident that he takes to be a matter of common knowledge: 'You put to death Socrates the sophist, because he was exposed as the educator of Critias, one of the Thirty who overthrew the democracy' (in *Timarchum* 173).

Roughly, then, we may say that the *Apology* and the purported official indictment present religious and moral charges, and that Xenophon and Aeschines imply a political dimension. We ought to ask how credible these different sources are.

Evidence for the Political Dimension

We can deal most briefly with the credibility of the two texts—from Xenophon and from Aeschines—that offer us specific evidence for a political dimension.

Xenophon offers us good evidence only if the 'accuser' he quotes was an actual accuser at the trial. But we cannot simply assume the authenticity of the 'accuser'. Many critics suppose that Xenophon is drawing on Polycrates' pamphlet against Socrates, probably written at least five years after the trial.[9] We have no direct access to Polycrates' pamphlet, but we have some reason to believe that he was careless about historical accuracy. Favorinus accuses him of an anachronism (Diog. Laert. ii 39).

A further doubt about Polycrates' attack arises from the earliest dateable explicit reference to it, in a speech of Isocrates. According to this speech, Polycrates' attack on Socrates for his association with Alcibiades is an inept innovation, because no one was aware of Alcibiades' having been educated by Socrates.[10] We should not rashly assume that Isocrates is telling the truth; but his objection to Polycrates would be strange if the association with Alcibiades had been well known as a ground of objection to Socrates. If, then, Xenophon's 'accuser' is Polycrates, we cannot rely on the 'accuser' for an accurate account of what was said or thought at Socrates' trial.

Nor should we trust Aeschines without question. He is trying to incite the jury to punish a companion of Demosthenes; and he claims that Demosthenes attacks supporters of democracy who exercise their right of equal speech (*isêgoria*). He reminds them that they put Socrates to death for being a companion of an earlier opponent of democracy.[11] This story is helpful to Aeschines' case; for, as he presents it, it shows that the Athenians had been ready in the past to take strong action against opponents of democracy. The fact that it helps his case does not show that it is false; but it shows that we ought to hesitate, in the absence of corroborative evidence, to accept it as true. Aeschines probably would not have mentioned the example of Socrates if he believed that the jurors would immediately reject it; but it would not matter to him if they would have rejected it on careful consideration and inquiry. We can assume, then, that this story would not evidently contradict any impression that the jury might retain, on the spur of the moment, about events of over fifty years earlier. That does not make it good evidence for the view that the Athenians in 399 were moved by these suspicions to prosecute and to convict Socrates.

Xenophon and Aeschines, therefore, do not provide good evidence for a political dimension in the trial of Socrates. Since these are the only sources that even appear to offer evidence for the political dimension, we have no good evidence for it.

Many critics find this conclusion too hasty. Three further points in favour of the political dimension have been presented:

(a) The admitted fact (if we accept Plato's dialogues on this point) that Critias, Charmides, and Alcibiades were among the associates of Socrates must have influenced both the prosecutors and the jury, even if we have no direct evidence on this point.[12]

(b) We can explain why we lack direct evidence. The amnesty of 403 would have prevented a prosecution of Socrates on explicitly political grounds and would have prevented explicit mention of his politically unreliable associates.

(c) The religious and moral charges mentioned in the purported official indictment do not explain why an Athenian jury would have voted for the death penalty. Something else must have influenced the jury; specifically, the political dimension must have influenced them.

'Must haves' are the last refuge of historians whose devotion to a thesis outruns their evidence for it. No doubt, they are sometimes legitimate; but do we need them to understand the trial of Socrates?

The Amnesty

To evaluate the argument that appeals to the amnesty of 403, we need to consider the unfortunately complex and puzzling evidence. This amnesty, following the restoration of the democracy after the fall of the Thirty, prohibited 're-calling evils' (*mnêsikakein*) from the past ([Aristotle] *Ath. Pol.* 39.6). It is not clear whether this prohibition would make it illegal to mention Socrates' relation to members of the Thirty in the years before they actually held power, provided that one did not make this relation part of an explicit accusation. Speakers in Athenian courts did not stop dragging up the behaviour of their opponents under the Thirty.[13]

Still, a prosecutor might be unwilling to test the precise limits of the law, since the amnesty had a wide scope and was sometimes vigorously enforced. In one case Archinus, a leading defender of the amnesty, denounced someone to the Council for violating the amnesty, and had him summarily executed. In this incident the offender may not even have brought a formal charge against anyone—he may have just been stirring up controversy (*Ath. Pol.* 40.2). This Archinus also introduced a procedure that allowed a defendant who believed he was being accused in violation of the amnesty to seek a preliminary hearing on this issue; the case could not go on if the hearing went in favour of the defendant.[14]

Some reasonable conclusions about the amnesty and the trial of Socrates may be drawn: (1) The prosecutors probably took the amnesty seriously. One of them, Anytus, is said to have observed it especially scrupulously.[15] In any case, one might expect supporters of the amnesty (such people as Archinus) to be eager to prevent violations in letter or spirit in the first few years when feelings were strong. (2) It would not have prevented a prosecution of Socrates on political grounds, as a companion of oligarchs and supporter of oligarchic revolution, if the prosecutors could show that he had continued these activities after the time covered by the amnesty. (3) The prosecutors would have been ill advised to prosecute Socrates on non-political charges, if they really intended these charges as a pretext for political charges that were prohibited by the amnesty. If the amnesty had strong popular support (as the actions of Archinus suggest), the prosecutors might expect many of the 500 jurors to support it; hence they might not want to damage their case by appearing to disregard or to circumvent the amnesty. (4) Even if the amnesty explained why the prosecution would not mention political offences, it does not explain why Socrates would not mention them if he thought that they were the opponents' basic objection to them or that many of the jury would take them seriously. Answers to objections that were not mentioned at the trial would not violate the amnesty.

For these reasons, the apparent facts about the amnesty do not explain why we have no reliable direct evidence to show that Socrates' trial had a political dimension.

Why Is Socrates Silent on the Political Dimension?

We are now in a better position to discuss a question that we raised but did not answer earlier: If the trial had a real political dimension, and if the *Apology* is historically accurate about the content of Socrates' defence, ought we expect Socrates to mention the political dimension? If we can explain his silence, it does not tend to show that the trial had no political dimension.[16]

Some reasons might be given for saying we ought not to expect this: (1) Socrates decided to confine himself narrowly to the official indictment. (2) He thought he would weaken his case by calling attention to suspicions aroused by his political activities. (3) The amnesty inhibited him from referring to such questions. (4) He decided to avoid political issues altogether, confining himself to philosophical questions. (5) The *Apology* is inaccurate; either through negligence or by a deliberate decision, Plato leaves out anything that Socrates might have said on the political associations that were held against him.

None of these arguments is cogent: (1) Socrates does not in fact confine himself narrowly to the official indictment. He goes back over twenty years to discuss the 'old accusers', because these have aroused prejudice against him. But he does not mention any suspicions connected with the Thirty. If these suspicions were well known to the jurors, and if they also aroused prejudice against him, why does he not mention them? (2) If political suspicions about oligarchy and the Thirty were so widespread that they prompted Socrates' opponents to bring the indictment, they would already be in the minds of the jury; Socrates would not be calling attention to them if he responded to them. (3) We have seen that the amnesty left Socrates free to defend himself against any prejudices that he might have thought were aroused by his associations with the Thirty. (4) In fact he does not avoid political questions. He mentions two sensitive issues: the trial of the generals after Arginusae, and the arrest of Leon by the Thirty. He could have used this part of his speech to answer the charges about oligarchy if he had thought them relevant. (5) We do not avoid the difficulties that arise from Socrates' silence if we treat the *Apology* as a Platonic fiction. If we suppose that Plato intended to write his own defence of Socrates, rather than Socrates' actual defence, we ought still to be puzzled at his failure to omit such an important source (according to those who favour the political dimension) of prejudice against Socrates. We might suppose that he took the charge that Socrates supported oligarchic revolution to be so obviously true that it was unanswerable; but in that case the emphasis that Plato lays on the episode of Leon is puzzling. What would be the point of mentioning a small act of protest against the Thirty, if everyone believed that Socrates had favoured them?

Admittedly, it is often difficult to present a cogent argument from silence. But in this case it gives us a plausible objection to the 'must have' defences of the political dimension. If what 'must have' happened actually did happen, we would reasonably expect to hear about it in the *Apology*; since we do not hear about it in the *Apology*, we have reason to conclude that what 'must have' happened probably did not happen.

If, then, we cling to the belief that the trial 'must have' had a political dimension despite the weakness of the positive evidence, we must dismiss the *Apology* not only as a fiction, but also as a strangely inept fiction.

The Religious Charge

One argument for the political dimension appeals to the alleged inadequacy of the official charges. Do we need to attribute political motives to prosecutors or jurors? Or do the official charges, as they are recorded by Plato and others, explain why people wanted to prosecute Socrates and were willing to convict him?

In the first charge Socrates was accused of not recognizing the gods of the city, and of introducing new divinities; and he says the Athenians believed this charge partly because of Aristophanes' *Clouds* (*Ap.* 19c). Each of these claims is open to doubt: (1) The Athenians did not characteristically persecute anyone for unorthodox beliefs.[17] Indeed, ancient Greek and Roman religion was usually a matter of practice and cult rather than belief. It is difficult to find a clear precedent for prosecution for unorthodoxy in Athens. Plutarch mentions a decree moved in the Assembly by Diopeithes at the beginning of the Peloponnesian War (*Pericles* 32.2) to prosecute those who did not recognize (*nomizein*) the gods or who taught accounts of celestial beings. A fourth-century source mentions the prosecution of Anaxagoras. But these stories have aroused the suspicion of modern critics.[18] (2) The *Clouds* may appear irrelevant. No one prosecuted Socrates for impiety immediately after the play; why should it have caused anyone to prosecute him over twenty years later? In any case, it was meant to be funny, not to level a serious charge against Socrates.

These arguments do not cast reasonable doubt on the historicity and the seriousness of the religious charge. It is probably unreasonable to reject all the evidence of prosecution for unorthodox beliefs before the trial of Socrates. But even if we reject it, the Athenian law allowed prosecution for impiety and left considerable freedom of interpretation (as did Athenian law in general) to juries. Even if Athenians did not normally bother to prosecute people for statements of disbelief in the gods of the city, they might not look with indifference on someone who was widely reputed to disbelieve in the anthropomorphic gods accepted by most Athenians, and to believe only in the cosmological principles of the Presocratic natural philosophers.[19] If Socrates had a reputation for holding such views, he might easily be subject to suspicion.

At this point the *Clouds* becomes relevant. The fact that it is meant to be funny does not show that it cannot also have been intended as a serious attack on Socrates.[20] Aristophanes conveys, and probably meant to convey, an unfavourable impression of Socrates as a disbeliever in the traditional gods and a believer in quasi-personal or impersonal natural forces. The charge of not recognizing the gods of the city and introducing new superhuman agents (*daimonia*) fits the Socrates of the *Clouds*.

Is Socrates' reference to the *Clouds* just a red herring, irrelevant to the trial? This is difficult to believe. The two charges in the indictment are so similar to the themes of the *Clouds* that it would have been amazingly foolish of Socrates to take the initiative in reminding the Athenians that the very same charges had been brought against him years ago, before anyone knew how Critias and Alcibiades would turn out. His comments are far more intelligible if other people remembered the *Clouds*, and if he needs to show that it does not support the current charges against him as strongly as it appears to.

Alternatively, should we suspect that Socrates never mentioned the *Clouds* at his trial, and that Plato introduced it in the *Apology* with no historical warrant? This suspicion also seems misplaced. Just as it would have been foolish of Socrates to take the initiative in referring to the *Clouds*, it would have been foolish of Plato to invent such a reference; for the *Clouds* is such damaging evidence against Socrates that any defence of Socrates—either his own or Plato's—would be inept if it gratuitously drew the jury's or the reader's attention to the play.

But we might still be suspicious about the relevance of the *Clouds*. If it really gave Socrates a bad reputation, why did no one prosecute him in the 420s? Why was he not prosecuted for twenty more years? These questions allow reasonable, though conjectural, answers. It is familiar fact in the 20th century that many people take religion more seriously under the pressure of war or disaster than they do in other circumstances.[21] In the first few years of the Peloponnesian War (431–27) the Athenians suffered invasion and the Plague; both the *Oedipus Tyrannus* and the *Clouds* were produced in the 420s. The *OT* does not refer overtly to current events; but it involves a plague, punishment for it, punishment for impiety, and the refutation of scepticism about religion (cf. 898–910, 945–49, 964–83).[22] Later in the 420s, however, Athenian fortunes improved, before the *Clouds* appeared in 423.

If some Athenians might have regarded the Plague as a sign of divine displeasure, they could hardly have thought the gods were any more pleased with them at the end of the Peloponnesian War, when they had not only lost their expedition in Sicily, and then lost the war, but had twice lost the democracy as well. Religious anxieties might easily revive in these circumstances.[23] Though Greek polytheism might tolerate some religious speculation, a world-view that left the gods with no power of intervention or influence, and made it a waste of time to pray to them or consult their oracles, could hardly be regarded as a way of honoring the gods. Many Athenians might easily have regarded the views attributed to Socrates in the *Clouds* as an insult to the gods.

The trial of Socrates is not the only sign of Athenian anxiety about religious questions in the last years of the Peloponnesian War. The fragmentary works attributed to Plato's relative Critias include a speech from his play the *Sisyphus*, in which the main character (presumably) explains belief in the gods as the product of human invention designed to restrain secret injustice and lawlessness. According to one ancient source, Critias used Sisyphus to express his own atheistic sentiments, not daring to avow them openly for fear of the Areopagus.[24] The remark about the Areopagus is perhaps significant, since it implies that in the last years of the War this Athenian 'House of Lords' took on more than a purely ceremonial role. It seems to have used its prestige to maintain morale in the conduct of the war, and especially in defence of the democracy that was already under internal attack before the defeat of Aigospotamoi.[25] The story about the *Sisyphus* suggests that in the last years of the War many Athenians were alarmed by open expressions of impiety.

The fragment also suggests what many Athenians might find alarming about expressions of atheism. It was certainly insulting to the gods to suggest that they did not exist, or that they existed and did not punish impiety. But in so far as the atheist rejected religious sanctions supporting moral principles, he might also be thought to be undermining those moral principles. The Athenians would not have been reassured if Critias had insisted that he believed in the gods of some of the Presocratics, closely identified with natural forces and altogether without any concern to punish particular acts of injustice.[26] Sisyphus' speech might be taken to suggest the view upheld by some characters in the *Clouds*, that once the fear of divine punishment is removed, there is no reason to refrain from profitable secret injustice; for if there had been some other good reason for an individual to refrain from injustice, why should anyone have bothered to fabricate gods? The apparently subversive aspects of the *Sisyphus* might have focused people's attention on Socrates and on the *Clouds*.

The evidence of an attempt to prosecute Critias for the *Sisyphus* is rather slight. But we have evidence of an actual prosecution for impiety in Pseudo-Lysias 6, a speech delivered at the trial of Andocides in 399. The speaker urges the Athenians to avoid divine anger by punishing impiety with death (53–5); he treats impiety itself as a sufficient threat to the city to deserve death.[27] When Socrates' accusers demanded the death penalty for impiety, they had a very recent precedent.

The speech against Andocides raises some further intriguing possibilities. The accuser of Andocides was Meletus; this is also the name of one of Socrates' accusers. The Meletus who accused Andocides was alleged to be one of those who went to arrest Leon, in the incident described by Socrates (Andocides, *Myst.* 94; cf. *Ap.* 32cd). One of Andocides' supporters in this trial was Anytus (*Myst.* 150), another of the accusers of Socrates. If the same Meletus accused both Andocides and Socrates, it is not surprising that he prosecuted Socrates for impiety. Moreover, the prosecution of Socrates was an act of cooperation between two people who had been on the opposite side both in the case of Andocides and in their attitudes to the Thirty; for Meletus at least went along with them, whereas Anytus was a strong opponent. If these two opponents combined forces to accuse Socrates of impiety, their accusation might appear all the more credible and might arouse less suspicion of being politically motivated (and hence of violating the spirit of the amnesty).

Unfortunately, these are just intriguing possibilities, since they assume that we are dealing with one and the same Meletus, and this assumption is not secure.[28] But whether or not the accuser of Andocides also prosecuted Socrates, his speech against Andocides gives us good evidence for religious attitudes that might intelligibly have turned people against Socrates.

The Moral Charge

Socrates was also charged with corrupting the young men (*Ap.* 24b9). What does this mean? It is not clear what law he was supposed to violate in corrupting young men, or what his prosecutors thought he was doing to corrupt them.

Socrates suggests that his accusers have no clear idea of what they mean, but are just appealing to stock charges against philosophers; when asked to explain 'corrupting' they mention 'things in the heavens and below the earth', 'not recognizing the gods', and 'making the weaker argument stronger' (*Ap.* 23d2–7).[29] This partly answers our question about the legal status of the charge; for he suggests that the accusers regard impiety as the primary instance of corruption. When the accusers say 'Socrates does injustice corrupting the young men and not recognizing the gods . . .' (24b9–c1), they may mean that he corrupts the young men with his own impiety.

Another aspect of corrupting the young men is not mentioned in the official charge, but Socrates implies that the accusers have it in mind: making the weaker argument stronger.[30] Socrates dismisses this charge as a stock accusation against philosophers, but he does not actually answer it; and evidently the fact that it could be brought against other people does not show that it was not especially appropriate for Socrates.

The charge might be levelled against anyone who practised a wide variety of argumentative techniques. A skilled rhetorician would be able to argue on both sides of the case, in the manner of a Euripidean debate; but one could also become skilled in supporting or undermining a position by the use of techniques of examination and objection. Zeno practised these techniques; and so, presumably, did Protagoras.[31] It is a matter for controversy how far Socrates himself contributed to the development of the various techniques called 'eristic', and how far they were already practised by his contemporaries. At any rate, Plato is anxious to distinguish the genuine methods and aims of Socratic cross-examination from the techniques of eristic, and acknowledges that many people found it hard to tell the difference.[32]

Socrates remarks that some young men learnt techniques of cross-examination from him and then practised them on others (82, quoting *Ap.* 23c). In a famous passage of the *Republic* Plato recognizes this fact about Socratic cross-examination (537e–539c). The significance of this passage is often exaggerated. Plato does not say that Socrates was wrong to do what he did, and he does not imply that he thinks young men in contemporary Athens should not be taught techniques of cross-examination—he is legislating for the ideal state. But the reference to the charges in the *Apology* is clear. Plato concedes that practice in argument leads some people to despise the moral and political norms and practices they were brought up in (539a).

If the charge of 'corrupting the young men' should be understood in this way, it is not sharply separate from the religious charge. Sophistical, rhetorical, and eristic arguments might readily be used to undermine both belief in the gods and belief in divine sanctions for moral principles and practices; the *Clouds* offers obvious examples. It would be natural to mention Socrates' argumentative techniques (or rather, a malicious or ignorant collection of half-truths about them) to explain how he undermined belief in the gods and in conventional morality.

This explanation of 'corrupting the young men' does not imply that the Athenians thought Socrates himself was sympathetic to oligarchy, or that they thought he advocated the immoral outlook that (in their view) his methods of argument tended to inspire. Athenians could well believe that he was a bad influence without believing that he was also an apologist of oligarchy. The explicit charge explains all that needs to be explained. It is a serious and relevant charge that might have seemed plausible to many Athenians, quite independently of any suspicions of Socrates' political outlook or influence.[33]

There is no good evidence, then, to suggest that Socrates' accusers regarded him as teaching an anti-democratic political theory. Objections to the use or abuse of Socratic argumentative technique explain quite well by themselves why people might suspect Socrates of corrupting the young men. There is no reason to suppose that the explicit or implicit political content of Socrates' teaching played any role in the accusations against him. The official charges, properly understood, satisfactorily explain why Socrates was prosecuted and condemned.

The Extent of Socrates' Political Doctrines

But even if we reject the historical claim that Socrates' anti-democratic teachings were elements of the actual objections to him, we must still consider the philosophical claim that Socrates' views are anti-democratic. If the philosophical claim is correct, a political dimension to the trial becomes more probable, despite the lack of direct evidence.

What are we to count as evidence of Socrates' political views? Our view about which dialogues of Plato are authentically Socratic is bound to affect our view of Socrates' political doctrines. If we are allowed to treat the *Republic* as evidence of Socrates' views, then it is fairly easy to argue that he is in *some* sense against democracy. If, on the other hand, we restrict ourselves rigidly to the early dialogues, the evidence looks quite different, and the case for supposing that Socrates is against democracy is at least much less clear.[34]

According to some critics, Socrates actually supports democracy, and the anti-democratic elements in the Platonic dialogues are entirely Plato's contribution.[35] The early dialogues do not advocate the political system that is described in the *Republic*. Socrates sometimes criticizes or questions some of the procedures and results of the Athenian democratic system, or of democracy generally (e.g., *Pr.* 319b–d, *Ap.* 31d6–32a3); but he does not claim that some other system would be preferable.

One passage in the early dialogues states Socrates' preferences between different contemporary regimes. On the one hand, Socrates is in the habit of praising Sparta and Crete as well governed. On the other hand, he has always remained in Athens (except for military service). The Athenian laws say: 'So much above the other cities you approved of the city of Athens and of us the laws, as is clear—for who would approve of a city without the laws?' (*Crito* 53a3–5). Socrates preferred the democratic laws of Athens (despite whatever faults he saw in them) over the non-democratic laws of Sparta and Crete (despite whatever virtues he saw in them). This preference does not imply that Socrates thought democracy was in principle preferable to all other forms of government.

This description of Socrates' outlook is supported by the available evidence about his participation in public and political life. He was not a political activist; he was the sort of person who was generally called 'inactive' (*apragmôn*). Pericles, as reported by Thucydides, says that if someone has no share at all in political activity, 'we' count him 'not as minding his own business, but as useless' (*ouk apragmona all'achreion*, Thuc. ii 40.2). Now '*apragmôn*', 'minding one's own business', is often a term of praise, opposed to '*polupragmôn*', 'busybody'; and in saying what 'we' think, Pericles is obviously replying to those who think that active involvement in politics is a sign that someone is an interfering busybody.[36] Socrates' 'inactive' attitude was not freakish or sinister, and there is no reason to suppose that anyone thought it was.[37]

But did Socrates arouse suspicion by failing to leave Athens during the regime of the Thirty? He certainly failed to take some positive action he could have taken in support of the democracy. But unless we knew that Athens was deserted by everyone except a hard core of collaborators with the Thirty, we could not use Socrates' failure to leave as a reason for special animosity against him, or as a reason for thinking he favoured the Thirty and did not prefer the democracy.[38]

Our view of Socrates' outlook, however, has to take account of the *Gorgias*. Many regard this as a late Socratic dialogue; and it provides much more prima facie evidence of anti-democratic views than we can find in any other early dialogue. It is difficult to decide whether Socrates is criticizing particular aspects of Athenian democracy and particular Athenian democratic leaders, or intends a more general theoretical criticism of democracy. If we take the second view, and if we suppose that the *Gorgias* is authentically Socratic, then we have good reason to believe that Socrates took some of his views about knowledge and virtue to justify rejection of democracy.[39] I am inclined to think that in this dialogue the basic principles of the *Republic* are developed out of unimpeachably Socratic doctrines. I would be inclined to say, then, that Plato's political theory is basically faithful to Socrates, though I would be much less confident about how much of it Socrates thought of by himself.

Socrates' Anti-Democratic Outlook

Suppose, then, that we take the *Gorgias*, and even the *Republic*, to capture Socrates' main political principles. What follows about the extent to which he is anti-democratic? He is surely a theoretical critic of democracy. For he believes that most people do not know what is in their own interest, and that it would be better for them to be ruled by people who know their interest better than they know it themselves. People are qualified to rule, therefore, if and only if they know what is in the interest of those they are to rule. In Socrates' view, no existing form of government governs in the interest of the governed; and the appropriate sort of knowledge is meant to produce rulers who meet this condition.

How, then, does Socrates think the relevant kind of knowledge is to be reached? The *Republic* imposes an extraordinarily demanding curriculum on future rulers. But even before he devises the elaborate scheme of the *Republic*, Plato has something to say on this question. His view emerges from his presentation of a character who is especially relevant to Athenian politics around 399. Callicles in the *Gorgias* despises the moral basis of democratic law and justice, dismissing it as mere propaganda by the masses to deceive the stronger people about their real interests (483bc); his 'unmasking' of democratic values is rather similar to the speech of Sisyphus. In contrast to Socrates, he values wealth, power, and the opportunity to satisfy one's appetites, for oneself and one's friends (491ab, 491e–492c). His friends include one of the Four Hundred.[40] He is sometimes represented as an aspiring demagogue (481d–482a); such aspirations are quite consistent with willingness to overthrow a democracy, in pursuit of one's own ambitions.[41]

Socrates asks Callicles how much he knows about virtue and justice, and how far he has produced them in himself or in any other citizen, in his private capacity; and he suggests that some preparation in this area should be a prerequisite for the politician's task of cultivating virtue and justice in the citizens in general (513e5–515b4). This Socratic demand is the background for the criticism of democratic politicians and makes that criticism intelligible.

An attack on democratic politicians is not itself an attack on the democratic system. We might argue that a politician who meets Socrates' conditions could also form people's outlook so that they would prefer to be ruled by him than to be ruled by politicians who do not know what is in their real interest. But it is difficult to see any place for the democratic use of election and sortition within Socrates' theory; if we allow a decisive voice to people who may not yet understand their own interests, we are in danger of undoing the efforts of the Socratic politician who has the relevant knowledge.

Anti-Democratic Practice?

If Socrates' political outlook is anti-democratic on the points we have mentioned, it does not follow that he was anti-democratic in practice, or that he advocated the replacement of the democratic system by the regime of the Thirty. We have no reason to suppose that if Socrates rejects democracy, he thereby favours oligarchy of the sort that he was familiar with in the Greek world. He rejects democracy on the ground that election and sortition do not guarantee rulers with the moral and political knowledge that is needed to promote the interests of all the citizens. But he does not suggest that if the wealthy dominate the political system, they will produce rulers who meet the Socratic criteria. He argues against both democracy and oligarchy by appeal to the choice of experts in a craft. It would be irrational to choose experts in a craft by lot or by the vote of ignorant people; but it would be equally irrational if they were chosen either for their own wealth or by the vote of wealthy but ignorant people. Nor should we distribute goods to the ruler, or in general to the expert, without reference to the needs and interests of the recipients (*Gorg.* 490b-e). If we take Socrates' anti-democratic views seriously, we should also attribute anti-oligarchic views to him.[42]

It is difficult to imagine, then, that the Thirty would have been pleased by Socratic political principles. Xenophon represents the Thirty as warning Socrates to stop drawing his comparisons between rulers and experts, since they seem to convey implicit criticism of their regime (*Mem.* i 2.32–8). Though Xenophon's story may well be historically unfounded, it captures the conflict between Socrates' political outlook and the views of the Thirty. We have no reason to assume, on the basis of his political views, that Socrates supported the Thirty before, during, or after, the time when they were in power.[43]

Admittedly, the Thirty were hardly a good advertisement for oligarchy. Plato favours the rule of a class with moral and political knowledge and without private property, because he thinks this is the only way to end the class struggle between the rich and the poor, which divides every city into two cities (*Rep.* 422e3–423a5). The rule of the Thirty is a rather lurid episode in the sort of class struggle that Plato describes. However, we have no reason to suppose that Socrates was friendly to oligarchy in general. His objections to oligarchy do not suggest that he favoured revolution—violent or peaceful—to replace the democracy with any form of oligarchy.

This conclusion should not be surprising. A political theorist may present theoretical objections to a form of government without claiming that in the actual circumstances the best thing to do would be to replace it with one of the actually available alternatives. The distance between the theoretical criticism and the practical strategy and tactics is a well-known source of dispute. Most French Socialists in 1914 decided to support bourgeois democracy. German Communists in 1933 opposed it. British Communists leaped nimbly from opposition in 1939 to support in 1941.

These examples are not meant to suggest that Socrates or Plato had a coherent strategy for social and political revolution or reform. They simply suggest that the task of deciding what to do about one's political convictions in a particular situation is often complicated. Theoretical criticism may be sharp, fundamental, and sincere without implying that the critics also advocate immediate and drastic political change.

But even if Socrates himself did not support the Thirty or other forms of oligarchic regime, might his friends or enemies have supposed he supported them? Did Socrates' companions honestly misunderstand him? Or did they willfully select and twist Socratic arguments and views for their own purposes? We cannot rule out honest misunderstanding; but someone like Critias might easily see an advantage in distorting Socrates' views for his own purposes.

This, however, is no more than speculation. We have no evidence to suggest that Critias or any of the Thirty claimed to have learnt anything about political theory or practice from Socrates. Nor did they need any lessons from him. Their methods and aims are no more ruthless than we would expect from an oligarchic clique with Spartan support; they could find all the support they needed in Greek history and tradition, without any help from Socratic arguments.

Conclusion

I have defended Socrates against the charge that he favoured the Thirty or the oligarchic circles from which they emerged. But I have not been trying to construct another *apologia* for Socrates. I have certainly not argued that his moral and political outlook or his political actions are not liable to serious criticism. I have not even raised all the main questions that bear on this more general issue. I have confined myself to one specific criticism of his political outlook and action.

I have also defended the more purely historical claim that Socrates' prosecutors and jurors did not hold him responsible for the oligarchic outlook and actions of the Thirty. I cannot claim to have proved that the trial did not have a political dimension. But I have argued that the most plausible conclusion from our available evidence is that it had no political dimension. Discussion of Socrates' trial and of his political beliefs and actions should proceed without the distraction of pseudo-historical political interpretations of the trial.

Notes

1. This essay is a revised version of 'Socrates and Athenian democracy', *Philosophy and Public Affairs* 18 (1989), 184–205. This was a discussion of I. F. Stone, *The Trial of Socrates* (Boston, 1988). I have revised it so as to make the detailed criticisms of Stone less prominent (either by deletion or by relegation to footnotes) and to cite a few of the many important publications on relevant issues from the last 15 years. But it is certainly not the paper I would write if I were writing afresh on the topic today. It remains a survey, at an elementary level, of a few issues raised by Stone's book, rather than a detailed treatment of any of them. At different times I have benefited from comments by Hugh Benson, Susan Meyer, William Prior, Gregory Vlastos, and Gail Fine.

A full and careful discussion of questions about the trial may be found in T. A. Brickhouse and N. D. Smith, *Socrates on Trial* (Princeton, 1989). They also print some relevant sources and secondary discussions in *The Trial and Execution of Socrates* (Oxford, 2002). The religious context may be studied in R. Parker, *Athenian Religion: A History* (Oxford, 1996), ch. 10.

2. Stone says: 'Getting a grip on the historical Socrates is only part of our task. Equally important is reconstructing the missing case for the prosecution, and seeing how Socrates appeared to his fellow citizens' (5). The same desire to find the Athenian point of view on Socrates appears in M. H. Hansen, *The Trial of Socrates—from the Athenian Point of View*, Historisk-filosofiske Meddelelser det Kongelige Danske Videnskabernes Selskab 71 (1995). This book is severely reviewed by S. R. Slings, *Mnemosyne* 51 (1998), 501–5. Slings, however, agrees with Hansen on the political dimension of the trial, on the strength of the *Apology* (which Slings regards as fiction) together with Aeschines (discussed below).

3. Stone takes an absurdly exaggerated view of the importance of Socrates' trial and execution. He takes it to be the climactic event in Socrates' life, just as the Crucifixion was the climactic event in the life of Christ: 'Had Socrates been acquitted, had he died comfortably of old age, he might now be remembered only as a minor Athenian eccentric, a favourite butt of the comic poets' (3). If this were true, then either (a) Plato would never have written his dialogues if Socrates had not been tried and condemned, or (b) the dialogues would have been forgotten if they had not included the *Apology* and *Crito*. Both (a) and (b) are baseless.

4. These three claims are accepted by (inter alios) Stone and Hansen.

5. The *pôs* in 24b8, and the use of *oratio obliqua*, show that Socrates does not claim to be quoting directly.

6. See Diogenes Laertius ii 40. Xenophon, *Mem.* i 1.1 gives the same wording, except that it substitutes *eispherôn* for *eishêgoumenos*. Diogenes cites the statement by Favorinus of Arles that the original indictment was kept in the archives in the Metroon at Athens. One might be tempted to infer that Diogenes is quoting the indictment from Favorinus, and that Favorinus had seen the actual document. Diogenes says nothing explicit on either point, but his other references to Favorinus in this context (ii 38–39) suggest that Favorinus took some trouble to find out the facts about the trial of Socrates.

7. Doubts about the significance of this suspicion in the charges against Socrates are expressed by R. Hackforth, *The Composition of Plato's Apology* (CUP, 1933), 73–79; M. I. Finley in 'Socrates and Athens', in *Aspects of Antiquity* (London, 1968), ch. 5; Brickhouse and Smith, *Socrates on Trial*, 69–87.

8. I use 'political dimension' to refer to the suspicions of Socrates' associations with oligarchs, and especially with the Thirty. As I remark below (on Arginusae and Leon), Socrates does not leave politics out altogether.

9. Polycrates' attack was written after 394 (Diogenes Laertius ii 39; see Dodds, *Plato's Gorgias* [Oxford, 1959], 28) and before Isocrates' *Busiris* (between 391 and 385?), which contains (3) the first reference to it. Further conjectures about Polycrates depend on the *Apology* of Libanius, which is presumed to paraphrase Polycrates (at 53 he mentions the accusation that Socrates was a 'hater of the people', *misodêmos*). We do not know how accurate the paraphrase is. An over-confident account of Polycrates is given by A. H. Chroust, *Socrates, Man and Myth* (London, 1957), ch. 4.

Hansen, 'Trial', 8–14, denies that Xenophon's 'accuser' is Polycrates. He assumes, without further support, that the 'accuser' must have been one of the accusers in 399. Similarly, Vlastos, *Socratic Studies* 89, assumes without question that the 'accuser's' charges must have been presented at the trial.

10. . . . *hon up'ekeinou* [sc. Socrates] *oudeis ê(i)stheto paideuomenon*, Busiris 5.

11. Hackforth *Composition*, 74n, gives a sober and justified warning about this passage: '. . . it is illegitimate to treat such a remark as the assertion of an incontrovertible fact as has frequently been done.' Unfortunately, his warning is ignored by Hansen, 'Trial', 30, who calls the passage 'perhaps the best and least biassed source for the trial of Socrates' (30), and by Vlastos, *Socratic Studies* 87ff.

12. Parker, for instance, reaches his conclusion by general scepticism about the specific sources on the trial: 'Plato's *Apology*, of course, does not imply that political factors had any importance (except perhaps in one passing aside). But we have no reason to take Plato's defence any more seriously as a historical record than whatever accusation underlies the 'accuser' of Xenophon. It is therefore hard to doubt that the names Critias and Alcibiades, and the word 'hater of the people', were spoken at the trial. Beyond this point we can scarcely go' (*Athenian Religion*, 207). David Lewis, in *Cambridge Ancient History* vi (2nd ed., Cambridge, 1994), 40, is even more inclined to attach importance to political factors: 'That the associations of Alcibiades and Critias with Socrates were in some way relevant seems certain, though 'corrupting the young' is not likely to have been part of the formal charge.' The mention of Alcibiades and

Critias suggests that Lewis takes Xenophon's 'accuser' to be historically reliable, and his doubt about 'corrupting the young' suggests that he rejects the evidence of Diogenes (and probably of Favorinus). It is difficult to see what reasonable principle guides Lewis's attitude to the different sources.

13. Athenian observance of the amnesty is briefly discussed by Brickhouse and Smith, *Socrates on Trial*, 73ff., and at more length by P. J. Rhodes, *A Commentary on the Aristotelian Athenaion Politeia* (Oxford, 1981), 471–73. Rhodes remarks that the Athenians went on mentioning people's past career, including their behaviour during the regime of the Thirty, in speeches at trials; but he concludes that they probably never actually convicted anyone in violation of the amnesty. For observance of the amnesty see Lysias 26.2 (from 382; a grudging admission by a speaker who thinks the amnesty might well be regarded as foolish). The past could be mentioned at the scrutiny of officials, Lys. 26.10 (Evandrus was listed among the cavalry under the Thirty; cf. 16.3–8), but it did not stop people with associations with the Thirty from being elected to offices (Lys. 16.8 [generals and cavalry commanders]; and despite Lys. 26 Evandrus passed his *dokimasia* and served as archon). See M. Ostwald, *From Popular Sovereignty to the Sovereignty of Law* (Berkeley, 1986), 503. (Some of these examples come from some time later than the trial of Socrates, when old grievances had perhaps subsided; on the other hand, there were special reasons to be especially scrupulous in observing the amnesty in 399 when the dangers of violating it were especially vivid.)

14. On this procedure of *paragraphê* see Isoc. 18.2–3; Rhodes, 473; A. R. W. Harrison, *The Law of Athens*, ii (Oxford, 1971), p. 106ff.

15. See Isoc. 18. 23–4. (This does not show that Anytus approved of the amnesty.)

16. See, e.g., Gregory Vlastos, *Socratic Studies* (Cambridge, 1994), 90: 'Scholars like R. Hackforth, . . . who adduced evidence of the former as though it constituted evidence against the latter, were simply confused. . . . ' 'The former' refers to the religious and moral charges, and 'the latter' to the political dimension. Vlastos refers to Hackforth, *Composition* 73ff.

17. Stone suggests that the religious charge might reflect Socrates' failure to observe the cults especially characteristic of Athenian democracy (201ff.). He acknowledges that no historical evidence supports his suggestion.

18. The alleged 'Decree of Diopeithes' is discussed sceptically by Stone (231ff.), who relies on K. J. Dover, 'The freedom of the intellectual in Greek society', in *The Greeks and their Legacy* (Oxford, 1988), ch. 13, from *Talanta* 7 (1976), 24–54. A less sceptical position is taken by Ostwald, *Sovereignty*, esp. at 196 nn. 72–73. Let us concede for the sake of argument that Dover is right, and that the whole story results from confusing comedy with historical fact; what must the postulated comedy have said? It was presumably similar to the attacks on Pericles through Aspasia that appear in other comedies; presumably Pericles was attacked not only for sexual irregularities, but also for having friends with weird and unfamiliar views about the gods. If there is this minimal basis for the story of Diopeithes, it suggests that at the time when even Thucydides admits Pericles was under attack (ii 65.2–3), it was thought natural to make fun of him and to attack him for association with strange religious views. It clearly does not follow that the Athenians were ready to engage in a 'witch hunt'; but it does follow that if you wanted to make someone look ridiculous or untrustworthy in the eyes of

many Athenians, you might try challenging his religious beliefs. And if this was a way of making someone seem ridiculous or untrustworthy, then many Athenians must have been suspicious of religious beliefs that might appear seriously irregular.

19. The meaning of *nomizein tous theous* is sensibly discussed by Hackforth, *Composition*, 60–63.

20. The political content and intentions of Aristophanes' plays have been widely disputed. (The best discussion I know is by G. E. M. de Ste Croix, *Origins of the Peloponnesian War* [London, 1972], 231–34, 355–71.) It is hard to believe, for instance, that in writing the *Knights* or *Wasps* he had nothing against Cleon, and was just using him to get a few laughs. His political remarks (even outside the *parabaseis* of the plays) often go far beyond the requirements of plot or humour. Something similar may be true about the *Clouds*.

21. The same is true of the 21st century, if one considers the aftermath of the attacks on the United States in September 2001.

22. B. M. W. Knox, *Oedipus at Thebes* (New Haven, 1957) plausibly connects the Athenian situation with the dramatic situation of the play. Agreement on this point does not imply agreement with Knox's identification of Oedipus with Pericles.

23. Pseudo-Lysias, for instance, assumes that the Athenians ought to be indignant at one of their own citizens who insults their own religious rites, and shows that 'he does not recognize the gods' (*theous ou nomizei*, 6.19); they can expect that the gods will punish impiety even if the punishment is delayed (20).

On religious anxiety at the end of the Peloponnesian War see Dover, *Greeks and Legacy*, 158. In the original paper 'Freedom of the Intellectual', Dover emphasized the political dimension of the trial of Socrates, but in his later 'additional note' he says: 'I now consider that I attached too much weight to the political aspects of the trial, and not enough to the mood of superstitious fear ('What has gone wrong? Are there after all gods who can be offended?') which is very likely to have descended on Athens between 405 and 395.'

24. See DK 88 B 25 = *TrGF*, ed. Snell, 43 F 19. Some ascribe the play to Critias (as Sextus does), others (including Aetius, the source who mentions the Areopagus) to Euripides (Diels, *DG* 298.8–27). See Dover, 'Freedom of the Intellectual' (leaning towards Critias); A. Dihle, 'Das Satyrspiel 'Sisyphos', *Hermes* 105 (1977), 28–42 (for Euripides, supported by H. Lloyd-Jones), *Justice of Zeus* (2nd ed., Berkeley, 1983), 192ff.); M. Davies, 'Sisyphus and the Invention of Religion', *Bulletin of the Institute of Classical Studies* 36 (1989) 16–32 (not convinced by the case for Euripides).

The overall point of the play is hard to guess from a single fragment. Since the play is a satyr-play, the sentiments expressed by Sisyphus are probably not represented as entirely serious (see Davies). Moreover, he may well have been shown receiving the traditional punishment for his impiety. Still, these aspects of the play may not have prevented the Athenian audience from being shocked by the atheism of this particular speech.

25. This claim about the Areopagus does not rest simply on the doubtful evidence of Aetius. Lysias' speech against Eratosthenes accuses Theramenes of secret negotiations with the Spartans at a time when 'the Council of the Areopagus was acting to promote your safety' (*prattousês sôtêria*, 12.69). The considerable status and prestige of the Areopagus would make it a suitable body to organize some opposition to the se-

cret and treacherous activities of the oligarchs; and the remark of Aetius about Euripides suggests that among its functions the Areopagus exercised some control over subversive and immoral public speech and propaganda. Comparisons with wartime conditions in other societies accustomed to a considerable degree of freedom of speech suggests that there is nothing inherently unlikely in this, and that a good deal can be done in such circumstances without any definite legal enactment.

If the *Sisyphus* fragment could be unequivocally ascribed to Critias, we would have some plausible evidence to show that many Athenians feared and distrusted the atheist views of someone within the Socratic circle. But even if the fragment is not Critias' work, the story about the Areopagus may provide some clue to the fears and anxieties of the Athenian public.

26. This helps to explain why Socrates would be under suspicion for believing in 'new divinities'. It was not because he believed, say, in foreign divinities with a traditional attitude to prayer, sacrifice, and morality (e.g., the Thracian goddess Bendis mentioned in *Rep.* 327a1–3), but because he believed (supposedly) in the amoral, non-personal gods of the natural philosophers. See Parker, *Athenian Religion*, 214–16.

27. See Lewis's comment in *CAH* vi 39: 'in the prosecution speech which we possess . . . religion is not a mere political weapon, but the whole breath of the accusation. This speaker at least is convinced that the evils which have defeated Athens indicate that special care is needed to make her right with the gods.'

28. For a good defence of the view that the two trials involve just one Meletus see H. J. Blumenthal, 'Meletus the accuser of Andocides and Meletus the accuser of Socrates', *Philologus* 117 (1973), 169–78. See also K. J. Dover, *Lysias and the Corpus Lysiacum* (Berkeley, 1968), 80 n. 30; Ostwald, *Sovereignty*, 495; Lewis in *CAH* vi 39. The identification is doubted by Brickhouse and Smith, *Socrates on Trial*, 27n.

29. In his remarks about 'corrupting' (28) Stone ignores this passage, and relies on Polycrates (whom I discuss below).

30. Socrates implies in his use of the present tense in 23d (cf. 19b4–6 on the 'old accusers') that the accusers still have this charge in mind.

31. Protagoras' 'overthrowing arguments' (*kataballontes logoi*) are mentioned in DK 80 B 1.

32. See *Gorgias* 457cd, *Meno* 75cd, the *Euthydemus*, and Isoc. *c.Soph.* 7. I have discussed this a little more in 'Coercion and Objectivity in Plato's Dialectic', *Rev. Int. de Phil.* 40 (1986) 49–74, at 61.

33. Stone attaches great importance to the allegations of 'the accuser', as reported by Xenophon: ' . . . "the accuser" charged that the antidemocratic teachings of Socrates had "led the young to despise the established constitution and made them violent". (64) Stone quotes Xenophon as saying that '"his accuser" said Socrates "taught his companions" to look down upon the laws of Athens. . . "' (29).

Stone fails to point out that the historical credentials of the passage in Xenophon are not secure. If 'the accuser' is Polycrates in his pamphlet against Socrates, we have no reason to believe that he gives an accurate account of the actual grievances against Socrates in 399; he may well have invented further ones to strengthen his reply to defences of Socrates. If we can explain what happened without resort to Polycrates' charge, we have no reason to believe it.

But even if we concede the historical accuracy of 'the accuser', he does not say what
Stone takes him to say; for the passage from Xenophon cited by Stone does not mention teaching. According to Xenophon, the accuser said that Socrates 'tended to make'
(or 'was in the habit of making'; *epoiei*) his companions despise the established laws,
and that his arguments 'provoked' them (lit. 'raised them up', *epairein*) to despise the
established constitution, and 'made' (*poiein*) them violent (Xen. *Mem.* i 2.9). The difference between Xenophon's verbs and Stone's 'taught' is not trivial. Xenophon's verbs
indicate an actual (alleged) effect of what Socrates said, not a conclusion that Socrates
intended to be drawn.

Perhaps this will seem a small point when we look at the arguments that the accuser
attributes to Socrates; for he charges that Socrates said it was stupid (*môron*) to choose
rulers of the city by lot, when we would never choose craftsmen by lot, and political
rulers are capable of doing far greater harm than craftsmen do if they are incompe-
tent. We might well ask: must Socrates not have intended these arguments to cause
disloyalty to the democracy? This need not be so, however, and it is not what the accuser says. It is quite plausible to suppose that a Socratic line of questioning involves
a comparison between political rule and the various specialized crafts; and it is easy to
see why, in the light of this comparison, the choice of rulers by lot might seem a foolish anomaly. It does not follow that Socrates rejected democracy in Athens, or that he
encouraged his companions to reject it. All that the accuser says is that the sorts of objections that Socrates raised actually caused his companions to despise the established
laws; and this could be true simply because of the objections that he raised and the
techniques of argument that he practised, not because he advocated some particular
political position.

34. I have said briefly what I think about Socrates, Plato, and the dialogues, in
Plato's Ethics (Oxford, 1995), ch. 1.

35. See K. R. Popper, *The Open Society and its Enemies*, (5th ed., London, 1966) vol.
1, ch. 10; R. Robinson, *Essays in Greek Philosophy* (Oxford, 1969), ch. 4 (a review of Popper); Vlastos, *Socratic Studies*, ch. 5 (a more moderate defence of a pro-democratic interpretation). This line of interpretation is criticized in R. Kraut, *Socrates and the State*
(Princeton, 1984), ch. 7, and Irwin, 'Socratic Inquiry and Politics', *Ethics* 96 (1986),
400–15.

36. Socrates actually has to defend himself against the charge of *polupragmosunê*,
Ap. 32c5.

37. A. W. Gomme, *A Historical Commentary on Thucydides*, vol. 2 (Oxford, 1956)
ad Thuc. ii 40.2 quotes some apposite examples of complimentary uses of *apragmôn*.
See esp. Dem. 40.32, Antiph. iii 2.1, Plato, *Rep.* 565a. In speaking of 'inactivity', I mean
(as Stone does [99]) the relative inactivity in Socrates' failure to *seek* political office
and failure to put himself forward in debates in the Assembly. Socrates never shirked
the ordinary obligations of a citizen. It is not even clear that he was so inactive that he
would be covered by Pericles' phrase 'no share at all in political activity', *mêden tônde
metechonta*. The sense in which he was *apragmôn* is discussed further by L. B. Carter,
The Quiet Athenian (Oxford, 1986), 183–85.

38. Stone correctly (153ff.) cites evidence showing that in later years orators sometimes tried to cast suspicion on a person by mentioning his behaviour under the

Thirty. But such efforts to arouse suspicion did not (or at any rate did not always) exclude people from high public office. See Lysias 16.8, discussed above. I do not see any reason to believe that suspicion of Socrates' behaviour during the regime of the Thirty is likely to have been a major influence on the jury. I doubt if we can even safely assume that the prosecution would have alluded to it; for against the benefits of arousing suspicion some jurors against Socrates they would have to count the cost of antagonizing fair-minded jurors who took the spirit of the amnesty seriously.

An interesting possibility arises if it is reasonable to believe that Socrates' accuser is the same Meletus as the man who, in contrast to Socrates, (allegedly) helped to arrest Leon, but afterwards became an ostentatious supporter of the democracy (see p. 136 above). Such an accuser could ill afford to encourage the jury to suspect Socrates for his remaining in the city under the Thirty, since any such suspicions could be far more justly directed at Meletus himself. It would be far more dangerous for Meletus than for Socrates if the jury were to violate the spirit of the amnesty.

39. One might especially appeal to the description of the 'true orator' and politician in 504d5-505b5.

40. Andron, father of the Atthidographer. See Dodds, *Gorgias*, ad 487c.

41. Critias himself provides a good parallel to this flexible attitude to democracy and oligarchy. When he was exiled on the motion of Cleophon, he went to Thessaly, and tried to set up democracy, arming the serfs against their masters (Xen. *Hell.* ii 3.36, spoken by Theramenes when he was being denounced by Critias). He seems more like an adventurer than like the fanatical oligarch depicted by Stone. For a recent discussion of Critias in Thessaly see Ostwald, *Sovereignty*, 464ff., who goes further than I would think necessary to discover consistency in Critias' political positions. (Abrupt transitions from left to right are not unknown in more recent history.)

42. One should not suppose that Socrates' and Plato's praise of certain aspects of Sparta commits them to wanting to replace the Athenian democracy with a regime of the Spartan type. Both *Republic* viii and the *Laws* contain severe criticism of Sparta. The fact that the Thirty were pro-Spartan would not necessarily recommend them to Socrates.

43. Some readers take *Epist.* vii, 324c–325a to describe Plato's view of the Thirty. Since I believe this letter is not authentic, and that this passage reflects the apologetic purpose of the author, I do not believe it is historically reliable.

8

The Impiety of Socrates

M. F. Burnyeat

ONE DAY IN 399 B.C. Socrates went on trial in Athens, charged with impiety and corrupting the young, and spoke certain words to the jury in his defence. Some time later—no one knows how much time later—Plato wrote *The Apology of Socrates,* in which Socrates again speaks certain words to the jury in his defence.

No sensible scholar believes that the relation between the first set of words and the second is the relation of identity. It is most unlikely that what Socrates said and what Plato wrote are exactly the same, if only for the trivial reason that unprepared spoken discourse very seldom comes out as a sequence of syntactically perfect, complete sentences.[1] The written and the spoken speeches could of course be partly the same. Plato could have preserved the gist of what Socrates said and re-presented it in his own inimitable prose. That indeed is what many scholars think the *Apology* does. But it is equally possible that Plato, like Xenophon and perhaps others as well,[2] devised his own independent defence of Socrates, that had little or nothing in common with what Socrates said on the day.

The scholarly literature on this topic is a paradise of inconclusive guesswork. I have no new guesses to offer here. Instead, I want to propose another way of reading Plato's *Apology.* Rather than taking the text as a historical challenge and wondering about its relation to what Socrates actually said on the day, or, more generally, about whether it gives a historically faithful account of Socrates' life and thought, I suggest that it would be more appropriate to the present occasion, and to everything George Steiner has stood witness for over the years, to read it as a personal challenge.[3]

If the words spoken by Socrates in the written defence are not identical with the words spoken by Socrates on the day of his trial, then the jury to which the written defence is addressed need not be identical with the jury of 501 (or 500) male Athenians to whom the spoken defence was addressed. Plato's writing the *Apology* in the form of a defence speech by Socrates puts the reader— any reader—in the position of juror. To read the *Apology,* whether in ancient times or today, is to be challenged to pass judgement on Socrates.

He is charged with impiety and corrupting the young. Is he guilty or not guilty? And if he is guilty, what should the punishment be? How would you have voted if you had been on the jury in 399 BC? How in your imagination do you vote now?

This, I propose, is the challenge the written defence presents to its reader, by virtue of the forensic form—the standard form of a court speech—that Plato gave it. Xenophon's *Apology,* by contrast, is plain narrative, like an investigating journalist's account of the trial, with soundbites from the most dramatic moments of Socrates' speech and interviews with various interested parties. Plato's *Apology* opens with one of the common forms of address to jury or assembly, 'You, men of Athens' (ὦ ἄνδρες 'Αθηναῖοι),[4] and continues throughout in the forensic mode we are used to from surviving speeches of Lysias or Demosthenes. This is decidedly not a dialogue. Readers are not invited, as the dialogues properly so called invite us, to join in a philosophical discussion about virtue, knowledge, and reality. We are invited to reach a verdict on the case before us.

Very well. Let us start reading. At the end of the first paragraph (18a) Socrates says that the virtue (ἀρετή) of a juryman, what a good juryman will do, is to concentrate his mind on the justice of the defence he will present. The manner and rhetorical skill with which it is presented should be disregarded. In other words, if you are sitting—in reality or in imagination—on this jury, the only thing that should weigh with you is the justice of the case.

Imagine, then, that you are a good member of the jury in the sense defined. You already know something of Socrates' activities, from listening to him in person or from reading the dialogues of Plato. How, let me ask, do you now think you would have voted then? Guilty or not guilty?

[At this point the audience in Geneva voted 'Not guilty' by a majority of many to one. Other audiences in Durham, Lille, and London, and in biennial lectures at Cambridge, have invariably voted 'Not guilty' also, though not always by so dramatic a margin.]

In 399 BC the vote was something like 280 against Socrates, 221 in favour. If only 30 votes had gone the other way, he would have been acquitted (36a).[5] All the same, 280 or so to find him guilty is a large number of people.

They will not all have voted 'Guilty' for exactly the same reasons.[6] Some, perhaps, were motivated by political hostility to Socrates, because of his association with Alcibiades and the tyrant Critias; others perhaps by malice, having had the unpleasant experience of being made to look a fool by Socrates' questioning; others again may have been swayed by the caricature of Socrates in Aristophanes' *Clouds,* which Socrates at 18a-19c says is the chief prejudice he has to combat. But how far do these still standard explanations take us?

Socrates says that many of the jury have heard him talking and know the sorts of things he says (17c, 19d). Many of you have read him talking in Plato's dialogues and know the sorts of things he says. They know—you know—he is not like the Socrates of Aristophanes' *Clouds* who studies things in the heavens and under the earth and who teaches people to make the weaker argument the stronger (19b-c). Socrates was such a familiar figure in the community, for so many years, that we have to probe deeper.

Imagine a reasonably conscientious member of the jury: one who has heard Socrates in discussion, who understands the difference between him and the Socrates of the *Clouds,* who is not activated by political vengefulness or personal malice, who concentrates as a good juryman should on thinking exclusively about the justice of the defence Socrates offers. Someone who genuinely cares about the welfare of the city and about whether it is good or bad for the young to listen to Socrates. My question is: Could *such* a person have voted to find Socrates guilty of impiety and corrupting the young?

I want to suggest that the answer is 'Yes'. Indeed, that we shall not understand Socrates, or the enormous and permanent impact he has had on human thought, unless we realize that he was guilty of the impiety charge for which he was condemned. But first, a word of caution.

Socrates' impact on subsequent thought is due largely to the writings of Plato, so it is the Socrates of the writings of Plato we have to understand, and that same Socrates whose guilt I propose to argue for. This will be no historical hypothesis about the flesh-and-blood snubnosed personality who died in 399 BC, but an invitation to make your own imaginative judgement on the literary Socrates whose defence Plato immortalized in the *Apology,* perhaps many years later.

The exact charge is specified at 24b: Socrates ἀδικεῖ (does wrong, s. c. to the city) by corrupting the youth and not believing in the gods (θεοί) which the city believes in but other new divinities (δαιμόνια καινά). I suggest it is true that Socrates does not believe in the gods the city believes in, and that a large part of what is involved in his corrupting the young is that they end up not believing in them either (so 26b and *Euthyphro* 3a-b). Part of my evidence is that the written defence never rebuts this part of the charge. Nowhere in the *Apology* does Socrates say he does believe in the gods the city believes in.

He proves to his prosecutor Meletus that if he believes in new δαιμόνια (divinities) he believes in gods, because δαίμονες are θεοί (gods) (27a-28a). On the strength of this proof he claims the indictment is self-contradictory: it says that Socrates does not believe in gods but believes in gods (27a). The question before the jury, however, is whether Socrates believes in the gods the city believes in, not whether he believes in gods. Socrates makes fun of Meletus for confusing him with Anaxagoras and claiming he says the sun is a stone and the moon earth, not gods as other people believe (26d-e). But he does not say he does believe that the sun and moon are gods.

He *refers* constantly to Ὁ θεός, which can mean 'god' in a generic sense or 'the god'. It is ὁ θεός who told Chaerephon at Delphi that no-one is wiser than Socrates (21b), which Socrates eventually interprets to mean that Ὁ θεός has ordered him to philosophize, testing himself and others (28e-29a; cf. 33c). It is also ὁ θεός who is responsible for Socrates' 'divine sign', that mysterious inner voice which from time to time warns him off something he is about to do (31c-d, 40b). Since the first mention of Ὁ θεός is the phrase 'Ὁ θεός at Delphi' (20e), the jury will assume he is talking of Apollo. But he never speaks of Apollo by name.

Apollo, of course, is one of the gods the city most centrally believes in. He presides over the basis of its social structure. Each member of the jury can speak of 'my Apollo Patroos (Ancestral Apollo)', meaning the altar to Apollo that is focus to the organization of his 'fratry' (group of families, subdivision of a tribe) through which he has his citizenship. Apollo is as important at Athens as he is at Delphi. But nowhere in the *Apology* is he mentioned by name.

When interrogating Meletus Socrates makes a point of swearing by Hera (24e), by Zeus (25c, 26e), and by 'these very gods of whom we are speaking' (26b). On the other hand, in his address to the jury the only time he names a deity is when he mentions that Achilles' mother Thetis was a god (θεός, 28c). This is to explain why she could foresee what would happen if he avenged Patroclus; it has nothing to do with Thetis being one of the gods the city believes in. (There is in fact no evidence of Thetis having had a shrine, or any civic role, in ancient Athens.) All the important references to divinity in the *Apology* are indeterminate references to Ὁ θεός or, once or twice, to θεοί-'gods' in the plural, without the definite article (35d; 41d).[7] Socrates might as well be speaking of 'god' and 'gods' in a quite generic sense. He might almost be a monotheist. There is little or nothing to show that *the* gods, the numerous particular and highly individual gods the city believes in, mean anything to Socrates at all. Yet that was the central charge of the indictment, the part on which the rest depends.

How is a conscientious 'juror-reader' to interpret Socrates' silence on the central issue we have to make up our minds about? Would it be unjust to interpret it as an admission that the charge as levelled is true?

What Socrates does say about divinity is as damning as what he does not say. His central theme is that his philosophical activity is undertaken at the bidding of Ὁ θεός whom it would be wrong to disobey (23c, 28d-30a, 33c; 37e). That is his interpretation of the oracle. Ὁ θεός wants him to go around Athens asking his questions and showing people they do not know what they think they know. Socrates is a gadfly god-sent to sting the Athenians into caring for virtue above all else (29d-31b; 36c; 41e). And the best way to exercise this care is to spend every day in philosophical discussion about virtue: 'For a human being the unexamined life is not worth living' (38a). Ὁ θεός wants everybody every day to be *questioning:* examining and re-examining the values by which their life is led.

In other words, what divinity minds about, in Socrates' view, is two things: (1) that people should try to be virtuous, (2) that they should realize they do not yet know, but have to find out, what it is to be virtuous. In yet other words, Socrates' divinity lays it down that the accepted values of the Athenian community are to be put in question. Neither in private nor in public life are the Athenians living as they should—the *Apology* is one long counter-indictment charging the Athenians with rampant injustice. Few modern scholars have seen this as clearly as the author of the following excerpt from an ancient rhetorical treatise:

> Since we are on the subject of deliberative and judicial speeches, you may also take from Plato examples of further complex disputes, which combine, in some fashion, all the branches of rhetoric. The *Apology of Socrates* has as its primary purpose (πρότασις) an apology, as its title makes clear, but it is also an accusation of the Athenians, seeing that they brought such a man to court. And the bitterness of the accusation is concealed by the moderation (τῷ ἐπιεικει) of the apology; for the things spoken in self-defense are an accusation of the Athenians. These are two strands (συμπλοκαί) in the speech.[8] A third is this: the speech is an encomium of Socrates, made inoffensive by being covered up as a requirement of self-defense. This is the third strand. The result is two interconnected judicial themes (ὑποθέσεις), the apology and the accusation, together with one encomiastic theme: the praise of Socrates. The fourth strand, which was, as Plato saw it, the most important theme, with a deliberative or counselling function and philosophical content, is this: the book is an exhortatory proclamation (παράγγελμα) of what sort of a person the philosopher ought to be.[9]

Seldom has the *Apology* been summed up so well.

I am sure this ancient rhetorician is right that accusation is as important a theme as defence. Witness especially the section 31d-32e where Socrates says it would be impossible for anyone who puts justice first to take part in Athenian politics (or democratic politics anywhere) without perishing (cf. also 36b-c). The death sentence at the end of the *Apology* is the most vividly present reminder of how vice and injustice dominate the city (see 39a-d). But every-thing Socrates says about the value of his philosophic mission is by implica-tion an indictment of the Athenians for resisting the call to virtue. And in making this counter-indictment Socrates claims to be speaking on behalf of divinity. What his divinity wants from the Athenians is their singleminded dedication to justice and virtue.

But would not Zeus want the same? Yes and no. In the *Iliad* Zeus sends Athene to *break* the truce sworn in his name (iv 71-72 with iii 276-280, 298). In due course he will punish the violation he has himself decreed (iv 168, 235-240). Apollo, god of medicine, is also god of the plague. The traditional gods both help and harm in the relationships and activities they are interested in.[10] Socrates' divinity, by contrast, appears to be as singleminded as Socrates.

Now let us return to our conscientious, decent-minded jurors, be they many or few, listeners then or readers today. When they have heard all this that Socrates says about Ὁ θεός, they are bound to agree that Socrates is not ἄθεος (godless). It is clearly not the case that he believes in no gods at all, that he has no religious beliefs. But does he believe in the gods that the city believes in? Does he share the religion of the Athenian people? Recall how closely a Greek community's sense of its own identity and stability is bound up with its reli-gious observances and the myths that support them. If Socrates rejects the city's religion, he attacks the city. Conversely, if he says the city has got its pub-lic and private life all wrong, he attacks its religion; for its life and its religion are inseparable.[11] Let our jurors ask themselves this question: What would be left of traditional (fifth century) religion, hence what would be left of tradi-tional (fifth century) Athenian life, if the city accepted Socrates' view that what divinity demands from human beings is not propitiation and sacrifices, festivals and processions, but the practice of moral philosophy? I submit that our jurors are bound in good conscience to say to themselves: Socrates has a religion, but it is not ours. This is not the religion of the Athenians.

Socrates almost said the same at 35d: 'I believe in gods as do none of my ac-cusers'. These words can be understood to mean that he believes more piously than they do. But they can also be taken to mean that he believes in a differ-ent way from them.

Perhaps the most disturbing statement, calculated to make the jury roar, is that Socrates is immune from harm by the court (30c). Nothing they inflict—death, exile, disenfranchisement—will touch him where it counts. Rather, they will be the ones to suffer from the injustice they will have committed. Even a juror who does not roar could be disturbed by this. The jury's task, re-member, is not to admire Socrates' courage and strength; still less to attempt, as modern scholars do, a rational reconstruction of Socratic moral philoso-phy. It is to judge whether Socrates does harm to the city he claims cannot do harm to him. And that claim clearly goes against the grain of the traditional culture, as expressed by and mediated through the poets. One of the reasons poetry will be censored in the ideal city of the *Republic* is precisely because the poets instill the idea that a good and just person can suffer harm and tragic loss through divine or human agency and thereby lose their happiness (379d-380b, 387d-e, 392b with 364b; the tale of Zeus and Athene breaking the truce is expunged at 379e).

Socrates' rival claim is not of course that you cannot lose your money, your children, be struck by disease, and so on, but that a good and virtuous person will cope with whatever happens in the best possible way, turning it to something good: 'Virtue does not come from possessions but from virtue possessions and *all other things* come to be good both for individuals and for a city' (30b).[12] And it is clear that one becomes virtuous, in Socrates' view, by one's own efforts, through philosophizing.

Now it is a traditional idea that humans cannot prosper without the help of the gods. The paradigm of hubris (arrogant pride) is the belief that you can. When Ajax boasted he could succeed without the gods, and spurned Athene's aid, her anger struck him with madness and death (Sophocles, *Ajax* 756-778). Connected with this is that the word εὐδαιμονία, which we translate 'happiness', originally meant 'being favoured by divinity (δαίμων)'. Yet in the written speech Socrates comes perilously close to saying you must and can prosper on your own, by your own efforts: you are to gain *eudaimonia* without the help of god or gods. Divinity's role is an ancillary one only, to protect the just—or at any rate to protect Socrates through the 'divine sign'—from certain unforeseeable worldly consequences of their own justice. If the 'divine sign' is a special gift to Socrates (as is implied at *Republic* 496c), even so the just will not suffer harm for the lack of its protection. Being just, they will always prefer death to doing what is unjust, and will never regard death as a harm that matters. But divinity cannot make people just and virtuous. It can only wait upon humans to be virtuous by their own efforts, and then it is well pleased. The question is, might not our decent-minded juror think this the most frightful hubris? And does not hubris land not only the hubristic individual but also his city in trouble? The city of Athens has recently been through terrible troubles. Are not the jurors menaced, directly or indirectly, as a consequence of having this hubristic philosopher in their midst?

I have argued that Socrates' god demands a radical questioning of the community's values and its religion. I want now to move the discussion to a more theoretical level, to gain a better understanding of the confrontation between traditional Athenian religion and the singleminded divinity of Socratic religion. The text that seems designed to help us reach this understanding— although we do not know whether it came out after, in conjunction with, or before the *Apology*—is Plato's *Euthyphro,* to which ancient editors gave the subtitle 'On piety: a testing dialogue'.

Euthyphro, whose ideas about piety Socrates will put to the test, is prosecuting his own father. At their farm on the distant island of Naxos a hired labourer killed one of the house slaves in a drunken brawl. Euthyphro's father tied the man up, threw him into a ditch, and sent a messenger to Athens to ask the religious authorities what he ought to do. By the time the messenger returned, the labourer was dead from hunger and cold. One question a reader of this dialogue is invited to think about is this: Does Euthyphro act piously in bringing a charge of homocide against his own father on behalf of the labourer?

The magistrate before whom Euthyphro has come to lay his charge is about to give a preliminary hearing to the charge against Socrates, who is accused, so he tells Euthyphro, of corrupting the young by making new gods and not believing in the old ones. So another question a reader of this dialogue is invited to think about is the question, Is Socrates guilty of impiety?

Clearly, both questions should be thought about together. They invite a contrast between the standards of the old religion, strongly—even fanatically— supported by Euthyphro, and those of Socratic religion. It would be difficult to imagine a more dramatic context for the theme—question of the dialogue: 'What are piety and impiety both in relation to murder and in relation to other things?' (5c-d).

Euthyphro's first properly formulated answer to the question 'What is piety?' is: Piety is what is pleasing to the gods (6e). Now if by 'definition' you mean what many modern philosophers mean by it, an analysis of the meaning of a word in ordinary discourse, then Euthyphro's definition is as good a definition as you will find in the Platonic corpus. Greek religion was much occupied with propitiating and pleasing gods. The snag was, how can humans know what gods want? Worse, different divinities often want different and incompatible things, as when Euripides' Hippolytus was caught in the cross fire between the chaste goddess Artemis and Aphrodite, goddess of sexual love. The conflict of religious obligations may be tragically unresolvable.

More troubling still is the prospect of conflict between different aspects of the same divinity. At a difficult moment on the way back from his expedition, Xenophon sacrifices to Zeus Basileus (Zeus the King) and dutifully does what the entrails prescribe (*Anabasis* vii 6.44). Not long afterwards, and still struggling, he learns from a seer that his difficulties are due to Zeus Meilichios (Zeus the Merciful): he has not sacrificed to him (vii 7.4).[13] In the *Euthyphro* it is enough for Socrates to fasten on the first type of conflict. Not on the lack of singlemindedness in an individual god but on the fact that the gods quarrel and disagree—at least according to the stories that Euthyphro believes.

Socrates has already said he is reluctant to accept the religious narratives of his community (6a-b—a very significant admission for the question before us). But, given Euthyphro's beliefs, Socrates is entitled to argue:

> It would not be surprising if, in punishing your father as you are doing, your action is pleasing to Zeus [who tied up his father, Cronus, for eating his own children] but hateful to Cronus and Uranus [Zeus' grandfather, whom Cronus castrated], pleasing to Hephaestus but hateful to Hera, and similarly with respect to any other gods who are at variance with one another over your action. (8b)

In short, the same things may be both pious (because pleasing to some gods) and impious (because displeasing to others).

I need not remind you that these very stories of the gods and goddesses doing violence to one another are the paradigm examples of what will be banned by the censors of the ideal city of the *Republic* (377c-378d), who will not even permit an allegorical interpretation of these central narratives of Greek religion. Plato knew very well that he was proposing an ideological reconstruction of the entire Greek tradition. What Euthyphro, as a fanatical spokesman for the old ideology, should have replied when faced with Socrates' conclusion that the same thing may be both pious and impious is: 'Yes, that's life. Remember the story of Hippolytus.' Instead, Plato asserts his authorial control and makes Euthyphro allow Socrates to change the definition of piety so that it now reads: 'What is pious is what is pleasing to all the gods' (9e).

This is fatal. Why have many gods if they think and act as one? Were this revised definition of piety to gain acceptance at Athens, it would destroy the community's religion and its sense of its own identity.

Worse follows. Socrates asks: Are the gods pleased by what is pious because it is pious, or is it pious because it pleases the gods? This is the intellectual ancestor of the question that exercised the theologians of later, monotheistic times: Does God command what is good because it is good, or is it good because God commands it? A knotty, abstract, but enormously influential piece of reasoning forces Euthyphro to endorse the first alternative and reject the second. He accepts that the gods are pleased by what is pious because it is pious, not the other way round. This is another blow to traditional polytheism. Piety becomes a moral quality prior to and independent of divine pleasure or displeasure. The gods not only think and act as one. They all single-mindedly love virtue and hate vice. If you want to know how to please the gods, moral philosophy will tell you more than the sorts of divination on which Xenophon had to rely.

Such gods would never have brought about the Trojan war, which goes back, you remember, to the judgement of Paris and Aphrodite's promise that, if he gave the prize for beauty to her rather than to Hera or Athene, she would get him the love of Menelaus' wife Helen. And where would we be now without the Trojan war? I am tempted to say that, with gods as singlemindedly moral as Socrates', Greek culture would have been impossible and, in consequence, Western civilization would not be what it is today.

A less flamboyant way of putting the same point is to quote Gregory Vlastos:

> What would be left of her [Hera] and of the other Olympians if they were required to observe the stringent norms of Socratic virtue which require every moral agent, human or divine, to act only to cause good to others, never evil, regardless of provocation? Required to meet these austere standards, the city's gods would have become unrecognizable. Their ethical transformation would be tantamount to the destruction of the old gods, the creation of new ones—which is precisely what Socrates takes to be the sum and substance of the accusation at his trial. (Vlastos 1991, 166)

Back, then, to the trial. The question before us as 'juror-readers' of the *Apology* is not whether Socrates has a better religion than the Athenians, but whether he believes in the gods the city believes in. The discussion in the *Euthyphro* may—or again it may not—leave you siding morally and/or intellectually with Socrates, but it was Socrates himself at the beginning of the *Apology* who said that a good jury member should consider nothing but the justice of the case presented. And the case for the prosecution is that Socrates does wrong to the city by rejecting its religion, not believing in the gods the city believes in and corrupting the young by leading them not to believe in them either. So I ask you again, Is he guilty or not guilty as charged?

> [The vote at Geneva now was 26 against Socrates, a few in his favour and a number of abstentions. Previous versions of this speech have invariably secured a similar reversal of opinion. A good illustration for Plato's strictures on the power of rhetoric.]

After the verdict, the penalty. In ancient Athens this was decided by the jury too, and they accepted the death sentence the prosecution had demanded from the start. Although I have argued that Socrates was guilty as charged, I certainly would not ask anyone to support the further decision to impose the death penalty. What I want to do, by way of concluding, is to connect the case of Socrates with a recent, continuing tragedy of our own society.

Socrates was put to death by and on behalf of a traditional religion that was both polytheistic and (let us say) not particularly focussed on what we would call morality. When in book 10 of Plato's *Laws* an ideal society is recommended where the gods are conceived in terms Socrates would approve, as 'good and honouring justice more than humans do' (887b), Plato is quite happy to impose the death penalty on those who refuse to adhere to the creed of his new religion if they cannot be cured of their unbelief (909a). In this sense, the new religion ushered in by Socrates and Plato proved even less tolerant than the old. We know that Christianity turned out no better. A few years ago an English newspaper (the *Independent)* published a letter in which the Pope of the time of Queen Elizabeth I advised two Catholic English noblemen that, were they to assassinate the Queen, Head of the Church of England, it would increase, rather than decrease, their prospects of everlasting bliss in Heaven.

That, of course, was a conflict between two brands of Christianity. But in the fictional world of Salman Rushdie's *Satanic Verses* we meet again a confrontation between a traditional polytheistic religion and a new highly moralistic monotheism. In all that has been written about the Rushdie affair, I have not seen it sufficiently emphasized that the now notorious scenes of blasphemy in Gibreel's dream are not a mindless insult to the Prophet and his wives, but an act of symbolic, passive resistance by the adherents of the traditional polytheistic religion, after this has been prohibited by the Prophet, the old gods' statues thrown down, and their temples closed. 'There were more ways than one of refusing to Submit' (p. 381). The death sentence which in the novel's dream is actually carried out on Baal, the poet at the centre of the resistance, is a fictional anticipation of the sentence pronounced upon Rushdie in the real world of our day—the world in which it was appropriate to remind *Independent* readers of religious conflict in their own European past.

Both Socrates and Rushdie's polytheists speak, think, and act in ways that the opposing religion is bound to consider impious. But the converse is also true. One group's piety is another's impiety. The *Euthyphro* lays the groundwork for Plato's own denunciation in the *Republic* of the impiety of traditional Greek religion, from which in turn he derives his notorious proposals to censor literature out of existence. Euthyphro himself may be a fanatical enthusiast, but what he is an enthusiast for is the traditional religion. (In the *Cratylus* his 'expertise' enables him to understand the meaning and significance of the names of lots and lots of gods.) Numenius of Apamea (second century AD), the first pagan philosopher we know of to take an interest in the Bible, imagined that Plato chose so 'boastful and dull-witted' a character in order to be able to criticize 'the theology of the Athenians' without incurring the same fate as Socrates (frag. 23 Des Places). A fanciful idea, perhaps, but better than denying all connection between Euthyphro's views and the religious basis for accusing Socrates of impiety.[14]

It is perhaps less obvious that the *Apology* is on the same side as the *Euthyphro* and *Republic.* We are so accustomed to reading it as the testimony of one who dies for the freedom of inquiry and the freedom to proclaim in the marketplace the results of inquiry, no matter how upsetting to received opinion. Indeed, as an unreconstructed liberal I like to think of the historical Socrates as doing just that, dying for the cause of free thought and free speech. But here I am speaking of the Socrates of Plato's *Apology*. And there is no doubt that the relation between the author of the *Apology of Socrates* and the author of *Euthyphro, Republic,* and *Laws* X, is the relation of identity.

This brings me to the final suggestion I want to leave you with. I offer it as no more than a possibility to think about, a rather sobering hypothesis concerning the verdict Plato himself had in view when he wrote the *Apology*. The verdict was this:

Yes, Socrates was guilty as charged of not believing in the traditional gods and introducing new divinities. But what is shown by the fact that so good a man as Socrates was guilty of impiety under Athenian law? The impiety of Athenian religion. What the Athenians, from within that religion, inevitably saw as his wronging the city was the true god's gift to them of a mission to improve their souls, to educate them into a better religion. They judged as they did, and could do no other, out of ignorance. For they had the wrong religion, and he was the first martyr for the true religion. So what we should do, as readers of Plato's brilliant and moving defence, is join with him in promoting the new religion. *In cauda venenum.* If we can get political power, we will make this new religion compulsory for all—especially the poets.

Notes

1. We need not believe either Xenophon's statement *(Apol. 4)* that Socrates was prevented by his 'divine sign' from preparing the defence beforehand, or the report in Diogenes Laertius ii 40 that he turned down an offer from Lysias to write the speech for him. It is nevertheless evident that the interrogation of Meletus at 24c-28a could not have been fully prepared ahead of time, yet syntactic propriety is preserved as beautifully as in any Platonic dialogue, even with the audience interrupting at 27b. The same holds for Socrates' response to the verdict (35e ff.). It would be absurd to try to read the *Apology* as a verbatim transcript of the spoken speech.

2. Xen. *Apol.* 1 refers to others (plural) who have written about Socrates' defence of death, but gives no indication as to who they were or the character of their writings, save that they all conveyed the lofty (or haughty) tone (μεγαληγορία) of his speech.

3. 'The present occasion' refers to a colloquium at Geneva in honour of George Steiner. This address in a slightly different version originally appeared in the colloquium proceedings, Dykman and Godzich 1996, 13–36.

4. The main alternative, 'Gentlemen of the jury' (ὦ ἄνδρες δικασταί), is used only in Socrates' valedictory address to the jurors who voted against the death penalty (40a, 40e, 41c); they have earned the title 'juror'.

5. On the problems of determining the exact figures, see the still unsurpassed edition by Burnet 1924, *ad loc.*

6. For more on the importance of this point, see my review of Stone 1988.

7. I say 'once or twice' because at 35d the word θεοί is a semi-quotation from the indictment; in the next and final sentence Socrates restores Ὁ θεός in the singular.

8. A bold translation, but forced upon me by the context. The enumeration 'one, two, three' prevents συμπλοκή carrying its normal meaning 'combination'; despite the dictionaries, here it must mean 'element in a combination'.

9. From the first of two books 'On figured speeches' (Περὶ ἐσχηματισμένων, date and author unknown) which have come down to us in the corpus of Dionysius of Halicarnassus (Usener and Radermacher 1904–1929, 305.5–23. For the reference and help with the translation, I am indebted to Janet Fairweather.

10. For more on this principle, I may refer to Padel 1992, esp. 166.

11. One way to gain some sense of this inseparability is to read through Parke 1977.

12. Burnet's construal of the sentence, my italics. Both the construal and the italics are confirmed by the negative expression of the same idea at 41c-d: 'To a good man nothing bad happens either in life or in death, nor are his affairs uncared for by gods'. This famous declaration of faith (it is introduced as something the worthy jurors ought to hold true) is the closest Socrates comes in the *Apology* to the idea of divine providence. But you must acquire virtue first.

13. For more on the conflictedness of Greek divinity, see Padel 1995, ch. 20.

14. For an extreme case of this denial, see Burnet 1924, 5–7.

Bibliography

Burnet, John. 1924. *Plato's Euthyphro, Apology of Socrates, and Crito.* Oxford: Clarendon Press.

Burnyeat, M. F. 1988. rev. Stone 1988. *The New York Review of Books* 31 March 1988: 12–18.

Dionysius Halicarnassus. H. Usener and L. Radermacher edd. 1904–1929. *Dionysii Halicarnasei opuscula.* Leipzig: Teubner.

Dykman, Aminadav and Wlad Godzich edd.1996. *Platon et les poets: hommage à George Steiner.* Faculté des Lettres. Université de Genève.

Padel, Ruth. 1992. *In and Out of the* Mind: *Greek Images of the Tragic Self.* Princeton: Princeton University Press.

———. 1995. *Whom Gods Destroy: Elements of Greek and Tragic Madness.* Princeton: Princeton University Press.

Parke, H.W. 1977. *Festivals of the Athenians.* London: Thames & Hudson. Stone, I.F. 1988. *The Trial of Socrates.* Boston: Little, Brown; London: Cape.

Vlastos, Gregory. 1991. *Socrates: Ironist and Moral Philosopher.* Cambridge: Cambridge University Press.

9

Socrates and Obedience to the Law

Thomas C. Brickhouse and Nicholas D. Smith*

IN THE *CRITO*, SOCRATES SEEMS TO ARGUE that one ought never to disobey the law, or any legal power or body. The strongest such obligation is suggested at *Crito* 51 B-C, where Socrates says of the state:

> ... if she orders you to be scourged or imprisoned or if she leads you to war to be wounded or slain, her will is to be done, and this is right, and you must not give way or draw back or leave your post, but in war and in court and everywhere, you must do whatever the state, your country demands, or you must show her by persuasion what is really right ... [1]

It is on such grounds that he refuses Crito's offer to assist him in escaping prison (and thus execution). Yet in the *Apology*, there is at least one instance where Socrates seems to say that he would, under the right circumstances, disobey a legally constituted authority. At *Apology* 29C-30C, Socrates says that were the jurors to tell him that he could go free, on the condition that he discontinue the practice of philosophy, his reply would be:

> Men of Athens, I respect and love you, but I shall obey the god rather than you, and while I live and am able to continue, I shall never give up philosophy or stop exhorting you and pointing out the truth to any one of you I may meet ... (29D)

Critics have been led, by comparing such passages as these, to argue that there is a contradiction in Socrates' view of the moral acceptibility of civil

*We are indebted to Terence Irwin, Henry Teloh, and Gene James for comments on earlier drafts of this paper, and to the National Endowment for the Humanities for funding that helped to make this research possible. All errors are, of course, ours alone.

disobedience.[2] Others have urged that this shows Socrates' arguments with Crito to be intended less as decisive philosophically than as rhetorically adequate to persuade Crito himself.[3] Still others have sought to defend the consistency and sincerity of Socrates' arguments by providing a variety of interpretations of the problematic arguments that either weaken their apparent conclusions or recast their focus, and thus purport to allow a consistent formulation of Socratic philosophy.[4] In this brief discussion, we do not want to evaluate all of these interpretations as such, but rather to point out an aspect of Socrates' arguments that has gone wholly unnoticed in the considerable literature on this issue. If we are right, giving proper attention to Socrates' legal situation in the *Apology* removes the apparent contradiction, even if we assume for these purposes the strongest possible reading of Socrates' professed commitment to the law in the *Crito*.[5] In this way, we shall show that no reading of the *Crito* conflicts with Socrates' vow in the *Apology*. We shall conclude by arguing that no non-trivial conflict between god and law can even be imagined.

I

The general question is whether or not in the *Apology* Socrates is prepared to do things that would defy legal authority, and thus his own proscriptions in the *Crito*. The passages cited above *(Apology* 29C ff.) is not the only one in the *Apology* where Socrates appears defiant of authority, but it is the only one that can be argued plausibly to cause serious concern for consistency with the arguments of the *Crito*. For example, at 32B-C, Socrates recalls the time when he alone opposed the plan to try *en masse* the eight generals responsible for leaving their dead after the sea-battle at Arginusae, although the other prytanes were in favor of such an action. This is not a problem, however, because such a trial would be illegal, despite its appeal to the populace. Similarly, at 32C-E, Socrates recalls the time when the thirty tyrants were in power and directed him to go out and bring Leon of Salamis for execution—a man who had apparently done no wrong and had never been tried for his alleged offenses. Socrates did not carry out their order, however, since neither was their order legal according to the laws under which he had grown up,[6] nor did they have legal authority under those laws to give any such command (despite their manifest political power). The same goes for all other cases of apparent arrogance or defiance in the *Apology,* with the sole possible exception of his resistance to the jurors at 29C ff.: none commit Socrates to defying law or legal authority. If there is a contradiction to be found between the *Apology* and *Crito,* therefore, it can be found only in this one passage.

But these other cases provide at least some grounds for deciding what will count as a problem for the claim that the two dialogues contain an inconsistency. For example, if it can be shown either that the directive Socrates imagines the jurors to issue could never be a legal one, or that the jurors had no legal authority to issue such an order, Socrates' vow to disobey would be no more inconsistent with the doctrine that one ought always obey the law than his resistance to the mass trial of the generals or to the tyrants had been. Though we concede that there might be other ways to resolve the paradox, for example, by construing his obligation to the law as only *prima facie,* and capable of exception where there is a conflict with the dictates of piety[7] or even morality in general,[8] we shall argue that no such moral hierarchies need to be constructed in order to maintain consistency in Socrates' view.

II

It is important to recognize the circumstances under which Socrates makes his controversial vow: He is on trial for impiety and corrupting the youth of Athens. More immediately, it has been claimed by the prosecution that either he should not have been brought to trial (were he innocent), or given that he has, he should surely be found guilty and sentenced to death (29C). Socrates imagines that the jury is not persuaded by Anytus, but is also not utterly convinced of Socrates' blamelessness and harmlessness, and thus offers to let him go on the condition that he give up philosophy. Socrates responds by saying that he would never obey.

There are two possible ways in which such a situation could occur: Either (a) the jury offers to acquit Socrates of all charges, with this provision, or (b) the jury finds Socrates guilty of the charges, but elects to sentence him to silence rather than the death-penalty proposed by the prosecution. Let us consider these in order.

If the situation Socrates has in mind is of sort (a), then what is supposed to occur is that Socrates is found innocent of any charges, but is nonetheless required to eschew philosophy, on pain of death (29D). But there is not the slightest historical evidence that the jury was empowered to provide any such conditional acquittals; nor is there any sense in supposing that there should have been provisions for this. After all, if the man is legally guilty of no crimes, then he surely deserves no penalties or restrictions. If, on the other hand, he would deserve death for repeating his actions, then surely those actions are blameworthy and should thus merit a conviction, and not an acquittal. Of course, it might be that one who is charged as Socrates was, and put forward for trial,[9] should, whatever the outcome, feel warned that whatever he had done had the potential of getting him in serious trouble. But, again, there is excellent reason to believe that Athenian juries in trials of this type did not have the authority to find a man innocent, on the one hand, and yet issue a directive having the effect of a penalty, should the directive be disobeyed. Had they made such a directive anyway, Socrates' vow to disobey it would commit him to no disobedience of the law—for no law allowed the jury to make such a directive.

Now it might be that what the situation demands is that the jury acquit Socrates without a provision of any kind, but then subsequently pass a law saying either that philosophy was a crime punishable by death, or that Socrates practicing philosophy was a crime punishable by death. The effect of this would be that while they found Socrates guilty of no crime (for what he had done was not against the law), they had become convinced that it *ought* to be against the law, and thus had resolved to make it so. Thus, they say to Socrates, "we will let you go now, for you have broken no law, but we will make it so that if you go out and repeat the actions that have brought you before us, you *will* be breaking the law—a law the breaking of which earns the death-penalty". This would provide a reasonable reading of the jury's directive, without committing them to the problems considered above, but it would still require them to take on prerogatives that they do not have. Juries are not empowered to pass laws, but rather may only acquit or condemn those brought before them on formal charges, and, under certain circumstances (and with certain restrictions, about both of which we will have more to say below), select the penalty to be paid by those that are convicted. Thus, if the jury acquitted Socrates, they would have no further power over him as a group, nor could they contrive as a group to maintain any such power over him. Of course, as citizens, some or for that matter all of the members of the jury could propose legislation of the relevant sort to the council. But, as jurors, they could not guarantee its passage, and so they could not with any legal authority, actual or potential, issue such a directive as Socrates imagines, having found him innocent. Hence, were the jury to find Socrates innocent, his continued practice of philosophy would violate no law or legally constituted authority, no matter what the jury had otherwise proposed to him. His vow to continue, therefore, would in no way violate his avowed commitment always to obey the law.

But Socrates may have had situation (b) in mind, where the jury convicts him, but then sentences him to give up philosophy, threatening death if he disobeys. This not only makes more conceptual sense than situation (a) (for now they would be assigning such a penalty as a sentence for a convicted criminal), but coincides well with Socrates' discussion at 37E-38A, where having been convinced, he reconsiders the proposal that he quit philosophy, as the appropriate sentence.

Now it is clear that the jury is empowered to penalize convicted criminals through the assignment of sentences. And were a sentence assigned, the convict would be in violation of the law, or at least disobedient of a legally constituted authority empowered to make such assignments, were he to fail to behave accordingly. Were Socrates legally sentenced to eschew philosophy, disobedience would then at least *prima facie* violate his purported view that he ought always to do as his country commands.

We do not know all of the limitations on what sentences juries were permitted to assign, though we can be fairly certain that at least some minimal restrictions were in effect. But we do know that there was an important distinction between types of trial procedures, a distinction that is crucially relevant to this case. Although there was apparently not a clear distinction made between civil and criminal proceedings, Athens did have a provision for two different sorts of cases: those for crimes the penalities for which were set by law, and those for crimes the penalties for which were not set by law. The trial procedure for the first sort of case was called an ἀγὼν τιμητός; the latter was an ἀγὼν ἀτίμητος. The procedure for impiety, Socrates' alleged crime, was of the latter sort.

There is a good deal that is not known about Athenian legal practices, and much that is not known about trial procedures of this sort. But we do know enough to see in Socrates' vow of disobedience an aspect never noticed in the vast literature concerning it. In an ἀγὼν τιμητός, the prosecution would propose a penalty at the end of the indictment.[10] If the defendant is then found guilty in the initial part of the trial, he proposes a counter-penalty.[11] One thing that seems secure in our knowledge of this procedure, as it is presented clearly and consistently in each source on this issue,[12] is that the jury was then required by law to have a second vote in which they chose the penalty from those proposed by the prosecutor and the defendant. There was no provision for them to concoct yet another possible penalty, and then assign that one.

But given this, Socrates' vow to disobey the jury, were they to proscribe further philosophical activity, would in no way commit him to disobeying either law or legally constituted authority, for the jury could in no way legally make such a proscription, even, as in situation (b), as the sentence for the crimes of which they had convicted him. On the one hand, the prosecution has asked for death. Telling Socrates that his sentence is to cease philosophizing is not, therefore, to select the penalty proposed by the prosecution. But it is not the penalty proposed by Socrates either, for when he is called upon to propose a counter-penalty, he explicitly says that he will not propose to quit philosophy. Rather, he offers a fine. Were the jury to sentence him to silence, therefore, they would be assigning a penalty proposed by neither of the parties empowered to offer an alternative. Hence, were they to direct Socrates to quit philosophy, their directive would not be legal. Socrates' commitment to obey the law would thus not be in even *prima facie* conflict with his refusal to obey this directive.[13]

Of course, if Socrates proposed such a penalty, the jury could legally select it, and subsequent failure to act accordingly would be a violation of the law (or legal authority) to which Socrates professes to owe utter obedience. But Socrates does not do this when given the opportunity, and there is no reason to suppose that he ever would do such a thing. After all, the heart of his defense against the charges brought by Meletus is that he will never disobey the command of the god, a command he interprets to require him to philosophize. Alternatively, if the prosecution had suggested that an abandonment of philosophy be the penalty, the jury would have had the opportunity legally to command Socrates to do what he says he would never obey. But the prosecution manifestly did not do this, and their failure to do so was already established by the time Socrates made his vow to disobey any such directive. In any case, such an event would require a number of unlikely conditions. First, that any indictment for as serious a crime as impiety would allow for even a conditional release of the accused is absurd. Impiety was far too serious a charge. Secondly, if other charges had been made—less serious charges—it is not certain that Socrates would have been found guilty of them, or that charges could have been found where such a penalty could be legally assigned. Thirdly, all of these problems aside, were this the penalty sought by the prosecution, it is not clear that Socrates could not have proposed an alternative that would have better suited the jury—even death[14]—and thus avoided the conflict that way. In short, the number of suppositions, all contrary to fact, that need to be made, even to get the problematic case off the ground, renders the problem prohibitively speculative.

One final point remains which might be used as an objection to our view that no serious paradox is to be found in Socrates' vow. After all, whatever truth there is in the above observations, the fact remains that Socrates does not say that he would disobey because any such directive to cease philosophy would not be legal; he says that he would disobey because such a directive would conflict with his duty to the god. If the fact that the jury could not legally require Socrates to quit philosophy had anything to do with his vow, surely he would have said so.

Such an objection is based upon a misunderstanding of our argument, however, and in any case ignores the specific purpose of Socrates' vow. First, we have not attempted to argue that there could be no moral principle overriding that which obliges Socrates to obey the law, though we will consider this point in the next section. Secondly, we have not claimed that the fact that the imagined directive from the jury would not be legal is what motivated Socrates to vow disobedience. We have only argued that in vowing to disobey any such directive, he is not vowing disobedience to the law or legal authority, and thus his vow causes no conflict with the arguments of the *Crito*.

But more importantly, Socrates does not raise this topic to explain either his feelings of obligation to the law, or any inclination he might have to violate the law. Rather, he raises this topic to underscore two points of fundamental significance in his defense: He wishes to show how much more deeply he fears doing that which is evil and shameful than death, and he wishes to highlight the seriousness with which he takes his mission for the god. In doing so, he uses the device of considering what he would do if the jury let him go unharmed, provided that he gave up this mission. His answer is that to do so would be shameful and impious. The irony of this is that it is on the grounds of piety that he will not promise to cease what has led to his being charged with impiety, and this irony would not likely have been lost on his audience, the jury. The gist of his vow, then, is only this: Even if it meant freedom for him were he to give up his "mission", and death were he to continue it, he would continue it—so much does he fear disgrace more than death. And even if the citizens of Athens would never forgive him for his actions, the will of the god means more to him.

The reason that Socrates would make such claims is that it is vital to his defense that the actions that have offended his accusers (and many others besides) are the will of the god, and thus cannot provide grounds for the charge of impiety. And were he seen to be saying all of these things out of a fear of death, the jurors could doubt the sincerity of his repeated professions to the effect that his work is serious and vital to the welfare of the state. Thus, Socrates urged both that he serves the god and that he has no fear of death in the strongest possible terms—so strongly that it even overrides an openly expressed love and respect for his fellow citizens. His vow to disobey the imagined directive does not reflect an arrogant disregard for the jury or their wishes. Rather it stresses the extent to which he is deeply pious, contrary to the claims of the prosecution. Indeed, it is a repeated feature of his defense that his actions are designed to better the state and those that compose it—so far are his commitments from defiant disregard for those that would have him stop behaving as he does.

III

We have not argued that there is no need to consider the commitments of Socratic philosophy on the issue of conflicting duties to god and law. Rather, our claim thus far is only that no such conflict arises from Socrates' vow in the *Apology*. The grounds for saying this, however, do not entail that no such conflict could occur. Though such speculation, according to the argument above, is not required by the juxtaposition of the *Apology* and the *Crito*, it is worthwhile asking whether such a situation could arise and, if it did, what Socrates' response would be.

The options seem to be three: (i) Socrates' principles would require him to obey the law even if it entailed defying the god's command; (ii) Socrates' principles would require him to obey the god's command even if it entailed defying the law; and (iii) there is no conceivable situation, once properly understood, in which obedience to the law and to the god conflict.[15]

Establishing which of these would be the Socratic position is made at least problematic by the fact that the text offers nothing explicitly addressed to this issue—for according to our argument above the statements of the *Apology* and *Crito* that have caused such controversy on this point are not, once properly seen in context, sufficient really to raise the question directly. Rather, they leave only the feeling that such a conflict could occur. But (i) on its face appears to conflict with at least the sense of Socrates' defense in the *Apology*; a defense that is founded upon repeated assertions to the effect that he has given up all else in favor of pursuing his duty to the god. Moreover, even if our argument above is correct, Socrates ignores the illegality of the jury's imagined directive, citing only the god's will in his vow to disobey. These features of the *Apology* at least suggest that Socrates took his duty to the god as foremost. And just as such observations would seem to render (i) an unlikely candidate for Socratic commitment, they would also seem to lend support to (ii), the option unanimously chosen by those scholars inclined to attribute a hierarchy of commitments to Socrates. But there is an homologous difficulty with (ii). In the *Crito*, Socrates' arguments never explicitly allow exceptions; they say only that one must obey the law, at least where those responsible cannot be persuaded that the law in question ought to be changed. Of course, it might be argued that the suggested exception is not provided in the *Crito* only because such religious questions are not at issue at that point.[16] The unqualified character of Socrates' conclusions, however, strongly suggest that the arguments are not intended to be applicable solely to those specific questions raised by Crito.

On these grounds, then, (iii) appears to be the most attractive option, though for it to work, grounds must be given for ruling out possible conflict between civic and religious duties. Let us consider, then, what evidence might be cited for this. First, it was generally supposed that the foundations for the legal code were divine in origin.[17] But more importantly, Athenian law directly proscribed impiety, without proscribing particular acts or beliefs.[18] The conflict between the laws and the god such speculations suppose, therefore, would be, to Socrates, conflicts within the laws themselves, since any law that required Socrates to disobey the god would direct him in a way exactly contradictory to the legal directive prohibiting impiety. Socrates' categorical duty to obey the law could not in principle conflict with his categorical duty to the god under these conditions, for the latter was built into the former.

Let us consider, for example, what would be the effect of this account on Socrates' position were he to face a duly enacted law prohibiting the practice of philosophy.[19] Certainly he would disobey such a law, yet in the *Crito* Socrates plainly asserts that each of the state's laws must be obeyed (51C-D). But in this situation, the imagined law requires what is to Socrates a manifest impiety; thus it contradicts a prior law prohibiting impiety. When laws contradict one another, even the most steadfast adherent to civil authority cannot find a way to comply with both. Necessarily, to comply with one is to disobey the other. That Socrates could not defy a law of logic is no evidence that he would defy a law of Athens, yet it seems the former is what would be required in this case, in order to achieve the latter in a non-trivial way. Thus, Socrates could argue that both duties—to the law and to the god—are such as to allow for no exceptions. Given that Socrates makes no exceptions to such duties, and that Athenian law provides for their compatibility, we see no reason not to assume the literality of Socrates' claims, at least so far as they apply to these problems.

This does, however, suggest one possible set of circumstances in which Socrates would encounter the conflict we have so far ruled out: We can generate such a case if we imagine Athens to repeal her proscription of impiety and subsequently outlaw philosophy. We have shown that no such conflict can be generated from a proper understanding of the *Apology*, even when conjoined with the strongest rendering of the arguments of the *Crito*. We have further argued that given the Athenian legal system as we know it, and as it was when Socrates argued the views for which we have come to know him, no such conflict can be generated. Though we concede that interest might be found in speculations as to how Socrates might have had to modify his views were Athens to undergo one or more drastic changes (or, for these purposes equivalently, if the god were to demand that Socrates attempt to destroy the laws), such speculations lie considerably beyond the scope of philosophical exegesis.[20] And though it may be desirable on other grounds to interpret Socratic claims in such a way as to weaken the commitments we have taken here to be categorical, we have shown that in context, Socrates' arguments can be taken at face value, with no violence to sense or logic.

Notes

1. This and the next quote are the Loeb Classical Library translation by H.N. Fowler (Harvard, 1971).

2. Cf. for representative examples of this view, Rex Martin, "Socrates and Disobedience to Law", *The Review of Metaphysics* XXIV, 1970, pp. 22 ff.; Gene James, "Socrates on Civil Disobedience and Rebellion", *Southern Journal of Philosophy* XI, 1973, pp. 119–127; and Howard Zinn, *Disobedience and Democracy* (New York, 1968, p. 28).

3. Cf. for representative examples of this view, Gary Young, "Socrates and Obedience", *Phronesis* XIX, 1974, pp. 1–29; Ann Congleton, "Two Kinds of Lawlessness: Plato's *Crito*", *Political Theory* II, 1974, pp. 432–466; Frederick Rosen, "Obligation and Friendship in Plato's *Crito*", *Political Theory*, I, 1973, pp. 307–308. George Grote, in *Plato and the Other Companions of Socrates* (London, 1888, Vol. I, Chapter 10) holds that the positions regarding obedience to law found in the *Apology* and the *Crito* are inconsistent. But Grote attempts to explain the inconsistency by arguing that the *Apology* is a faithful account of the speech Socrates actually gave at his trial, while the *Crito* represents Plato's attempt to portray his master in a far more favorable light by writing an imaginary discussion between Socrates and Crito in which Socrates defends the prerogatives of the state. A position similar to that of Grote is found in J. Dybikowski, "Was Socrates as Reasonable as Professor Vlastos?", *The Yale Review* LXIV, 1974, pp. 293–296.

4. Cf. for representative examples of such interpretations, Gregory Vlastos, "Socrates on Obedience and Disobedience", *The Yale Review* LXII, 1974, pp. 517–534; Frances C. Wade, S.J., "In Defense of Socrates", *The Review of Metaphysics* XXV, 1971, pp. 311–325; Gerasimos Santas, *Socrates* (London, Boston, and Henley, 1979, pp. 54–56); R.E. Allen, "Law and Justice in Plato's *Crito*", *Journal of Philosophy* LXIX, 1972, pp. 557–567; A.D. Woozley, "Socrates on Disobeying the Law", in *The Philosophy of Socrates,* ed. by Gregory Vlastos (Garden City, New York, 299–318). A somewhat different version is taken by Woozley in his recent book, *Law and Obedience: The Arguments of Plato's Crito* (Chapel Hill, 1979, Chapter III, esp. pp. 44–46).

5. There is a variety of interpretations of the specific conclusions that the arguments of the *Crito* are supposed to reach, and we shall not attempt to take sides on this issue. Rather, we shall take at face value what Socrates proclaims of his view in numerous places in the *Crito*, namely, that he is morally obliged to obey the laws and legal structures of his country. It is worth noting, however, that many of the arguments of the *Crito* seem to derive this obligation from higher ones, and so our argument should not be taken as an attempt to refute any of the more detailed interpretations of the *Crito* that take this into account. Rather, we seek only to show that such moderating interpretations are not required for consistency with the problematic vow in the *Apology*.

6. That one aspect of Socrates' feeling of duty to the law is that he had grown up under its protection is evident in his argument at *Crito* 51C ff. The degree to which this in particular is vital to his duty is somewhat unclear, though we can be certain that Socrates' commitment to this law would entail acquiescence to the established process by which any new laws were to be made. Thus, it would reasonably be hypothesized that any new law or legal decision would, by this same argument, prohibit Socrates' disobedience. Cf. pp. 11–12 for the limits of this, however.

7. Cf. Vlastos and Santas, for examples. Though not explicit in arguing that Socrates holds a "hierarchical view" of moral obligation, such an attribution to Socrates seems to be implied by both positions taken by Woozley. Unfortunately,

whatever philosophical merits such a view might have, nowhere in the *Crito* does Socrates allow that his obligation to the state could be overridden by any other obligation, though cf. note 5, above.

8. Cf. Wade, for example. Again similar considerations apply to this view as any other "hierarchical view". (Cf. notes 5 and 7 above.)

9. Not all plaints were actually brought before the court for trial. The king archon, whose function it was to hear preliminary evidence against a defendant in impiety actions, could for a variety of reasons refuse to forward a case to the court. (Cf., A.R.W. Harrison, *The Law of Athens*, Vol. I, Oxford, 1971, p. 90).

10. Cf., John Burnet, *Plato's Euthyphro, Apology of Socrates and Crito*, Oxford, 1963, p. 152, note on 36B3.

11. The penalty proposed by the prosecution is called the τίμησις; that by the defendant, the ἀντιτίμησις. It is not entirely clear whether this was a legal requirement for the defendant, or merely an option that he had.

12. Cf., for examples, Burnet, *op. cit.*, p. 149; Harrison, *op. cit.*, pp. 80–82; J.H. Lipsius, *Das Attische Recht und Rechtsverfahren* (1905, pp. 248–253); Louis Gernet, *Droit et Societe dans la grece Ancienne* (1955, pp. 61–81, esp. 78–79); Otto Schulthess, *RE* cols. 1251–1255; Harpokration, s.v., ἀτίμητος ἀγὼν καὶ τιμητός. The principal ancient source is Demosthenes, 52.18, 53.26, 56.43, 58.70, and 59.6.

13. Moreover, the jury could not sentence Socrates to death, but then suspend it under the provision that it would be executed if Socrates continued practicing philosophy. We haven't the slightest evidence that Athenian law provided the jury the power to assign and suspend a sentence. But in any case, even if the jury did legally have the power to do this, and opted to exercise it in Socrates' case, his failure to cease philosophy would not then be a violation of a law, but rather the choice of death over silence—a choice provided by the terms of the suspension.

14. It is unlikely that Socrates would ever propose such a penalty, despite his professed lack of fear of death, but the supposition that he might, under these conditions, is surely no more unlikely than are the conditions we have imagined.

15. Though he is not necessarily committed to the view that follows, Terence Irwin's helpful comments had a great effect on the way we have structured it.

16. This is the move made by Santas to explain why Socrates does not mention in the *Crito* what Santas takes to be the overriding nature of his obligation to the god. Though we should not be taken here as refuting this view by fiat, see notes 5 and 7, above.

17. Cf. K.J. Dover, *Greek Popular Morality in the Time of Plato and Aristotle*, Berkeley and Los Angeles, 1974, pp. 255–56.

18. Cf. D.M. MacDowell, *The Law in Classical Athens*, Ithaca, N.Y., 1978, pp. 199–200.

19. Initially, Socrates might not consider it a law at all. In cases where one believed that a law was passed that contradicted a prior law, one could endeavor to have it cancelled by proposing a παρανόμων, a legal procedure in which the initiator of the later law is charged with having created such a contradiction, and during which that later law is suspended. At least at the outset, Socrates might well have initiated such a procedure. However, it is conceivable that even if he did this, the offending law would be upheld, leaving Socrates to face a duly enacted—and now upheld—law forbidding

him to philosophize. The fact that the jury trying the imagined case did not see the contradiction does not entail that there is no contradiction, however, and this is crucial to the situation Socrates would now face. For a more detailed discussion of how such a legal procedure would work, cf. MacDowell, pp. 50–52.

20. Even on the most superficial reading of the *Crito,* however, some provision is made for this: Socrates could always choose to leave Athens, though it is not clear that this would not compromise his religious mission in Athens. (Cf. *Crito* 51D, but cp. *Apology* 30D-E, and 37C-E.)

10

Dokimasia, Satisfaction, and Agreement

Richard Kraut

1
Agreement: Some Unsolved Problems

ALTHOUGH THE LAWS ASSERT AT AN EARLY POINT in their speech (50c5-6) that
Socrates agreed to abide by the judgments of the courts, they do not immediately defend their claim. They say only as much as is needed to discourage
Socrates and Crito from pursuing a line of reasoning that will get them
nowhere. Admittedly, Socrates has recently suffered an injustice at the hands of
his city, but if, as the Laws allege, it is an injustice he agreed to risk, then his un-
fortunate trial will give him no legitimate reason to try to destroy the city. But
to defend immediately their claim that Socrates made such an agreement
would take the Laws too far away from their present task. They first need to
complete their "argument from destruction" by showing that Socrates would
be unjustified in acting violently or destructively against Athens, regardless of
the injustices inflicted on him by the city. And, as we have seen, that brings
them to the analogy between offspring and citizens. But once this business is
taken care of, the Laws can return to the point they left hanging. What makes
them say that Socrates agreed to abide by the judgments of the courts? By
which acts, undertaken or omitted, did he make this agreement? Furthermore,
what reason do they have for saying that it was a just agreement? The Laws now
devote sixty lines (51d1-53a7) to these questions. They proceed as follows.

(A) 51d1-e4: They first explain the process by which all citizens make an
agreement with the city. When an Athenian comes of legal age and observes
the political practices of his city, he is, if dissatisfied, allowed to expatriate, and

he may even take his property with him. But whoever is aware of the city's institutions and decides to stay has agreed, through what he does, to abide by its
commands.

(B) 51e4-52a3: They next assert that this creates a third argument against
escape, and they repeat their earlier point that everyone is given two choices:
to persuade or obey. But Socrates refuses to do either.

(C) 52a3-d7: The argument now turns more specifically to the relationship between Socrates and Athens. By escaping, he would be more guilty
than anyone else, for he especially has agreed to live as a citizen, and he has
been especially satisfied with the city. Unlike others, he has rarely left
Athens; furthermore; he has had children there; and most recently, when he
could have proposed exile as a punishment, he claimed instead that he
would rather die.

(D) 52d8-53a7: Finally, the Laws add some further facts about the agreement Socrates has made. He was not forced, rushed, or tricked into this agreement, but in fact had seventy years during which he could have left, if he was
dissatisfied or thought his agreements unjust. But he did not prefer even
Sparta or Crete, cities he has always thought to be well governed. This satisfaction with his native city shows that he has been satisfied with its laws, for
no one can be satisfied with a city apart from its laws.

I have already made some use of the material presented in (B) and (D). In
(B), the Laws are saying that even when someone breaks an agreement and
disobeys the city, he must persuade. (See III.1.)* In (D), they are arguing that
the agreement Socrates made was just. (See II.2-3.) But several questions were
previously shelved, and now they must be answered. First, we want to know
whether it is ever permissible for a citizen to violate an order on the grounds
that it does him an injustice. (See II.4.) Obviously, if the citizen voluntarily
agrees to every order Athens gives, then he is agreeing to risk such suffering.
But can a citizen remain in Athens and legitimately refuse to agree to certain
laws or orders? Can he refuse to agree to a law because it does him an injustice? Or must he leave the city and go into exile if he is dissatisfied with any
laws? Second, we want to know whether the argument from agreement com-
pensates for the weakness of the parent-city analogy. (See IV.6.) As I argued
earlier, that analogy gives the city the right to issue orders to and to demand
explanations from its citizens. But it does not give the city the right to kill or
imprison its citizens for disobedience, since this is not a right that parents
have in relation to their adult offspring. If the city has this right, it must be
given to it by the agreement of its citizens. But what if the citizens refuse to

---

* References are to Richard Kraut's *Socrates and the State* (Princeton University Press, 1984), from
which this piece is reprinted.

give it? In that case, the city will have too little power. On the other hand, if a citizen who continues to reside in Athens has no choice but to agree to the judicial system, in what sense is his agreement voluntary and therefore just? Is it voluntary only in the sense that he can leave Athens if he wants to? In that case, the Laws are adopting the highly authoritarian doctrine that departure is the only way to avoid making an agreement to obey one's city. It seems that the Laws are caught between two equally unappealing extremes: either agreement is too easy to avoid, in which case the city has too little power; or agreement is too difficult to avoid, in which case the citizen has too little freedom. Must the Laws fall into one or the other of these two traps?

To answer these questions, it will be necessary to look carefully at the mechanics by which an agreement is made. What is the precise role of residence in the argument of the Laws? Does residence constitute an agreement to obey, or is it merely a sign of satisfaction? Do they think that being satisfied with a law is the same thing as agreeing to it? Are there any other factors besides residence and satisfaction in the mechanics of making an agreement? We are forced to tackle these questions if we want to determine whether permanent departure from Athens is the only way to avoid making an agreement to obey the city.

2
Implied Agreement

The Laws say that an Athenian who conducts himself in a certain way "has agreed with us, by what he does (*ergôi*), to carry out what we command . . ." (51e3-4). Later, at 52d5, they expand on this *ergôi*: Socrates has agreed to be a citizen "by what he does and not by what he says" (*ergôi all' ou logôi*). So they do not claim that Socrates ever said, in so many words, "I agree to do whatever the city commands," or "I agree to be a citizen."[1] Rather, their point is that his nonverbal behavior gave rise to such an agreement; as we might put it, his agreement was tacit or implied, though it was not expressed in words. Now, I take it to be quite uncontroversial that agreements can be made by what we do, and not merely by what we say or write. A nod of the head, to take a trivial example, can express assent as easily as "yes." Or a speaker at a meeting can ask his listeners to rise if they agree to the conditions he has just described. We can fix upon any convention we like to serve as a signal of agreement: a green tie can mean "I agree to join the club" and a red tie can mean "I refuse."

But in addition to these obvious examples, there are others that are less straightforward and more interesting. Suppose someone agrees to play a game of chess with me. While the game is in progress, I am out of the room, and he alters the positions of some of the pieces. No doubt, this is a case of cheating, but can we also describe it as the breaking of an agreement? True, my opponent never explicitly said, "I will play by the rules," but that hardly seems to matter. He did agree to play chess, and what does that agreement come to if it is unaccompanied by the understanding that certain rules will guide our conduct? Of course, players can agree to change the rules if they want to, but in the absence of such an arrangement, the agreement to play chess is an agreement to pursue a certain goal by means of certain rules.

Consider a second example. A man enters a restaurant, looks at a menu, and orders a certain dish, which, as the menu indicates, costs $10. When the waiter brings the bill at the end of the meal, the customer refuses to pay, and claims in his defense that he never agreed to pay $10 or any other amount; he merely requested a certain dish, and the waiter was nice enough to bring it to him. Now, if this man understands the conventions by which restaurants operate, then he is obviously guilty of sophistry. He knows that the restaurant requires payment for his meal, and by ordering that particular meal he created the legitimate expectation that he would pay for it. Any court of law would hold that he had made an agreement to pay $10, even though he merely said, "I'll have that dish."[2] And surely the courts are right that valid agreements do not always have to be spelled out in so many words.

One final example. The rules of a certain club are prominently displayed on the walls of its admissions office, and membership is granted to anyone who pays a certain fee and submits some information about himself. Does an individual who joins thereby agree to abide by the rules posted on the walls? The application form does not include a statement of allegiance to the club's rules, and so the act of joining does not involve an *explicit* agreement to obey. But does it *imply* an agreement? Of course, we are not asking whether the new member *ought* to abide by the rules of the club. Perhaps, if the organization is evil or its rules absurd, he should not. What we want to know is whether someone who violates those rules is also violating—justifiably or not—an agreement implied in the act of joining.

Surely our previous two examples suggest that an implicit agreement has been made. Neither the chess player nor the restaurant customer explicitly agreed to abide by any rules or conventions. If they implied an agreement when they accepted a match or ordered a meal, then our club member has also implicitly agreed to the rules of the organization. He knows what will be expected of him when he joins, for the club has gone out of its way to make sure that new members are aware of its regulations. So, by joining, he gives the others to understand that he will abide by those rules. And this understanding is appropriately called an agreement.

3
The Club of Athens

I have dwelled on these examples because I think the last of them is relevant to the *Crito*. During the late fifth century, becoming an Athenian citizen was not something that happened automatically either at birth or at any other time. Male children born of citizen parents had to take positive steps to enroll themselves as citizens at the age of seventeen, and unless their names appeared on the official lists of citizens, they could not legally exercise the judicial and legislative privileges of adult Athenians. The process of registration was carefully regulated. The candidate for citizenship had to provide evidence of his age and citizen parentage at the year's first official meeting of his deme. If the deme members were not satisfied with his credentials, the case could be appealed to a court, but if the case went against the candidate, he was enslaved. If the deme was satisfied with his credentials, his name was registered on the official lists, but the deme's decision to do so was reviewed by the Council, which could fine deme members for inaccurate judgments. If anyone tried to exercise the rights of a citizen without having gone through this process, he was imprisoned, and if found guilty, sold by the city to the highest bidder. The whole process was called a *dokimasia*, which literally means a "testing."[3]

So, becoming a full-fledged Athenian citizen was very much like joining a club. Not only did one need certain qualifications (that is true of the citizens of every state), but one also had to take positive steps to enroll as a member. Merely reaching a certain age, merely being eligible for citizenship, was not enough: one actually had to apply for membership. Now, this fact about Athens provides the Laws with a sounder basis for argument than we might have thought available to them. If citizenship had merely been a matter of reaching a certain age, then it would surely have been absurd for an Athenian philosopher to say, "You are now seventeen, and therefore you have agreed to obey the city." If citizenship is conferred on you whether you like it or not, then becoming a citizen cannot involve a voluntary agreement. But what if you actively apply for citizenship status: won't you be committed thereby to the laws of the city? At any rate, won't you be committed to the laws if you show that you understand them? Might the *Crito* be relying on this idea when it argues that the Athenian citizens have agreed to obey the city?

Let us now look at the passage which describes the mechanics by which citizens make an agreement to obey the city.

We make this proclamation, by giving freedom to any Athenian that wants it: When he has passed the test for citizenship [*dokimasthêi*] and has observed the affairs of the city and us the Laws, if we do not satisfy him he is free to take his

belongings and go wherever he wants. No law prevents or forbids you, if one of
you wants to settle in a colony [*apoikia*], should we and the city not satisfy you.
Or if you want to go somewhere else and be a resident alien [*metoikein*], you can
go wherever you want and take your belongings. But whichever of you remains,
seeing the manner in which we decide court cases and the other ways in which
we manage the city, we say that by this time he has, by what he does, agreed with
us to carry out whatever we command. (51d1-e4)

The verb, *dokimasthêi*, that appears at the beginning of this passage is cog-
nate to the noun, *dokimasia*. So the Laws are definitely referring to the testing
procedure by which Athenians applied for admission to the citizenry.[4] But
they do not say that this act of enrollment is the sole act by which one makes
an agreement to obey the city, nor do they claim that this agreement is made
at the very moment one is accepted as a full-fledged citizen. In addition to the
dokimasia, they talk about the citizen's grasp of legal institutions, his freedom
to leave, his satisfaction with the city, and his decision to remain. Any interpretation of the argument from agreement must explain how these various
factors are supposed to combine to constitute an agreement to obey the city.
What I propose is that the process by which one makes this agreement takes a
good deal of time, and that the initial step is going through the *dokimasia*. It
is no accident that, in the above quotation, the *dokimasia* is mentioned first,
and the activity of observing the city's affairs comes second. The idea is that
at the time someone enrolls as a citizen, he does not yet understand the way
his city works. The new citizen, in other words, is now being given an opportunity to observe the legal machinery of Athens, and he cannot be taken to
have agreed to the city's laws until he has had sufficient time to understand
them. This same point is implied when the Laws say, in the above passage,
". . . whichever of you remains, seeing the manner in which we decide court
cases . . . by this time . . . has agreed with us. . . ." Until one was seventeen and
had passed one's *dokimasia*, one was not allowed to take part in legal proceedings; one could not bring a case to court, and in all legal matters one was
represented by one's father or guardian. Furthermore, the temporal adverb,
"by this time" (*êdê*) reinforces the idea that some time elapses between the
dokimasia and the completion of the agreement to obey the city. Finally, at a
later point in their argument, the Laws explicitly say that the agreement made
by Socrates was not the result of deception or lack of time for reflection (52e2-
4). The implication is that one is justified in breaking agreements if one is
tricked into them, or if one had to make a snap decision. It is unlikely that the
Laws would claim that a citizen who has just emerged from his *dokimasia* has
already agreed to obey the city. Were they to take this line, they would be vulnerable to the charge that the citizen has had too little time to understand and
evaluate the organization he has just entered.

None of this shows that enrolling as a citizen is not one of the steps by which one agrees to obey the city; rather, it shows that this act is not by itself sufficient to constitute agreement.[5] The Laws must therefore mean that undergoing the *dokimasia* for citizenship is the act that initiates the process of committing oneself to the city's orders. That process goes on for some time longer, and there is no fixed time at which it terminates. But at some point or other, the new citizen has gathered enough understanding of the club he has entered; from then on, if he is satisfied with the city and does not quit, he has in effect agreed to its rules. The act of making this agreement therefore consists of three stages: the *dokimasia*, the period of increasing political awareness, and the point at which one has stayed so long that one can fairly be said to have agreed. No agreement has taken place until stage three has been reached, and the boundary between stages two and three is indeterminate. Evidently, the Laws have a complex theory of implied consent, but it is intelligible and even appealing. Some clubs are so simply organized that their rules can be explained to any prospective member, and in these cases, those who join with full information have thereby agreed to obey the rules. This was my thesis in the preceding section, and the Laws are relying on a variant of that thesis. Some clubs are so complex that they can be understood and evaluated only by those who have had some first-hand experience as members. In these cases, anyone who has voluntarily joined and has remained a satisfied member for a certain period of time has in effect agreed to abide by the rules.[6]

4
Socrates and Locke

As we have seen, the agreement made by the citizens is an agreement "to carry out whatever we [the Laws] command" (51e4). But the next three times the *Crito* specifies the content of their agreement, it uses different words: it is an agreement "to live as a citizen in accordance with us" (*kath' hêmas politeusesthai*: 52c2, 52d2-3, 52d5). Surely this is merely a change in verbal formulation; the Laws say nothing to suggest that a single pattern of behavior gives rise to two different implicit agreements.[7] An agreement "to live as a citizen in accordance with us" is the same thing as an agreement to do what is commanded by the laws that govern the behavior of citizens.

Nonetheless, an important fact is brought out by the words, "to live as a citizen in accordance with us." The Laws are obviously confining their attention to the way in which citizens have become committed to the city through their voluntary acts. Only such individuals could be described as having agreed "to live as citizens." Contrast a resident alien who has lived in Athens for a good

deal of time: he may understand the way the city works, he may be satisfied
with its laws, and he has decided to stay in Athens rather than reside elsewhere. In other words, he differs from the citizen who has agreed to obey the
city in only one respect: he has not passed the *dokimasia* for citizenship. And
because of this single difference, the Laws would never say that the resident
alien has agreed "to live as a citizen." Furthermore, there is no way of telling
whether the Laws take such resident aliens to have implicitly agreed to obey
the city, for they simply do not address this issue. Of course, the Laws are not
hinting that individuals who are not citizens of Athens but who nonetheless
reside there (resident aliens, women, slaves) ought to dishonor the city and
covertly violate its laws. Rather, they simply ignore the problem of why these
groups should feel any commitment to the city. Notice that their analogy between cities and parents is similarly restricted in scope. The laws that concern
marriage and education apply to citizens only, and therefore citizens are the
only ones who have been shown to owe a debt of gratitude to Athens. The
Laws are quite aware of this limitation. They say, "We begat, nurtured, and educated you, and gave all the fine things we could to you and all the other citizens . . ." (51c8-d1). Those who have not received these benefits have been
given no reason to obey or persuade, even though they live on Athenian soil.

It might be suggested, however, that the argument from agreement can easily be extended to cover a great many resident aliens. Suppose we simply drop
the *Crito*'s reference to the *dokimasia* and retain everything else. According to
this new theory, anyone has agreed to obey the city if he has fulfilled these
three conditions:

(A) He understands and is satisfied with the laws.
(B) He is legally free to leave the city.
(C) He chooses to remain a resident.

Adult citizens and many resident aliens satisfy these conditions, and so this revised theory has greater scope than the one we actually find in the *Crito*. But
the trouble with this new theory is that (A), (B), and (C) do not constitute
jointly sufficient conditions for implied consent. We can grant that if someone
resides in a city and is satisfied with its laws, then he has probably benefited
from them. And it might be argued that whoever has willingly benefited from
an organization owes some debt of gratitude to it. But even if we concede these
points, they do not show that the individual made an agreement to obey the
organization from which he benefited. Consider an example. A man may think
that his community's rescue squad is doing a good job, but he may refuse to
join it or help it financially. If he later voluntarily accepts its help, that does not
show that he thereby agreed to join it, obey it, or contribute to it. No doubt, he

owes the squad some gratitude for its help, but we should not automatically treat such debts as implicit agreements. Similarly, a man who lives in Athens and who has benefited from the city does not agree to obey it merely because he voluntarily chooses to remain there. When we drop the *Crito*'s reference to the *dokimasia*, what remains is not enough to constitute an implied agreement.

It is Locke, not Socrates, who wants to show that visitors and resident aliens, no less than citizens, have agreed to obey the laws. In a well-known passage from the *Second Treatise of Government*, he says:

> . . . Every man that has any possessions or enjoyment of any part of the dominions of any government does thereby give his tacit consent, and is as far forth obliged to obedience to the laws of that government, during such enjoyment, as any one under it; whether this his possession be of land to him and his heirs for ever, or a lodging only for a week, or whether it be barely travelling freely on the highway; and, in effect, it reaches as far as the very being of anyone within the territories of that government. (Sec. 119)

We can sympathize with Locke's desire to show that citizens are not the only ones who ought to obey the laws of the state in which they reside.[8] The failure of the Laws to tackle this question is one of the limitations of their theory. Nonetheless, the *Crito*'s conception of implied agreement has more intuitive appeal than Locke's, for those who enroll as citizens of a state are more plausibly held to have agreed to obey its laws than are those who merely travel on its highways. Suppose the state bans all abortions: could we say that those who walk down the street thereby tacitly agree to obey this law? We cannot easily avoid the use of public property, and for this reason, if no other, "travelling freely on the highway" is not an act of tacit consent to a nation's laws. By contrast, there are many states in which one can live comfortably without becoming a citizen. And if a country does offer someone citizenship and he accepts that offer, doesn't he agree to abide by its terms, as he eventually comes to understand them? This suggestion, I will argue (VI.13), does not quite work, but nonetheless it is based on a perfectly reasonable assumption: when an offer of membership is made and its terms are understood by the eligible candidates, then those who voluntarily accept the offer are also accepting those terms, even if they say nothing to this effect.

5
Completing the Agreement: An Authoritarian Reading

We come now to a serious difficulty. According to the *Crito*, what is the precise relationship between agreement and satisfaction? Does remaining in the city complete one's agreement to obey its laws, regardless of one's attitude toward those laws? Or does remaining complete one's agreement only because it demonstrates one's satisfaction with the city? May a person who is dissatisfied with certain laws continue to reside in Athens, or is he required to leave? Is leaving the only way to avoid completing one's agreement? The remainder of this chapter will be devoted to these questions.

Let us begin with the observation that the parties to an agreement often accept a certain voluntary act as the sole vehicle by which their agreement is ratified. Suppose I tell you, for example, to shine your lights three times at midnight if you agree to join the club. If you fail to signal but tell me the next day how much you want to join, your expression of enthusiasm has no contractual effect, for you have failed to perform the only act designated as the vehicle of agreement. Conversely, if you tell me, while you shine your lights three times at midnight, that you object to some of our rules, you are nonetheless agreeing to join; disclosing your dissatisfaction does not diminish your commitment. And there are many other examples in which a single, mutually understood, voluntary act bears the entire burden of conveying one's agreement. If you write up a contract and I tell you how happy I am about it but refuse to sign, then I am as uncommitted to its terms as I would be had I said nothing; and if grumblings of dissatisfaction accompany my voluntary signature, I am nonetheless as bound to the document as would be the happiest of signatories. Until and so long as the act of assent is voluntarily performed, public signs of satisfaction or dissatisfaction are just so much noise.

It is a worthwhile experiment to apply this model to the *Crito*. Let us assume then that freely remaining in Athens is the sole act by which a citizen completes his agreement to abide by the laws, and self-exile is the sole act by which he can break off that agreement. On this interpretation, voluntarily remaining in Athens is understood by the Laws and the public to be a fairly reliable sign of one's satisfaction with the political system, but even if one is dissatisfied, remaining nonetheless commits one to obedience. Satisfaction, in other words, is the normally expected concomitant of the act by which one completes one's agreement, but after one's *dokimasia*, the sole vehicle of agreement is one's continued residence in Athens for a certain length of time. Accordingly, if one has become a full member of this club, then publicly disclosing one's dissatisfaction with some of its rules in no way cancels one's agreement. Others may be surprised that one remains a member, if one is dissatisfied, and they may even think that the dissatisfied citizen should quit. But in any case, they will insist that so long as one remains, the rules of the club must be observed.

If we look again at the *Crito*'s initial discussion of consent (51d1-e4), it seems to fit this interpretation nicely.

(A) . . . We make this proclamation, by giving freedom to any Athenian that wants it: When he has passed the test for citizenship and has observed the affairs of the city and us the Laws, if we do not satisfy him he is free to take his belongings and go wherever he wants.

(B) No law prevents or forbids you, if one of you wants to settle in a colony, should we and the city not satisfy you. Or if you want to go somewhere else and be a resident alien, you can go wherever you want and take your belongings.

(C) But whichever of you remains, seeing the manner in which we decide court cases and the other ways in which we manage the city, we say that by this time he has, by what he does, agreed with us to carry out whatever we command. . . .

The first two sections, (A) and (B), portray the developing citizen as someone who is in the process of making a decision. He is studying the political system to determine whether he should be satisfied with it. Their implication is that departure is a sign of dissatisfaction with the laws, and conversely, remaining is a sign of satisfaction. But then, in sentence (C), satisfaction is no longer in the picture: the sole act that is mentioned is remaining. It is as though the Laws are saying that although remaining is a sign of satisfaction, the really important thing is the remaining, and not the satisfaction. Freely remaining is the act that solely constitutes one's finally assenting to the city's orders, and accordingly departure at the right time is the only way to prevent one's agreement from being completed.

After the Laws describe the mechanics of agreement in (A), (B), and (C) above, they state the persuade-or-obey doctrine for a third time (51e4-52a3), and having done that, they return to the topic of agreement. But now they do not rest content with the claim that Socrates agreed to obey the city. Rather, they insist that he is among the Athenians who made this agreement most of all (52a6-8). To justify this claim, they point out that there is a great deal of evidence that they and the city satisfied him (52b1-2). Since he stayed at home more than any other Athenian, he must have been especially satisfied with the city (52b2-c1), and in this way he emphatically (*sphodra*: very much, exceedingly, strongly) chose the city and agreed to live in accordance with its laws (52c1-2). Furthermore, Socrates had children in the city, again indicating that it satisfied him (52c2-3). And at his trial, he chose death rather than exile, so great was his unwillingness to live outside of Athens (52c3-8).

In their attempt to show that Socrates "most of all agreed," the Laws are evidently not confining themselves to actions he performed in the earliest stage of his political life; he had children and spoke at his trial long after his enrollment as a citizen at the *dokimasia*. And the later remark (52e2-3) that Socrates had seventy years of opportunities to leave Athens again indicates that the

Laws are searching for signs of agreement within the whole range of his political career. Their assumption is that there never comes a point when the behavior of a citizen residing in Athens can no longer be taken as giving assent
to the laws. If remaining for three years after one's *dokimasia* is enough to
show that one agrees to obey the city, then remaining for ten years or twenty
shows this all the more. The more one stays, the more one agrees, and accordingly the less one travels outside the city, the more one agrees. All of this
attention to the length of a citizen's presence in Athens seems to fit nicely with
the interpretation we are exploring, for that reading makes voluntary presence
the sole vehicle of agreement. If freely remaining constitutes the completion
of one's agreement, what better way to show that someone "very much
agreed" (52a68, 52c1-2) than to point out how very much he remained?

   It is important to realize how authoritarian the *Crito* becomes if we read it
this way. Consider a young citizen who has recently passed his *dokimasia* and
is examining the city's laws. He sees that there are many good ones, but also
finds that a few are unjust, and he decides that he would never obey those few.
What is he to do? He would like to agree to most of the laws without agreeing
to a few others—but there is no way to do that. There is no such thing as re-
maining-with-respect-to-law-A and leaving-with-respect-to-law-B. So if this
citizen remains for a sufficient length of time, he will have agreed to obey all
the laws that exist, including the ones that he considers unjust. If he can never
bring himself to obey those unjust laws, then remaining in Athens will be
agreeing to do what he has no intention of doing. But surely the Laws could
not countenance such dishonest agreements: assenting to an order that one
intends to disobey is hardly a way of showing respect for the laws. Accordingly,
the *Crito* must mean that if a person knows of a law that he would refuse to
obey, his only permissible course of action is self-exile. That is, if quitting the
club of Athens is the only way to avoid completing one's agreement to obey its
rules, then the virtuous citizen of an imperfect city must leave—a harsh legal
doctrine, if ever there was one.

   Now, the Laws never quite say in so many words that a disgruntled citizen
should pack up and leave Athens. The closest they come to this idea is 52e3-5:
". . . you had seventy years in which you could have gone away, if we did not
satisfy you and the agreements did not seem just to you." They do not say that
he *should* have left if he was dissatisfied—only that he was *free* to leave.
Nonetheless, it has to be admitted that the *Crito* mentions only one way to
avoid completing one's agreement to obey the city: taking up residence elsewhere. Their silence about any other way of preventing one's agreement from
being completed suggests that there simply is no other way.

   When we put all of these considerations together, they create an argument
that deserves serious consideration. To summarize:

(i) Whether someone is satisfied with an agreement is never relevant to the question of whether he made it. The Laws must surely realize this.

(ii) The sentence that claims that Socrates agreed to obey the city makes no mention of satisfaction.

(iii) If continued residence in Athens is what constitutes the completion of an agreement, we can understand why the Laws say that Socrates agreed more than anyone else.

(iv) The Laws mention only one way in which a citizen can prevent his agreement from coming to completion: taking up residence in another city.

But as I will show, the authoritarian interpretation that is based on these four points is faced with grave difficulties. The text is better explained by a reading that gives satisfaction a significant role to play in the *Crito's* theory of consent. When we later reconsider points (i) through (iv), we will see how unconvincing they are.

6
Problems for the Authoritarian Reading

On the authoritarian reading, the *Crito* is saying that a citizen should not agree to a law that he knows he will not obey; and the only way to avoid completing one's agreement to such a law is to leave the city. It should be obvious that this interpretation is completely at odds with the persuade-or-obey doctrine no matter which way that doctrine is understood. Suppose my argument in Chapters III and IV was correct, and the doctrine means that disobedience can be justified, so long as one persuades. Socrates, for example, may disobey an order to give up philosophy, so long as he is willing to persuade a jury that his conduct is justified. Obviously, if this is what the *Crito* means, then the Laws cannot also be insisting that Socrates must leave if he is dissatisfied with any Athenian command. But suppose my interpretation of the persuade-or-obey doctrine is wrong, and Grote's is correct. Then that doctrine means that anyone may try to persuade the Assembly to change the law, but that until he succeeds he must obey. Even this conservative reading of the persuade-or-obey doctrine cannot be reconciled with a love-it-or-leave-it political philosophy. For the Laws cannot both welcome dissent and tell the dissatisfied citizen to get out. Athens allowed any citizen to try, for as long as he wished, to have a statute repealed and the Laws cannot pretend to represent the city if they insist that dissidents must leave.

Furthermore, the authoritarian reading does not explain why the Laws are interested in showing that Socrates demonstrated his satisfaction with the city frequently, and in several ways. Recall that, according to this interpretation, to show that someone agreed to obey the city it is neither necessary nor sufficient to prove that he was satisfied with it. Correspondingly, the fact that he was *very* satisfied should be irrelevant to the conclusion that he *very much* agreed. But if this is so, then much of what the Laws say to Socrates is pointless:

> We say, Socrates, that if you do what you have in mind, then you are among those who are not the least but the most guilty of these accusations. If I should then ask why, they might justly upbraid me by pointing out that I have been among those Athenians who most of all made that agreement. They could say: Socrates, there were many indications [*tekmêria*] that we and the city satisfied you. You would not have stayed in the city so much, compared with other Athenians, if it had not satisfied you so much. . . . (52a3-b4)

As we can see, they use (A) his almost constant presence in Athens as evidence that (B) he was especially satisfied with the city, and from this they infer that (C) he has very much agreed to obey the laws. Why not skip the middle step, and say that since he was present so often he agreed very much? And why go on to say (52c2-8) that having children in Athens and refusing exile also demonstrate satisfaction with the city? By citing these acts as evidence of satisfaction, the Laws are implying that *any* act by which a citizen displays satisfaction with the city is an expression of his agreement to obey its laws. At any rate, the Laws clearly believe that a citizen's voluntary presence in a city is not the only sign by which he completes his agreement.

7
From Residence to Satisfaction

To reinforce the conclusion we have reached, let us look at another portion of the text. After the Laws have referred to the trial of Socrates and have pointed out that he then refused exile but now seeks it, they make these fundamental points:

> (A) Are you doing anything . . . but transgressing the compacts [*sunthêkas*] and agreements [*homologias*] that concern us? You did not agree out of compulsion nor were you tricked or forced to decide in a short time. Rather, you had seventy years in which you could have gone away, if we did not satisfy you and the agreements did not seem just to you. (52d8-e5)

> (B) But you preferred neither Sparta nor Crete, which you frequently say are well governed, nor any other Greek or foreign city, and you made fewer visits outside

the city than do the lame, the blind, or others who are crippled. In this way, it is clear that the city and we, the Laws, have especially satisfied you, of all Athenians. For whom could the city satisfy, apart from its laws? (52e5-53a5)

Part of (B) is mere repetition, for we have already been told that Socrates wins the award for most days spent in Athens by a single citizen. But part of this section gives us important, new information: Socrates thinks that there are well-governed cities outside of Athens, yet he prefers his native city. And the Laws rely on this when they infer (53a3-4) that he has been satisfied with Athens. We will examine this inference more carefully in Section 9, but for now let me suggest that the Laws are making the following concession. If someone believes that there are no well-governed cities, then the fact that he stays in his own city does not show that he is satisfied with its laws. Continued residence may reflect the belief that one's city is merely the best of a bad lot; and if that were the attitude of Socrates toward Athens, then none of the alleged signs of agreement—residence, children, trial—would show his satisfaction with the city's laws. So, the statement about Sparta and Crete is not incidental, but rather fills an important gap in the argument of the *Crito*. Socrates is indeed satisfied with Athens, since he prefers it even to well-governed cities elsewhere. The important point is that the Laws are moving beyond residence to satisfaction. That Socrates remained in Athens by itself shows nothing; what counts is the satisfaction displayed by his residence.

Turning back now to (A), we can begin with a point that everyone would admit. Although the Laws do not explicitly say so, they clearly mean that if an agreement is coerced or rushed or arises through deception, then it is not valid. They would hardly bother mentioning the unforced nature of the agreement Socrates made unless they were willing to concede that, had it been forced, their criticism of him for breaking an agreement would fail. But the next point I want to make is less obvious. It seems to me that (A) initiates a line of thought that is continued in (B). Throughout the whole paragraph, the Laws are concerned to show that Socrates' residence in Athens expressed his satisfaction with the city. They want to prove this because they admit that, had residence not reflected satisfaction, it would not have conveyed any agreement to obey the city. So what we have, when we put sentences (A) and (B) together, is a list of four factors that can block the inference from residence to satisfaction: force, deceit, insufficient time, and the belief that there are no well-governed cities. The role of the paragraph is to point out that since Socrates was bothered by none of these problems, the inference from residence to satisfaction is legitimate.

Now, this reading is obviously in direct conflict with the authoritarian interpretation we have been examining. For that interpretation holds that, according to the Laws, the agreement Socrates made is to be respected whether the acts constituting agreement express satisfaction or not. A person signing a mortgage contract cannot justify the violation of its terms by pleading that his signature did not express any enthusiasm; the fact that he signed the contract only because it was the best of a bad lot does not diminish his obligation. Similarly, the Laws are saying, according to the interpretation under scrutiny, that Socrates would be bound to his commitment whether there were worthwhile alternatives to Athens or not. The presence or absence of such alternatives is relevant to the question of whether satisfaction can be inferred from residence; but residence constitutes agreement so long as it is voluntary, i.e. unforced, unrushed, and open. And if the agreement is voluntary, then Socrates must abide by it, whether he was satisfied with it or not.

If we adopt this interpretation, then we will have to say that passages (A) and (B) serve different purposes. The first tries to show that the agreement was voluntary, the second that Socrates was satisfied with the laws. The first is crucial, for without it the agreement Socrates made would not be one he must respect; but the second is peripheral, serving only to show that the laws Socrates agreed to are ones with which he is satisfied. By contrast, the interpretation I propose unifies the paragraph, since each sentence is designed to help show that Socrates was indeed satisfied with the city and its laws. Now, surely it is *ad hoc* to hold that (A) and (B) serve such different purposes: such a view is justified by nothing in the text, and it is designed only to salvage the theory that agreement requires no evidence of satisfaction. In fact, the text suggests that *both* segments are equally designed to show that residence reflected satisfaction. (A) points out that Socrates had a great deal of time to leave if the laws did not satisfy him. That is, to the question, "Did he have enough time?" the Laws reply, "Yes—seventy years, if he was dissatisfied." This suggests that the full question being asked is, "Did Socrates have so little time to make up his mind that we can't tell whether he was satisfied?" In other words, both (A) and (B) are concerned with the question whether Socrates' residence expressed his satisfaction. The idea that (A) is concerned solely with the voluntary nature of his agreement, and (B) with his satisfaction, has no support from the text. The word for voluntary (*hekôn*) does not occur in (A); but both segments explicitly refer to satisfaction.[9]

I conclude that the authoritarian reading does a poor job of explaining the text. As we saw in the preceding section, and as we have now seen again, the Laws point to various and frequent signs of satisfaction as evidence that Socrates agreed to obey the city. Remaining in Athens, when one is legally free to leave, does not by itself constitute the completion of one's agreement. Rather, one's presence in the city completes one's agreement only when it provides evidence of one's satisfaction with the laws. And there are other ways of demonstrating satisfaction besides continued residence: e.g. having children and statements one makes about the relative merits of cities. The authoritarian interpretation goes wrong by underemphasizing the role of satisfaction in the *Crito*'s argument, and by failing to recognize the variety of ways in which satisfaction can be shown.

8
Implicit Agreement Revisited

If the interpretation we have been examining is flawed, what should we put in its place? It might seem that only one alternative is available to us: the Laws are saying that the citizen completes his agreement by being satisfied with the city. In other words, what completes the agreement is the fact that the citizen is in a certain mental state. His behavior—remaining in the city, having children, refusing to propose exile—gives us evidence that he has completed the agreement, but his actions do not themselves constitute its completion.

Yet surely this is an interpretation that we should be reluctant to attribute to the *Crito*. For any reasonable thinker ought to realize that what counts in the making of agreements is observable behavior rather than a person's inner satisfaction. If I ask someone whether he will do me a favor and he nods, then he has made an agreement even if he was not satisfied with my request. After all, a person who explicitly says, "I agree to do it," cannot void the effect of his words by saying to himself, "But I don't really agree to do it." Someone who voluntarily undertakes certain observable acts, knowing that others will regard these acts as the making of an agreement, *has* in fact agreed, whatever his inner mental state. Can the Laws have been too stupid to realize this? And yet, if we credit them with the realization that it is external behavior and not satisfaction that counts, we will be making the same mistake that was made in the authoritarian reading. The text simply does not allow us to eliminate satisfaction as a crucial element in the *Crito*'s conception of implicit agreement. We seem forced to choose between an interpretation (satisfaction alone completes the agreement) that is silly and an interpretation (residence alone completes the agreement) that is refuted by the text. We might try to avoid the defects of these two extremes by saying: what is essential is *both* remaining *and* being satisfied; and the Laws simply assume that the two go along with each other. But that cannot be right, for as we saw in the preceding section, the Laws mention four factors (compulsion, deceit, lack of time, lack of alternatives) that can explain why a citizen who remains might nonetheless be dissatisfied. So we seem to have reached an impasse.

I think we can solve this problem if we deepen our understanding of the variety of ways in which people can make agreements. Consider the following example. John asks Anne whether she would like to take a trip with him to-morrow to the mountains; he tells her to decide quickly, because if they are to go, he has to cancel his earlier plans, rent a car, and make other preparations. Anne has laryngitis, but to indicate her reaction to John's proposal, she smiles, gives him a hug and a kiss, and begins to pack her bags. John takes these actions as expressions of agreement, and prepares to leave. The question I want to ask is this: has Anne in fact agreed to take this trip? I believe that there is a strong case for saying that she did. To begin with, the fact that she has *said* nothing does not show that she failed to agree. Had she nodded, for example, that would certainly have indicated agreement. But if a nod would have sufficed, then why shouldn't the actions she performed also suffice? It might be said, in reply to this question, that a nod is a generally recognized sign of agreement, whereas hugs, kisses, and the packing of bags are not. And, the argument might go, whenever someone tacitly agrees to do something, that person must use either a generally recognized sign of agreement (e.g. nodding), or an *ad hoc* signal accepted by the parties to the agreement (e.g. the flashing of lights). But Anne has not used either kind of signal. She has merely acted in a way from which it can be inferred that she plans on going. If she has no such intention, then she is misleading John and acting wrongly, but her wrong should not be described as the breaking of an agreement.

I see no good reason, however, for using the word "agreement" in such a restricted way. Suppose Anne did not have laryngitis, and had said to John, after hearing this proposal, "Thanks so much—I'll run and pack my bags right away." Obviously, these words, uttered in the proper tone of voice, would have constituted an agreement, even though they are not a promise, nor a generally recognized sign of agreement (like a nod or a handshake), nor an *ad hoc* signaling device (like the flashing of lights). What matters is that Anne's verbal and nonverbal behavior are intended to show that she is delighted with John's offer, and in these circumstances the communication of this fact is all that is needed for an agreement to be made. She does not have to say, "I hereby accept your offer," if she wants to agree to go; in fact, had she made such a stiff remark, it would have been reasonable for John to wonder whether she really was accepting. We cannot make a list of words and phrases (e.g. "I hereby agree," "yes," "okay") that have to be used to ratify agreements, and similarly it is wrong to insist that a nod can ratify an agreement (since it is a conventional signal) but that a hug and a kiss cannot. People can convey assent and register agreement in both conventional and unconventional ways, and it is overly rigid to stipulate that implicit agreements must rely on standardized signals.[10]

My suggestion, then, is that there is a kind of agreement that is expressed by nonverbal signs of satisfaction, and that the agreement to obey the laws is of this sort. The *Crito* is saying that after an individual has enrolled as a citizen, and has had sufficient time to evaluate the city's legal processes, it is fair to count his public signs of satisfaction as the completion of his agreement to obey the laws. But which actions will indicate agreement and which will not? It would be unreasonable to demand an abstract criterion from the Laws. No one can delimit the class of words that signal assent, and similarly the Laws need no definitive list of actions that will count as signs of agreement. *Any* actions that publicly express satisfaction with the laws will complete one's agreement to obey them. Remaining a resident can express satisfaction, given the right background conditions. So can the infrequency of one's trips abroad, one's decision to raise children in the city, and what one says about the relative merits of cities. Thus, on my interpretation, remaining is merely one of many possible signs of agreement; it is not, as the conservative interpretation holds, the unique act by which one's agreement is completed. Here, my interpretation fits the text better: for although the Laws emphasize the citizen's presence more than any other signal of agreement, they do point to other signs as well. Furthermore, it is central, on my interpretation, that the acts that complete one's agreement be acts from which one's satisfaction with the city can be inferred. Here too it has an advantage over the authoritarian reading, which treated satisfaction as the expected but inessential concomitant of the act by which one ratifies one's agreement. As we have seen, satisfaction plays a larger role in the *Crito* than that.

Notice that, on my interpretation, the Laws are not adopting the absurd position that agreements to obey the city are completed only if the citizen actually *feels* satisfied. Rather, what count are the visible actions that express satisfaction, together with the background conditions that allow us to interpret that behavior. If a citizen is not in fact satisfied, but has only tried to create that impression, he has nonetheless agreed to obey the city. So too in the case of John and Anne: perhaps all of her actions were simply an act, and she had no intention of going with him. Even so, she did express satisfaction, and therefore she did agree to go. John had every reason to interpret her behavior as a signal of agreement, and Anne was responsible for leading him to that interpretation. Similarly, in the *Crito*, it is not the feeling of satisfaction, but the public signs of satisfaction, that complete the process of agreement.

A further point should be noticed. Whenever an agreement can be ratified by only one type of act, that is because the parties are relying on some mutually recognized signaling device. Without some such convention, many different types of act would convey agreement, and sometimes it is useful to reduce this variety and thereby lessen the possibility of misunderstanding. So, in certain cases, agreements must be written and notarized; in other cases, we introduce a signal to suit the occasion. Now, if residence is the sole act by which the citizen can complete his agreement to obey the laws, then that would have to be a convention generally recognized in Athenian society. Surely the *Crito* cannot *stipulate* that residence constitutes agreement; rather, Socrates and every other citizen would have to be aware that remaining is generally recognized as the sole act by which one gives one's assent. But as a matter of historical fact, there is no evidence that there was any such convention. By contrast, the interpretation I favor has no need to presuppose the existence of such a convention. For it says that agreement is ratified not by the performance of certain designated acts, but by anything that expresses satisfaction with the laws. The case of John and Anne is helpful here: he did not have to say, "If you agree to go, give me a hug and a kiss, and start getting ready." She conveyed her agreement by expressing her satisfaction, rather than by relying on some long-standing or *ad hoc* convention. Similarly, the Laws can infer an agreement from the citizen's behavior, even though the citizen did not learn ahead of time that acting in certain ways would constitute an agreement.

In Section 5 of this chapter, I said that the authoritarian interpretation is supported by four points. But now we have seen how hollow three of them are:

(i) No one can seriously believe that agreements are ratified by feelings of satisfaction rather than by behavior. And so we originally took the Laws to mean that satisfaction can be expected to accompany residence, but that it is residence and not satisfaction that constitutes the agreement. But now we see that we were using a misleading model of agreement. In certain cases—as when someone signs a contract—satisfaction is indeed peripheral; but as the case of John and Anne shows, signs of satisfaction can sometimes constitute agreement. And even in such cases as these, what counts is the behavior that expresses satisfaction, and not the mental state itself.

(ii) The sentence that claims that Socrates agreed to obey the city makes no mention of satisfaction. Out of charity, we originally took this to mean that what completes an agreement is residence, and not satisfaction. But since then we have seen how great an effort the Laws make to show that Socrates was satisfied with the city. To understand the Laws, we must take account of everything they say about agreement, and not concentrate entirely on the first sentence in which they claim that an agreement was made.

(iii) There is one point that the Laws emphasize more than any other in their effort to show that Socrates agreed to obey the city: military campaigns aside, he has practically never left Athens. But we were wrong to infer from this that residence alone constitutes agreement. For one thing, the Laws point to other signs of agreement as well. For another, they realize that residence does not count as a sign of agreement unless it is also a sign of satisfaction.

We are now left with one remaining argument on behalf of the authoritarian reading. The Laws mention only one way in which a citizen who has passed his *dokimasia* can avoid making an agreement to obey the city: he can take up residence elsewhere. Now, we must not infer from this that residence in Athens is the sole act that constitutes agreement, for we have seen how much evidence there is against this hypothesis. Nonetheless, there is still a possibility that part of the authoritarian reading can be salvaged. The Laws might mean that there are many ways of showing one's satisfaction with the city, but only one way of showing dissatisfaction, namely, by self-exile. But as I will argue in Section 10, this hypothesis has little to recommend it.

9

The Preference for Athens

I would like to backtrack for a moment and consider some important details that were passed over in Section 7. There we saw the Laws making the following points:

(A) Socrates has said many times that Sparta and Crete are well governed.
(B) But he has always preferred Athens to these and all other cities.
(C) He has made very few visits to cities outside of Athens.
(D) Therefore, it is clear that the city has especially satisfied him.
(E) No one could be satisfied with a city apart from its laws.
(F) Therefore, it is clear that the laws of the city have especially satisfied him.

(E) presents one possible way of rendering 53a4-5; essentially the same reading can be found in Grube (". . . for what city can please if its laws do not?") and Croiset (". . . car comment une ville plairait-elle à qui n'aimerait pas ses lois?"). But there is an alternative in Tredennick, Woozley, and Allen: "Who would care for a city without laws?" as Tredennick puts it. On philological grounds, there is no reason to choose one translation rather than another. But which makes the best sense of the argument? Our choice is between (E) and

(G) No one could be satisfied with a city without laws.

Surely (E) is preferable, since it justifies the move from (D) to (F), whereas (G) does not. An analogy may help. It would be a mistake to argue that whoever likes Chicago also likes its police force since no one can like a city without a police force. We ought to give the *Crito* the benefit of the doubt, and acquit it of such a fallacy. By contrast, (E) is precisely the premise needed to smooth the way from (D) to (F). The basic idea is that a person's attitude toward the laws of a city determines his attitude toward the city itself. And so if we are satisfied with a city, that is because its laws please us; if the laws do not please us, then neither will the city itself. Thus, from (D) and (E), the *Crito* validly moves to (F).

Now let us look at a consequence that is suggested by (A), (B), and (E). Socrates prefers Athens to Sparta and Crete, though he thinks the latter two well governed. What can be the basis for this preference? (B) and (E), considered together, suggest that he thinks more highly of the laws of Athens than the laws of any other city. For if a person's attitude toward the laws of a city determines his attitude toward the city itself, then we can expect his preference between cities to be determined by his ranking of their legal systems. So Socrates must think that the laws of Athens are more satisfactory than the laws of Sparta, Crete, or any other city.[11] And this is no empty compliment, for he takes Sparta and Crete to be well governed. *Why* Socrates has such a high opinion of the Athenian legal system is a mystery that will exercise us in Chapter VII. For now, I take it to be an undeniable and significant fact that Socrates gives the laws of Athens high marks.

One further point. The Laws do not say what evidence they have for statement (B). Perhaps they think that Socrates has verbally expressed his preference for Athens over Sparta and Crete. Or perhaps they infer (B) from his utter lack of interest in visiting these foreign places; whoever praises the legal system of another city but shows no interest in visiting that city or attending its festivals must think even more highly of his own city. Or perhaps the Laws are relying on both the verbal statements of Socrates and his habit of staying within the walls of Athens. In any case, there is no need for them to assume that Socrates could have taken up permanent residence in Sparta or Crete. The Laws do say, at an earlier point, that Socrates was legally free to live in a colony, or to be a resident alien somewhere outside of Athens (51d7-8). I take them to mean that certain cities would have allowed Socrates to enter and to settle permanently. But the *Crito* never says that Sparta and Crete are among such cities, and its argument has no need for such an assumption. When the Laws talk about possible destinations for an escaping Socrates, they mention Thebes and Megara (53b4). It is understandable that Sparta and Crete are not considered, since they are closed, exclusive societies in which Socrates could not have expected to settle down.[12] Sparta and Crete are benchmarks in the evaluation of Athens, but they are not real alternatives as permanent residences. They are used to make the point that Socrates is satisfied with the laws of his native city; but the *Crito* has other cities in mind when it says that Socrates can permanently leave Athens if he so chooses.

The Laws show that Socrates was satisfied with Athens by pointing out that he preferred it to two other cities that he considers well governed. Naturally, this same argument cannot be applied word-for-word to every citizen of Athens, for surely there were many ardent democrats who considered Sparta and Crete poorly governed. But so long as these individuals publicly indicate their preference for Athens over some well-governed city or other, they are expressing their satisfaction with its laws. Of course, someone who publicly indicates that Athens is, in his opinion, the only well-governed city there is, also shows his satisfaction with the city. But what if an individual thinks that there are no well-governed cities at all? Or suppose someone thinks Athens poorly governed, but is barred from whichever cities he does consider well governed? The *Crito* has to admit that in these cases continued residence in Athens does not signal any agreement to obey its laws, since it does not reflect satisfaction with those laws. I suspect that the Laws simply do not think that these cases will occur very often, or at all. They assume that everyone, or nearly everyone, will think that some existing city or other is well governed. They themselves think that Athens has good laws; after all, those laws have done as much for the citizens as laws can (51c8-d1). They also consider Thebes and Megara to be well governed. And these (unlike Sparta) were cities in which any Athenian could take up residence; that is why they are mentioned as possible destinations for an escaping Socrates (53b3-c4). A citizen of Athens who continues to reside there, when he could live in some other city that he takes to be well governed, is thereby indicating that in his opinion Athens is well governed. Why would he stay, if he could live under a better legal system?

Residence, then, is a sign of satisfaction only when certain background conditions are presupposed. The citizen must be legally free to leave, and his decision to remain must not arise from deception or lack of time. Furthermore, it must be assumed that a citizen's decision about where to reside will be based primarily on his evaluation of various legal systems. He must also believe that some cities are well governed, and that he is living in or can move to one of them. The Laws make all of these points explicit. Obviously, they are aware that if the inference from residence to agreement is to be justified, several important assumptions must be made.

10
Dissent and Dissatisfaction

When Socrates says that Sparta and Crete are well governed, he does not mean that their legal systems are entirely without fault. After all, as we have just seen, he thinks that Athens is preferable, because of its laws; so he probably believes that Sparta and Crete are politically defective in some way or other. Similarly, when the *Crito* says that Socrates is satisfied with the laws of Athens, it can hardly mean that the city is faultless in his eyes. We know that Socrates was a critic of democracy, since he did not think the many competent to decide matters of right and wrong. The Laws must mean that, all things considered, Socrates was greatly satisfied with his city. With certain institutions and statutes he was no doubt dissatisfied. We should also recall that the persuade-or-obey doctrine, on either a liberal or a conservative reading, invites dissent. The Laws are thus quite aware that a citizen who remains in Athens may nonetheless be dissatisfied with certain statutes and commands.

Now, suppose a new citizen has become acquainted with the legal practices of his city, and is generally pleased by its laws. He plans on remaining in residence, but there are a few statutes to which he is vigorously opposed. He tries to persuade others to repeal them, but does not succeed. Would the *Crito* say that if this citizen remains in Athens, then he will have agreed to obey even those laws he vigorously opposes? Two textual points seem to suggest an affirmative answer. First, the Laws mention only one way to avoid completing one's agreement to obey a city's commands: permanent departure. So they must think that there is no other way to do so. Second, the Laws explicitly say that by remaining, Socrates agreed to carry out whatever the city commands (51e1-4). That means that he agreed to obey every law and every order of the city, without exception. Apparently, the *Crito* is saying that he agreed to obey even those statutes with which he is dissatisfied.

But neither of these arguments is convincing, once we examine them. Consider the first. It is quite true that the Laws mention only one way to express dissatisfaction with a city's laws, namely, through permanent departure. But the *Crito* would be an absurd document if it were to hold that sincerely expressed objections to a statute do not express dissatisfaction with it. After all, to show that Socrates is satisfied with the city, the Laws refer to statements he has made: he spoke against exile at his trial, and he has often said that Sparta and Crete are well governed. Surely, if a man's public statements can be used to build a case that he is satisfied with a city, then they can also be used to show that he is dissatisfied with some of its laws. As we saw before in Section 8, the Laws are not stipulating that such-and-such will count as a sign of satisfaction or dissatisfaction. Rather, they are saying that from certain behavior and background conditions we can reasonably infer that a person is satisfied. Obviously, if agreement is shown through natural expressions of satisfaction, then the Laws must concede that dissatisfaction can be manifested in the same way. And what more natural way to express dissatisfaction than through verbal dissent? It is of course not surprising that the Laws do not explicitly mention dissent as a way of expressing dissatisfaction. They are not concerned to make a definitive list of ways in which satisfaction and its opposite can be expressed—in fact, there can be no such fixed list. The Laws bring out only those points that are needed to support the conclusion that Socrates was satisfied with the city; the fact that dissatisfaction can be expressed through dissent is too obvious and too peripheral to be included in their economical argument. We should also recall a point made earlier, in Sections 5 and 6: The *Crito* cannot be counseling us to make an agreement that we have no intention of honoring, and therefore, if departure is the only way to avoid making an agreement, a conscientious dissenter must go into exile. But that severe position is obviously at odds with the persuade-or-obey doctrine. Surely then, there must be ways to remain a resident and avoid making unconscionable agreements. Sincere and public dissent from offensive laws is the obvious way.

But what of the second point? It is quite true that, according to the *Crito*, Socrates made a sweeping commitment: he agreed to "carry out whatever we command" (51e4). But this is far less significant than we may have realized, for the Laws equate making an agreement with giving indications of one's satisfaction. In the right conditions, residence is a sign of satisfaction with all the laws, but that does not mean that it is decisive evidence in each and every case. Rather, if someone is generally satisfied with a city's laws, then that merely creates a presumption in favor of agreement. Though there may be many statutes that such a citizen has not explicitly endorsed, it can be assumed that he agrees to all the ones he has not opposed. The burden of proof is on him to show that he is not satisfied, and so long as he remains silent, it is fair to infer that he is satisfied with a given law. So, for every Athenian law in force, Socrates has shown signs of his satisfaction with it, unless he indicates otherwise. The analogy with games is helpful here: a person who agrees to play chess thereby agrees to every rule of the game, unless he speaks up and proposes a variant. But notice that the proviso, "unless he proposes a variant," can be dropped and the preceding statement remains true. To state the conditions for *making* agreements, neither we nor the Laws have to refer to a method for *blocking* agreements as well. The *Crito* is saying that through a certain pattern of behavior the citizen undertakes a general commitment, from which he may make particular exceptions if he gives public notice. And this is all the Laws need to say to defend their assertion that Socrates agreed to the law that gives the courts authority. They know that he said nothing for or against that particular statute. But since he never criticized it, his general satisfaction with Athens commits him to it.

Why do the Laws think it so important to show that Socrates has been satisfied with his city? Surely they must be assuming that if Socrates was *not* satisfied, then he did *not* make an agreement to obey. Merely enrolling as a citizen, after all, does not constitute an agreement. But the Laws believe that if certain things happen after that enrollment, then the whole process will amount to an implicit agreement. One of the elements that must be added, beyond merely passing one's *dokimasia*, is understanding: the citizen who has not yet learned the laws and procedures of his city cannot be said to have agreed to them. And satisfaction, as we have seen, is a further ingredient. So it must have occurred to the Laws that if a citizen is dissatisfied with a statute and publicly expresses that dissatisfaction, then the claim that he has tacitly agreed to obey it is put in serious jeopardy. That is why they are so concerned to show that Socrates was satisfied with the legal system, considered as a whole. For that allows them to argue that he did agree to obey each and every law, barring evidence to the contrary. That is, every Athenian law which the citizen has not sincerely and publicly criticized is a law with which he has shown signs of satisfaction.

I am not attributing to the Laws the naive view that if a citizen merely says, "I am dissatisfied with this law," then that by itself prevents his agreement from being completed. For a citizen might be insincere in his expressions of dissatisfaction, and sometimes others can have good reason to believe that he is being insincere. To see whether a person is really dissatisfied with a law, we must look to all available evidence, including verbal reports, and we must search for the best explanation of that behavioral evidence. If a person says he is dissatisfied with a law, then we can expect him to state his reasons, and in appropriate circumstances he ought to support its repeal; his failure to do such things would suggest insincerity. Furthermore, if a law is obviously essential to the existence of the state, we would find it difficult to take at face value any expressions of dissatisfaction with it. Consider, for example, the Athenian statute that gave authority to the courts. That law orders the citizens to accept any lawful verdict brought by a jury, whether that verdict is favorable or unfavorable to the defendant. If someone objects to this, and says that he would like to live in a city where verdicts are enforced only when they are favorable to the accused, we would strongly suspect him of insincerity. For his proposal would in effect destroy the legal system and the city, and any sane person can be expected to see this.[13] So the Laws can assume that there is a core of legislation that will satisfy every adult in his right mind. A citizen cannot simply announce, "I am dissatisfied with all the laws of the state" and expect to be taken seriously. The only way he can, with a single act, prevent his agreement from being completed is to take up residence in a different city. That is why the Laws emphasize the fact that this option has always been open to Socrates. He can cancel all his agreements at once by leaving; but if he fails to leave, he must express his dissatisfaction in piecemeal fashion. The Laws would admit that many statutes are controversial, and in these cases expressions of dissatisfaction that are backed by argument and action will block agreement.[14]

11
Later Agreements and Reversals

I have argued that the *Crito* takes the *dokimasia* to be the initial step in the process of making an agreement, and that after a certain period of time has elapsed and one has shown one's satisfaction with the laws, one has agreed to obey them. But precisely which laws does the citizen agree to—only those that have already been passed, or all future laws as well? At some point, does the citizen who is generally satisfied with his city's legal system give it a blank check to do whatever it likes in the future? Or does he agree only to those laws that have been in force for a certain length of time? Surely the latter, if my preceding argument is correct. Since the Laws give the new citizen some time to evaluate the city before they claim that he has made an agreement, they must believe that a statute one has not yet been able to assess is not a statute one has agreed to obey. And of course that principle applies to future laws as well. The citizen has no way of knowing what sort of orders his city is going to issue in ten or twenty years; revolutions and deep-seated constitutional changes were not merely theoretical possibilities in fifth-century Athens. The Laws say nothing to suggest that at some point or other the citizens agree to obey the orders of any rulers that happen to acquire power in the future. Now, precisely how does an older citizen—suppose he is seventy—go about making an agreement to obey a law that has just been adopted? I assume that the *Crito* will answer this question in the familiar way: the citizen has become a member of the club of Athens, and therefore, if he is generally satisfied with its rules and does not quit, he agrees to obey all those laws that he has had time enough to understand. The older man, in other words, has the same relationship to new laws that a recently enrolled citizen has to all the laws with which he has not yet gained familiarity. He has not agreed to them yet, but he will have agreed if enough time goes by and he voices no dissent. We should notice, at this point, a small textual detail: at 52e3-5, the Laws tell Socrates that he has had seventy years in which to leave, if he did not think the agreements (I stress the plural) just. Evidently, they have no objection to thinking of the citizen's agreement to obey the city as a large multiplicity of agreements, each corresponding to one law or decree. Some of these agreements are made *en bloc*, as the citizen matures and becomes satisfied with the political system. As new laws are added, new agreements are made.

These points help us see that Socrates made no agreement to obey the tyrannical regime of the Thirty.[15] Elected in 404, through the pressure of a Spartan general, they were charged with the task of revising the laws and were given power to control the city in the meantime. They executed many, seized a great deal of property, and repealed a few laws; but the positive task of designing a new and permanent form of government seems never to have begun. Thebes and Megara harbored Athenian fugitives, who organized themselves into a fighting force; within about a year the Thirty were overthrown, and a Spartan king, Pausanias, allowed democracy to be restored. Socrates remained in Athens during this period of civil war, and that raises the question whether he was sympathetic to the regime of the Thirty. Since he did not become a refugee, did he tacitly show that he was satisfied with that government? Not at all. For Socrates accepts a legal philosophy according to which mere residence is not by itself a sign of satisfaction. The citizen never makes an agreement to obey all future laws and rulers, whoever and whatever they may be. Rather, he must always be given an opportunity to see what the laws of his city are, and the Thirty never did carry out this job of revising the laws. Either Socrates was waiting to see what they would produce, or he was waiting for them to be overthrown; in the meantime, he would obey no order that he considered unjust, and he would be willing to persuade them that his disobedience was necessary. (See V.2 on open disobedience.) We might think that, for strategic or moral reasons, Socrates should have joined the exiles, but at any rate we cannot take his decision to remain as a sign of satisfaction. The *Crito* shows that he did not view residence in this way.

One further point. A citizen's attitude toward his city may change not only because its laws change, but because *he* changes. Suppose a law has been in existence for some time, and by showing his satisfaction with it, the citizen has agreed to obey it. But then he gradually comes to realize that it is an unjust law, and he publicly expresses his dissent. Presumably he will try to have the law repealed, but whether he succeeds or not, an important conceptual question is raised by his change of attitude. Does his agreement to obey the law terminate when he publicly and sincerely expresses his dissatisfaction with it? We are not asking whether he did at an earlier time have an agreement; rather, we are asking whether that agreement continues to exist even when satisfaction is replaced by dissatisfaction. Is the *Crito* saying that a tacit agreement is made when satisfaction is shown during a certain *limited* period of time, come what may? In that case, signs of dissatisfaction that come too late cannot terminate an agreement. Or is the *Crito* saying that one has made a binding agreement only for those periods of time during which one exhibits satisfaction? In this case, a change of mind will destroy an agreement. I know which answer *I* would favor: it seems to me that an agreement cannot be unmade by a unilateral change of heart. It is essential to agreements that they are commitments to future behavior, and so if a contracting party can terminate his agreement merely by changing his mind, then there really was no commitment to begin with. Since I think the Laws have a reasonable view about agreements, I am inclined to believe that they would give the same answer. But of course there is no textual evidence on this matter, one way or the other. And in many cases the question is not critical, since the Laws concede that agreements can justifiably be broken. If a statute requires the doing of injustice, then the citizen must not obey it, even though he only recently came to the realization that it is unjust. He must not let his earlier attitude bind him to wrongdoing. On the other hand, suppose the issue is whether to *suffer* injustice: a citizen decides that a statute he once liked is in fact unjust to him, and he therefore becomes dissatisfied with it. In this case, the question of whether he still has an agreement is not academic, for if he has none, there is no reason why he should obey the law. Surely the Laws would say that his past satisfaction does bind him and that he must obey, even though he now regrets his earlier naivete. At any rate, that is what they must say, if they do not want to be absurdly lenient.

12
A Conclusion Drawn

At the beginning of this chapter, I posed two questions. First, does the *Crito* allow a citizen to violate a law on the grounds that it does him an injustice? We see now that it does. The Laws merely insist that when a citizen agrees to obey a law, he cannot break his agreement merely because it calls on him to suffer injustice. But since agreement is a matter of satisfaction and not mere residence, it is possible for a citizen to remain in the city and avoid making an agreement to obey a law that he thinks does him an injustice. If he publicly and sincerely objects to a particular statute soon enough after it has been adopted, or soon enough after he has passed his *dokimasia,* then he has not agreed to obey it. Of course, if he disobeys, he must do so openly, and when summoned to court he must try to persuade the jury that he was right to disobey. But if the law he disobeyed is in fact unjust to him, then the *Crito* contains not a word to the effect that he has violated the law for insufficient reason. It is therefore a far less authoritarian dialogue than we might have supposed.

Second, we wanted to know whether the Laws avoid falling into one or the other of two extremes: do they make it too difficult or too easy to avoid making an agreement? If a citizen can avoid giving his consent simply by taking no positive steps to make an agreement, then the state will have too little power—it will not even have the right to imprison wrongdoers. But if a citizen cannot avoid agreeing to obey the laws, short of going into exile, then he must leave the state whenever it gives orders that require the doing of injustice. Now, if the argument of this chapter has been correct, then the *Crito* cannot easily be accused of falling into either of these two traps. A citizen cannot avoid making an agreement merely by saying, "I refuse to agree to that law." Unless he publicly shows that he is dissatisfied with a law, he has agreed. And certain laws are so crucial to the existence of the city that it will be difficult, if not impossible, to demonstrate one's sincere dissatisfaction with them. But in many other cases, it will be easy for the citizen to show that he is genuinely opposed to a law, and in these cases he can avoid agreement.

We should notice how the parent-city analogy and the argument from agreement compensate for each other's weaknesses. Though each provides an independent argument against escape, neither by itself presents a complete picture of the state's powers. The parent-city analogy fails to provide the city with the right to use certain forms of punishment, and the argument from agreement tries to fill this gap. Conversely, the Laws would leave the city with too little authority, if, like Locke, they were to claim that all political authority must be based on consent. If one has reason to obey the law only when one has agreed to do so, then the citizen who sincerely dissents will have no reason to obey—even if his objection to the law is groundless. The *Crito* avoids this consequence, not by making agreement unavoidable for residents, but by recognizing a source of political authority that has nothing to do with consent. Both the parent-city analogy and the argument from agreement allow the citizen a fair degree of freedom, but when they are combined, they produce a powerful conclusion: Socrates has to accept his death, in spite of the fact that he is a victim of injustice.

13
How Good Is the Argument from Agreement?

Did Socrates and his fellow citizens really agree to obey the laws? Does the *Crito* succeed in establishing this conclusion? I think not, for there is at least one devastating defect in the argument of the Laws: they adopt the false assumption that if citizens are satisfied with their country, they must be satisfied with its laws (VI.9). In fact, there are innumerable reasons for being satisfied with and remaining in a country that have nothing to do with its legal system. A farmer, for example, can love his country for its rich topsoil. I suspect that Socrates overlooks this point because he generalizes from his own case: he sees no reason to like a city apart from its laws, for he thinks that the legal system shapes the moral outlook of the citizen (more on this in VII.6), and nothing is more important to him than one's attitude toward virtue. He preferred Athens to all other cities because of the legal system's effect on moral development, and he too quickly inferred that the comparative merits of legal systems must always be the determining factor in our civic preferences.

But suppose we set aside this error. Consider an Athenian citizen who has passed his *dokimasia*, has understood his city's legal system, and has shown by his behavior (including verbal behavior) that he is on balance satisfied with the laws. Did he thereby agree to obey the city's commands—excepting those he sincerely criticized? Our question is both historical and philosophical: we are asking whether a certain kind of person in fifth- or fourth-century Athens did in fact make a certain agreement; but we must also decide what counts as an agreement. It is plausible to assume that when an organization makes an offer of membership, and makes its rules known to prospective recruits, then those who accept the offer implicitly agree to obey the rules. The Laws realize, however, that the Athenian legal system is not well known to its newest members, and they claim therefore that an implicit agreement is completed only when the new citizen understands and shows his satisfaction with the way the city conducts its legal business. I doubt that this move, clever as it is, really works. Agreements exist only when offers are made and accepted, but after the citizen has passed his *dokimasia*, it is no longer true to say that his city is still making him an offer. If no offer is outstanding once the *dokimasia* has been passed, then the new citizen is not really in the business of evaluating the terms of an offer. And since there is no longer an offer for him to accept, there are no terms to which he gives his agreement, should he show his satisfaction with the laws.

For the sake of a philosophical experiment, let us change the historical facts. Suppose Athens had not only had a *dokimasia* for seventeen-year-olds, but had also required its citizens to take an oath when they were thirty and therefore politically experienced. In this oath, they promise to obey the city or persuade it as to the nature of justice, and those who refuse to swear allegiance are stripped of their citizenship, though they may remain indefinitely as resident aliens. If Athens had had this institution, and if Socrates had taken this oath, then of course he would have broken an agreement had he escaped from jail without persuading the city. But would it have been a just agreement? The Laws, I suspect, would say yes, for the citizen is not being forced, tricked, or rushed into agreement, nor does his oath require him to commit unjust acts. My own view, however, is that the adult children of citizens have certain rights—e.g. the right to vote—that cannot be taken away from them merely because they refuse to swear an oath of allegiance. When a child becomes a full-fledged participant in the political process of his native state, he is only getting his due, and if he must first make an agreement before he acquires his rights, then that agreement is unjust. By insisting upon such an agreement, the state is offering to the new citizen something that ought in any case to be his. The state is not a private club which may limit membership in any way it chooses and extend membership on any terms it likes. The state can require naturalized citizens to take an oath of allegiance; it can require its public officials to swear that they will uphold the laws; it can strip citizens of some important rights if they commit serious crimes; and it can make residents who engage in certain activities agree to abide by the relevant laws (for example, those who receive drivers' licenses can be required to agree that they will obey the traffic laws). But even when the state deserves the gratitude of its citizens, it cannot establish an oath of allegiance as a condition that native citizens must fulfill before they exercise such rights as the rights to vote.[16] For if it were appropriate for the state to require such an oath, then in effect there would be no right to vote: voting would be a privilege, like driving, which the state extends to citizens on reasonable terms. Once we start thinking in terms of natural rights, we part company with the whole political outlook of the Laws. The central idea behind their argument from agreement is that when someone joins an organization, he agrees to those rules with which he later shows his satisfaction. But there is something profoundly wrong here: the state is not just any organization, but one to which certain individuals have rights of membership. So even if the Laws had succeeded in showing that Socrates had implicitly agreed to obey the laws—even if Athens had required its citizens to make an explicit agreement—the contract in question would nonetheless have been unconscionable, because the state would have been offering a citizen what in any case ought to have been his.

We saw in Chapter V that something in the first type of argument against escape can be salvaged: there can be a significant debt of gratitude that citizens owe their state, just as they owe a debt of gratitude to their parents. But the second type of argument against escape, it now appears, is misconceived at its core.

Notes

1. In the second half of the fourth century, military recruits took an oath to "obey those who for the time being exercise sway reasonably and the established laws and those which they will establish reasonably in the future." In "The Ephebic Oath in Fifth-Century Athens," P. Siewert (whose translation I have just used) argues that fifth-century citizens also took the oath (*Journal of Hellenic Studies* 97 [1977], pp. 101–111). But the silence of the *Crito* is significant: though it would suit their purpose, the Laws never say that Socrates or others verbally agreed to obey them. So even if the oath is as early as Siewert thinks, it may have been taken by only some of the citizens. It is reasonably certain, at any rate, that Socrates never took it; for otherwise the Laws would have said so.

2. Such agreements are called "implied-in-fact" contracts. See Friedrich Kessler and Grant Gilmore, *Contracts: Cases and Materials,* Boston: Little, Brown and Co., 1970, pp. 116–117. For further discussion, see the references in Charles Fried, *Contract as Promise: A Theory of Contractual Obligation,* Cambridge: Harvard University

Press, 1981, pp. 142–143 n. 4. He says, "... offeree acceptance of a proferred benefit for which he knows payment is expected is the paradigm cas" of the "tacit acceptance" of a contract.

3. See Douglas M. MacDowell, *The Law in Classical Athens*, London: Thames and Hudson, 1978, p. 69.

4. To my knowledge, no English translation of the *Crito* properly alerts the reader to the institutional meaning of *dokimasthêi*. Grube, for example, has: "after he has reached manhood;" Tredennick "on attaining to manhood;" Woozley "when he comes of age." Allen's "when he has been admitted to the rights of manhood" is better.

5. Contrast R. E. Allen, *Socrates and Legal Obligation*, Minneapolis: University of Minnesota Press, 1980, pp. 111–112: "... Socrates by voluntarily assuming the status of citizenship has thereby entered into an implied agreement to abide by the decisions of courts. ..." Allen recognizes the institutional background of the *dokimasia* (pp. 90–91), but he seems to think that according to the Laws becoming a full-fledged citizen is sufficient for making an agreement to obey the city's orders.

6. Objection: "But the Athenian citizen did not think of himself as having made an agreement to obey the laws; he never formed the intention to do such a thing. And without an intention to agree, there can be no agreement. So the Laws are wrong." (Cf. the claim of A. John Simmons, *Moral Principles and Political Obligations*, Princeton University Press, 1979, p. 83, that there is no consent in the absence of a "*deliberate undertaking*" [his emphasis] to consent. See too p. 77: "... consent must be given intentionally and . . . knowingly.") Reply: One can discover that one's previous actions constituted an agreement, even though one did not at the time think of them in that light. For example, when we order food in a restaurant, we agree to pay the price on the menu, even though few realize that in ordering they are making an agreement to pay. Socrates is claiming to have discovered that his previous actions constituted an agreement, and it is irrelevant that neither he nor his fellow citizens realized, at the time, that their actions had this effect.

7. Contrast A. D. Woozley, *Law and Obedience: The Arguments of Plato's Crito*, London: Duckworth, 1979, pp. 97–98. He ignores the *kath'hêmas* and takes *politeuesthai* to mean not only obeying the law but making some fuller contribution to the political life of the city. I see no reason for such an interpretation.

8. See John G. Bennett, "A Note on Locke's Theory of Tacit Consent," *The Philosophical Review* 88 (1979): pp. 224–234, for a recent interpretation. According to Bennett, Locke's argument, though unsuccessful, does not depend on the notion that whoever resides within or visits a state thereby benefits from it and in fairness must repay those benefits in the coin of obedience.

9. At 52d6-7, Socrates and Crito concede that an agreement has been made, and this might suggest that the argument of the Laws can be neatly divided into two parts: prior to 52d6-7, they merely try to show that Socrates made an agreement; after that, they claim that it is an agreement he should honor. If this is the right way to break up the text, then it could be claimed that 52d8-53a7 has a certain unity, in that the Laws here give two reasons for keeping the agreement: it was just (52d8-e5), and Socrates was satisfied with the city (52e5-53a5). I reject this interpretation for several reasons. First, if Socrates' satisfaction with Athens is (as alleged) a reason for honoring his

agreement, then the Laws have been putting forward this reason far before 52e5-53a5. Second, after Socrates and Crito concede at 52d6-7 that an agreement has been made, the Laws assert that Socrates has been free for seventy years to leave Athens. Now, if he had not been free to leave, remaining would hardly constitute or provide evidence for an agreement. Evidently, even after 52d6-7, the Laws continue to support their claim that Socrates made an agreement. The fact that he was free to leave supports two points simultaneously: he made an agreement; and the agreement, being just, should be kept. Third and most important, it is hard to see why satisfaction with the city or its laws should be a reason for honoring an agreement to obey its commands. As the Laws know, Socrates will honor all just agreements, and this means that he will keep them even when he doesn't like the people or cities to whom he has given his word. It is far more plausible to regard satisfaction as a way of expressing agreement, rather than a reason for honoring an agreement already made in some other way. I conclude that the interpretation under consideration is inadequate. Though Socrates and Crito concede at 52d6-7 that an agreement has been made (in fact, they offer no resistance at 50c4-6 either), the Laws have not at that point completed their argument for that conclusion. After 52d6-7, they claim that the agreement was just, but in addition they add further support for their claim that Socrates was satisfied with the city and that he therefore completed his agreement to obey it.

10. Cf. Fried, *Contract as Promise*, p. 43.

11. Though the Greek tells us (52e5-6) that Socrates merely said, on many occasions, that Sparta and Crete were "well governed" (*eunomeisthai*), Tredennick's translation inflates the compliment: Sparta and Crete become Socrates' "favorite models of good government." The sense of the passage, if I am right, is just the opposite: it is, among existing cities, Athens that provides Socrates with his "favorite model of good government."

12. See Plutarch, *Life of Lycurgus*, 9, 27; Plato *H. Ma.* 283b4-286c2, *Laws* 634d7-e4. Aristotle (*Pol.* 1272b17-18) says that the distance of Crete from the rest of Greece had the same effect as the Spartan expulsion of strangers. For further discussion of Socrates' attitude toward Sparta and Crete, see VII.5-6.

13. But suppose we consider a far more specific law, e.g. one that requires the payment of a large fine as the penalty for a minor offense. And imagine a citizen who campaigns for the repeal of this law, on the grounds that the punishment is too severe; he argues that citizens convicted of such a crime would be justified in refusing to pay so large a fine. If my interpretation of the *Crito* is correct, the Laws are not committed to saying that this citizen agreed that, should he ever be convicted of the crime in question, he would pay the full penalty fixed by law. Presumably, Socrates never campaigned in this way against particular penalties, and given his general satisfaction with the legal system, the Laws infer that he has tacitly agreed to abide by all the judgments of the courts, both favorable and unfavorable (50c5-6). But a citizen who sincerely and publicly objected to certain penalties cannot be said to be satisfied with or to have agreed to the very law he fought against. Nor does the parent-city analogy require him to accept the penalty: if a father tells his adult children that if they do not listen to him he will shut them up in a closet, they are not required by the speech of the Laws to submit to that punishment. Of course, the parent-city analogy requires the citizen in

question to tell the jurors that he will not pay the fine required by law, and he must argue in court that the penalty is unjust in view of how small the offense is. Since his disobedience must be open, the city may find ways to exact the penalty from him, in spite of his noncompliance. Even so, it is important to realize that nothing in the *Crito* entails that such a citizen cannot be justified in refusing to pay the fine.

14. If my interpretation is correct, then one of Hume's points against contractual theories of political obligation does not apply to the *Crito* (David Hume, "Of the Original Contract," in *Essays: Moral, Political, and Literary*, Vol. I, New York: Longmans, Green, and Co., 1898). He considers the view that tacit consent is conveyed by continued residence, and objects that not everyone can afford to leave: "Can we seriously say, that a poor peasant or artizan has a free choice to leave his country, when he knows no foreign language or manners, and lives from day to day, by the small wages which he acquires? We may as well assert, that a man, by remaining in a vessel, freely consents to the dominion of the master; though he was carried on board while asleep, and must leap into the ocean, and perish, the moment he leaves her." "Of the Original Contract," p. 451. Hume indicates, on the last page of this essay (p. 460), that the *Crito* is one of his targets. But as we have seen, that dialogue does not require the citizen to leave the city if he wants to withhold his consent from particular laws. Contrast Woozley, *Law and Obedience*, pp. 106–109, who presses Hume's point against the *Crito*. Like Simmons, *Moral Principles and Political Obligations*, p. 99, he takes this to be a fatal flaw in any attempt to base political obligation on agreement or consent.

15. For background, see the works cited in Ch. I n. 29.

16. Can the state justifiably impose some lesser penalty on native citizens who refuse to agree to take some oath of allegiance? I can't think of anything that would be appropriate. Consider a fine, for example. If it were large, it would be an unfair burden, especially on the poor. If it were small, it would trivialize the oath and thus defeat its purpose, which is to increase the citizen's sense of allegiance to the state.

11

The Interpretation of Plato's *Crito*

David Bostock

SOCRATES GIVES AS HIS LEADING PREMISE in the *Crito* that one should do nothing wrong (οὐδαμῶς δεῖ ἀδικεῖν, 49b8). (He says, indeed, that he has lived his whole life in obedience to this premise, 49a-b.) He then proceeds to argue that it would be wrong for him to try to escape from gaol, thus evading the death penalty he had been sentenced to. But a central problem in interpreting the dialogue is that the arguments he offers for this conclusion appear to be designed to establish a very much stronger conclusion: it would *always* be wrong for *any* citizen of Athens to disobey *any* law of Athens. Such a conclusion is in itself distinctly unappealing, and apparently not consistent with the leading premise, for presumably a law might be an unjust law commanding the doing of what is wrong. Moreover, in the *Apology* Socrates apparently reports one such case and envisages another. At 32c-d he says that he did not obey an order from the Thirty Tyrants because what was ordered was wrong (ἄδικοv τι, 32d5); and at 29c-d he says that he would not obey a court order to cease philosophising, evidently on the same ground (though he does not here use the word ἄδικον, or a synonym). Here, then, it seems to be admitted that a law, or anyway a legally authoritative order,[1] may command one to do wrong, and that if so it should not be obeyed. This sets our problem: is it possible so to interpret the *Crito* that it does not enjoin obedience to any and every law? I propose and criticise three lines of interpretation which attempt to avoid this 'authoritarian' reading of the dialogue. They differ from one another most notably over the question of *how many* distinct and separable arguments the dialogue contains. I then consider the merits of the authoritarian interpretation.

The Dialogue Contains but One Argument

At 49c-d Socrates elaborates his leading premise to 'one should not wrong any person', adding to this 'not even if one has been wronged by him'. (ἀδικεῖν is used transitively from 49b10, and equated with κακουργεῖν and with κακῶς ποιεῖν at 49c.) At 49e5-7 he states a further premise 'one should do what one has agreed to do, provided that it is not wrong'. (δίκαια ὄντα evidently has the force of μὴ ἄδικα ὄντα.) He then proposes that it follows from these premises that it would be wrong for him to escape (49e9-50a3). Crito requests further elucidation, the personified Laws of Athens are brought upon the stage, and the argument proper begins.

Now it is clear that the first point that the Laws make is this: if Socrates tries to escape, he will be attempting, for his part, to destroy the Laws, and (thereby) the whole city; for a city could not survive if the verdicts reached by the courts were set aside and rendered powerless by individuals. They go on to add that much could be said on behalf of this *particular* law, that verdicts should be carried out (50a8-b8). This evidently suggests the following argument:

(i) The law that verdicts should be carried out is fundamental to the whole system of laws.

Hence (ii) Whoever attempts to disobey *this* law is attempting (for his part) to destroy the whole system of laws.

But (iii) It would be wrong for Socrates to attempt (for his part) to destroy the whole system of laws.

So (iv) It would be wrong for Socrates to attempt to disobey *this* law.

Thus (v) It would be wrong for Socrates to attempt to escape.

I shall call this suggested argument argument A. If we may grant the *(very* dubious) step from (i) to (ii), which receives no further elaboration in the dialogue, it would seem to be a valid argument (at least if we add, as a further and uncontentious premise, that in the present context escaping would be disobeying this particular law). Moreover, it clearly does not generalise to the conclusion that Socrates should obey any and every law of Athens, but confines attention to one law in particular, as specially fundamental.[2]

It is true that argument A does not entirely evade the problem we began with, since it is surely possible that obeying a verdict reached by a court would involve doing something wrong. Indeed one of our cases from the *Apology* was precisely a case of this sort: if the court had ordered Socrates to cease philosophising, Socrates could not have obeyed that order without doing something which was (in his eyes) wrong. (Or even if he would not quite have called it *wrong* [ἄδικον]—as I observed; he does not quite say this in so many words[3]—at any rate he does very clearly say that he would not have obeyed the order.) Now one might try to distinguish the cases in this way. In this particular example, Socrates imagines the court saying 'We will let you go, but on this condition, that you no longer . . . philosophise. But if you are caught still doing this, you will die' (29c7-d1). Perhaps we can see this as a kind of *disjunctive* order 'either cease philosophising and live, or continue to philosophise and die'. Then Socrates' proposed response is to *obey* this order by obeying the *second* disjunct, for he clearly does envisage that he would indeed be put to death (30c1). By the same reasoning, the order 'Do not litter; penalty £10' would count as being 'obeyed' by one who both littered and paid £10, and similarly with any law to which some definite penalty for infringement was attached. But in the case under consideration in the *Crito* the court will not have attached any penalty for failing to obey its order. The verdict evidently was not put in this way: 'Socrates is to be executed; and if he escapes this he will be banished'. So in this case we do not have a disjunctive order, and there is only one way of obeying it.

Clearly this is very special pleading, and wholly unconvincing. Moreover, it does not really attempt to meet the general issue, but merely to sidestep it, by making use of incidental features of the two cases in the *Apology* and the *Crito*. A *more plausible* reconciliation of the two dialogues would be to weaken the *Crito*'s argument A by qualifying step (ii)—and hence the remainder of the argument—by adding a *ceteris paribus* condition.[4] Then it may be said that in the situation envisaged in the *Apology* other things were not equal, since (a) the court order was countermanded by a divine order, and (b) Socrates' claim was that in continuing to philosophise he was attempting not to destroy the city (or its laws) but to do it good (30a5-6). But neither of these considerations would apply to the situation in the *Crito*. However, it cannot be maintained that any such *ceteris paribus* condition is in fact stated in the *Crito*, and so one has to admit that on a natural reading the two passages are simply in conflict. Looking a little more deeply, the place where a *ceteris paribus* condition would be even more welcome is as a condition on the *Crito*'s leading premise that one should never wrong anyone. For it may be that all the available courses of action do involve wronging someone (e.g. either the Laws, if Socrates disobeys the court order, or the God, if he obeys it), and then the proper course is to choose the lesser wrong. But again it cannot be said that the *Crito* shows any awareness of this complication; its argument has a naive simplicity that allows no place for a conflict of obligations.

Despite all this, an important point remains. Our argument A does focus on one law in particular, that verdicts should be carried out, and it claims only that that law ought always to be obeyed (at least, by one placed as Socrates is placed, on which we have more to come). This is a long way from the fully 'authoritarian' reading of the dialogue, and in fact the claim is not wholly implausible. Many of those who wish to preserve a place for the modern phenomenon of 'civil disobedience' would not feel that they were bound to deny it. Perhaps even the Socrates of the *Apology* might have been led to reconsider his position: it is not obvious that what someone sees as a command of God *ought* to be accepted as overriding this particular law of humans. This brings me, then, to the point of my first suggested interpretation.

The first interpretation is that argument A is the only argument to be found in the *Crito*. At 50a7-b8 the Laws state premise (i) and proceed to infer (ii). They do not, however, assert the remaining premise (iii), that it is wrong for Socrates, in his position, to seek to destroy the whole system of laws, and certainly they have not yet made any attempt to argue for it. On the first interpretation, the *whole* of the rest of their argument (down to 53a) is designed to provide support for this premise. They offer two subarguments for it: one I shall call the parent-city analogy, and this occupies 50c-51c; the other is the argument from agreement, occupying 51d-53a. But both of these are *subarguments* to the main argument, and both are designed to show that it is wrong for Socrates to attempt to subvert *the whole system* of laws. (He might, however, be right to disobey this or that particular law, so long as that disobedience does not threaten the whole system.[5]) In support of this interpretation I note three points.

(a) The ensuing discussion begins by raising an objection to the argument just suggested: Socrates might reply 'the city has wronged us, and the verdict was not correct' (50c1-2). This reply is best seen as an objection to the suggested premise (iii): if Socrates does attempt to destroy the laws as a whole, i.e. the city (50b1-2), then this is doing no wrong; it is rather a just retaliation for a wrong done.[6] A good part of the parent-city analogy is clearly designed as a counter to this reply: it claims that Socrates and the city (or the country, πατρίς, are not on an equal footing; rather, they are so related that it is wrong for Socrates to retaliate in this way (50e4 ff). Thus the argument concludes 'It is impious to offer violence to one's mother or father, and still more to one's country. . . . Consider then, Socrates, whether we are right in saying that you are trying to do us wrong (οὐ δίκαια) in trying to do what you are now trying to do' (51c2-8). Assuming that we may identify the country, the city, and the system of laws as a whole, and that 'destruction' is the extreme case of 'offering violence to', this conclusion to the parent-city analogy is exactly the required affirmation of premise (iii).

(b) Before the parent-city analogy gets under way (at 50c9), and immediately after it has been suggested that 'the city has wronged us, and the verdict was not correct' (50c1-2), the Laws make this remark: 'Was this too agreed between you and us, Socrates, or to abide by whatever verdicts the city should declare?' Clearly this introduces the idea behind the argument from agreement, which is to be more fully given later. Here at its first introduction the specific agreement that the Laws insist upon is an agreement to abide by whatever verdicts are declared (and this is contrasted—somewhat elliptically—with a suggested agreement to abide by such verdicts only when they are correct; the Laws claim that this latter is *not* what was agreed). Now it has been claimed that destruction of the law that verdicts be carried out is tantamount to destruction of the whole system of laws. Conversely, then, an agreement to abide by the law on verdicts should equally be implied by an agreement to abide by the system of laws as a whole. That, then, should be what the longer argument from agreement at 51d-53a is arguing for, and we should interpret it in that light if at all possible. This makes it a *part* of the argument given initially: as Socrates has agreed to abide by the system as a whole, it is wrong for him to try to destroy it.

(c) On this interpretation, the basic charge against Socrates is always that he is aiming (for his part) to destroy the laws, and that this is doing wrong, because in fact it is doing *them* wrong. In the concluding passage (53a8-54d1) the Laws are arguing that escape will bring none of the advantages that Crito apparently sees in it (44e-46a), and in the course of this they twice recur to this charge. Any well-governed city that Socrates may fly to will reject him as a destroyer of the laws (53b6-c1), and for the same reason he will not be welcomed by the laws of Hades (546-8). They refer also to the two bases for this charge, that Socrates will not have kept his agreements, and that he will have done harm to those whom he least ought to harm, in retaliation (54c2-5). But they treat the two coordinately, and as the second clearly is part of an argument to show that he is wrong to try to destroy the laws, we should see the first in the same way.

The Dialogue Contains Two Distinct Arguments

The obvious weakness in the first interpretation is that there really is no connection between argument A and the argument from agreement at 51d-53a. The considerations advanced in (b) and (c) above are wholly programmatic: they enjoin us to see the argument from agreement as part of argument A *if we can*, since there are some (not very strong) pointers to suggest this. But there is an equally strong pointer in the opposite direction, namely that before the Laws are brought upon the scene at all Socrates has introduced two clearly distinct premises. One is the premise that one ought not to wrong another, not even in requital for a wrong done to oneself, and this premise clearly is put to use in argument A. The other is the premise that one should keep one's agreements, provided that what is agreed is not wrong, and this premise is of course employed in the argument from agreement. These being two quite distinct premises, is it not natural to suppose that each will be the main premise of two quite distinct arguments? Indeed Socrates himself seems to imply this, as soon as he has introduced his two premises, for he then says: 'If we go away from here, without having persuaded the city, shall we or shall we not be wronging certain people, and indeed those whom we least ought to? And shall we or shall we not be abiding by what we have agreed, it not being wrong?' (49e9-50a3). This passage very clearly suggests that two distinct arguments are to come. The first of them is (perhaps) argument A, as outlined earlier, and the second is evidently the argument from agreement.

Moreover, when we do look in detail at the argument from agreement, we see that it cannot be brought under the wing of argument A. Its main claim is simply that Socrates *has* agreed to obey the laws, and therefore (in accordance with the premise on agreements) it would be wrong of him not to do so. There is no hint that he has agreed only to obey 'the system as a whole', thus leaving room for disobedience to one or another particular member of that system. On the contrary the Laws claim that any full citizen who remains in the city 'has agreed with us, in so doing, to do *whatever* we command' (51e3-4, cf. 52a1-2). Nor do they suggest in this passage (i.e. 51d-53a) that a failure to obey would amount to an attempt at destruction, and in fact the destruction of the laws is mentioned only once in this passage, where it seems to me clear that it is a reference back to the previous argument and not a part of the present one. (At 52c3 the Laws digress to a special *ad hominem* argument: at his trial Socrates could have proposed exile as an alternative to the death penalty, and so achieved with the consent of the city what he is now proposing to effect without it. But he had then said that he would prefer death to exile. Then they continue 'But as it is you do not respect what you said then, nor do you show regard for us, the laws, whom you are trying to destroy, and you are behaving like the most worthless slave, trying to run away in contravention of the compacts and agreements by which you have promised us that you will live as a citizen' [52c8-d3]. Here the *first* point [not respecting what you said then] sums up the newly introduced *ad hominem* charge, the *second* point [trying to destroy us] refers back to the accusation of argument A, and the *third* point reverts once more to the theme of agreement, which is then continued to 53a7. It is not being suggested that breaking agreements and running away is *itself* an attempt to destroy.) I conclude that the attempt to see this argument from agreement as merely part of argument A will not do, and there are (at least) two distinct and separate arguments in the *Crito*.[7]

This, then, introduces the second interpretation. On this view, *one* of the arguments is argument A, construed as before, and this is not fully authoritarian because it only claims of one particular law that it ought always to be obeyed. But we now construe argument A as running from the beginning (50a8) only to 51c8. The new sentence beginning on that line begins with a recapitulation of the salient points of argument A, but then moves on (at ὅμως in 51d1) to introduce a new line of argument, which we may now call argument B. This, however, is equally not a fully authoritarian argument. Though it may indeed seem so, from its main exposition in 51d-53a, we should remember that its leading premise is introduced at 49e5-7 with an important proviso: one should keep one's agreements, *provided* that what is agreed is *not wrong*. Thus even if Socrates has, by remaining in the city, agreed to obey each and every one of its laws, it does not follow that he is obliged to do so. On the contrary, if obedience to a law would involve doing something wrong, then by the proviso he is not obliged to obey it, and by the premise stated right at the beginning he is obliged not to obey it. Plainly, if this proviso is regarded as governing every claim made in argument B, then this argument cannot conflict with the major injunction 'do no wrong'.

It is difficult to give an accurate formulation of argument B, so I shall not try to set one out. For one thing, it is not quite clear *when* Socrates is supposed to have agreed to obey the laws of Athens. At 51d3, it appears that he made the agreement—presumably an agreement to obey the laws for so long as he was a resident of Athens—at the time when he was admitted to full citizenship. On the other hand one might take 52e3 as indicating that the agreement was continually being remade each day that he remained in Athens as a free man, and hence that he had agreed, at the start of the trial, to abide by its verdict. Thus he was bound, not just by a promise made long ago, when this particular outcome could not have been foreseen, but by a very recent promise, made in full knowledge of the dangers inherent in it. Another doubt is over just which of Socrates' 'deeds' (rather than 'words') constitute the agreement. Up to 52a4 it appears to be simply his choosing to remain in Athens as a citizen of that city, but thereafter the Laws increasingly stress his *satisfaction* with the city (and its institutions), as if this were highly relevant. Cleary there could be citizens of Athens who remain in the city while exhibiting considerable dissatifaction with its institutions, and there could be non-citizens who remain because they are well-satisfied. Would either of these types of people be held to have agreed to obey its laws? A much more serious difficulty is over just *what* Socrates has agreed to do. For most of the passage, it is natural to suppose that what he has agreed to do is simply to obey the laws, but at 51e4-52a3 it is said that there is another alternative open to him: he must either obey *or persuade*. I shall consider how this is to be interpreted in the next section.

But a genuine problem for the present interpretation is this. According to this interpretation, the proviso on keeping agreements, that what is agreed should not be wrong, is to be taken as applying to this whole argument. But in that case the Laws must show, somewhere during this argument, that it is not wrong for Socrates to do what the laws now require of him (namely to remain in prison until he is executed). It is clear that they make no attempt to show any such thing—the topic is simply never mentioned—and their argument therefore contains a very notable gap. Nor are we permitted, on this interpretation, to repair the gap by referring back to argument A (e.g. by claiming that argument A has already shown that escaping would be wrong, and inferring from this that not escaping would not be wrong, and hence inferring once more, by argument B, that Socrates is obliged not to escape).[8] For the present interpretation is that arguments A and B are wholly independent arguments. *Instead* of the claim that what is agreed is not wrong, what we find in argument B are several indications that the agreement was fairly entered into. Thus Socrates was free to agree or not, and was not in any way forced to agree, for he could instead have decided to live elsewhere, with no financial penalty (51d4-e5, 52e1). Again, there was no kind of trickery involved, since Socrates knew what he was agreeing to, and had plenty of time to observe, how the Laws of Athens did operate (51e1-2, 52e2-3). These, one might say, are considerations tending to show that the agreement was not wrongly made (was made δικαίως), but this by no means ensures that *what* was agreed was not wrong (was δίκαιον). Thus it appears that argument B, as developed by the Laws themselves, does *not* satisfy the proviso on keeping agreements introduced at 49e5-7.

There is only one passage in argument B which one might take to contain a reference to the proviso, and that is at 52e4-5. The Laws have been summing up their claim that the agreement was fairly entered into, and that Socrates could at any time have chosen to emigrate, and to this they add 'if we did not please you, and if the agreements seemed to you to be wrong' (εἰ μὴ . . . δίκαια ἐφαίνοντό σοι αἱ ὁμολογίαι εἶναι). Now the implied claim that the agreement was not wrong *could* be taken as claiming that *what* was agreed was not wrong, though it also, of course, could be taken as claiming that the agreement was fairly struck. It may be that the Laws are suggesting, in this ambiguous phrase, that the first (relevant) interpretation follows from the second. But in that case one can only say that they are mistaken: a perfectly fair agreement may yet be an agreement to do what is wrong. However it *may* be that we should see them as arguing in this way: the fact that Socrates has remained in the city shows that he has agreed to obey its laws, and the further fact that he is especially satisfied with the city—that its laws 'please him'—shows further that in his opinion what he has agreed to do is not

wrong. So this is an *argumentum ad hominem:* Socrates, at any rate, is bound
to accept that the proviso is satisfied because the Laws do in fact please him,
and if he had agreed to do something wrong he would not be pleased. On this
account, then, the crucial proviso is mentioned, and it is argued, not exactly
that it *is* satisfied, but that Socrates must *think* that it is.

Now this *may* be how Plato intended his argument to be taken, though if so
one can only say that the reasoning is wholly specious. For the sake of argument, let us suppose that until the time of his trial Socrates was indeed very
satisfied with the laws of Athens, and with the decisions reached in the courts
applying those laws. It evidently cannot *follow* that he was also pleased with
the verdict that convicted him of impiety and corrupting the young, and presumably he was not at all pleased with this verdict. Equally, it cannot *follow*
that he is now pleased to submit to the death penalty, and he is in no way
bound to think that what the agreement has led to *in this case* is not wrong.
More generally, the initial agreement is no doubt to be conceived of as a *general* agreement to do *whatever* the laws command. But the proviso, that one
should keep this agreement only where what is commanded is not wrong,
must be shown to be satisfied *in each particular case.* It is clear that the Laws
make no attempt to show that it is satisfied in *this* case, and thus argument B,
as stated, pays no attention to the relevant form of the proviso.[9] In fact, I think
it is more natural to say that it ignores this proviso altogether, in effect replacing it with the different proviso that the agreement be fairly made. It thus
appears to be of a fully authoritarian bent, requiring obedience to any and
every law from every citizen, who chooses to remain in the city, knowing what
its laws are. Unless, perhaps, we can save the situation by requiring *either* obedience *or* persuasion?

The Dialogue Contains Three Distinct Arguments

Since the alternative of either obeying or persuading also occurs within what
we are at present calling argument A, let us first reconsider this argument a little more thoroughly. Again, there are too many difficulties over the details for
it to be sensible to attempt a precise formulation.

At 50c9 the Laws ask Socrates 'What accusation do you bring against us
and the city, that you should attempt our destruction?' They then get him to
admit that he has no fault to find with the laws on marriage, and on the care
and education of children. Moreover, since these matters are regulated by
laws, they the Laws claim to *be* his parents, and to have been responsible for
his care and education as a child; he is their offspring and their slave (50d1-
e4). From this they infer that they and Socrates are not on an equal footing.

Just as a slave would be wrong to retaliate in kind against his master, and just as Socrates would have been wrong to retaliate against his father, so equally Socrates would be wrong to retaliate against the Laws; they are indeed trying to destroy him, but it is nevertheless wrong for him to try to destroy them in turn (50e4-51a7). So far, the discussion can easily be seen to be focused towards argument A as set out: what is at issue is whether Socrates has the right to (try, for his part, to) *destroy* the Laws, in his own self-defence, and the Laws claim that he has no such right.

Again, it is not quite clear what exactly is the basis of this claim. It may be suggested that, on orthodox Greek morality, a son is wrong to try to kill his biological parents, even in self-defence. Thus Oedipus should not have killed Laius when he met him at the crossroads, even if it was in self-defence, and even though Oedipus owed nothing to Laius for his upbringing and education (and did not know who he was). Of course, when the matter is put in this way, then the claim of the Laws to be Socrates' parents looks very thin indeed: they cannot reasonably say that their blood runs in his veins, or that without them he literally *could* not have existed. Besides, this makes it irrelevant that Socrates has no fault to find with the laws on marriage, upbringing, and education. Perhaps it is better, then, to suppose that the Laws are claiming much the same status as a foster-parent or guardian, to whom the child owes some debt of gratitude for benefits received. But in that case, of course, the analogy looks thin in a different way. If your guardian is murderously attacking you, surely you may kill in self-defence, if there is no other way of surviving? But I leave these issues unsettled, since my concern is not so much to criticise the argument as to determine what it is supposed to be.

Up to the present point (51a7), we can quite easily see the argument as concerned with the specific point of *destroying* the Laws, as argument A requires. We can also see the concluding lines (51c2-8, quoted above p. 213) as equally concerned with this point. But already a different theme has crept in. At 50e9-51a2, leading up to their claim that Socrates has no right to retaliate in kind on this question of destruction, the Laws have *also* mentioned that children and slaves ought not to answer back, or to hit back. This apparently leads them into making much greater claims for the rights of parents, and still more of the state. They claim that in *all* matters one should reverence, soothe, and yield to the state even more than to one's parents, and in fact one should do or submit to *whatever* it commands, no matter what the consequences to oneself (51a7-c1). This goes far beyond the previous claim that no one who has been born, brought up, and educated in Athens should seek to *destroy* its laws, and it really cannot be counted as part of our original argument A at all. It apparently claims for *all* laws the unquestioning obedience that argument A claims only for one particular law. Let us dignify this passage with the name 'argument C' (though really it does not deserve to be called an argument, but is simply a claim). We may regard argument C as slotted into the middle of argument A, or—perhaps better—we may regard argument C as following A, and developed out of it by pressing the parent-city analogy to further and stronger conclusions. In that case the concluding passage 51c2-8, which we previously took as the conclusion to A alone, may be seen rather as the conclusion to A and C together; it is elliptical enough to be taken in this way.

My third interpretation, then, recognises *three* distinct arguments in the *Crito*:-A, C, and B.[10] As before, A is not fully authoritarian, because it only claims obedience for one particular law, the law that verdicts should be carried out. (And it claims this obedience either from all who have been born in Athens, under its laws, or from all who have been born, brought up, and educated in Athens, and have no fault to find with its laws on these matters. Perhaps we ought to add here, in view of 51c9-d1, that it is not only these laws that are relevant, but also any further laws conferring benefits on the citizens. But it may be better to suppose that this mention of further benefits that the laws confer is more relevant to argument C [enjoining obedience to all laws] than to argument A [forbidding destruction of the laws].) Both C and B appear at first sight to be fully authoritarian, requiring obedience to any and every law. But, as this interpretation has it, they are not, for *both* are protected, by including the alternative 'either obey or persuade'. We have already noted that this alternative is explicit in argument B; we now note that it is also present in argument C (at 51b3-4, and at 51c1). How, then, is this alternative to be interpreted?

One thing that is clear is that the 'persuasion' alternative concerns persuasion as to the rightness or wrongness of the command in question ('or to persuade [the city] where τὸ δίκαιον lies' [51c1], 'or to persuade us [the Laws] if there is something we do μὴ καλῶς [51e7]). The traditional interpretation has been this. In the case of a law which a citizen regards as unjust, he is at liberty to persuade the assembly that it is unjust, and thus obtain its repeal. Similarly with a parental command regarded as unreasonable: the parent may be persuaded to rescind that command. It has recently been objected[11] that this account in effect never does allow disobedience, since it does not envisage one disobeying *first* and persuading *afterwards*. But we can readily extend the traditional account to allow for this, if we wish. In a Greek court of law (though not, of course, in an English one) it was permissible to plead that though one *had* broken the existing law, still one ought not to be condemned, because the law in question was a bad one. And such a plea is of course equally in order with a parental command. So we may certainly allow this much: one *has* done no wrong if one disobeys an existing law (or parental command), but afterwards succeeds in persuading the city (or the parent) that the disobedience was in this case justified. But, according to the traditional account, one has done wrong if one both disobeys and also does not *succeed* in persuading the city or parent—either before or after the event—that disobedience was or would be justified. In this case one has neither obeyed nor persuaded, and is therefore at fault.

However, my third suggested interpretation (which is in effect Kraut's interpretation)[12] will not rest content with this, for it clearly allows for the possibility of there being a command which it would be wrong to obey and yet one which the relevant authority could not be persuaded to see as wrong. That is, the authority could not be persuaded beforehand to withdraw it or afterwards to pardon infringements of it. So, according to this interpretation, the alternative should be construed in this way: one must either obey or *try to* persuade.[13] If one disobeys, but does *try to* persuade—either before or after the event—then one is not at fault, even though the attempt at persuasion may not be successful. No doubt, if what is commanded is not wrong, then one should obey the command, whether it comes from the state or from a parent. But where what is commanded is wrong, then one should not obey it, but try to persuade. In the case of a parental command addressed to an adult son or daughter, if the persuasion does not succeed then that, presumably, is the end of the matter. In the case of a law, if the persuasion does not succeed, then no doubt the appropriate penalty will be suffered. But in each case one has committed no wrong. That, at any rate, is what this third interpretation proposes. In its favour is the fact that it removes the authoritarian sting from arguments B and C. But what else may be said for it?

Kraut argues (pp. 91-103) that the analogy between parents and cities must be taken as drawing a parallel between on the one hand cities and their citizens and on the other hand parents and their *adult* offspring. If this is so, then indeed his interpretation of 'persuade or obey' seems preferable, since Greek society would hardly suppose that a fully adult man should obey his ageing father on *all* matters on which he did not succeed in persuading him otherwise. The consequence is no doubt fairly drawn, but the premise upon which it rests is insecure. The text nowhere *says* that the relationship it is concerned with is specifically that between parents and *adult* offspring, and there is a strong indication that it is not, since this same relation is held to obtain between masters and *slaves* (50e4, e8). It clearly cannot be said of slaves that they do no wrong by disobeying their master's command, so long as they have at least *tried* (but failed) to dissuade him from it. Kraut replies, if I understand him rightly, that the master-slave relationship is relevant only to argument A (concerning the *destruction* of the superior party), and not to argument C (concerning obedience to it) (pp. 105-8). But the two arguments cannot be so clearly separated, since it is undeniable that argument C grows out of, and develops, the consideration deployed in argument A. It is certainly open to us to hold that the thought in argument C, as in argument A, is that the relationship of a citizen to his city is comparable to the relationship of a *young* child to its parents, or a slave to his master: thus if persuasion fails, obedience is *required*.

Moreover this reading is very strongly supported by a point in the text that Kraut appears to overlook. At 51b2-3 it is said that one should reverence (σέβεσθαι) *and yield to* (ὑπείκειν) the state even more than to one's parents. On Kraut's account of 'persuading'—i.e. trying, but perhaps failing, to persuade—this may possibly be viewed as a way of 'reverencing' one's parents or one's state, but it can hardly be described as a way of *yielding* to them. As he himself explains, a father who has not been obeyed by his adult son, and who has not been convinced by the persuasion offered (either before or after), will generally do nothing further and expect nothing further. There is no penalty he can impose (save the extreme penalty of disinheritance, which anyway he can only impose once), and the son has entirely fulfilled his obligations. But a father in such a situation will hardly think 'he has *yielded* to me'. I conclude that Kraut's positive argument in favour of his interpretation is unconvincing: it is much more probable that the relationship between the citizen and the city is being compared (in argument C) to the relationship between a *young* child and its parents, which is in fact similar to the relationship between a slave and his master. In their case, obedience is expected, and disobedience is set down as *wrong*, unless it is justified by a *successful* attempt at persuasion.

There are two further arguments against Kraut's interpretation. One is that it is of course the personified Laws themselves who propound the alternative 'either obey or persuade', meaning presumably that they the Laws will be *satisfied* if either disjunct is fulfilled. But very clearly *the law is* not satisfied by an unsuccessful attempt at persuasion,[14] and what Kraut means to suggest is that the demands of morality are satisfied by this, at least when it would be wrong to obey, but not the demands of the law. Thus, as he sees it, the personified Laws have a double role: they both represent the actual laws of the city, and yet can keep a distance from them and represent morality instead (as when they admit that the verdict against Socrates was *not* a correct verdict, 54b8). However, where the 'obey or persuade' alternative occurs in argument B (at 51e7-52a3), it is surely as part of an account of what the actual laws of the city require, as is the permission to emigrate with no financial penalty, just above (51d5-e1). So there seems to me to be no escape from the objection this way: the actual laws evidently would not be satisfied by unsuccessful attempts at persuasion.

Finally, the Laws say that if Socrates escapes he will have both failed to obey and failed to persuade (52a3-4). Now quite a natural way of taking this charge would be to suppose that it claims that Socrates has not obeyed the law against impiety and corrupting the young, and also has not persuaded the jury that he should not be condemned on this account. If that is the correct way of taking it, then our proposed third interpretation must certainly be rejected, since Socrates evidently did *try* to persuade the jury that he should not be condemned. However, it may well be that this 'natural' way of taking the remark is mistaken, for after all our personified Laws do admit that the verdict was incorrect, and so apparently they should concede that Socrates *has* obeyed the Law against impiety and corrupting the young. So perhaps what they mean is this: having been found guilty on this charge, Socrates (if he escapes) will not be obeying the subsequent decision that he should therefore be executed, and equally will not have persuaded the jury that a different penalty would be more appropriate. But then again we can reply that he did *try* to persuade the jury to impose a different penalty. (It may well be said that he did not try very hard. Though the alternative that was *in the end* proposed may not have been too unreasonable,[15] the main tenor of his second speech in the *Apology* can hardly be described as a *serious* plea for leniency; it is more naturally seen simply as defiance. But this does not alter the fact that he did make an *attempt* at persuasion.) In response to this objection, Kraut claims that in order to count as 'persuading' the jury on this issue, Socrates should have urged, in his second speech, that his escape from gaol would be justified (p. 89). But that is evidently quite unreasonable. It is surely enough that he should have tried to persuade the jury that the death penalty was not an appropriate penalty, and that indeed he did (37a-b).

I conclude that there are too many indications that, in the *Crito*, merely trying (but failing) to persuade does not count as fulfilling the command either to obey or to persuade, and that our third interpretation must also be rejected. Let us take stock.

On all interpretations, the dialogue contains argument A. This is not a *fully* authoritarian argument, since it claims only that there is one particular law that ought always to be obeyed. Nevertheless it is authoritarian enough to produce a potential conflict with the leading injunction to do no wrong. It is not plausible, however, to see argument A as the only argument in the dialogue; at least we must admit that argument B is presented as a different and independent argument.

Argument B *should* be prevented from reaching a fully authoritarian conclusion by the fact that, when its premise is first introduced, an important proviso is attached: one should keep agreements, *provided* that what is agreed is not wrong. However, when argument B is actually developed, this proviso does not appear. In its place, two *other* provisos are suggested—one (by implication) is that the agreement should be fairly made, with no duress, ignorance, or trickery; and the other is that persuading the other party to alter the agreement is an acceptable alternative to keeping it. Neither of these provisos prevent the argument from conflicting with the leading injunction to do no wrong. Concerning the first of them, this point is uncontroversial; and I have just been arguing that the same point should also be admitted concerning the second, since what is intended is that disobedience is permitted only when there is a *successful* attempt at persuasion. Argument B, then, may fairly be characterised as a fully authoritarian argument, for its concessions fall far short of what we actually require.

Finally, there is also argument C. This is no less authoritarian than argument B, and it seems in fact to be a further and separate argument. Although it evidently grows out of a consideration that is relevant to argument A, it builds upon and develops that consideration so as to lead to a much more authoritarian result than A does by itself.

As my final question, I ask: was this what Plato intended? Did he *mean* to be arguing for the authoritarian conclusion that one should always obey any and every law (failing persuasion)? Or was it a mistake on his part that he allowed himself to use arguments that do (purport to) establish this strong conclusion, when all that he actually wished to argue for was a much more limited result?

The Authoritarian Interpretation

There are three points which may suggest that Plato did indeed mean to argue for the strong conclusion that one should always obey any and every law. Of these the first two would carry little weight by themselves, but the third is—it seems to me—of some significance.

In the concluding section of the dialogue, when the Laws turn to consider the disadvantages of escaping, one of the pertinent questions that they ask is this: when you are living in exile, Socrates, what will you say? 'Will you say the same as you said here, that virtue and justice, and customs and laws, are of most value to men?' (53c6-8). We of course expect to be told that Socrates, while in Athens, had praised virtue and justice above all else (ἡ ἀρετὴ καὶ ἡ δικαιοσύνη). But is it not a little surprising to be told that he had accorded *the same* praise also to customs and laws (τὰ νόμιμα καὶ οἱ νόμοι)? The implication must be that Socrates had supposed that the demands of the law and the demands of morality never would conflict with one another.[16] No doubt this is difficult to reconcile with *Apology* 32c-d, where Socrates appears explicitly to allow that morality may conflict with a legally authoritative order. But here we may turn to the second point.

Later in the same concluding passage the laws themselves are *distinguished* from their application by men. Socrates, admittedly, has been wronged, but he has been wronged 'not by us, the Laws, but by men' (54b8-c1).[17] In a similar vein it may be urged that the command of the Thirty Tyrants, though (perhaps) legally authoritative, was not a command of the laws themselves, but should rather be regarded as a command of men wrongly applying the law. Clearly, anyone who wishes to maintain that the laws are never morally in the wrong will need just such a distinction between the laws themselves and their application by particular men at particular times. It may be no accident that the *Crito* does indeed insist upon it.

These two points are perhaps suggestive, but equally they could not unreasonably be discounted, as reading too great a significance into a couple of stray remarks which surely were not intended to reveal the overall strategy of the dialogue. But my third point evidently is of importance for the interpretation of the dialogue as a whole. It goes back to the introductory section, where Socrates is setting the terms for the debate to come.

When Crito first pleads that Socrates should accept his offer of an arranged escape, he several times refers to 'what most people will think' (44b9-c5, 44d1-5, 45d6-46a1). From the first, Socrates rejects this appeal to the majority opinion (44c6-7), and he begins his reply by arguing for its worthlessness (46c6-8). He proposes, as an alternative, that one should pay attention only to the opinions of the one man who knows about whatever is at issue, the expert (Ὁ φρόνιμος, 47a10; Ὁ ἐπιστάτης καὶ ἐπαίων, 47b10-11). This, he says, applies equally where morals are concerned (47c9-10), for here too we should pay attention only to 'he who understands about right and wrong, this one person and the truth itself (Ὁ ἐπαίων περὶ τῶν δικαίων καὶ ἀδίκων, Ὁ εἷς καὶ αὐτὴ ἡ ἀλήθεια, 48a6-7).

Thus the *method* that Socrates suggests, for the proper consideration of the question before us, is that we should *consult the moral expert*. Moreover, since it is nowhere suggested that the method cannot be followed in the present case, we should presumably see the dialogue as pursuing this method. But who, then, is the expert who is consulted?

Well, the obvious suggestion is that it is the Laws themselves: the personified Laws are taken to be those who *know* about right and wrong, and whose opinions therefore should be listened to. If this is not the implication of the introductory section, then who *else* might be suggested as the moral expert whose advice is sought? There seem to be just two alternatives. One is that it is *Socrates* who is the expert, since after all the argument that is rhetorically put into the mouth of the Laws is presumably to be understood as being in fact Socrates' own reasoning. But (a) it would be distinctly odd, to say the least, if we are supposed to take Socrates as here implying that he himself is the moral expert, since everywhere else in Plato's dialogues he is consistently portrayed as *disclaiming* this status. Besides, (b) there seems to me to be altogether too much 'irony' in Socrates *saying* 'we must consult the expert' and *meaning* 'I must work it out myself, for I am the expert'. And finally (c) as the dialogue ends Socrates tells us that he *hears* what the Laws have been saying, as if it is indeed not his voice but another's (54d2-5), so as to preserve the impression that he has been listening not to his own advice but to someone else's. On the other side, one must of course agree that the Laws are presented as arguing from premises that Socrates himself has introduced at 49a-e (even if they do misrepresent his premise on keeping agreements). Thus it *may* be that we should understand Socrates as here claiming to be himself the expert, however improbable that may seem in the light of the other dialogues. But it seems to me rather more probable that the presumed expert is the Laws, who clearly can be regarded as a further and different source, available for consultation.

The other alternative is that the 'expert' who is consulted during the dialogue is neither Socrates nor the Laws but simply 'the truth itself', as the wording of 48a6-7 (quoted above) may perhaps suggest. If this was indeed Plato's intention, then (a) one can only say that the 'method' being proposed is a sham, and not in any way parallel to the method of consulting experts over bodily health and fitness (47a13-b3, 47d7-e1). In moral questions, there is no practical way of setting out to 'consult the truth itself', unless one can first assume some genuine expert who does know this truth. Moreover (b) the wording of 48a6-7 ('the expert *and* the truth') is surely not best understood as implying that the only expert in this area simply is the truth; rather, if one does consult a proper expert, then one will *thereby* have consulted the truth, because by hypothesis the expert knows the truth. More generally, the implication that there is an expert to be consulted is not satisfied merely by the supposition that there is a truth to be discovered, and I am unwilling to believe that Plato thought otherwise.

It must be admitted that the *Crito* is unique among Plato's early dialogues in implying that there is such a thing as the moral expert. Elsewhere it is explicitly claimed that there is no such thing (e.g. *Protagoras* 319b-320b, *Meno* 89e-96c). But at the same time the *Crito* is unique in attributing a serious moral argument not to Socrates nor to one of his interlocutors but to a personified abstraction, the Laws of Athens. It seems to me a very reasonable conjecture that these two features are related, and that the *Crito* does mean to imply that the laws are the experts—or, at any rate, that they are the best approximation to experts that is available to us. (The idea is perhaps this: the laws and customs of the city, though fallible—for they can sometimes be 'persuaded' that they are in the wrong—are nevertheless the only repository we have of 'the wisdom of the ages' in moral matters.) For that reason, their advice must always be treated with the greatest respect. No doubt the arguments of the *Crito* do push this line of thought too far, and the moral supremacy that they claim for the laws is not endorsed in any other early dialogue. Presumably Plato came to see that the implications, when strictly carried through, are unacceptable, and that there is a need to distinguish, much more firmly than the *Crito* does, between what is legally wrong and what is morally wrong.[18] But I suspect that he did quite seriously mean, in the *Crito* itself, to argue that the good man will never intentionally disobey the law.

Notes

1. It may of course be argued whether the orders of the Thirty Tyrants did have the appropriate legal authority, and it may be observed that the court could not legally make an order that Socrates should cease philosophising unless Socrates himself were to propose this as his alternative to the death penalty. But Socrates does not suggest that he did or would disobey these orders on the grounds of their illegality, but simply on the grounds of their wrongness.

2. The point is not always noticed. For example, it is ignored by both sides in the debate between R. Martin, 'Socrates on Disobedience to Law', *Review of Metaphysics* 24 (1970/1), pp. 21–38 and F. C. Wade, 'In Defense of Socrates', *Review of Metaphysics* 25 (1971/2), pp. 311–25.

3. Putting 29b6-7 together with 29d2-4 we can infer that obeying the supposed order, like doing wrong (ἀδικεῖν), would be bad and disgraceful (κακὸν καὶ αἰσχρὸν). But we cannot directly infer that it would *be* doing wrong.

4. This is, in effect, the solution adopted by G. X. Santas, *Socrates* (Routledge & Kegan Paul, London, 1979), pp. 48–51.

5. This first interpretation is to be found in Santas (op. cit.), p.18: 'Socrates' argument, in all its versions, is an argument to the conclusion that he must not escape, on the grounds that he would be disobeying *this* law [that the verdicts reached by the courts shall be supreme].... We do not know whether Socrates would make the same argument against disobeying *any* law'. (Santas does admit, however, that the arguments I distinguish as B and C below purport to establish much stronger claims. On this he remarks 'this over-arguing is puzzling, and we are unable to resolve the puzzle', pp. 26–28.)

6. Note that Socrates' remarks at 49b-d do not claim that retaliation is always wrong. Rather, they claim that retaliation is wrong *when* it involves *wronging* the person retaliated against.

7. So, for example, G. Vlastos, 'Socrates on Political Obedience and Disobedience', *Yale Review* 63 (1974), pp. 517–34, and J. Dybikowski, 'Socrates, Obedience, and the Law: Plato's *Crito*', *Dialogue* 13 (1974), pp. 519–35.

8. This, if I understand him rightly, is how Santas proposes to fill the apparent gap (op.cit., pp. 21–25).

9. No doubt the proviso is, in Socrates' own opinion, satisfied in this case. In his view, submitting to the death penalty will no doubt be *suffering* a wrong, but not *doing*

wrong. (The suggestion that it is doing wrong to his friends, his children, or—we may add—his wife, is one to which he pays no serious attention. Similarly with other suggestions that one might make, e.g. that it will harm the reputation of Athenian democracy if such a miscarriage of justice is not prevented, and the people given no opportunity to repent.) But although Socrates may indeed think that accepting death would not be wrong, still this point is not argued, or even mentioned, during argument B. And argument B would apparently have applied even if Socrates had taken a quite different view of his obligations to other people (and to himself).

10. I think this is now the most common interpretation. See e.g. the debate between Martin and Wade (op. cit., n. 2), and between G. Young, 'Socrates and Obedience', _Phronesis_ 19 (1974), pp. 1–29, and R. J. McLaughlin, 'Socrates on Disobedience: A Reply to G. Young', _Phronesis_ 21 (1976), pp. 185–97. Also R. Kraut, _Socrates and the State_, Princeton 1984.

11. E.g. Kraut, op. cit., ch. 3 (passim).

12. Op. cit., n.10.

13. It is well known that πείθειν can _mean_ 'try to persuade'. Success is not automatically implied (as it is with the English verb).

14. By contrast, the law _may_ be satisfied by a sincere but unsuccessful attempt to _obey_, as Kraut urges on pp. 69–70.

15. This question is discussed in T. C. Brickhouse and N. D. Smith, 'Socrates' Proposed Penalty in Plato's _Apology_', _Archiv fur Geschichte der Philosophie_ 64 (1982), pp. 1–18.

16. Quite how we are to understand 'customs' in this context is unclear. But perhaps it would not be unreasonable to take the reference to be to written laws (νόμοι) and to unwritten laws (νόμιμα).

17. By contrast, at 51a3-4 it is apparently the Laws who are seeking to destroy Socrates.

18. For all we know, the _Crito_ may have been his first dialogue, preceding even the _Apology_. (R. Hackforth, in his _The Composition of Plato's Apology_ [Cambridge, 1933], argues that there is reason to believe that the _Apology_ was not composed until six years after the speeches it purports to relate.)

12

Conflicting Values in Plato's *Crito*

Verity Harte

M Y PAPER HAS TWO AIMS. The first is to challenge the widespread assumption that the personified Laws of Athens, whom Socrates gives voice to during the second half of the *Crito,* express Socrates' own views.[1] (By 'Socrates' I shall always mean Plato's Socrates, not the historical Socrates.) I shall argue that the principles which the Laws espouse not only differ from those which Socrates sets out in his own person within the dialogue, but are in fact in conflict with Socrates' stated principles. This view has the consequence that no-one in the *Crito* spells out Socrates' own reasons for refusing Crito's urgent appeal that he escape from prison. If the personified Laws do not do so, nobody does. But it might be thought that the goal of the dialogue, the *Crito,* is to do just this: to show why Socrates did not escape. Hence the second aim of my paper, which is to give an alternative account of what the dialogue does instead.

First, then, let me set out the case for taking the arguments of the Laws to be in conflict with the principles which Socrates states in his own person.

Socrates and the Laws: The Case for Divorce

I begin at the end of the dialogue, not with the arguments, but with what Socrates says, back in his own person, in response to the speech of the Laws which he himself has delivered.

Know well, my dear friend Crito, that these are the things I seem to hear, like those who take part in Corybantic rites (κορυβαντιῶντες) seem to hear flutes, and the very sound of these arguments is buzzing within me (ἐν ἐμοὶ ... βομβεῖ) and making me incapable of hearing anything else. Know too that, if you speak against these things which now seem to me, you will speak in vain. Nonetheless, if you suppose you can accomplish anything further, speak. (54d2-7)[2]

In reference to this passage, Kraut says simply that 'Socrates applauds [the Laws'] arguments'.[3] I have no quarrel with the claim that Socrates presents himself as being powerfully affected by the arguments of the Laws. I do question whether this is best described as 'applause'. An argument can powerfully affect one, even render one speechless, without this implying that one endorses the argument. And this is the effect of the imagery Socrates uses: his comparing himself to those who take part in Corybantic rituals and his use of the metaphor of buzzing.

First, Corybants. Evidence about Corybantic rites has been usefully collected and discussed by Linforth, who suggests that most of what we know about Corybants comes from references in Plato.[4] In general, Corybantic rites are associated with madness and divine possession. Of course, madness, especially when divinely induced, can be an influence all to the good. But Socrates 'seems to hear' the Laws' arguments as those who take part in Corybantic rites 'seem to hear flutes'. If Linforth is right, the reference—despite the fact that flutes were involved in Corybantic rites—is to an hallucinatory experience associated with their devotion to the rites; and so, by analogy, in the case of Socrates. Socrates has been hearing voices—those of the Laws.

Further, other Platonic passages suggest that when someone is "Corybantically" affected by an argument, the argument is one they would not, or should not, endorse. For example, at *Phaedrus* 228b6-c1 Socrates describes himself as sickening of the desire to hear speeches. As such, he is the perfect partner to share in the Corybantic madness (συγκορυβαντιῶντα) with Phaedrus through hearing him repeat Lysias' speech. At the end of the report of Lysias' speech he refers again to their shared frenzy as the effect of the speech, although here he refers to Bacchic, rather than Corybantic frenzy (234d1-6). Even Phaedrus thinks that Socrates is being ironic and is making fun of Lysias' speech. Socrates does not endorse Lysias' speech. Instead, he offers a speech of his own, and then promptly condemns both his own and Lysias' speeches as offences against the god, Love. These passages are not straightforward in tone. But it should be clear that the frenzy which Lysias' speech induces is not an indication that Socrates believes it to be true.

Again, at *Symposium* 215e1-4, Alcibiades compares the effect which Socrates' conversation has upon him to the madness of those who take part in Corybantic rites: his heart leaps and the tears flow. Here, of course, it is Socrates himself who induces the madness, and one might assume it to be a positive result. However, the great tragedy of Alcibiades, in Socrates' eyes at least, is surely that, once away from the influence of Socrates, he does not endorse the principles of which Socrates speaks. Socrates is passionately committed to argument, to following where the argument leads. Are the symptoms which his arguments induce in Alciabiades the kind of response to argument that he would approve of? In the *Crito*, the effect of the Laws' arguments is to make Socrates incapable of hearing any other argument. Is this effect good? I suggest not. In line with other passages, I take Socrates' own claim to be Corybantically affected by the arguments of the Laws to be an indication from Plato that these are arguments he would not or should not endorse.[5]

The sound of the Laws' arguments, remember, is buzzing within Socrates. To us, in this age of electricity, things that buzz can be good things. In Greek things that buzz are not good things at all. Things that literally buzz are bees, wasps, mosquitoes, etc. So, in Aristophanes, the buzzing and biting of such insects are among the trials of poverty (*Plutus* 537–539). The connotation of dangerous irritants is preserved in metaphorical uses of the verb. So, in the *Republic*, Socrates describes the activity of the dominant class within a democracy—the class of idlers and spendthrifts—in the following terms:

> Its fiercest members do all the talking and acting, while the rest settle near the speaker's platform and buzz (βομβεῖ), and refuse to tolerate the opposition of another speaker.[6]

Notice, again, how buzzing can preclude hearing another point of view.[7]

Metaphorical buzzing is best interpreted in light of the core meaning of the verb. A bee buzzing around you is irritating, dangerous, and not to be welcomed. But it does have power, because it can sting you. For Socrates to say, in the *Crito*, that the sound of the Laws' arguments is buzzing within him, is to acknowledge their power, but not, I suggest, to endorse them.[8] But why should Socrates not endorse these arguments? I shall focus on two reasons—the main contenders. Socrates and the Laws each have a principle of non-retaliation, but not, I shall argue, the same principle.[9] They each have a principle of keeping agreements, but again, not the same principle. Further, these parallel principles do not just differ. The way in which they differ indicates a conflict of values between Socrates and the Laws.

Non-Retaliation

Socrates' principle of non-retaliation is stated absolutely, with no qualification whatsoever. At 49b10-11:

Since one must in no way do wrong (ἀδικεῖν), then one must not return a wrong (ἀνταδικειν) when wronged as the many suppose.

Again, at 49e4-5, Socrates says that one must never return harm (ἀντικακουργεῖν)[10] since doing people harm is no different from doing wrong. Finally, at 49c10-11:

One must neither return a wrong nor harm anyone no matter what one may suffer at their hands.

For Socrates, returning a wrong, or harming people is never justified.

As Vlastos has emphasised, Socrates' ban on retaliation is radically novel in his contemporary context.[11] And its novelty is emphasised within the dialogue. Socrates warns Crito not to agree to these principles contrary to what he really thinks (49c11-d1). Indeed, Socrates says that very few would agree (49d2). For Socrates himself, however, the ban on returning a wrong follows directly from the ban on doing wrong. And he is helped to this conclusion by the Greek terms involved. His term for returning a wrong (ἀνταδικεῖν) has at its core his term for doing wrong (ἀδικεῖν). Significantly, his term for returning a wrong is a neologism.[12] Significantly, because the novelty of Socrates' position is to take all cases of retaliation to be wrongful acts. To coin a term for retaliation with wrongdoing at its core brings this out.

This last point needs expansion. In contrast to my view, Bostock has argued that Socrates' ban on retaliation is in fact qualified; that Socrates claims only that 'retaliation is wrong *when* it involves *wronging* the person retaliated against'.[13] In so arguing, Bostock rightly pays attention to the root of the verb ἀνταδικεῖν, namely ἀδικεῖν or wrongdoing, but draws, I argue, the wrong conclusion. The α- privative in ἀνταδικεῖν is interpretative, not descriptive. Socrates refers generally to acts of retaliation in response to being wronged, and analyses them as acts of wrongdoing in themselves. Only thus is Socrates' position one which the majority would reject. The space which Bostock seeks to preserve for legitimate retaliation is possible only within a moral framework which sees no wrong, in certain contexts, in returning wrong. The Laws, I will argue, work within just such a framework: Socrates, I argue, does not.

Suppose I am one of the many who will reject Socrates' principle. There are two ways in which I might do so. I might agree with Socrates that returning a wrong is indeed a case of doing wrong, but one which, in certain contexts, may be condoned. That is, my defence of certain acts of retaliation may cause me to reject Socrates' outright ban on doing wrong. Alternatively, I may accept the outright ban on doing wrong, but deny, in certain contexts, that returning a wrong is in fact doing wrong.

Crito's responses are instructive at this point. He clearly and emphatically agrees that one should never do wrong. But in response to Socrates' inference—that one should not therefore return a wrong—he replies only 'it appears not' (49c1). Why so cautious? Crito is cautious at precisely the point at which Socrates takes the ban on returning a wrong to follow from the ban on doing wrong.[14] If Crito is cautious because he is uncertain, his uncertainty runs along the lines of the second possible response I described: that is, he is uncertain whether, in certain circumstances, two wrongs might not make a right. And his caution is instructive, because it cautions against supposing that every view of retaliation will take every act of retaliation to be a wrongful act, condoned or not. My contention is that the Laws' view of retaliation is a case in point. Their principle of non-retaliation does not imply that returning a wrong is, in all contexts, doing wrong. Indeed, it rather implies otherwise.

The crucial passage occurs in the first wave of the Laws' speech. The Laws argue that, since they have given Socrates birth, brought him up, and educated him, he is their 'offspring and slave' (50e2-3). In the light of this status, they ask him whether he thinks that justice is on an equal footing (ἐξ ἴσου) between him and them, and whether he thinks it just for him to do in return whatever they may attempt to do to him (50e4-7). And they invite him to consider this question by comparison with two other, morally asymmetrical relationships: the relation between father and son, and between master and slave.

In the two comparable cases—between father and son, master and slave—justice is not on an equal footing between the parties, or so it is claimed. This moral asymmetry has the consequence that retaliatory action on the part of the son or slave—the subordinate party—is not just. This conclusion carries over to the case of Socrates—the citizen—because his relation to the Laws is exactly comparable to that of a son or slave to a father or master, except that retaliation against the Laws would, if anything, be an even greater wrong. The weight of the argument that Socrates should not retaliate against the Laws falls entirely on the claim that justice is not on an equal footing between him and them; that he is their moral subordinate. And the principle of non-retaliation which emerges from this may be stated as follows: in certain morally asymmetrical relationships the subordinate person must never retaliate.

This principle of non-retaliation is clearly different from Socrates'. Socrates' principle of non-retaliation makes no issue of the relative status of the persons involved. The Laws' principle makes unequal status the central issue. But difference does not yet give conflict. Thus far, the Laws appear to be silent on the justice or otherwise of retaliation on the part of someone who is not a moral subordinate; on the part of one adult male citizen against another, for example. And this silence is critical. If the Laws *do* licence retaliation in morally symmetrical cases, their principle is clearly in conflict with Socrates'.

The Laws' silence about symmetrical cases might itself indicate consent to retaliation in such cases. But they also give this consent explicitly, at 50e7-51a2. The Laws have just asked Socrates whether he thinks that justice is on an equal footing between him and them, and whether he thinks it just for him to do in return what they do to him. The presumption is that, if he were planning to escape, he must answer, yes, in both cases. Now comes the riposte.

> Isn't it rather true that in the relation between you and your father, and between you and your master, should you have happened to have one, it was *not* the case that justice was on an equal footing between you, so that [it would have been just] to do in return the things which you suffered, [it] neither being [just] to speak back when badly spoken to, nor to strike back when struck, nor many such things? (50e7-51a2) (my emphasis; for the supplements, see end of previous sentence, 50e7)

What is crucial is the scope of the 'not' (italicised) in what was not the case, which includes everything in the positive, including the 'so that' clause: 'so that [it would have been just] to do in return the things which you suffered'. The effect is to give us a counterfactual claim: that, if it had been the case that justice were on an equal footing between Socrates and his father, it would have been just for him to do in return the things which he suffered. And so, the effect of these lines is to make two claims: a negative claim, that in morally asymmetrical relations like this, it is not right to retaliate, and a positive claim, in the form of a counterfactual, that in morally symmetrical relations, it is right to retaliate (or, at the very least, is not wrong to do so). And it is this twofold claim that carries over, mutatis mutandis, to the case of Socrates and the Laws.[15]

Of course, the Laws do not use the example of ἀδικεῖν and ἀνταδικεῖν in the passage quoted. Vlastos has argued that all that is legitimated here is ἀντιποιεῖν, as distinct from ἀνταδικειν.[16] Vlastos is right that the specific examples listed here—speaking back and striking back—are but examples to illustrate a general point about the circumstances in which, something having been done (ποιεῖν), one can do back (ἀντιποιεῖν). However, the specific type of 'doing' on the part of the Laws, which prompted the making of this general point, was an act of wrongdoing (ἀδικειν). Socrates suggests, and Crito agrees, that the best way to defend the act of destruction involved in breaking the law and escaping would be to point to the fact that the city has wronged them (50c1-2). Hence the specific type of 'doing back' (ἀντιποιεῖν) to which the general moral of 50e7-51a2 applies is indeed, pace Vlastos, ἀνταδικεῖν. And this is confirmed, when, in conclusion, the Laws refer back to this argument using Socrates' own terms (ἀνταδικεῖν and ἀντικακουργεῖν) at 54c2-3.

The way in which the Laws present their own principle of non-retaliation itself makes explicit that retaliation on the part of one who is not a moral subordinate either is just or is not unjust. Either way, this puts them in conflict with Socrates. Socrates warned us that few would agree with his outright ban on retaliation. The personified Laws are not among those few. This is the first reason why Socrates should not endorse the speech of the Laws. The second concerns keeping agreements. Here, it is Socrates' principle which is importantly qualified in a way that the Laws' principle is not.

Keeping Agreements

Socrates' principle of keeping agreements is established by getting Crito's assent to the following question:

> Should one do the things one agrees with someone [sc. to do]—these things being just—or should one deceive [sc. the person with whom the agreement is made]? (49e6-7)

I take the agreements in question in this context to be agreements to act. And I take Socrates' remarks about justice to specify the circumstances in which agreements to act should be kept. What must be just, if an agreement is to be kept, is the things agreed to be done. Socrates places no explicit conditions on the way an agreement is made (although certain conditions may follow simply from speaking in terms of an 'agreement' at all). But he does place conditions on what kind of action an agreement can demand. An agreement to act in certain ways obliges one to act in these ways, only if the actions it requires are themselves just.[17]

The justice of the actions concerned must be evaluated independently of the agreement which is made. Socrates cannot think that an agreement to act in certain ways in itself makes these actions just. His qualification would have no point were this the case. And his qualification is perfectly intelligible in the light of his earlier statements. Socrates has already said that one should never do wrong. In framing his principle of keeping agreements, he subordinates the obligations arising from agreements to the overriding principle that one should never do wrong. An agreement, by Socrates' principle, has no power to oblige one to do anything wrong. And this point is crucial as we turn to the Laws: that, for Socrates, the obligations of an agreement are subordinate to the claims of justice.

The Laws' argument that Socrates has entered into an agreement with them has been the subject of much discussion. For my present purposes, the question is simply this: do the Laws, like Socrates, think that agreements are binding only if what they require of one is itself just? I shall argue that they do not.

The Laws take Socrates—like any adult citizen who continues to reside in the city—to have entered into an agreement with them. It is an agreement in act, as opposed to an agreement by argument (ἔργῳ not λόγῳ, cf. 52d5).[18] The Laws' first and most general statement of its consequences is this: "Whoever among you [i.e. adult citizens] stays, seeing the way in which we judge legal cases and govern the other affairs of the city, we say at that point he has, by his action, entered into an agreement with us to do whatever we command" (51e1-4). The agreement here is a perfectly general one, and it obliges the citizen to do *whatever* the Laws command. Stated thus, the Laws' view of this agreement is clearly in conflict with Socrates' principle, provided one allows the following points: first, that it is perfectly possible that the Laws may command a citizen to do something which is independently evaluated to be unjust; second, that the opportunity afforded the citizen to consider how, in general, the Laws operate could never guarantee that each individual command they issue will not require an act of injustice. On the Laws' view, the agreement, once made, is absolutely binding.[19] And this conflicts with Socrates' principle, because his principle requires that a party to an agreement should be able to evaluate the justice of any action required by the agreement, and to break the agreement should a particular action not be just.

The Laws do say things which may be thought to qualify this account of the citizen's agreement. But nothing in what they say brings their position into line with Socrates' principle. First is their emphasis on the way the agreement has been made. It has, they argue, been freely and fairly made. But this does not help. An agreement can be fairly made—especially as general an agreement as the agreement in question—without this being any guarantee that what will be required of a party to the agreement will never be unjust. The Laws do say something about justice in this regard. When they stress that Socrates has had 70 years in which he could have left the city freely, he could have done so 'if [the Laws] did not please [him], or if the agreements did not seem to [him] to be just' (52e4f). But what he could have considered is the justice of the *agreement*. For Socrates, by contrast, it is the *actions* the agreement requires whose justice must be evaluated. And, again, the general nature of the agreement is such that the opportunity to consider the justice of the agreement itself does not give what Socrates' principle requires, namely the opportunity to establish whether any individual action, required by the agreement, might be unjust.

The second apparent qualification of their position is the Laws' notorious offer of an alternative to obedience, namely persuasion. Once, they describe the alternative to obedience as 'to persuade them as to the nature of justice'. This is at 51c1, before they have begun to discuss the nature of the agreement itself. Several times, they speak, elliptically, of the simple alternative 'persuade or obey'. The question is: does this alternative entitle the citizen to break the agreement if it requires an injustice, allowing them simply to persuade the Laws of the justice of doing so? So Richard Kraut has argued. He has even argued that such persuasion need not be successful: the attempt is enough.[20] I disagree on both counts. The persuasion envisaged remains entirely situated within the structure of the agreement by which the citizen is bound. The citizen's task is not to persuade the Laws of the justice of an act of disobedience after the fact. It is rather to persuade the Laws to alter or retract an unjust command. This, I think, is clear from the only other passage in which the Laws enlarge on the nature or goal of the envisaged persuasion. One of the three ways in which the disobedient citizen does wrong, they say, is this: ". . . having agreed to obey us, he neither obeys us nor persuades us if we are not acting well. . . ." (51e6).

The persuasion here is directed at the behaviour of the Laws: if *they* are not acting well. By implication, the injustice in question is the action of the Laws in making a certain command. It does not matter if the injustice of the act of making the command is a consequence of the injustice of the act required. The goal of the persuasion is to get the *Laws* to act differently, not to legitimate an act of disobedience on the part of the citizen. But if the target of the persuasion is the behaviour of the Laws, the default position on the citizen's part is to obey their command. The option to persuade gives the citizen the opportunity to attempt to influence the Laws' commands, and get some retracted: it does not offer him the opportunity simply to disobey. And, of course, on this view, the persuasion must be successful to have any point.

If this is the alternative the citizen is offered, then the conflict with Socrates still remains. Socrates and the Laws conceive the balance between the claims of justice and those of an agreement in different and conflicting ways. Socrates allows the claims of justice to override any obligation consequent upon an agreement: the party bound by an agreement may simply break the agreement in the event that the terms of the agreement require him to act unjustly. The Laws' conception of the agreement between themselves and the citizen does not allow this. Providing the agreement is freely and fairly made, the Laws retain their right of command. The citizen cannot break an agreement if it requires an act of injustice; he can merely seek to persuade the Laws to alter their unjust command. The power to decide questions of justice thus belongs to the Laws and not, as Socrates' principle requires, to the citizens themselves. Indeed I take this to follow from the introduction of the need to persuade: that decisions about questions of justice are to be worked out within the framework of the agreement, a hierarchical framework, in which the Laws, and not the citizen, have power. This conflict between Socrates and the Laws on keeping agreements is the second reason why Socrates should not endorse the speech of the Laws.

Three Voices: Three Value Systems

Once one gives up the assumption that the Laws espouse Socrates' own views, the *Crito* becomes a dialogue containing three separate voices: Crito's, Socrates', and the Laws'. Each, I suggest, speaks from the perspective of some system of value. Consider the closing wave of the Laws' argument: should Socrates escape, they argue, he will endanger his friends, who may lose both their property and their city (53b1-3); he will turn his children into exiles, or at best leave them neither better nor worse off than if he were dead (54a3-b1); and Socrates himself will cut a ridiculous figure, and one which makes a mockery of all his previous emphasis on justice and virtue (53b3-54a1).

These arguments appear to have more in common with Crito's arguments than with anything Socrates has said in his own person. Conversely, but within the same frame of reference, Crito had opened the dialogue by arguing that, if Socrates does *not* escape, he will harm his friends, both by depriving them of his companionship and by exposing them to the bad opinion of the many (44b6-c5); he will leave his children orphans, to suffer the fate of orphans (45c8-d4); and the whole affair will bring shame and ridicule upon Socrates, as well as his friends, that one who throughout his life has spoken of concern for virtue should be seen to act in this wicked and shameful way (45d4-46a4).

Between Crito and the Laws, then, we have a point by point comparison, although they argue to opposite conclusions. Socrates, by contrast, has explicitly denied the relevance to the decision to be made of concern for such things as loss of property and the welfare of children (48c2-6).[21] The only relevant consideration is whether or not it would be just for Socrates to escape (48b11-c1).

Socrates clearly supposes that considerations about prestige or children are not relevant to the consideration of whether or not it is just for him to escape. Crito and the Laws, by contrast, do both appeal to considerations such as these, although to different effect. What is less often noted is that Crito and the Laws, no less than Socrates himself, argue in terms of what it is just for Socrates to do.[22] For Crito, the very considerations which Socrates rejects formed the core of his argument that it would precisely be *just* for Socrates to escape. For the Laws, these considerations are part of their argument that it would *not* be just for Socrates to escape. All three speakers argue in terms of justice. But they employ different considerations in doing so, and argue with different results.

My question is: how can this be? Suppose they all agree that the question to be addressed is whether or not it is just for Socrates to escape, as indeed they appear to. This prompts a prior question about what considerations count as relevant when deciding what it is just for someone to do. And an answer to this question will in turn depend on what, in the first place, is understood by what is just. For readers of the Socratic dialogues, the train of thought should be all too familiar. If ever there were a dialogue that cried out for Socrates to stop the discussion and demand that we first clarify our notion of justice, the *Crito* to my mind is it. But Socrates nowhere does. And the omission, in my view, is both striking and marked. It is also the key to the alternative reading I propose.

Crito, Socrates, and the Laws each address (or in Socrates' case begins to address) the question of whether or not Socrates should escape from the perspective of some system of value. But their value systems are in conflict (all three of them with each of the others). As I have said, the *Crito* is a dialogue in which, for once, there is no attempt to define the central value under discussion, namely justice, on the basis of which Socrates' course of action is to be decided. The *Crito* is, however, a dialogue which shows a striking awareness of the consequence of conflicts of value. When Socrates warns Crito not to agree with his outright ban on returning a wrong against what he himself really thinks, he says that there will be no 'common will' or 'common deliberation' (κοινὴ βουλή) between himself and those (i.e. the majority) who do not agree with this outright ban (49d2-5). Vlastos has rightly emphasised that Socrates' point is not that he cannot *argue* with people who do not agree on this point. We know very well that he can and does. His point is that there can be no shared process of deliberation as to how to act.[23] But the *Crito* is precisely the dialogue whose apparent goal is to come up with a deliberated decision as to how Socrates should act.

There is no shared process of deliberation between Socrates and the Laws. They agree, or so I assume, on how Socrates should act; that he should not escape. But they do not agree on the reasoning by which they arrive at this conclusion, since they have conflicting conceptions of the justice of retaliation and of the obligations consequent upon an agreement.

Crito and Socrates

What about Crito and Socrates? They present a curious combination of agreement and disagreement. We are told that they have conversed together on previous occasions, and apparently agreed on certain ethical principles (49a5-b1). In the course of the *Crito*, Crito again agrees to several 'Socratic' principles: that it is not living, but living well that matters; that living well is living rightly and justly (48b4-10); that one must never do wrong (49a4-b9); that one must never return a wrong (with the hesitation noted above)[24] (49b10-c1); and, emphatically, that one must never do harm (49c2-3). At least initially, however, there had also been obvious disagreement between them. Crito, but not Socrates, had given weight to the opinion of the many, and the damage they can do. And Crito had based his argument on considerations about the welfare of Socrates' friends and family, considerations which Socrates deems irrelevant to the question at hand.

What should we make of this combination of agreement and disagreement? One might suggest that Crito is simply confused; his grief at the prospect of Socrates' death gets the better of him, at least at first. But while it is true that he argues with feeling, Crito, no less than Socrates, argues in terms of what it is just for Socrates to do. Alternatively, one might note how incredibly general are the agreements that he and Socrates have made. Two people could, I would think, quite readily agree that one should live rightly and justly, but have entirely different conceptions of what living rightly and justly consists in.[25] Crito's own initial arguments suggest that they do.

The most immediate point of disagreement between Crito and Socrates concerns their respective notions of harm, and can best be seen in their difference in attitude to the opinion and power of the many. Among several bad consequences which Crito says will follow from Socrates' refusal to escape is the shame Crito will suffer at being seen, by the many, to have put money before friends (44c2-3). It is this consequence to which Socrates responds, questioning whether the opinion of the many is worthy of concern. Time for a familiar Socratic lesson on the dubious qualifications of the many as guides to virtue.

But Crito, I suggest, is more than an unreflective crowd follower. He has a reason for thinking that the opinion of the many should be taken into account here, and a reason germane to Socrates' circumstances. Socrates should, he suggests, be able to see for himself that it *is* necessary to be concerned about the opinion of the many, for Socrates' own circumstances show him the harm, and that is the greatest harm, the many can do (44d1-5).[26] Socrates, by contrast, does not think the opinion of the many is worth considering. And he defends his position by simply denying that the many *can* do him or Crito genuine harm. The many, in his view, can neither do the greatest harm nor the greatest good, for they cannot make men foolish and they cannot make men wise (44d6-10). What is at issue, then, in this dispute about the power of the many is different understandings of harm. Crito's understanding of harm is external; harm is physical harm.²⁷ Socrates' understanding of harm is internal; genuine harm is harm to the soul.

At least at first, then, Crito and Socrates have fundamentally different understandings of what counts as harm. They will later agree, however, that there is no difference between doing harm and doing wrong, or acting unjustly. And this agreement has a linguistic connection with the earlier dispute. Earlier, they disputed whether or not the many could work the greatest harms or evils (τὰ μέγιστα κακὰ ἐργάζεσθαι) (cf. 44d7). Later, they agree that doing harm (or working evil) (κακουργεῖν or κακῶς ποιεῖν ἀνθρώπους) is no different from doing wrong (ἀδικεῖν) (49c2-8). So, if they have different conceptions of working evil, they should have different conceptions of doing wrong, and hence of right or justice.

Neither Socrates nor Crito spells out their respective conceptions of justice. But an impression of the difference between them can be extrapolated from what each of them says. Socrates' understanding of justice is closely bound up with his notion of harm. Harm, for Socrates, is harm to the soul. And he refers to the soul as 'what the unjust damages and the just benefits' (47e7). To refrain from injustice is in one's own best interest, because injustice harms one's soul. Injustice, he says, is 'in every way bad and shameful *for him who does it*' (49b4-6, my emphasis). For Socrates, then, when it comes to questions of justice, it is the individual agent who counts: it is their soul which is most at stake.

By contrast, Crito's conception of justice is bound up with the significance of specific groups of others: friends, enemies, and family. Of course, he too is concerned with what it is just *for Socrates* to do, but his conception of what it is just for Socrates to do is mediated by Socrates' relations to others. His first attempts to persuade Socrates to escape are all concerned with duties to friends. If Socrates does not escape, Crito faces a double misfortune: the loss of a friend along with the shame, considered before, in the view of the many. And Socrates has a duty as his friend not to put him in such a shameful position. Correspondingly, Crito and Socrates' other friends have a duty to run whatever risks are involved in helping Socrates escape. It would, he says, be just for them to run these risks (45a1-2). Helping friends is a significant component of his conception of justice. Instead of helping his friends (and letting his friends help him), Socrates is ensuring that his enemies get what they want, namely his death (45c5-8). To do this, Crito says, is not just. That Crito is accusing Socrates of precisely the reverse of the conventional Greek view of justice—of harming friends and helping enemies—has been well remarked by Bentley.²⁸ One last group of significant others concludes Crito's plea: Socrates' sons. Socrates has a duty to his sons. Having given them birth, he must be prepared to endure hardship with them, to raise and to educate them. This is what a 'good and brave man' would choose (45c8-d8).

The contrast between Crito's and Socrates' conceptions of justice might be characterised in terms of the different domains to which each thinks justice applies. Socrates cashes out justice solely in terms of its effect on an individual's soul: justice is what benefits the soul. Of course, just acts may involve others, but here at least Socrates has nothing to say on this front. A fortiori, there is no suggestion that others—and their relation to the agent in question—have a role to play in determining the justice of an action. For Crito, by contrast, the justice of an agent's action is differently assessed according as it relates to other specific groups: friends, enemies, and family. This contrast is based upon what Crito says in his opening argument and what Socrates says in response. But Socrates' response takes the familiar form of question and answer. And there is a further question as to whether, in the course of these questions and answers, Crito is brought to revise his conception of justice.

Crito does accept, during their discussion, that the view of an expert is, in every sphere, more worthy of attention than that of the crowd. In particular, he accepts that this is so in the sphere of what is just and unjust, shameful and honourable, good and bad, that is, precisely the sphere in which the decision to be made resides (47c8-d3). Crito also accepts that not to follow the advice of the moral expert, if such there be, would irrevocably damage 'something we used to say becomes better by justice and is harmed by injustice' (47d4-5).[29] What they 'used to say' is improved by justice and damaged by injustice is clearly the soul. But Socrates never says as much. Nor, when he proceeds to elaborate an analogy between harm to the body and (greater and more significant) harm to 'what the just benefits and the unjust corrupts', does he name the soul directly (47e6-7). Why is Socrates so coy? And does Crito truly understand what is meant?

If Crito does understand that Socrates is referring to the soul in these passages, then he has been brought to accept that harm to the soul is greater and more significant than harm to the body, in contrast to his stance in the earlier dispute about the significance of the many. Notice, however, how resistant is Crito's impression of the power of the many. At the end of a lengthy argument against the significance of the power of the many, Socrates remarks that 'someone might say: but the many can kill us' (48a10-11). And Crito responds: 'That's clear. Someone might indeed say that, Socrates. You're right.' (48b1-2). This seems the response of someone who still has considerable sympathy with such a view.

If Crito is really to change his view of the power of the opinion of the many, especially in view of the part this has played in Socrates' circumstances, he needs to reevaluate the notion of harm with which he began. If he is to reevaluate his notion of harm, he needs some concrete alternatives. Socrates leads him towards his own conception of harm as harm to the soul, but does not spell it out for him. And Crito is not much helped by Socrates' characterising the soul as 'what the just benefits and the unjust harms', unless he has also revised his conception of justice. The problem throughout their conversation is that, while both agree that Socrates should act in accordance with justice, it is not at all clear that they are agreed upon what justice consists in. As yet, no one has spelled out a working conception of justice. By the end of his conversation with Socrates, Crito may well be less certain of his own unarticulated conception of justice. I do not think he has yet acquired a contentful alternative. As the dialogue proceeds, it seems to be the Laws, rather than Socrates, who provide him with a conception of justice he cannot dispute.

Crito and the Laws

Next, then, consider Crito and the Laws. They argue to opposite conclusions. But they appear to share at least some of the same domain of values. It is Crito and the Laws, remember, who show a point by point correspondence on appeals to Socrates' image, and to the welfare of his family and friends. So, are their values the same? I shall argue that they are not, but that the gap between Crito's conception of justice and that of the Laws is readily closed. In the course of their argument, the Laws appropriate and subsume Crito's values within their own.

To characterise the difference between Crito and the Laws, I shall talk in terms of 'concentric circles of justice'. I have in mind a picture of conventional Athenian morality as described by Dover, in the following terms: ". . . an Athenian felt that his first duty was to his parents. . . , his second to his kinsmen, . . . his third to his friends and benefactors; after that, in descending order, to his fellow citizens, to citizens of other Greek states, to *barbaroi*, and to slaves."[30] Here we have a series of concentric circles of significant others, hierarchically arranged: the closest circle containing those most important, to whom obligation is most strongly felt.[31]

Crito's opening arguments implied his own, less extensive, concentric circles over which Socrates' obligations extend. First came Socrates' friends; then his family, specifically, his sons; and out on the edge of the circles, Socrates' enemies, whom he has no obligation to assist: quite the reverse. The Laws' conception of justice can also be construed in terms of concentric circles. But their circles extend further than Crito's, insofar as they include the political community in which Socrates resides. And they have a different hierarchical arrangement. The Laws argue that the political community is owed allegiance of the same kind, but to a greater degree, than one's family and friends. And it is by so arguing that the Laws both incorporate and challenge Crito's values.

Consider the way in which the Laws characterise the laws: citizen relation and the obligations the citizen thereby incurs. The Laws claim that the citizen (Socrates) is their 'offspring and slave' (50e3-4). They claim this on the basis of their having given him birth, nurtured, and educated him. Crito too had referred to the bringing up and educating of children, but had described them as the responsibility of a parent, not of the Laws. That Socrates has such responsibilities formed part of his argument that Socrates should escape.

The Laws' claim to these responsibilities is carefully prepared for. Their first claim is to be the *means* by which Socrates' parents and educators fulfilled their roles as such (cf. δι'ἡμῶν at 50d2), referring to the laws by which his parents married and gave him birth, and to the laws directing his father to educate him in music and gymnastics. Having stated this carefully, however, the Laws go on to speak as if they themselves were Socrates' parents and educators, and make various claims upon him on the basis of being so. Are they simply speaking loosely? Or, in the process of identifying themselves as the means by which Socrates' parents did these things, do they seek to appropriate these roles from their biological counterparts? I suggest that they do, and that this is the first evidence of their strategy of argument: that of characterising the laws: citizen relation in terms familiar from life in the Greek household or οἶκος. Such a strategy is helped, of course, by the personification of the Laws.

The Laws compare the laws: citizen relation with two other relations: that of father to son and master to slave. What is striking about these two relations is that they are the two key asymmetrical and hierarchical relations in the Greek household which are between men. (The third, according to Aristotle, being that between husband and wife.)[32] They are also the two relations, comparison with which is used to demonstrate that it would be wrong for Socrates to retaliate against the Laws. The argument trades on the claim that Socrates owes the Laws, qua fathers and masters, the same kind of obedience he is expected to understand that he would owe to a (biological) father or master, no matter what he experiences at their hands. Reverence towards parents, and an injunction against harming them, is, of course, deeply rooted in Greek morality. (Consider the Oresteia, to name but one tragic exploration of this theme.) The Laws' strategy is to translate this convention into a civic context. And the Laws claim something more than that the citizen owes precisely the same obedience and reverence to them as a child to a father or a slave to a master. They claim to be owed such obedience and reverence to a greater degree.

> . . . are you so wise that you have failed to recognise that your fatherland is more to be honoured than your mother, father and all your ancestors; that it is more to be revered, more holy and of greater worth among both gods and men of sense. . . ? (51a7-b2)

... it is not holy to use force against a mother or father; and even less so than in these cases to do so against one's fatherland. (51c2-3)

The Laws appeal to the felt obligation towards parents and kin, and claim a greater obligation towards themselves. Their values overlap with Crito's, insofar as both appeal to obligations to members of the household. But they are not the same. The Laws exploit Crito's values to their own ends. The obligations he appealed to are real, but they are not the most important obligations Socrates has.

The Laws' appropriation of the traditionally felt obligation towards friends and family within a civic context occurs within the first wave of their argument. Their claim to a parental role is also the source of the obligations owed by a citizen who has entered into an agreement with them. If one then considers the final wave of their argument, with its point by point correspondence with Crito, it becomes clear how they can use such similar arguments to opposite conclusions.

The Laws do, like Crito, consider Socrates to have an obligation towards his friends and family, as well as himself. But he has a prior and greater obligation towards the Laws and his city. Having already argued that he would be failing to fulfil this greater obligation, and thus acting unjustly, were he to attempt to escape, the Laws conclude by arguing that he would, in consequence, harm his friends and his family also. He would do so, because to fail to fulfil his own obligations to the city would embroil his friends and his family in his own injustice. His friends would be implicated in the injustice of his attempt to escape; his sons would be condemned to his life of exile in a lawless state. The Laws' assessment of Socrates' obligations towards his friends and family arrives at a different conclusion from Crito's, because they assess these obligations in the context of their own different system of values.

The Argumentative Strategy of the Laws and the Orators

Many parallels can be found in the rhetoric of the day for the argumentative strategy of the Laws. The term πατρίς, literally 'fatherland', already contains the germ of the idea that a citizen has an almost familial relation to their country. And this idea has a special place, and a corresponding vocabulary, in the minds of Athenians. While I have found no direct parallels for the claim that the relation between citizen and laws is like that of child to father or slave to master, the Athenians' claim to be earthborn or aboriginal (αὐτόχθονες) leads several writers to refer to Athens—the city and political community with which the Laws of the Crito identify themselves—as father, mother, and nurse: e.g. Demosthenes *Funeral Oration* LX.4, 5; Isocrates *Panegyricus* 24-25; Lysias

Funeral Oration II.17. These characterisations of the citizen: city relation in familial terms underlie the suggestion that the citizen owes certain obligations to
their city as a result of the special relation between them. So, for just one example, Lysias, in his *Funeral Oration*, II.70, praises those who have died for
ending their lives as good men must, 'repaying the fatherland for their nurture'.[37] Such rhetorical tropes are part of a broader pattern of analogies, in the
rhetoric of the day, between household (οἶκος) and city (πόλις).[38]

Household and city may be compared. They may also conflict.[39] The locus
classicus is Sophocles' *Antigone*, which explores precisely this conflict. Sources
can be found which take the friends and family side of this debate. But one can
also find voices on the other side, the side, as I have argued, which the Laws of
the *Crito* take. Creon, in the *Antigone*, is one: 'whoever places a friend above
the good of his own country, he is nothing: I have no use for him' (182-83).[40]

Connor cites two pieces of evidence to suggest that the conflict between obligations to kin and obligations to the city may have been particularly at issue in
the turbulent period at the end of the 5th century and turn of the 4th, the period in which the dramatic date of the Crito falls.[41] Thucydides, in his account
of the troubles associated with the civil war in Corcyra in 427 as well as similar
disruptions elsewhere, says that at this time 'Family relations (τὸ συγγενές)
were a weaker tie than faction membership (τὸ ἑταιριχόν) . . .' (III.82).[42]
Xenophon puts the following remark into the mouth of Euryptolemus, speaking in 406 in favour of there being a trial for the generals involved in the battle
off Mytilene, including his relative Pericles (jr.): 'it would be shameful for me to
think more of him than of the whole city' (Hellenica vii.21).

Neither of these passages need be taken as supporting the side of the city
against kin. Thucydides certainly should not be, since he lists the decline of
family ties among his catalogue of the devastating effects of civil conflict.
Euryptolemus' proud show of putting the interests of the city ahead of that of
his kinsmen must also be taken in context. He argues that the generals should
be put on trial, but he does so against a motion that they should simply be
sentenced by vote.[43] One may suspect that his emphasis on his own self-deny-
ing patriotism is a rhetorical move designed to support the least unfavourable
outcome for the generals. Thus these two passages are not sufficient to show
that there was a widespread move in Athenian society towards the position
adopted by the Laws of the *Crito*. Nor are they sufficient to establish a particular connection between the adoption of such a position and the period in
which Socrates' trial occurred. However, they, along with the other evidence
considered, do show that the Laws' argumentative strategy is comparable to
the many ways in which contemporary rhetoric sought to exploit the analogy
between οἶκος and πόλις; that the strategy is one which would have been
recognisable to a contemporary Athenian reader of the Crito; and that the po-

sition adopted on the relative place of city and kin is one which some Athenians may have seen reason to defend. And this is enough for them to be used as contemporary parallels for the case I have made regarding the strategy of the Laws.[44]

One final piece of evidence is found in lines from a (largely) lost Euripides play, *Erechtheus*, cited in Lycurgus' speech, *Against Leocrates*.[45] These lines, in which the speaker lists their several reasons for sacrificing a child for the good of the city, collect together several of the themes recurrent in the texts I have been considering. They appeal to the special relation an Athenian has to their city through being earthborn (8). They trade the good of the household off against that of the city, and conclude that the loss of a single household weighs low in the balance against the welfare of the whole city (19-21). And they construe the love for his city of a citizen as a prime example of filial love (53-54).

The Laws and Crito espouse two different, but importantly related systems of value. Crito appeals to the traditionally felt obligations towards friends and family; the Laws appropriate these values within a civic context and place an obligation to law and the city ahead of obligations to family and friends. In doing so, they trade on their characterisation of the Laws: citizen relation in familial terms. The Laws take one side—indeed the obvious side for them to take—in what appears to be a recognisably Athenian debate about the relative value of household and city. Their values are not those of Socrates or Crito, but are a kind of Athenian civic piety.

The Three Value Systems in Review

The participants in the Crito, both real and imagined, are confronted by the practical question of what, in his current circumstances, Socrates should do. Crito, Socrates, and the Laws all think that Socrates should act in accordance with justice. But each has a different conception of what justice amounts to. Crito's value system might be described as involving 'kinship values';[46] he treats the justice of an agent's action in terms of their relation to a specific community of family and friends. Socrates' value system is, of course, 'Socratic'; he treats the justice of an agent's action in terms of its benefit or harm to the agent's soul. The Laws' value system may be described as 'civic'; they treat the justice of an agent's action in terms of their relation to the political community, first, and only afterwards to family and friends.

All three value systems are different. But they all have deep roots in the philosophical, personal, and political communities of the characters in the dialogue, the dialogue's author, Plato, and its Athenian audience. In presenting these different, but deeply Athenian value systems, what the Crito does, I suggest, is set up a conflict between them.

This conflict has two aspects: one static, one dynamic. If one treats the dialogue as static, the three value systems are laid out in turn, provoking one to reflect on the relations between them. But there is also a dynamic process during the course of the dialogue, which is the process of Crito's apparent change of mind. It is Crito who begins the dialogue urging Socrates to escape. It is Crito who ends the dialogue unable to dispute the Laws' case against that escape. Crito's value system is challenged, first by Socrates, and then by the Laws. But it is the Laws, rather than Socrates, who give Crito an alternative system of value he cannot dispute.

The Structure of the *Crito*: Some Authorial Signposts

The conflict between the values of Crito, Socrates, and the Laws is written into what Plato has each of them say. The staging of the conflict between them is written into the structure of the dialogue as a whole. The dialogue juxtaposes several systems of value: Socrates' in the middle, flanked by Crito's on the one side and the Laws' on the other. Surrounding all—at the beginning of the dialogue and again at the end—there is also brief but intriguing reference to god.

Almost immediately the dialogue opens, Crito and Socrates get involved in a debate as to the date of the expected arrival of the ship from Delos, whose arrival heralds Socrates' death. Crito has evidence from people recently arrived from Sounion that the ship will arrive that very day, and that Socrates must die, therefore, on the following day. Where Crito's evidence (and his consequent anxiety) are thoroughly human, Socrates, by contrast, refers all such matters to the lap of the gods, simply saying 'may it happen, with good fortune, in the way that is dear to the gods' (43d7-8). His own evidence for his belief that the ship will not in fact arrive that day is a prophetic dream, on which more below. At the end of the dialogue, Socrates again appeals to the divine order. His closing line, and that of the dialogue as a whole, makes sudden and striking reference to god: '. . . let us act thus, since it is thus that god guides (or instructs)[47] us' (54e1-2). Inclusion of the divine order completes the dialogue's roll call of the values most deeply rooted in Plato's Athens. It also makes passing reference to a matter close to the explicit subject of Socrates' trial. It is at least tempting to suppose that Plato has Socrates characterise his action of accepting execution as an act of piety in full and ironic awareness that Socrates will die convicted of impiety.[48]

The *Crito* itself presents us with a set of concentric circles of the values most important in Plato's Athens. The position of Socrates' values, in the centre of the dialogue, dramatically represents the bind that Socrates is in, trapped within a community whose values are not his own, neither the kinship ethics of Crito, nor the civic ethics of the Laws. But this is his community nonetheless: the community in which he engaged in philosophical conversations with the likes of Crito, and the political community which sentenced him to death. It is at just this point that Plato has Socrates drive home a point about conflicts of value: that there can be no common will or common deliberation (no κοινὴ βουλή) between him and those (the majority) who do not agree with his statement of values (49d1-5). And this reference to commonality (τὸ κοινόν) is not without a certain poignancy in the context of the dialogue as a whole. Socrates had insisted that he and Crito inquire in common (κοινῇ) into the question of whether or not it is just for him to escape (48d8). And the personified Laws are introduced as τὸ κοινὸν τῆς πόλεως (what's common in, or belonging to, the city) (50a8).

If the *Crito*'s structure is a powerful presentation of the bind that Socrates is in, the dialogue also begins by challenging our expectation of how to evaluate the consequences of that bind for Socrates himself, namely his imminent death. It is Crito's values, and in particular Crito's conception of harm, which suggests that for Socrates to be executed is for him to experience the greatest harm. According to Socrates' conception of harm, such a physical penalty cannot really harm him. If he does not commit an injustice, his soul is unharmed; and thus he is unharmed in the way that he thinks counts. It is for this reason that Socrates had warned the jurors at his trial that, if they should kill him, they would harm themselves more than they harm him (*Apology* 30c6-8). This is the paradox of Socrates' action in accepting execution; he does something which, in practice, in his circumstances, few Athenians would do—namely, does not escape[49]—and thus accepts what to most Athenians might seem the ultimate harm, physical death. To Socrates, however, the greatest harm is to act unjustly. And thus it is those, like his accusers, who attempt to kill a man *unjustly*, who do themselves the greatest genuine harm (cf. *Apology* 30d2-5).

Socrates' paradoxical approach to his circumstances and his imminent death is reflected in the opening scene of the *Crito*, both in the contrast between his own and Crito's state of mind and in his puzzling dream. Crito is sorrowful and sleepless, whereas Socrates has been sleeping peacefully, a contrast on which Crito himself remarks, explaining why he did not wake Socrates when he first arrived (43b3-5). If Socrates' composure surprises Crito, it is because Crito cannot understand the attitude to death which lies behind it. Crito's distress and Socrates' calm reflect the contrasting conceptions of harm which will shortly be disputed between them. In letting Socrates sleep on, Crito has given him time for a prophetic dream, the dream on which his conviction that the ship from Delos will not arrive that day is based. The dream itself captures several dimensions of the contrast between Crito's and Socrates' different attitudes to his imminent death.

Socrates reports his dream as follows: "A woman appeared to come towards me, beautiful and fair in appearance, and wearing white. She called to me and said: 'on the third day you shall come to fertile Phthia'" (44a10-b2). The dream quite clearly foretells the day of Socrates' death, 'on the third day'. But the way in which it does so challenges Crito's expectation that Socrates' death will be a sorrowful event. The pronouncement is made by a woman, probably divine. In Greek thought, beautiful figures in dreams, and figures wearing white, suggest divinity.[50] White clothes are also expressive of joy, in contrast to mourning.[51] Thus the dream foretells Socrates' death, but it does so in a way suggestive of joy, rather than sorrow. The dream figure's pronouncement—'on the third day you shall come to fertile Phthia'—echoes *Iliad* IX. 363. In the *Iliad* the words are spoken by Achilles in the course of his refusal of Agamemnon's offer, conveyed by Odysseus, intended to assuage his anger over the loss of Briseis and persuade him to remain and fight. Phthia is Achilles' home; his words anticipate his arrival home 'on the third day'.

In evoking Achilles' words, Socrates' dream figure brings new meaning to the idea of going home. Achilles, famously, has two possible futures: an heroic death or an unheroic life. For Achilles, to go home to Phthia would be precisely to avoid imminent death. In Socrates' dream, by contrast, going to Phthia— going home—refers to Socrates' death. A suggestive parallel for such dream symbolism is found in a dream of Eudemus, reported by Cicero, following a lost work of Aristotle (*De Divinatione* I.53). Here too one finds the same symbolic use of the returning home of the physical body for the returning home of the soul at death that is at work in Socrates' dream. The dream predicts his death. But it also characterises death as a return home, not of the physical body, the focus of Crito's anxiety and of his conception of harm, but of the soul, the focus of Socrates' interest.

If this interpretation of Socrates' dream is right, it suggests a more decisive view on the afterlife of the soul than Socrates had himself been prepared to assert in the *Apology*. There, death is something about which Socrates claims not to know whether it be good or evil (*Apology* 37b6-7). But the *Apology* is not therefore in conflict with the *Crito*. It is not Socrates in the *Crito* who suggests that death is not an evil, but the homecoming of the soul; an occasion for joy more than sorrow. Rather, it is the tone of Socrates' dream that suggests this. Here, then, is an occasion when Socrates dreams in anticipation, at least on any conventional chronology of Plato's dialogues, anticipating a view of the afterlife of the soul which he will himself defend, on the day of his death, in the *Phaedo*.

The tenor of Socrates' dream, along with his quiet composure, confounds the expectation that death is something to be sorrowful about and to try to avoid, the expectation reflected in Crito's obvious distress, and in his mission in arriving at the prison so early. At the start of the dialogue, then, Plato challenges our expectations of how we should evaluate what will be the outcome of the dialogue: Socrates' refusal to escape and consequent death. But Socrates' dream also does something else. It suggests, with its tone of finality and its divine portent, that the decision regarding Socrates' fate has already been made; he will die, 'on the third day'. This same tone is found again, at the end of the dialogue, when Socrates ends the dialogue proposing to act 'in the way that god guides (or instructs) us' (54e1-2). But nothing in the intervening dialogue has referred to the guidance of god as a basis for deciding how Socrates should act.

Socrates' decision has been made outside the context of the dialogue we read, and before the discussion with Crito we find within it has even begun. Perhaps, then, it is no surprise that the discussion ends, as it does, with the apparent agreement of all parties that Socrates should not escape. Perhaps, too, it is no surprise that, on the interpretation I am proposing, Socrates nowhere spells out his own motivation for refusing to escape. His decision has already been made, and made outside the scope of the dialogue.

Crito's response to Socrates' dream is instructive, both about its apparent reversal of our expectations as to how we should feel about Socrates' death, and about its signalling a decision already taken. Crito declares that the dream is 'absurd' or 'strange', literally 'out of place' (ἄτοπον) (44b3). And so it is, for someone like Crito, who grieves at the prospect of Socrates' death, and who has come to try to dissuade him from it. But the implication of the dream—that Socrates will die—is clear even to Crito, 'too clear' indeed (44b5). It is too clear, because Crito cannot accept the implication. Even as he acknowledges the dream's meaning and apparent finality, he launches into a last-ditch attempt to persuade Socrates to unmake the decision he has already made (44b5-6). The remainder of the dialogue does not show Socrates making that decision, but does something else. The something else it does, I have argued, is present a conflict between the different value systems of Crito, Socrates, and the Laws, all of which are deeply rooted in Plato's Athens.

Conclusion: The Results of the Reading Proposed

It is, of course, an historical fact that Socrates was executed by the Athenians in 399BC. But the *Crito* is not a work of historical fact. It is a philosophical work written by Plato with reference to the occasion of Socrates' death. The goal of the *Crito* on the reading I have presented is to portray the lack of consensus of values between Crito, Socrates, and the Laws. What results from this reading is two challenges, one for the dialogue's readers—its Athenian audience and ourselves—and one for its author, Plato.

The challenge for the reader concerns the reader's values and is appropriately Socratic. The Socrates of Plato's Socratic dialogues presents a constant challenge to the values held by the different individuals he meets and by the community in which he lives. But he never gives simple straightforward answers. The *Crito* too, I suggest, presents such a challenge. In staging a conflict between these different, but deeply Athenian values, the dialogue provides an occasion, within and without the dialogue, to reflect on the values by which one ought to live. And this seems to me a thoroughly appropriate challenge for the dialogue to raise. After all, if *the* Socratic question is, how should I live my life?, what could be more appropriate than for Plato to use the way in which Socrates 'died his death' as an occasion to ask this question once again?

The second challenge is for Plato. By the end of the *Crito*, the kinship ethics of Crito have been successfully appropriated and subsumed into the civic ethics of the Laws. But there remains a conflict of values between Socrates and the Laws: Socrates has no consensus of values, no κοινὴ βούλη, with the political community in which he lived.[52] The challenge for Plato is to resolve this conflict between Socrates and his political community. His response will await the *Republic*, the dialogue in which Plato has Socrates embark on the discussion of the nature of justice so absent from the *Crito*; and the dialogue which, in the course of this discussion, builds a political community in line with a value system which treats justice in terms of the benefit or harm to an individual's soul. The *Republic* is, of course, the dialogue which trades precisely on an analogy between the structure of an individual's soul and that of the political community in which he or she lives.[53]

Notes

1. This assumption motivates the entire volume of literature addressed to the apparent conflict between Socrates' attitude to obedience to law in the *Apology* and that of the Laws in the *Crito*, since the apparent conflict is worrying only if both attitudes are Socrates' own. For a representative sample of works which make this assumption, see Allen (1980), Bostock (1990), Kraut (1984), Vlastos (1991) ch.7 and (1994) ch.4, and Woozley (1979). Exceptions include: Bentley (1996), Calvert (1987), Jones (unpubl.), Lane (1998), Miller (1996), and Young (1974). In general, those who depart from the assumed consensus between Socrates and the Laws take the Laws to add something to what Socrates says in his own person, but to depart from strictly Socratic argumentation for the purposes of persuading Crito. I too think that the Laws' arguments have special significance for Crito, but in a different way. And I shall go further than most in identifying genuine conflicts between the arguments of the Laws and those of Socrates, and in making these conflicts central to what the dialogue is about.

2. Cf. Linforth (1946) p.136, in particular for his argument in favour of taking οἱ κορυβαντιῶντες as a reference to people who have some direct connection to Corybantic rites, as opposed to a general term for being mad or hallucinated.

3. R. Kraut (1984) p.4 and elsewhere in the same work.

4. I.M. Linforth (1946).

5. The Corybantic passages considered above, along with others, are discussed by Linforth (1946). The only other passage which draws a direct comparison between Corybantism and the effect of an *argument* is *Euthydemus* 277d4-e2. Here Socrates compares the effect of the opening arguments of the two sophists to the effect of Corybants, and again, the invitation is to suspicion of the argument concerned. Here, however, the comparison is to the *preliminary* stages of a Corybantic rite, not the rite itself.

6. Tr. Reeve-Grube.

7. Miller (1996) esp. pp. 121–122 also draws attention to some of the oddities of the Corybants passage. He focuses on the suggestion that 'another perspective', which he takes to be the Socratic perspective, is being suppressed. I read his paper late in the development of my own, but note that, while he arrives at a different interpretation overall, there is much that is in sympathy between his reading and my own.

8. Linforth (1946) also cites two passages in later authors which link Corybantism and buzzing (here, buzzing around someone/thing—περιβομβεῖν) in ways exactly comparable to their use in the *Crito*: Celsus ap. Origen *Contra Celsum* III.16 and Lucian *Lexiphanes* 16. Both passages use a comparison with Corybantism and the metaphor of buzzing of speeches which are clearly not being endorsed: quite the reverse.

9. That there is a discrepancy between Socrates' and the Laws' attitudes to retaliation was first suggested to me in conversation by Mary Hannah Jones. The development of the argument as presented here is my own. Jones' own interpretation is elaborated in her (unpublished) paper, 'Reading the *Crito*'.

10. Kraut (1984) p. 26, n. 2, rejects the translation 'injure' or 'harm' for κακουργεῖν as liable to mislead one into thinking that Socrates condemns all physically damaging acts, whatever their context. I agree that Socrates should not be taken to be so committed. Nonetheless, the translation 'harm', suitably indeterminately construed, seems appropriate here, especially in comparison with an earlier passage, in which Socrates and Crito debate whether or not the many can τὰ μέγιστα κακὰ ἐργάζεσθαι (work the greatest harms/evils) (44d3-4, d7). Here, what is at issue, as I shall argue below, is precisely a dispute about different conceptions of harm. Elsewhere in Plato, one may compare *Republic* I 332d4-e4, where κακῶς ποιεῖν—Socrates' other term in the *Crito* passage in question (49c7)—is treated as equivalent to βλάπτειν, connoting harm. In forensic speeches, the verb κακουργεῖν has an almost technical sense, referring to the acts of a particular class of criminals, often belonging to the lower classes (see discussion in Hansen [1976], esp. ch. II). In this regard, it seems worthy of note that Crito's most emphatic agreement relates to Socrates' suggestion that one should never κακουργεῖν, nor ἀντικακουργεῖν (49c2-6), in contrast to his tentative agreement that one should never ἀνταδικεῖν (49c1), on which more below.

11. G. Vlastos (1991) ch. 7.

12. As is the term ἀντικακουργεῖν. Plato is the only author cited by LSJ in connection with this latter verb (citing *Crito* 49c, 54c). He is the earliest author cited by them in connection with the verb ἀνταδικεῖν (citing *Crito* 49b,e and *Theaetetus* 173a along with Maximus of Tyre 18.5 (= 12.5 in Trapp's Teubner, 1994). A search of the TLG on CD-Rom revealed 28 occurrences in other authors or collections, all later than Plato. 14 of these occurrences are quotations of the *Crito* passage. A survey of the other occurrences suggests that the *Crito* passage is the cornerstone, more or less explicitly, for many later discussions of retaliation. E.g. Maximus uses the term when arguing that the just man will never retaliate, in a dissertation rightly described by Thomas Taylor as one whose 'whole foundation . . . is taken from the *Crito* of Plato' (Taylor [1994] p. 40, republication of his 1805 translation). The *Crito* is also used by both Christian and non-Christian writers, as Platonic precedent for the doctrine of 'turning the other cheek': Eusebius *Praeparatio Evangelica* XIII.7, 9, *Demonstratio Evangelica* I.6.69; Theoderet *Graecarum Affectionum Curatio* XII.42 (= IB, pp. 309–10, Raeder's Teubner [1904]); Celsus ap. Origen *Contra Celsum* VII.58. Significantly for what follows, all these writers use the term ἀνταδικεῖν for positions which condemn *all* acts of retaliation when wronged.

13. D. Bostock (1990) p. 5, n. 6, his emphasis.

14. If this seems to read a lot into one reply—'it appears not'—it may be noted, further, that to gain Crito's agreement Socrates reformulates the inference in terms of κακουργεῖν and ἀντικακουργεῖν; invites him to agree to an equation between κακῶς ποιεῖν and ἀδικεῖν; and only then reinserts ἀνταδικεῖν into his overall conclusion. Even so, Socrates goes on to caution Crito against agreeing to what he does not believe, and it is not until several lines later (49e4) that Crito gives his endorsement to 'the foregoing' (τοῖς πρόσθε, 49e1-2). Is 'the foregoing' everything which has just been said, some of what has just been said, or simply Crito's and Socrates' agreement in conversations prior to the *Crito* (cf. 49a8) that one should never do wrong, from which Socrates has now inferred that one should never return a wrong either?

15. That Plato could actively exploit a distinction between the behaviour appropriate between moral equals and that appropriate between parent and child is shown by *Republic* 464e4-465b3. There, of course, the morality is that of the ideal city, not Athens. But it shows an awareness of the logical space required for my view of the Laws' position.

16. Vlastos (1994) ch. 4, p. 90, n. 8.

17. This conditional reading of the participle clause in 49e6 seems to me the correct reading of the Greek and not: 'should one do whatever one agrees to be just . . . ?' where one would expect an accusative infinitive construction. Even in this case, however, the emphasis would be on the justice of the *actions* agreed and not the agreement itself. Miller (1996) p. 124, n. 8, arrives at the same conclusion as I do as to the best interpretation of this passage.

18. The contrast between agreement in act and agreement in argument is central to Melissa Lane's reading of the *Crito* (1998).

19. Here and elsewhere in my discussion of the Laws' conception of the binding power of agreements, I have been much persuaded by Bostock's interpretation (1990),

although Bostock differs from me in taking the Laws' argument to express Socrates' (or Plato's) own views.

20. R. Kraut (1984), esp. III.

21. This need not mean that Socrates would never have any thought (or feeling) for the welfare of children. Conversely, we would be wrong just to assume that Socrates thinks of the welfare of children in the ways that 'we' might. In any case, he is quite explicit here that considerations about children, along with questions of reputation and property, should not form the basis of the decision to be made regarding the proposed escape; they are, he says, the sort of considerations on which 'the many' would judge.

22. For direct references to justice by the Laws and Crito, see, e.g., the Laws at 50e7, 51a6, 51b7, 51e5; Crito at 45a1-3, 45c5-8.

23. G. Vlastos (1991), ch.7, p. 195.

24. And see note 14 above.

25. This is not to say these principles are trivial: Thrasymachus, for one, would disagree (*Republic* I).

26. Recall that, in the *Apology*, Socrates identifies 'the many' as his first accusers (19d6-7) and their charge is the first charge he speaks against (18a7-e4).

27. Not exclusively, perhaps. Paul Cartledge reminds me that Crito is also concerned about shame (pers. comm.) (cf. above). But his concern is about the shame caused by what the many will think—that he values money over friends—even though they will think this only because they misunderstand the nature of the case—that it is not a question of money, but of Socrates' refusal to escape (44c3-5). Shame, then, may be an internal consideration, but it is bound up with external considerations of how one appears to others. Contrast Glaucon's grasp of the distinction between *being* just and *appearing* just (*Republic* II).

28. Bentley (1996) p. 4. Cf. also Young (1974) p. 5. For the conventional view— helping friends and harming enemies—see Polemarchus' advocacy of it in *Republic* I.

29. Following Allen's translation (1980) *ad loc.*, to reflect the imperfect verbs.

30. K. Dover (1974), p. 273. Dover uses the phrase 'concentric fortifications' (1974) p. 273, n. 1, which he takes from Earp (1929), p. 32.

31. Cf. the Stoic Hierocles, who chooses precisely this image of concentric circles to depict a person's relations to others; in Hierocles' version, the smallest and innermost circle contains immediate family, the largest and outermost circle contains the entire human race. Hierocles ap. Stobaeum IV. 671ff Hense.

32. Aristotle *Politics* 1253b5-7.

33. Cf. Miller (1996) p. 127 with n. 16.

34. Both do so in ways most suited to their particular case. Crito appeals to Socrates' obligations to his friends, first, and only thereafter to his kin, his sons, no doubt because he is Socrates' friend. The Laws appeal to obligations towards parents, as well as to those of a slave towards a master. For the purposes of their analogy, the use of asymmetrical and hierarchical relations best makes their case.

35. Without wishing to enter into the debate about the precise structure of the arguments of the Laws, on which see Bostock (1990), I take it that the argument of the Laws, broadly speaking, has three waves: (i) that for Socrates to escape would be (wrongly) to retaliate against the Laws; (ii) that he would (again, wrongly) be breaking

his agreement with them; (iii) and that he would in fact harm himself, his friends, and his family were he to do so. Together these three waves constitute the Laws' response to Crito/Socrates' contention that the city has wronged them, in reply to the Laws' opening charge that to escape would be to destroy the city 'for his part' (50a9-b5). The latter suggests that the Laws envisage yet another kind of harm, harm to an institution or to the social fabric, to add to the conceptions of harm which were earlier in dispute between Crito and Socrates. Below, I shall mention a contemporary parallel for the claim that an individual might destroy the city 'for his part'.

36. Does 'in consequence' overstate the case? I do not think so. Notice that, at 53a8-b1, when Socrates is invited to consider the consequences of escape, at this stage for himself and his companions, he is to consider it under the description 'contravening these [sc. agreements and compacts, vide 52e1] and committing a wrong', that is, assuming the result of the previous arguments.

37. As to the master : slave relation, I have again been unable to find any direct parallels for the use of this analogy for the Laws : citizen relation. However, the germ of such an idea may be present in claims that the laws are κύριοι (e.g. Antiphon I.1; Lysias I.29, the latter cited by Strauss [1993] pp. 48–9). Athenian perceptions of law, as well as attitudes to punishment, are the subject of Danielle Allen's doctoral thesis, *A Situation of Punishment—the Politics and Ideology of Athenian Punishment* (Cambridge, 1996). I am grateful to her for allowing me to read sections of her work while still in progress.

38. As argued in the valuable discussion of Strauss (1993) esp. ch. 2. See also Due (1989) pp. 210–13, 219–21 who refers to Cyrus' characterisation as a father in Xenophon's *Cyropaedia* as part of a positive exploitation of the οἶκος/πόλις analogy.

39. See the useful discussions in Dover (1974) esp. pp. 301–6, and Connor (1971) ch. 2.

40. Tr. Fagles.

41. Connor (1971) ch. 2.

42. Tr. Warner, modified with advice from Paul Cartledge.

43. The context of Euryptolemus' speech has another intriguing connection to the dramatic context of the *Crito*. The generals for whom Euryptolemus seeks a trial are the same generals whose trial *en bloc* Socrates voted against on the grounds of the illegality of such a proposal (*Apology* 32a4-c3).

44. To clarify: I am not suggesting that there is nothing at all distinctive about the particular arguments Plato has put into the mouth of the personified Laws, but rather that they are part of a recognisable family of arguments which exploit (no doubt often for different ideological reasons) analogies and disanalogies between household and city. Paul Cartledge has suggested to me that the Laws' claim that the citizen is like a slave is counterculturally paradoxical in the context of Athenian democracy in which a citizen defined himself in part as free (non-slave) (pers. comm., and cf. his [1993]). Perhaps here, Plato, whose anti-democratic sentiments are no secret, takes Athenian democratic commitment to the power of the *demos* or law-making body to what, for him, is its logical conclusion. Cf. Xenophon (another anti-democrat) *Memorabilia* I.2.40–46, where the will of the majority in a democracy is said to tyrannize the minority, i.e. to treat them like slaves.

45. Lycurgus' speech, which no doubt postdates the *Crito*, is itself replete with parallels to the arguments of the Laws. In particular, it provides an analogue for the Laws' contention that Socrates is attempting to destroy the city 'for his part': compare 63–67 with e.g. *Crito* 50b1-2.

46. I am grateful to Sylvia Berryman for the label.

47. The verb is ὑφηγέομαι which has both these senses.

48. This is not to say that Socrates' expressions of piety contradict the charge of impiety made. That Socrates appeals to god(s) does not mean that he recognises the Athenians' gods. The view that the *Apology* presents Socrates as guilty of impiety as charged has been defended by Burnyeat (1997).

49. Within the dialogue remarks by Crito and the Laws imply that escape from prison was both common and what most people would expect Socrates to do: see Crito's remarks on what the many will think (44c3-5) and the Laws on escapees (53d5-7). That escape from prison was common is confirmed by the references to such escapes in the orators (e.g. Demosthenes *Ag. Timocrates* 126; *Ag. Aristogeiton* I. 56). In cases of murder, the defendant had the right to go into exile after the first defence speech (Antiphon V.13; Demosthenes *Ag. Aristocrates* 69; cf. Bonner & Smith (1938) vol. II, pp. 120, 202). Successful escape into exile put the murderer beyond the reach of lawful killing (Demosthenes *Ag. Aristocrates* 37ff.). Escaping into exile, particularly escaping to avoid execution, was clearly common and recognised practice in contemporary Athens.

50. For the association between beauty and divinity for dream figures, cf. Pease (1973) on Cicero *De Divinatione* I.40, p. 165. White is the colour of the clothes of goddesses and demi-goddesses in Homer. Interestingly, given the fatalistic tenor of Socrates' dream, white is also the colour of the garments worn by the Fates, daughters of Necessity, in Plato *Republic* X 617c1-2.

51. LSJ list the meanings 'bright, fortunate, happy' for the metaphorical use of λευκός . On the Greeks' attitudes to white in general, see Snowden (1983) pp. 82–83. Aristophanes (*Acharnians* 1024) plays on the assumption that white clothes are worn in times of joy, not sorrow.

52. Here is it worth remembering the political resonance of the term βουλή in Plato's Athens.

53. The evolution of the interpretation of the *Crito* presented here was much helped by numerous conversations about the dialogue, especially with Myles Burnyeat, Peter Garnsey, and Melissa Lane, as well as by their comments on written drafts. For advice on matters relating to the historical context or to particular details of interpretation, I am also indebted to Danielle Allen, Luke Beckett, and Doreen Innes, and, for initiation into the mysteries of searching the TLG on CD-Rom, to Ian DuQuesnay. For written comments on the final drafts, I am grateful to Paul Cartledge, Malcolm Schofield, and the anonymous reader for the *Archiv*. A shortened version was presented to audiences at mini-conferences at King's College London and at Aarhus University in Denmark. I am grateful to the audiences on both occasions, and especially to my commentator at King's, Raphael Woolf, and to my colleague, M.M. McCabe, to the latter, both for her comments and her judicious wielding of a red pen. While all the above have proved to me again what an enjoyable and

cooperative venture the business of ancient philosophy can be, none of them, of course, should be presumed to agree with the result.

Bibliography

Allen, D. (1996). *A Situation of Punishment: The Politics and Ideology of Athenian Punishment*. Dissertation, Cambridge University.

Allen, R.E. (1980). *Socrates and Legal Obligation*, Minneapolis.

Bentley, R. (1996). "Responding to Crito: Socrates and Political Obligation", *History of Political Thought*, vol. 17, no.1, pp.1–20.

Bonner, R.J. & Smith, G. (1938). *The Administration of Justice From Homer to Aristotle*, 2 volumes, New York: Greenwood, repr. (1968).

Bostock, D. (1990). "The Interpretation of Plato's *Crito*", *Phronesis* XXXV, pp. 1–20.

Burkert, W. (1985). *Greek Religion: Archaic and Classical*, tr. by John Raffan, Blackwell, Oxford.

Burnyeat, M.F. (1997). "The Impiety of Socrates", *Ancient Philosophy* XVII, no.1, pp. 1–12.

Calvert, B. (1987). "Plato's *Crito* and Richard Kraut", in Panagiotou ed. (1987), pp. 17–33.

Cartledge, P. (1993). *The Greeks*, Oxford, new edn. (1997).

Connor, W.R. (1971). *The New Politicians of Fifth-Century Athens*, Princeton, repr. (1992) with new intro., Hackett.

Dodds, E.R. (1951). *The Greeks and the Irrational*, University of California Press, Berkeley.

Dover, K.J. (1974). *Greek Popular Morality in the Time of Plato and Aristotle*, Blackwell, Oxford.

Due, B. (1989). *The Cyropaedia*, Aarhus University Press.

Earp, F.R. (1929). *The Way of the Greeks*, London.

Hansen, M.H. (1976). *Apagoge, Endeixis and Ephegesis against Kakourgoi, Atimoi and Pheugontes: A Study in the Athenian Administration of Justice in the Fourth Century BC*, Odense University Classical Studies, vol. 8, Odense University Press.

Jones, M.H. (unpubl.). Reading the *Crito*.

Kraut, R. (1984). *Socrates and the State*, Princeton.

Lane, M.S. "Argument and Agreement in Plato's *Crito*", in *History of Political Thought* 1998.

Linforth, I.M. (1946). "The Corybantic Rites in Plato", *University of California Publications in Classical Philology*, ed. Alexander, Green & Linforth, vol. 13, no. 5, pp. 121–162.

Miller, M. (1996). "The Arguments I Seem to Hear: Argument and Irony in the *Crito*", *Phronesis* XLI, pp. 121–137.

Panagiotou, S. (1987). "Justified Disobedience in the *Crito*", in Panagiotou ed. (1987), pp. 35–50.

Panagiotou, S. ed. (1987). *Justice, Law and Method in Plato and Aristotle*, Edmonton, Alberta, Canada.

Pease, A.S., ed. (1973). *M. Tulli Ciceronis De Divinatione Libre Duo*, reprint of University of Illinois Studies in Language and Literature vol. VI (1920) & vol. VIII (1923), Wissenschaftliche Buchgesellschaft Darmstadt.

Snowden, F.M. (1983). *Before Color Prejudice: The Ancient View of Blacks*, Harvard University Press.

Strauss, B. (1993). *Fathers and Sons in Athens: Ideology and Society in the Era of the Peloponnesian War*, London.

Taylor, Thomas (1994). *The Dissertations of Maximus Tyrius*, translated by Thomas Taylor, vol. VI of the Thomas Taylor Series, The Prometheus Trust, republication of Taylor's 1805 translation.

Vlastos, G. (1991). *Socrates: Ironist and Moral Philosopher*, Cambridge.

Vlastos, G. (1994). *Socratic Studies*, ed. Myles Burnyeat, Cambridge.

Woozley, A.D. (1979). *Law and Obedience: The Argument of Plato's Crito*, Duckworth.

Young, G. (1974). "Socrates and Obedience", *Phronesis* XIX, pp. 1–29.

About the Editor

Rachana Kamtekar is assistant professor of philosophy at the University of Arizona. She is the author of various articles on ancient ethics, politics and psychology. She is co-editor, with Sara Rappe, of the forthcoming *Blackwell Companion to Socrates*.

About the Contributors

David Bostock has been Fellow and Tutor in Philosophy at Merton College, Oxford, and Lecturer in Philosophy at the University of Oxford since 1968. His publications include *Plato's Phaedo, Plato's Theaetetus, Aristotle's Metaphysics, Books Z and H*, and *Aristotle's Ethics*.

Thomas C. Brickhouse is professor of philosophy at Lynchburg College. He is the author (with Nicholas D. Smith) of three books, *Socrates on Trial, Plato's Socrates*, and *Socrates the Philosopher*, as well as of many articles.

M. F. Burnyeat is Senior Research Fellow at All Souls College, Oxford University and formerly Laurence Professor of Ancient Philosophy at Cambridge University. He is the author of *A Map of Metaphysics Zeta, The Theaetetus of Plato* and numerous articles on a wide variety of topics in ancient philosophy.

S. Marc Cohen is professor of philosophy at the University of Washington. He is co-author of *Ammonius on Aristotle's Categories* and co-editor of *Readings in Ancient Greek Philosophy*. His articles on Plato and Aristotle have appeared in various journals and anthologies.

Peter Geach is Honorary Fellow of Balliol College, Oxford University. His publications include *Mental Acts, Reference and Generality, God and the Soul*, and, most recently, *Truth and Hope*.

Verity Harte is lecturer in philosophy at King's College London. She is the author of *Plato on Parts and Wholes* and of articles on various topics in ancient philosophy.

Terence Irwin is Susan Linn Sage Professor of Philosophy and Humane Letters, Cornell University. He is the author of *Plato's Gorgias* (translation and notes), *Aristotle's Nicomachean Ethics* (translation and notes), *Aristotle's First Principles, Classical Thought,* and *Plato's Ethics.*

Richard Kraut is professor of philosophy and Classics and holds the Morrison Chair in the Humanities at Northwestern University. Among his publications are *Aristotle: Political Philosophy, Aristotle on the Human Good,* and *Socrates and the State.* He also edited the *Cambridge Companion to Plato.*

Donald Morrison is professor of philosophy and Classical Studies at Rice University. His recent publications include articles on Socrates, classical political philosophy, and philosophical method in later Greek philosophy. He is editor of the forthcoming *Cambridge Companion to Socrates.*

Mark L. McPherran is professor of philosophy at the University of Maine at Farmington. He is the author of *The Religion of Socrates,* the editor of *Wisdom, Ignorance, and Virtue: New Essays in Socratic* Studies and *Recognition, Remembrance, and Reality: New Essays on Plato's Epistemology and Metaphysics,* and many articles on Socrates, Plato, and ancient skepticism.

S. R. Slings was Chair of Greek at the Free University at Amsterdam. His publications include the new Oxford Classical Text of Plato's *Republic* and an edition with commentary of Plato's *Clitophon.*

Nicholas D. Smith is the James F. Miller Professor of Humanities at Lewis & Clark College. He is the author, coauthor, editor, or coeditor of numerous papers and books in several areas of Greek philosophy and literature, and the coauthor with Thomas C. Brickhouse of *Socrates on Trial, Plato's Socrates, The Philosophy of Socrates,* and *Plato and the Trial of Socrates.*

E. de Strycker, S. J., taught at St. Ignatius College at the University of Antwerp. His publications include various articles on Socrates and Plato.

Gregory Vlastos held various distinguished professorial posts during his lifetime and wrote *Socrates, Ironist and Moral Philosopher* and *Plato's Universe;* some of his most influential papers are collected in his *Platonic Studies.*